Legalizing Gender Inequality
Courts, Markets, and Unequal Pay for Women in America

Equal pay for men and women in the work force suffered a series of defeats in U.S. courts during the 1970s and 1980s and became the object of attack by a conservative administration and conventional economic wisdom. Yet the issue persists, unsolved, and continues to attract scholarly and popular attention. Building upon a new generation of research about institutions and the social construction of the market, the authors of *Legalizing Gender Inequality* challenge the existing theories of gender-based pay inequality and present a new, more realistic way to analyze the relationship between the market, pay differentials, and the law.

Major legal precedents have been built upon the notion that labor markets, not employers, are the source of inequality. Robert Nelson and William Bridges contend that the courts have, by uncritically accepting the market explanation for male–female wage disparity, tended to legitimate and legalize a crucial dimension of gender inequality in American society. The authors argue to the contrary that male–female earning differentials cannot be explained adequately by market forces, principles of efficiency, or society-wide sexism.

Through a careful, sophisticated examination of data on wage-setting practices from four landmark pay discrimination cases, Nelson and Bridges demonstrate that employing organizations tend to disadvantage workers in predominantly female jobs by denying them power in organizational politics and by reproducing male cultural advantages. Much of the gender inequality in the system is, therefore, the direct result of organizational decision making. The authors argue further that comparable worth is an inappropriate remedy, as it misdiagnoses the causes of gender inequality and often falls prey to the same organizational processes that initially generated this differential.

In addition to its new theory on wage determination, this book contains important insights into how the dynamics of litigation affect the use of social science theory and data. This book promises to change the way that scholars and analysts – whether from the perspective of sociology, law, labor economics, or gender studies – think about wage inequality.

Robert Nelson holds a J.D. and Ph.D. from Northwestern University. He is a Senior Research Fellow of the American Bar Foundation and Professor and Chair of the Department of Sociology at Northwestern. He has published widely in the sociology of law, with particular attention to studies of the legal profession, organizations, and inequality. His most recent book is *The Hollow Core: Private Interests in National Policymaking* (with John Heinz, Edward Laumann, and Robert Salisbury) (1993).

William Bridges is Professor and Head of Sociology at the University of Illinois at Chicago. His research interests span the sociology of labor markets, the sociology of employment relationships, and the more general study of social inequality. With Wayne J. Villemez he is author of *The Employment Relationship: Causes and Consequences of Bureaucratic Personnel Administration* (1994).

Structural Analysis in the Social Sciences

Mark Granovetter, editor

Other books in the series:

The series *Structural Analysis in the Social Sciences* presents approaches that explain social behavior and institutions by reference to *relations* among such concrete entities as persons and organizations. This contrasts with at least four other popular strategies: (a) reductionist attempts to explain by a focus on individuals alone; (b) explanations stressing the causal primacy of such abstract concepts as ideas, values, mental harmonies, and cognitive maps (thus, "structuralism" on the Continent should be distinguished from structural analysis in the present sense); (c) technological and material determinism; (d) explanations using "variables" as the main analytic concepts (as in the "structural equation" models that dominated much of the sociology of the 1970s), where structure is that connecting variables rather than actual social entities.

The social network approach is an important example of the strategy of structural analysis; the series also draws on social science theory and research that are not framed explicitly in network terms, but stress the importance of relations rather than the atomization of reductionism or the determinism of ideas, technology, or material conditions. The structural perspective has become extremely popular and influential in all the social sciences, and this series brings together such work under a single rubric. By bringing the achievements of structurally oriented scholars to a wider public, the *Structural Analysis* series hopes to encourage the use of this very fruitful approach.

Structural Analysis in the Social Sciences | 16

Legalizing Gender Inequality

Courts, Markets, and Unequal Pay for Women in America

Robert L. Nelson
American Bar Foundation and Northwestern University

William P. Bridges
University of Illinois at Chicago

CAMBRIDGE
UNIVERSITY PRESS

PUBLISHED BY THE PRESS SYNDICATE OF THE UNIVERSITY OF CAMBRIDGE
The Pitt Building, Trumpington Street, Cambridge, United Kingdom

CAMBRIDGE UNIVERSITY PRESS
The Edinburgh Building, Cambridge CB2 2RU, UK http://www.cup.cam.ac.uk
40 West 20th Street, New York, NY 10011-4211, USA http://www.cup.org
10 Stamford Road, Oakleigh, Melbourne 3166, Australia

© Robert L. Nelson and William P. Bridges 1999

First published 1999

Printed in the United States of America

Typeface Sabon 10/12   *System* QuarkXPress [BTS]

*A catalog record for this book is available from
the British Library.*

Library of Congress Cataloging in Publication Data

Nelson, Robert L., 1952–
Legalizing gender inequality: courts, markets, and unequal pay for
women in America / Robert L. Nelson, William P. Bridges.
p.   cm. – (Structural analysis in the social sciences; 16)
Includes bibliographical references and index.
ISBN 0-521-62169-0 (hb). – ISBN 0-521-62750-8 (pbk.)
1. Pay equity – Law and legislation – United States.   2. Pay equity –
United States.   I. Bridges, William P.   II. Title.   III. Series.
KF3464.N45   1999
331.2′153′0973 – dc21   98-38432
                                                                CIP

ISBN 0 521 62169 0 hardback
ISBN 0 521 62750 8 paperback

To Lisa and Barbara

Contents

ix

Figures and Tables

Figures

Tables

xi

Acknowledgments

Over the long course of this project we have benefited from the support and advice of many institutions and persons. The American Bar Foundation provided significant financial and scholarly support from the very inception of this work, which dates back to the time John Heinz was director, through the tenures of William Felstiner and Bryant Garth. Jack, Bill, and B.G. not only offered institutional support, but important intellectual guidance as well. The project also was supported by grants from the National Science Foundation (SES-8800627) and by a year at the Center for Advanced Study in the Behavioral Sciences for the first author (SES-9022192). Under Philip Converse and Robert Scott, the Center proved a wonderful environment for developing and writing the ideas that make up the core of this book. Northwestern University and the University of Illinois–Chicago provided several kinds of resources for this project, including most crucially a set of colleagues and students who were interested in the work we were doing.

Several individuals were essential to the production of this book. Most important is Lorrie Wessel, who typed several drafts of this manuscript and its constituent chapters and articles. Bette Sikes skillfully edited the manuscript and organized the presentation of the tables. Kathleen Much of the Center for Advanced Study edited an early draft of chapter 5. Mark Dubnoff, Elizabeth Warren, and Monique Payne provided excellent research assistance. Bill Bielby gave thorough comments on the entire manuscript. Ian Ayres, Jim Baron, Dick Campbell, Lisa Douglass, Lauren Edelman, Paula England, Carol Heimer, Robert Inman, Aldon Morris, Laura Beth Nielsen, Deborah Rhode, Dorothy Ross, Peter Siegelman, Art Stinchcombe, and Don Treiman read and commented on various parts of the manuscript. We also are grateful to our editors at Cambridge University Press. Mark Granovetter, editor of this series, offered inportant intellectual encouragement and advice. Elizabeth Neal guided us through the first stages of submitting our manuscript. Mary Child gave us valuable substantive and editing suggestions. Brian MacDonald carefully copyedited the final manuscript. While all the above institutions and individuals were invaluable to this effort, we bear ultimate responsibility for our claims and mistakes.

Finally, we want to thank our families for the emotional and intellectual support they have given us throughout this project. Their patience, love, and understanding sustained us throughout this work.

1

Law, Markets, and the Institutional Construction of Gender Inequality in Pay

The pay equity movement won its largest legal victory in 1983, when Judge Jack Tanner of the federal District Court of Western Washington found that the State of Washington had discriminated against workers in predominantly female jobs and awarded the plaintiffs a $400 million judgment.[1] The *AFSCME* decision (so named because the American Federation of State, County, and Municipal Employees brought the lawsuit) catapulted the pay equity issue into instant prominence. In its immediate aftermath, the number of states conducting pay equity studies doubled to thirty-four, and the number of articles on pay equity in leading newspapers quadrupled (McCann 1994, 54–59). The victory was shortlived, however. In 1985, the Ninth Circuit Court of Appeals reversed the *AFSCME* decision. Then judge, now justice, Anthony Kennedy pronounced, "Neither law nor logic deems the free market a suspect enterprise. . . . Title VII does not obligate [the State of Washington] to eliminate an economic inequality it did not create" (*AFSCME*, 1407). According to Justice Kennedy, the plaintiffs not only lacked a legal basis for redress, but the very nature of their thinking – their logic – was wrong. The Ninth Circuit authoritatively denounced plaintiffs' theory of gender-based wage inequality as inconsistent with a core institution of American society – the free market.

The reversal of the *AFSCME* decision had a devastating effect on the pay equity movement. Other courts followed the *AFSCME* precedent in rejecting similar claims. Reform activity in states and municipalities slowed to a trickle. Media coverage of pay equity matters fell by more than one-half (McCann 1994, 54–59). Some wage reforms were won through state legislation and collective bargaining, but even these garnered only mixed results. The conventional view among the press, policy makers, and academics was that comparable worth was essentially dead

---

1 *American Federation of State, County, & Municipal Employees v. Washington*, 578 F. Supp. 846 (D. Wash. 1983), rev'd, 770 F.2d 1401 (9th Cir. 1985) (hereinafter *AFSCME*).

on arrival, an unrealistic reform program that lacked broad-based political support and now had lost its tenuous foothold within federal antidiscrimination law. Reflecting on the aftermath of *AFSCME*, the director of the National Committee on Pay Equity summed up the common perception in the media: "I thought this issue died in 1985" (McCann 1994, 85).

Fourteen years later we are attempting to probe more deeply into the circumstances that surrounded the sudden death of pay equity as a law reform movement. Pay equity reform was derailed by the dominant discourse on the role of law in addressing between-job wage inequality.[2] Justice Kennedy's opinion can be taken as representative of that discourse. His views were echoed by a chorus of prominent judges, scholars, and policy makers who dismissed the claims of pay equity advocates as empirically unfounded and potentially dangerous to the American economy (see, e.g., Killingsworth 1985; Livernash 1980; O'Neill 1984; Fischel and Lazear 1986). Clarence Pendleton Jr., chairman of the Civil Rights Commission, may have coined the most colorful phrase when he referred to comparable worth "as the looniest idea since Looney Tunes" (Bureau of National Affairs 1981, 35–46).

The legal and ideological success of the dominant view revolves around the analysis of an empirical question: What is the source of wage differences between jobs held primarily by women and those held primarily by men within the same organization? The legal opinions and orthodox labor economics that make up the dominant discourse give two answers. First, differences in wages are produced outside the employing organization – that is, they are the product of "the market" rather than of decisions by the employer. Second, differentials are based on efficiency considerations – that is, the reasonable, noninvidious, economic motivations of employers. If one accepts the dominant interpretation of male-female wage differences, doing so mutes the entire policy debate on pay reform, for it follows that neither the courts nor legislatures should intervene in the pay policies of employers.

This book argues that the core empirical claims of the dominant discourse are largely untested, have far more limited application in the American economy than the discourse acknowledges, and, in several significant organizational contexts, are demonstrably wrong. We assert that a substantial portion of the pay differences between "male" and "female" jobs, especially in large organizations, cannot be attributed to the market and does not rest on efficiency principles. Rather the differ-

2 By "between-job" inequality we mean the differences in pay between different jobs, such as the truck drivers versus the secretaries of a firm. "Within-job" pay differences, by contrast, consist of pay differences among workers within one job category, such as the truck drivers employed by the same firm.

ences are the product of organizational processes for which employers could be held legally responsible and which could be the target of political action by groups of women within the workplace.

Our results also raise questions about the role of courts in offering authoritative interpretations of the reasons for gender inequality in organizations. As we confronted the empirical data in the pay discrimination cases, we were led to wonder why the courts so quickly and uncritically accepted the dominant conception of between-job gender inequality in the face of relatively weak evidence to support it. We have come to see the courts as important participants in the institutional construction of markets and the gender gap in pay. The courts adopted and reinforced the orthodox explanation of male-female earnings differentials. In doing so, they contributed to the construction of a false dichotomy between "markets" and gender equality. And they gave legal sanction to a persistent aspect of gender inequality in organizations. Without a sound basis in market necessity or efficiency principles, the courts legalized gender inequality in pay.

Our analysis does not, however, lead us to support comparable worth as the solution for gender inequality in pay. Our reasons are theoretical and practical. First, although many of the criticisms that comparable worth advocates mount about orthodox labor economic explanations of earnings differentials are valid and have been enormously important to the theoretical debate, we think they have failed to develop a persuasive theory of the wage gap. In short, they misanalyze the sources of male-female wage differences. Second, we see other avenues of change as more promising and politically feasible. The call for comparable worth as the touchstone of wage reform contributed to a false opposition between the market and the law against pay discrimination: It accepted the orthodox economic view that pay differentials originated in the "market," but it also entailed the intractable position of rejecting markets as a valid basis for wage setting. Despite our disagreement with comparable worth, we suggest that the death of pay equity in the law was premature. Our findings imply the need to reopen the question of how antidiscrimination law should be applied to sex-based, between-job pay differences.

We revisit the relationship between law, markets, and gender inequality in organizations through empirical case studies of four significant pay discrimination lawsuits that were litigated in the 1970s and 1980s. These case studies provide a unique vantage point on organizations as systems of gender inequality. They also reveal how litigation and legal judgments construct competing images of both gender relations in organizations and the role that antidiscrimination law should play in organizational practices.

Our argument thus touches on three significant concerns: theories of gender inequality in organizations; theories of law, markets, and gender inequality; and social policies on pay equity. In the remainder of this chapter we locate this project with respect to these theoretical and practical concerns, outline our methodological approach, and describe the organization of the book.

Gender Inequality in Organizations

This book is foremost an analysis of gender inequality. We seek to advance theories of inequality by explicitly examining the relationship between market and organizational processes and by explicating the mechanisms through which organizations reproduce gendered pay hierarchies.

The economic inequality of men and women is a fundamental aspect of the stratification systems of modern societies. In the United States gender-based pay inequality is intimately connected to the nature of gender relations. At least in part because women tend to make less than men, women are more likely to stay at home to care for children than are men, women are more likely to follow their spouses when they pursue career opportunities than the reverse (even though such moves may have a destructive effect on women's careers or wage-earning prospects), and, if unmarried, women are more likely than men to subsist at or below the poverty line. These tendencies are part of a broader culture of male dominance that tends to relegate women to "women's roles," both in the family and the workplace. It is sometimes difficult, therefore, to disentangle the causes and effects of gender-based wage inequality. Yet in any number of real-life contexts, the simple material reality that men earn more reinforces the unequal position of women in society.

It is not surprising then that the wage gap in pay between men and women has been a central, recurrent topic for empirical investigation and theorizing by economists and sociologists. The two disciplines offer divergent interpretations of the phenomenon. Most labor economists, while recognizing the possibility of sex discrimination in pay (see, e.g., Becker 1971), argue that whatever gender inequality exists reflects differences in choices men and women make about investment in human capital, occupational selection, and labor force participation, and the rational responses of employers to labor market conditions (see, e.g., Polachek 1975; Mincer and Ofek 1982; O'Neill 1985).

In the sociological literature, the role of markets is minimized on the basis of the view that large segments of the work force are employed in internal labor markets (Doeringer and Piore 1971; Althauser and

Kalleberg 1981) or bureaucratic personnel systems (Edwards 1979; Jacoby 1985), each of which institutionalizes nonmarket, organizational influences that hinder the market determination of wage rates. Indeed, a significant portion of organization-specific research in the field, that done on government agencies, is sometimes justified explicitly on the grounds that wages in this context (net of "background characteristics") reflect only employer discretion and are unaffected by market forces (see, e.g., Taylor 1979; Grandjean 1981). The difficulty is that these studies assume away market influences on compensation rather than examine how organizational compensation systems interact with the labor market. Other sociologists theorize about the structural characteristics of labor markets that serve to disadvantage women. They posit that premarket socialization and discriminatory hiring practices limit women to stereotypically female jobs. As a result, female occupations tend to be "crowded" and to receive lower wages. Other scholars argue that labor markets are segmented between better-paying, stable jobs at the core and low-paying, unstable jobs in the periphery. Women and minorities, it is argued, are denied access to jobs in the core of the economy, and consequently suffer economically marginal employment (generally see Marini 1989; England 1992).

Thus there is a tendency for economists to reify the effects of markets on wages, while sociologists either ignore market forces or construct alternative aggregate models of tainted markets. Theories of inequality need to consider both organizational and market factors. In our view, the impasse between these contrasting viewpoints stems from the failure to develop and test theories of income determination in large organizations that address the relationship between organizational and market influences on compensation systems.

While much of our argument will be conducted in the negative by presenting evidence that counters market and efficiency-based explanations of female-male wage differentials, we seek to develop a new sociological framework for the analysis of gender inequality – what we call the organizational inequality model. We propose that much can be gained analytically by thinking of gender inequality in pay as an aspect of organizational systems of inequality. Our approach has its roots in a classic Weberian conception of organizations as systems of legitimate domination. In this conception organizations involve hierarchical relationships between leaders and staff that must be legitimated by appeals to shared values. Modern institutional theorists, from Selznick (1969) to Meyer (Meyer and Rowan 1977) to DiMaggio and Powell (1983), have elaborated on the basic theme that organizations cannot be understood solely as a set of exchange relationships or as a configuration of vested interests. Rather, they also are normative entities that give rise to shared understandings and expectations about organizational practices. The crucial issue then becomes what (or whose) values become institutionalized as organizational practice, with what consequences for various members of the organization and for the survival of the organization as a whole.

What both the classic tradition and more recent institutional theory has slighted, however, is the role of gender in structuring these relationships, as well as the consequences of organizational practices for gender inequality. Steinberg (1992, 576) asserts the feminist view:

> Masculine values are at the foundation of informal and formal organizational structures. Masculine styles of authority are legitimated by reliance on bureaucratic and hierarchical organizational forms. Images of masculinity and assumptions about the gendered division of labor organize institutional practices and expectations about work performance. . . . Regardless of their position in the organizational hierarchy, men have a vested interest in maintaining their gendered advantages. Men are not just passive recipients of organizational advantages but also actively recreate their dominance every day. They maintain organizational arrangements and institutional policies that appear to be gender neutral, but that, in fact, advantage men.

Contemporary scholarship on organizations and inequality has not made much progress on this theoretical front, despite an infusion of interest in gender inequality and some rethinking of organizational theory by feminist theorists. It has been more than fifteen years since Baron and Bielby (1980) called for "bringing the firm back in" to studies of gender inequality. Still, most research on male-female wage differentials is done in the aggregate, using cross-sectional samples of individuals, occupations, or subgroups within particular industries (see, e.g., Anderson and Tomaskovic-Devey 1995). Case studies in particular organizations provide insight into the local dynamics of gender inequality and demonstrate that there is considerable variability in the character of gender inequality in organizations, depending on historical and industrial contexts (see, e.g., Kanter 1977; Cohn 1985; Diprete 1989; Milkman 1987; Baron et al. 1991; Cockburn 1991). But they stop short of developing a general organizational approach to gender inequality. Organizational analyses of the diffusion of equal employment opportunity structures have not investigated the effects of structural changes on pay inequality within organizations (Edelman 1990, 1992), although such work has begun to examine how legal rights become transformed in the context of employing organizations

(Edelman, Erlanger, and Lande 1993; Edelman, Abraham, and Erlanger 1992).

One reason for the underdevelopment of organizational theories of gender inequality is that some feminist and critical theorists reject bureaucratic forms of organization as inherently antithetical to their visions of justice and individuality (Ferguson 1984; Frug 1984). In their view, women and minorities should not formulate strategies for succeeding within bureaucratic hierarchies but must instead seek to dismantle bureaucracies. While radical critiques of bureaucracies are valuable for unearthing various ways in which bureaucratic structures operate as gender and race hierarchies, they do not develop a theory that would explain variations in the quantity or character of inequality in bureaucratic organizations. We see such theory as important because bureaucratic organization dominates in society. Such organizations not only impose systems of inequality; they also can promote values of gender equality and fairness. As Selznick observes in response to contemporary critics of bureaucracy:

> In our preoccupation with subtle forms of oppression and with high aspirations for fairness and well-being, we may forget that resistance to domination must begin with the obvious and the unsubtle. Arbitrary power is all too often blunt and crude; the pain it inflicts is readily apparent; there is no need for a guide to suffering, no need for consciousness-raising. Rather we require elementary constraints on the abuse of power. When these are discounted – as "mere structures" or as "liberal legalism" – people are left unprotected where protection is most urgent. This posture often signals a failure to appreciate the gains other generations have won and that are now taken for granted. (1992, 263–64)

Indeed, there are indications that women and minorities may find bureaucratic employment settings more congenial. Bridges and Villemez (1994) found that women and minorities were more likely to work in firms with developed personnel systems.

Perhaps the main reason why organization-level analyses have not played a more prominent role in the pay equity debate is that such analyses are inconsistent with how comparable worth advocates have theorized the problem of between-job, male-female wage differences. Advocates of comparable worth tacitly assume that employers follow similar cultural templates in devaluing work done primarily by women. Accordingly, they have concentrated their efforts on aggregate-level demonstrations of such effects (see England 1992). They have shown little interest in analyzing whether organizations vary in the nature of between-job wage differences or whether such differentials are produced through different mechanisms in different organizations. They have been satisfied that such variation is probably not important, given that most job evaluation studies show about the same level of "underpayment" to female job categories.

In our view this has left a serious gap in our understanding of how gender inequality is produced at the organizational level. As we note later, the lack of an organizational theory of pay setting can frustrate attempts to make pay systems more fair. Ironically, this theoretical tack also may have made pay equity proposals vulnerable to market-based arguments. By attributing wage differentials primarily to society-wide forces that operate outside the employing organization, comparable worth advocates come perilously close to reaching the same conclusion as orthodox economists: employing organizations are not individually responsible for the wage gap that exists in their organizations. For the economists, the employers are price takers. Comparable worth advocates might agree, with the added stipulation that the employers' pricing behavior is based on cultural bias against women.

We suggest that it is valuable to begin to theorize explicitly about how organizational characteristics influence patterns of gender inequality in organizations. Among the variables of interest are whether the organization is in the public or the private sector, the size and complexity of the work force, the degree to which the firm constitutes an internal labor market or otherwise has a large number of skilled jobs that are idiosyncratic to the firm's operations, the role of unions in management-employee relations, the degree to which the firm has developed a bureaucratic personnel system that attempts to centralize and rationalize personnel decisions, the nature of the product and labor markets in which the organization is located, and the historical and social characteristics of the industry in which the organization is embedded.

The configuration of these variables and the nature of their effects on gender inequality in organizations is likely to vary by historical period. For the most part, our case studies concern large bureaucratic organizations in the early to mid-1970s. Although we are examining only a small number of organizations, we detect discernible period effects. Most obvious is the relatively recent application of antidiscrimination laws to these organizations in the early 1970s. The cases all represent new efforts to determine the reach of laws against pay discrimination. Another period effect is the historically specific shape of managerial ideologies as it affected pay systems. For example, the four organizations we studied redesigned their pay systems based on the advice of consultants. The pay consultants literally acted as agents for disseminating similar pay rationalization schemes among organizations in the same economic sector.

The role of consultants raises another potentially important variable: the effect of organizational field on pay-setting practices. The neo-institutionalist school of organization theory (see Meyer and Rowan 1977; DiMaggio and Powell 1983) asserts that the structures and practices of organizations, including those relating to equal opportunity, are significantly influenced by what similar organizations do (Edelman 1990). This, too, is apparent in our cases.

In asserting the importance of organizations in generating gender inequality, we do not mean to deny the significance of forces external to organizations. Indeed, one task of an organizational theory of gender inequality is to map variation in how organizations incorporate or mediate the nature of gender relations in the broader society. Some organizations have crudely exploited categories of workers – minorities, immigrants, children, and women – through their monopsonistic position in the labor market (see, e.g., Thomas 1985; Milkman 1987). Cohn's (1985) insightful comparison of the British Railways and the British Postal Service in the nineteenth century illustrates how one organization pursued an overt strategy of "feminizing" its work force as a means of reducing labor costs, while another did not, in a period when women were at least informally (and sometimes formally) barred from certain kinds of work.

In contemporary American society, these processes typically occur in more subtle ways, as organizations recruit from gender-stratified occupational labor markets, as organizations construct firm-specific models of skill and capability that build on and transform gender stereotypes, as groups of management or groups of workers compete for resources within organizations by deploying "gendered" strategies (e.g., hard bargaining) or invoking "gendered" values (e.g., the family wage, "aggressiveness").

Some of these practices may be intentional. But many aspects of gender hierarchy in organizations are the "naturalized" products of gender relations from an earlier period in the organization (Bourdieu 1977). The gendered character of these practices is rendered invisible to the current incumbents of organizational positions. They often did not invent them. They merely are working within a set of taken-for-granted understandings that do not explicitly concern gender. Only in certain moments will the "hidden" dimension of gender emerge. In our case studies those moments included a time when a frustrated employee claimed a promotion was based on politics, not merit, when an outside consultant analyzed pay and promotion data by gender and found unexplained gender differentials, and when a woman unwittingly learned over a drink with a male co-worker that he mysteriously made more than she did even though they were doing the same job.

The gender ideologies of organizations are likely to be continuous with gender ideologies in the organization's environment. This is true in part because organizations are populated by professionals and other experts who were trained outside the organization. Personnel officers in large organizations, for example, will be imbued with the personnel philosophy of their organization. But their practices also are likely to reflect prior experience and training in other organizations, such as the military. Thus theoretical and practical understanding of gender inequality will depend on the interaction between organizations and environments on employment issues.

While there is a need for sociologists to begin to develop a systematic theory of gender inequality in organizations, this book proceeds inductively. We selected our case studies to tap aspects of organizational and market differences that we think are salient determinants of between-job gender inequality. But these four cases are only a beginning. We cannot claim to have captured the kinds of variations in organizational characteristics that would form the basis for a comprehensive theory. Instead, we have gone into as much depth as possible in a small number of cases. This approach allows us to discover and evaluate mechanisms that contribute to or alleviate gender-based pay inequality in these organizations.

The four case studies illuminate how organizational processes interact with and mediate market forces in the generation of gender-based wage inequality. There is a sharp contrast between public sector and private sector organizations in how this mediation takes place. In public sector organizations, in which the wage structure is more rigidly determined by job, we find explicit interest group behavior with respect to the pay levels for particular jobs. Female-dominated jobs tend to be less well represented in these political processes. The politics of pay are more muted in private sector firms, in part because there is less information available about who gets what, in part because norms of equity and employee participation are less salient than in the public sector, and in part because pay levels are less rigidly set by job. Nonetheless, organizational politics of a different kind play a pivotal role in structuring pay levels and producing and reproducing patterns of gender inequality in pay.

The *Sears* case represents an instance in which the tension between different parts of the organization (the "field" and the "parent"), along with the organizational imperative of rapid growth and deployment during an earlier era, produced a highly decentralized pay system. By entrusting almost total wage-setting discretion to subunit managers, this system fostered a pattern of discriminatory pay premiums to male workers. In the Coastal Bank case (a pseudonym), we find patterns of gender inequality produced in an organization that consists of a large, nonprofessional sector at the bottom, a modest-sized professional strata in the middle, and a small group of all male manager/owners at the top. In the nonprofessional sector, gender inequality in wages is largely the product of job (much like in the public sector organizations we studied). Moreover, female jobs tend to be disadvantaged in part because the organizations tend to play tough with market rates for female jobs (i.e., they pay further below the market than they do for less numerous, mostly male-occupied jobs). At the middle professional level, pay is much less structured by type of job and far more determined by rank within the professional corps. While top management may be committed to lowering labor costs in this stratum, department heads compete to gain higher incomes for their professional subordinates. In practice, these appeals favor male officers proportionally more than female officers. Moreover, the clublike character of top management encourages a definition of "performance" and "potential" that matches the status-class attributes of existing management: white, male, Gentile, and upper class.

The case studies support the need for organizational theories of gender-based wage inequalities. All four organizations studied employed sophisticated efforts to evaluate jobs and survey market rates. All invoked at least the idiom of market wage rates in justifying their pay structures. Yet each organization produced a pattern of gender inequality that was significantly independent of market forces and efficiency considerations. Our results suggest the value of mapping variations in gender and racial inequality across different market and organizational contexts.

In this book we have not ventured into the study of racial inequality in organizational pay systems. The organizational approach to inequality we advance here may well be usefully applied to race-based pay discrimination, as well as to the particular difficulties produced at the intersection of race and gender. We would not presume, however, that race and gender work the same way in occupational systems, labor markets, or organizational pay systems. Just as we have attempted to theorize about gender differences in pay at the level of organizations, additional research is necessary to theorize about racial (and race by gender) differences in pay in organizations. We settled on a singular focus on gender in part to make this a manageable project. The legal and empirical literature on gender inequality alone is complex and difficult to marshal. It is also the case that legal and policy debates in the wage discrimination field have, since the early 1970s, focused primarily on gender discrimination.

Law, Markets, and Gender Inequality in Pay

In both method and substance, this is a study in the sociology of law. Not only do we rely on law cases as windows through which we view organizational dynamics, but we see each case as representing a legal challenge to gender inequality in an organization. The resolution of these cases thus has implications for larger theoretical issues concerning law and inequality. Is the law an instrument for change, a hollow symbol of justice presiding over a manifestly unfair system of wage inequality, or part of an ideological apparatus that denies and legitimates aspects of gender inequality that are pervasive in organizational life?

One of the central tensions within the American legal system in the modern era has been the question of what role the law should play in redressing patterns of social inequality. In the area of sex-based pay discrimination, the most intense debate has concerned the question of whether employers can be liable for discrimination in how they pay men and women who hold different jobs in the same organization. The passage of the Equal Pay Act of 1963 established the principle that employers could not pay men and women different wages for the same job. (The act allowed exceptions for piece-rate systems, seniority-based pay differences, and for reasons other than sex.) The Civil Rights Act of 1964, as amended in 1972, set in place a broader antidiscrimination rule that prohibited employers from discriminating against women and minorities in any aspect of employment, including pay. Title VII's ban on wage discrimination did not contain an "equal work" requirement. But until 1981, when the Supreme Court decided the *Gunther* case,[3] it was not clear whether an amendment to Title VII that sought to reconcile it with the Equal Pay Act imported the equal work requirement into Title VII as well. *Gunther* ruled that Title VII could apply to between-job pay differences. It thus opened the door for comparable worth lawsuits in which plaintiffs used job evaluation results as a means of attempting to demonstrate sex-based pay discrimination.

In its pure form, a comparable worth lawsuit argues that employers are required to pay equal wages for jobs of the same evaluated worth (typically as measured in terms of skill, effort, responsibility, and working conditions). *AFSCME* sounded the deathknell for "pure" comparable worth theories. In its aftermath, plaintiffs moved away from sole reliance on job evaluation results in cases alleging between-job pay discrimination and sought rather to bring in other evidence of disparate treatment and intentional discrimination. Their efforts failed every time,

---

3 *County of Washington v. Gunther*, 452 U.S. 161 (1981).

as courts insisted on characterizing the plaintiffs' claims as "comparable worth claims" and cited the same market explanation given for between-job wage differences invoked in *AFSCME*.

The rise and fall of comparable worth as a legal theory of discrimination must be understood in the context of the broader set of cases alleging sex-based pay discrimination in the post-*Gunther* era. As a predicate to the in-depth analyses of the four cases, we reviewed and classified all reported opinions in such cases for the period 1982–96. This analysis reveals that, although the courts never overruled *Gunther*, after the defeats in *AFSCME* and similar cases plaintiffs largely abandoned efforts at more ambitious, between-job claims of discrimination. Scrutiny of the opinions issued in the cases involving between-job claims indicates that, with the exception of a few cases in which there is something approaching an empirical analysis of market issues, the courts rejected the plaintiffs' claims based on a conviction that the employers' pay policies were reasonable and nondiscriminatory given labor market conditions. The courts adopted what we call the free market paradigm of the relationship between labor markets and employing organizations.

Our project has two kinds of legal implications. The first pertains to the internal logic of antidiscrimination law. By reanalyzing the market explanation for between-job wage differences in these cases, we are questioning the empirical underpinnings of the leading precedents in the case law. To the extent our interpretations take hold, future commentators and courts may reconsider the authority of these cases and adopt a more critical stance toward market and efficiency explanations offered by employers.

Our results thus may reopen doctrinal debates about the appropriate standards to apply in determining sex-based pay discrimination. In recent years the courts increasingly have moved away from notions of liability based on disparate impact in favor of tests based on intentionality and specific institutional culpability.[4] The courts have explicitly rejected disparate impact approaches to allegations of systemic discrimination in pay.[5] This judicial stance is fully compatible with the dominant conception of between-job gender inequality, for the dominant conception locates the source of wage disparities outside the employing organization.

But what if empirical research challenged the validity of the dominant conception? In our view, the question of the source of gender disparities in organizations is an empirical issue to be determined on a case-by-case basis. The organizational inequality framework we propose argues that

4 See, e.g., *Wards Cove Packing Co. v. Atonio*, 490 U.S. 642 (1989); partially overridden by the Civil Rights Act of 1991.
5 See *Spaulding v. University of Washington*, 740 F.2d 686 (1984).

there often is a link between organizational pay practices and gender-based pay differences. Our framework blurs the comfortable distinction between forces internal and external to the employing organization by focusing on specific mechanisms within organizations that generate between-job pay inequality. Given that employers typically are aware of such practices, are in a position to study their consequences for gender inequality, and have the power to alter the practices, our framework may lead to a reconsideration of the responsibility of employing organizations for gender-based pay differences.

The second set of legal implications relates to social theories about law and gender inequality in American society. The empirical record generated by the case studies, including court documents, transcripts, interviews with participants, organizational documents, work force statistics, and local labor market data, allows us to evaluate the official descriptions of gender inequality in the defendant organizations offered by the judicial opinions in these cases. Our examination of these data suggests that in at least three of the four cases the courts played a profoundly conservative role. The judges deployed the authority of law to legitimate institutionalized forms of gender inequality in the workplace. The decisions were not merely institutionally cautious, in the sense that the courts declined to enter a judgment that would have required a complicated, judicially taxing remedy, as in litigation concerning prisons, schools, and other institutions. Rather, the opinions offered a sweeping, some might say "sociological," interpretation of the organizational and market context presented in the case before them.

In three of the four cases the opinions ratified the status quo as just. If similar logic and proof had been used to reach the opposite result in these cases, the opinions would have been pilloried in the press and in legal commentary as instances of inappropriate judicial activism. The one case that ended as a legal victory for the plaintiffs was decided on quite narrow grounds of intentional discrimination in the initial placement, promotion, and pay of women and minorities as a group. Neither the plaintiffs' theory nor the remedy adopted attacked some basic aspects of gender inequality in the defendant's pay system.

We see the courts in these cases acting as conservators of institutionalized patterns of gender inequality. This is a different, although not entirely an inconsistent, conclusion from that proposed by Michael McCann (1994) in his pathbreaking study of the pay equity movement. McCann judged pay equity litigation a key element in raising the rights consciousness of female workers and an inspiring source of rights discourse. While the activists McCann spoke to may have taken inspiration from a legal rights framework, they represent but the vanguard of a reform movement that has gained limited victories in relatively isolated contexts. In our view, the legal discourse that has had a broader effect, in policy and in society's perception of gender inequality, has been voiced by judges denying the responsibility of employers for pay differences between male and female workers. By attributing the gender gap in pay to a faceless monolith, the market, for which no identifiable group of individuals is responsible, this discourse located the problem beyond the reach of collective action by workers within the workplace. Rather than empowering female workers, the discourse tended to silence them.

Why did the courts assume such a posture? Several models of judicial decision making might be invoked to explain this pattern. We conclude that the most persuasive account rests on an ideological explanation. The courts saw the evidence presented in these cases through the lens of the dominant discourse on between-job gender inequality. The certainty of this vision is revealed in the texts of these opinions, such as that quoted from Justice Kennedy. With few exceptions, the courts do not merely say that the plaintiffs failed to carry their burden of proof. Instead, the opinions offer sweeping pronouncements that market forces and efficiency considerations explain the wage differences at issue, despite often powerful evidence to the contrary. This is an instance of what Kim Scheppele (1987) refers to as perceptual fault lines. The courts in these cases would acknowledge the antidiscrimination principle articulated by *Gunther* but were largely unwilling to question the dominant explanation of "the facts" before them.

We do not mean to attribute some kind of universal intention to the courts. The conclusions they reached were not predetermined. A small number of judges ruled in favor of plaintiffs in between-job cases. Others described the kinds of evidence they were looking for in the plaintiffs' case, which they did not find. In a few early cases the plaintiffs invited the courts to assume that market forces were at work by asserting (1) "the market discriminates" and (2) the employer had discriminated by "following the market." Yet most of the opinions cannot be explained away on tactical grounds. Most of the opinions reflected an unquestioning assumption that market forces produced the gender inequality plaintiffs complained about.

Our analysis thus calls for both a rethinking of the law against sex-based pay discrimination and a reconsideration of the role of law in maintaining gender inequality. Our results suggest the need to expand the legal responsibility of employers for between-job wage differences. Under the current regime, the courts have functioned to deny and legitimate existing patterns of gender inequality in organizations, even though these patterns do not appear justified by market or efficiency factors.

Social Policy and Pay Equity

Finally, our investigation is relevant to policy debates about antidiscrimination policy. How our society confronts between-job gender inequality depends on theoretical understandings of the relationship between law, labor markets, and employing organizations. The emphasis in this work is on these underlying theoretical constructs and the evidence that supports one theoretical perspective over another. Yet our conceptual framework and our findings have implications for what concrete steps might be taken through the courts, regulation, and political organization to address this problem.

The debates about existing laws against sex discrimination in pay is a subset of a broader issue in social policy: How should this society regulate the pay practices of employers for predominantly male and predominantly female jobs? According to free market theorists, pay practices should be left to the discretion of employers. It usually is irrational for employers to discriminate on the basis of sex; the market will cure itself by driving less efficient, discriminating employers from the market. Besides, any attempt at regulation would entail costs that would outweigh potential benefits, even for the intended beneficiaries of such regulation (see Epstein 1992). Advocates of comparable worth, in contrast, argue that market prices and employer practices are so thoroughly infused with sexism that the only cure for gender inequality is to abandon market systems in favor of job evaluation. When properly cleansed of sexism and racism, job evaluation will reward workers fairly based on their evaluated worth to the firm.

We enter this broad debate with what we take to be a set of relevant empirical findings. First, the free market theorists exaggerate the degree to which market forces determine wage levels within large organizations. Second, we find that organizational politics significantly shape the outcomes of pay systems, whether based on market principles or principles of comparable worth. These findings suggest the need to move the policy debate about pay equity beyond the simple juxtaposition of market and nonmarket systems. This society cannot rely on labor markets to cure the problem of between-job sex discrimination in pay. Yet, for a number of political and practical reasons, including difficulties of implementation, comparable worth also does not appear to be the solution.

Just as the organizational inequality model identifies organizational processes that generate gender inequality, it implies a set of procedural reforms that can alleviate institutional tendencies toward sex discrimination in pay. It may seem ironic, given our questioning of the link between markets and organizational pay systems, but we think there may be much to be gained by harnessing the transformative energies of markets. Gender hierarchies in organizations often have functioned to distort and deflect the progressive effects of market change on male-female wage differences. If organizations more consistently and fairly incorporated market principles in their wage determination systems, we expect it would have progressive gender consequences. It also is useful for policy to encourage the sometimes powerful tendencies within organizations to develop pay practices that are more rational and just. While antidiscrimination law is not the only, or necessarily the preferred, instrument for change, it can play an important role in stimulating significant organizational change. We expand on these ideas in the conclusion of the book, based on what we have learned from the case studies.

Some analysts may argue that gender-based wage inequality is no longer a pressing problem that requires renewed attention by policy makers. They can cite trends over the past decade that reveal a shrinking gender gap in pay, in which women earned about 60 percent of men in 1974 but 76 percent by 1994 (see Chapter 3). We would counter that a substantial portion of the economic "progress" of women in the past decade has resulted from the stagnation and decline in the earnings of male workers (see Chapter 3). Moreover, there is no guarantee that without an active antidiscrimination policy sex-based discrimination and inequality will not increase. In this period of increasing hostility to affirmative action, both by the courts and politicians, there is some evidence that women workers are more pessimistic about equal opportunity in the workplace than they have been since the 1970s (*New York Times*, Sept. 12, 1995, p. C2, cols. 1–3; Rhode 1997). Indeed 1997 saw the first widening in the gender gap in many years, although female earnings rebounded in 1998 (*Chicago Sun Times*, June 10, 1998, p. 1). We should not assume that gender-based wage inequality is a problem that will go away by itself.

Methods

Our empirical analysis is based on in-depth examinations of four legal decisions that dealt with claims of gender discrimination in pay. The use of law cases as empirical case studies is relatively novel in the sociology of law, although more common among legal historians and other observers (see, e.g., McEvoy 1995; Noonan 1976; Mnookin 1985; Kluger 1976; Stewart 1983). Our approach is somewhat distinctive. Typically when sociolegal scholars are researching a case, they are primarily interested in the law. We are at least equally interested in aspects of the employing organizations that are the defendants in these lawsuits.

We exploit litigation to gain data on the origins, functioning, and gender effects of organizational pay systems that otherwise are very difficult to obtain. Of course, we also enjoy a unique opportunity to study law in action. The case studies reveal the conditions that gave rise to the lawsuit, the kinds of organizational data that found their way into the legal record, and, to some extent, the consequences the legal results have for the organization.

Case study approaches have gained popularity in sociology, as historical sociologists, feminists, and other critical theorists have called for analyses that explicitly recognize the historical contingency of social action and that give agency to the human actors involved (see, e.g., Sewell 1992; Abbott 1992; Burawoy 1991). Steinberg (1992, 580) explicitly extols case studies of organizations as a superior method for feminist research compared with surveys and other "mainstream" methods. (See Reinharz 1992 for a more catholic perspective on the use of various methods to pursue feminist research.) Sociolegal scholarship also has seen increasing emphasis on critical narratives that attempt to analyze the legal consciousness of nonelite segments of society (see, e.g., Silbey and Ewick 1995; Merry 1990). McCann (1994), for example, pursues an "interpretive" approach in his interviews with pay equity activists, meaning that he allowed his informants to tell their own stories of how they came to perceive injustice and the steps that led them to get involved. His effort is part of a larger movement within law and society research that seeks to "decenter" official law by shifting attention from formal legal institutions to the effects of law and legal values in everyday life (Sarat and Kearns 1993; Trubek 1984). Many scholars working in this new vein frame their research in terms of domination and resistance (Scott 1985, 1990) and thus see their intellectual enterprise as raising counterhegemonic interpretations of law in social context. (For an excellent review, see Hirsch and Lazarus-Black 1994.)

Our approach embraces many aspects of this critical turn. Context is crucial to our analysis. The framework we propose posits that the specific configuration of politics and gender within an organization is an important source of gender inequality. The search for intraorganizational mechanisms of inequality requires an examination of local conditions. Moreover, our framework leads to explanations of inequality that run counter to the dominant interpretations offered within organizations and within legal opinions in most pay cases. In that sense, our project has a counterhegemonic message.

Yet in many ways our research involves conventional social-scientific methods. First, although we insist on the need to move below the level of aggregate data on gender inequality, we still seek to build a more general theory about inequality in organizations that maps variations in gender inequality by market and organization contexts. Second, our analysis is based on "mainstream" methods of qualitative and quantitative research, including focused interviewing and regression analyses of work force and labor market data. Third, our case studies probe into the specific dynamics of organizational pay systems but hardly could be characterized as involving thick descriptions of organizational life. In the case studies we are primarily engaged in elite, intellectual debates about the determinants of sex-based pay differences. The data made available to us from the cases are the by-product of what the legal and personnel professionals in these matters deemed relevant to the question of discrimination. We have analyzed that material to address an ongoing debate within law and social science about the roots of gender inequality.

Whatever epistemology one subscribes to, our project faces difficult problems of proof. One could crudely characterize what we do in the case studies as relitigating lawsuits outside the presence of a judge, without giving the defense the opportunity to interrogate our sources, present alternative explanations, put their own experts on the stand. How can we claim to offer an empirical account that is more valid than that accepted by a court under the glare of scrutiny from opposing counsel and a public record? To that specific charge we plead nolo contendere. There is no guarantee that our results would prevail if these cases were to be litigated again. But that also is not the standard by which we have analyzed these data or by which we choose to have our work evaluated. We have approached these cases with the canons of social scientific proof in mind. The validity of our results ultimately rests on the ability of others to replicate our findings or to offer more compelling interpretations for what we present (for a general discussion, see King, Keohane, and Verba 1994, 7–9). Our results may not convince a given judge in a given case. We will settle for trying to persuade an intellectual community that we have added new insights into an old problem.

By far the largest problem with our research design from the standpoint of conventional methods is the difficulty of making generalizations to a large and complex universe of organizations from a set of four cases. When the cases become available because of litigation over claims of sex discrimination, there is a considerable risk of selection bias as well. How do we know that the conditions that led these organizations to be sued do not make them highly idiosyncratic among the population of organizations?

In the chapter on methods (Chapter 4) we pursue these questions at length. Suffice it to say here that our selection of cases was driven in part by necessity and in part by theoretical interests. We were limited to litigated cases that did not contain protective orders concerning organizational data. Because of our theoretical interest in markets, we thought it essential to include both public and private sector cases. For a variety of reasons, public sector organizations can be expected to operate their pay systems differently than private firms. Profit pressures, for one, do not play the same role in public sector organizations as in private firms. Thus we might expect private firms to follow the market more closely in setting wages than would public sector organizations. In the process of screening potential cases against private employers, we discovered that comparable worth litigation – that is, broad-based allegations of discrimination in paying different male and female jobs – has been limited to the public sector. We decided to press on with two private sector cases, even though they contained different sorts of pay discrimination claims than the public sector cases. The data in these cases still allowed us to investigate market, efficiency, and organizational inequality models. More important, they allowed us to test our theoretical framework in the private sector.

Despite some obvious limitations, we think these four cases carry substantial weight in theoretical debates about gender inequality. First, they represent fundamentally important variations in organizational and market contexts. In addition to the public-private variable just mentioned, they also vary by size: Two are very large organizations, two are more modest in size. Taken as individual entities the four organizations comprise an interesting collection of organizational types: a large state employment system, a small state university, a Fortune 500 retailing giant, and a money center bank. Not surprisingly, each organization's pay system contains some unique elements. What is more striking theoretically, however, is that all four also exhibit significant commonalities in how they determine the pay of workers and the mechanisms that produce male-female pay differences.

Second, there is little to suggest that these organizations are atypical among similar sorts of organizations in this time period on issues of gender discrimination. What may be most unusual about these organizations is the nature of the pay claims raised and the fact that they actually came to trial. Government reports suggest that a very large proportion of large organizations have been sued for sex discrimination in some aspect of their employment practices (Dunworth and Rogers 1996). Mere status as a defendant to a discrimination lawsuit does not render these organizations unusual. Also, we know from Bumiller's work (1988) building on the findings of the Civil Litigation Research Project that, of all perceived injuries, employment discrimination has the lowest odds of leading to the filing of a formal complaint. Just because other organizations were not sued for pay discrimination does not mean that women within those organizations did not experience wage injustice. Moreover, the defendants in these cases defended their pay practices on the grounds that other employers did the same thing. While our results contradict the notion that they were just following the market in setting wages, our reading of these and other pay cases, as well as reports of pay consultants that compare these organizations with others in their industry, lead us to conclude that these are not especially deviant organizations.

Finally, the fact that the plaintiffs lost three of the four cases suggests that these are not "easy" cases from which to argue for an organizational inequality approach.

Plan of the Book

The remainder of the book has three parts: theory and method (Chapters 2–4); the case studies (Chapters 5–8); and the conclusion (Chapter 9). In Chapter 2 we analyze legal theories of sex-based pay discrimination. After briefly sketching the development of the statutory and case law leading up to the *Gunther* opinion, we examine all reported cases involving claims of sex discrimination in pay in the post-*Gunther* period. This analysis reveals that only a handful of between-job cases were adjudicated after *Gunther*. After the defeats in *AFSCME* and other cases, plaintiffs largely abandoned such theories. In the recent era, plaintiffs have limited their claims to more conventional Equal Pay Act issues. We then review the opinions in the cases involving between-job claims. These cases did not overturn *Gunther*, but were resolved based on the factual question of whether market or efficiency considerations explained the wage differences complained of. Our reading of these cases suggests that the courts, with a few exceptions, were heavily influenced by the dominant conception of between-job, male-female pay differences. We close the chapter by presenting three paradigms of sex-discrimination law that link empirical conceptions of employing organizations and labor markets to different regimes of antidiscrimination law: the free market paradigm, the comparable worth paradigm, and the organizational inequality paradigm.

Chapter 3 develops an organizational theory of gender inequality in pay. After summarizing historical and comparative data on the gender gap in pay, we examine the connection between the wage gap and sex segregation by job. We conclude that a substantial portion of the male-female wage gap is attributable to between-job pay differences – the focus of the pay equity movement and our empirical analyses in this book. After reviewing the literature in economics and sociology on male-female wage inequality, we present the organizational inequality model that informs our approach.

Chapter 4 discusses the research design of the study, including the unusual issues raised by using materials generated from litigation to perform empirical analyses of inequality in organizations. After we assess the problem of selection bias, we describe how the cases were selected and summarize the similarities and differences among them. We conclude the chapter with a comment on the intellectual approach we take in this book, what we call critical empiricism, and locate our approach within sociolegal studies.

Part II of the book consists of four case studies. Each case study analyzes an organization as a system of gender inequality. Each chapter describes the litigation that framed the issue of sex discrimination in the case. Using different kinds of data, in each organizational study, we examine the relative explanatory power of market, administered efficiency, and organizational inequality models of gender inequality. In Part III of the book, we synthesize the findings from the case studies and discuss the implications of our results for theories of gender inequality, for the sociology of law, and for policy debates on pay equity.

Part I

Theory and Method

2

Legal Theories of Sex-Based Pay Discrimination

The decisions of federal courts in cases alleging sex-based pay discrimination reflect the tension between the law's normative commitment to equality and the courts' reverence for markets and efficiency. *County of Washington v. Gunther* (452 U.S. 161 [1981]), the Supreme Court ruling that fostered comparable worth litigation in federal courts, can be seen as a response to the antidiscrimination imperative. The Court would not countenance blatant discrimination against women workers just because they held different jobs from the male workers with whom they were compared. In the cases that followed *Gunther*, however, the lower courts limited its practical effect. They rejected comparable worth theories that relied on job evaluation studies to prove discrimination or that argued that employers were obligated to correct inequities identified in job evaluation results. Moreover, they consistently found that between-job pay differentials reflected market wages or acceptable business judgments rather than invidious, gender-based policies. The courts rendered these judgments case by case. Yet the opinions contain either sweeping references to the "economic realities" confronted by employers or only the most cursory analyses of market conditions. Our reading of the opinions is that the final outcomes of these cases were influenced by a deeply held, promarket ideology that may have extended beyond the facts in particular cases.

Much of the rest of this book examines whether the courts' belief in markets and efficiency as the primary determinants of the male-female wage gap is well founded empirically. The focus of this chapter is the law itself. One of our objectives here is to set the legal context for the social-scientific analyses that follow. We briefly describe the evolution of the law against sex-based pay discrimination, examine the judicial treatment of comparable worth lawsuits, and report the frequency and success rates of various types of pay discrimination theories in the post-*Gunther* era. This analysis establishes the significance for law of our empirical investigation of the four cases. It also allows us to locate our case studies within pay discrimination cases as a group. The analysis of existing cases also provides a foundation for our presentation of three models of pay discrimination that link different legal approaches to between-job wage differences and different theoretical conceptions of labor markets and employing organizations. These models serve as a bridge to the next chapter, where we review the social-scientific literature on labor markets and gender inequality in organizations.

Another objective of this chapter is to begin to develop a sociological narrative on the law of sex-based pay discrimination. How the federal courts have dealt with pay discrimination claims has significant implications for theories of inequality and law. We reserve extended theoretical discussion until we have analyzed the four cases in depth and have seen how the litigants and judges behaved in context. Yet the overall pattern of cases and legal doctrine we review in this chapter is grist for theoretical work. It provides the basis for some preliminary theoretical formulations that we revisit throughout the case studies and confront more centrally in the concluding chapter of the book.

The Evolution of Federal Laws against Gender-Based Pay Discrimination

The two principal federal laws against gender-based wage discrimination are the Equal Pay Act of 1963[1] and Title VII of the Civil Rights Act of 1964.[2] The Equal Pay Act prohibits employers from paying men and women employees differently for "equal work on jobs the performance of which requires equal skill, effort, and responsibility, and which are performed under similar working conditions, except where such payment is made pursuant to (i) a seniority system; (ii) a merit system; (iii) a system which measures earnings by quantity or quality of production; or (iv) a differential based on any other factor other than sex." The Equal Pay Act contains something close to a strict liability standard. If a female employee establishes that there is a wage differential for the same job that does not fall within one of the four exceptions, that is sufficient to win. The employee is not required to prove the employer's intent to discriminate based on gender.

The main limitation of the Equal Pay Act with respect to gender-based wage differences is the equal work requirement. While the courts interpret the act to reach "substantially similar jobs," even though they may have different job titles, it only applies to contexts where men and women work in the same jobs. Given the high levels of sex segregation by job in the American economy, the act has a limited purview. As

1   29 U.S.C. §206 (d) (1990).   2   42 U.S.C. §§2000e-1 to 2000e-17 (1982).

recently as 1991, 53 percent of either working women or working men would have to change jobs to produce a fully integrated American labor force (Reskin and Padavic 1994, 54). Thus a large portion of the gender gap in earnings appears to reside in differences between traditionally female jobs and traditionally male jobs rather than in the earnings differences of men and women doing the same job.

Title VII of the Civil Rights Act of 1964 is not so limited on its face. It contains a blanket prohibition against discrimination in compensation because of an individual's sex, race, religion, or national origin.[3] Title VII's broad wage discrimination rule is limited by the so-called Bennett amendment, which sought to clarify the relationship between Title VII and the Equal Pay Act. The Bennett amendment excuses sex-based wage differentials "if such differentiation is authorized by the provisions of section 206(d) of title 29 [i.e., the Equal Pay Act]."[4] The language of the Bennett amendment is ambiguous. Did it import only the affirmative defenses to Equal Pay Act claims into Title VII? Or did it also import the equal work requirement? Until the Supreme Court's decision in *County of Washington v. Gunther*, there was considerable division among the lower courts on this question.

The logic and outcome of the *Gunther* decision may have been foreshadowed by *I.U.E. v. Westinghouse* (631 F.2d 1094 [1980]). The plaintiffs in *Westinghouse* were workers in predominantly female jobs in Westinghouse's Trenton, New Jersey, factory. They alleged that in the 1930s Westinghouse maintained separate job and wage categories for "male" jobs and "female" jobs. Even though some of the female jobs received the same point ratings as male jobs, they were placed in lower wage-grade categories. In 1965 the company established a new, unitary job-grade system that merged the male and female jobs. But some 85 percent of female workers were placed in grades that were lower than the grade of any male workers, and only one of the seventy-seven workers in higher job grades was a woman. The plaintiffs conceded that they were not doing the same work as the incumbents of male jobs but argued that Westinghouse had intentionally paid female jobs less than male jobs because of the sex of the workers and thus had committed intentional pay discrimination in violation of Title VII. The district court dismissed the plaintiffs' case before trial. It held that because the plaintiffs were not alleging that they did the same work as male workers, they could not state a valid claim under either the Equal Pay Act or Title VII. The Third Circuit Court of Appeals, with Judge Leon Higginbotham writing the opinion, reversed.

At the core of Judge Higginbotham's opinion was the view that a

3   42 U.S.C. §2000e-2.   4   42 U.S.C. §2000e-2(h).

narrow reading of Title VII's wage discrimination provision would allow serious injustice of the sort the civil rights laws were meant to combat. He introduced his interpretation of the significance of the Bennett amendment for Title VII with a comparison between gender-based wage discrimination and other forms of wage discrimination.

> Westinghouse's position would permit employers to discriminate against women even though they could not pursue similar discriminatory practices against others on account of race, religion, or national origin. As an example, it is clear that Title VII prohibits an employer from paying more per hour to welders than plumbers *if* the reason for the employer paying higher wages to the welder is that the majority of the welders are Protestants and that the majority of the plumbers are Catholics. . . . While Westinghouse presumably would not challenge the illegality of the scheme outlined above, it asserts that the scheme would be permissible if the reason for the wage disparity is that the majority of welders are men and the majority of plumbers are women. . . . In the absence of explicit statutory language or Supreme Court holdings to the contrary, we are hesitant to conclude that Title VII would allow discriminatory behavior on the basis of sex, when the same behavior would be prohibited if made on the basis of race, religion, or national origin. (I.U.E. v. Westinghouse, 631 F.2d 1094, 1100 [1980])

The court of appeals remanded the case to the trial court for further proceedings that would allow the plaintiffs to prove intentional discrimination. The case settled before going to trial.

The *Gunther* case also presented an instance of allegations of blatant between-job wage disparities that might go unpunished if Title VII were interpreted narrowly. The County of Washington paid its prison matrons (all females) only 70 percent as much as it paid its prison guards (all males). The guards and matrons did much the same work. And the county's job evaluation study assigned the matron position 95 percent as many job evaluation points as the guard position. When the matrons sued under Title VII, the district court dismissed the case, in large part due to its interpretation of the Bennett amendment. Both the Ninth Circuit Court of Appeals and the Supreme Court disagreed. By a 5 to 4 majority, the Supreme Court held that Title VII's wage discrimination provisions could extend beyond those of the Equal Pay Act. The Court specifically refused to endorse "the controversial concept of comparable worth" (452 U.S. 161, p. 166), but ruled that an employer could be liable for discrimination in how it paid two different jobs, one held by men, one by women. Over the strenuous objections of the dissent, the majority in *Gunther* read the Bennett amendment as bringing only the affirmative defenses to the Equal Pay Act into Title VII, while leaving the equal work requirement out.

The Court appeared moved by a concern that some egregious forms of wage discrimination might go without effective remedy if the equal work requirement were made part of Title VII wage claims. "As Congress itself has indicated, a broad approach to the definition of equal employment opportunity is essential for overcoming and undoing the effect of discrimination. . . . Respondents' claims of discriminatory undercompensation are not barred . . . merely because respondents do not perform work equal to that of male jail guards" (452 U.S. 161, pp. 178, 180–81). The Supreme Court's decision gave the jail matrons an opportunity to prove discrimination based on gender. The county settled the lawsuit after it was remanded to the trial court.

Gunther was a doctrinal turning point for wage discrimination claims under Title VII. It meant that employers could be liable for between-job pay disparities if plaintiffs established that they resulted from gender-based discrimination. Although *Gunther* was a weak precedent, in the sense that the opinion commanded a bare majority of the Court and was coupled with a vigorous, often-cited dissent by Justice Rehnquist, it reaffirmed the purposive nature of Title VII's antidiscrimination principles. At a minimum, egregious forms of pay discrimination against women would not be tolerated just because male and female workers held different jobs. But how far would the courts go to redress between-job pay disparities? What would they recognize as evidence of employer discrimination? Could job evaluation studies be employed to establish gender-based pay discrimination? If such disparities were detected in a job evaluation study, did employers have an obligation under Title VII to remedy such disparities? The answers to these questions would determine the practical effect of *Gunther's* doctrinal turn.

Post-*Gunther* Cases

The Rejection of Comparable Worth Theories

After *Gunther*, a series of cases were filed, all against public sector organizations, that employed comparable worth theories of pay discrimination. By "comparable worth" we mean that the plaintiffs primarily relied on job evaluation studies in making their claims of between-job pay discrimination. The lawsuits also typically included other allegations of intentional discrimination, such as job segregation, refusals to hire and promote women employees for various jobs, and discriminatory pay practices within job categories. But these allegations assumed a relatively minor role in the lawsuits; the plaintiffs' key allegation concerned pay differentials between predominantly male and predominantly female jobs, after controlling for job evaluation points.

Before we describe the judicial treatment of comparable worth claims, some background on Title VII theories of discrimination is necessary. The Supreme Court has formulated two broad theories of employment discrimination under Title VII: disparate treatment and disparate impact (generally see Sullivan, Zimmer, and Richards 1988, 1:38–46; Larson and Larson 1994, 2: July 1996 Cumulative Supplement). Disparate treatment involves instances in which employers treat some people less favorably than others because of their race, color, religion, sex, or national origin. "Proof of discriminatory motive is critical although it can . . . be inferred from the mere fact of differences in treatment."[5] Systemic disparate treatment cases focus either on formal policies that discriminate among various groups or practices that use race or gender to discriminate despite the employer's denial that such factors are used. Plaintiffs may establish a prima facie case of discrimination employing either statistical evidence of disparate treatment or anecdotal evidence or some combination of both. The burden of proof then shifts to the employer to rebut the evidence of discrimination by disputing the showing of a disparity or showing valid, nondiscriminatory reasons for the disparity in employment outcomes.

Disparate impact cases involve employment practices that appear neutral on their face, but result in differing employment outcomes for different groups. Proof of discriminatory intent is not required. A plaintiff makes out a prima facie case by showing the disparate impact of an employer practice on a protected group. The employer must then respond by challenging the showing of a disparity, by claiming that the disparity results from a practice that is excepted from Title VII (such as a bona fide seniority system), or by demonstrating that the practice is justified by business necessity. Disparate impact theories potentially have broad application because they could be used to challenge a wide range of employment practices that produced different outcomes for different groups, even in the absence of proof of discriminatory intent.[6]

5 *International Brotherhood of Teamsters v. United States*, 431 U.S. 324, 335 n. 15.
6 In *Wards Cove Packing Co. v. Atonio*, 490 U.S. 642 (1989), the Supreme Court significantly narrowed the doctrine by holding that only certain kinds of comparisons would be considered relevant to the question of discrimination. The Civil Rights Act of 1991 legislatively reversed *Wards Cove*, mandating that the law on disparate impact was to be returned to what existed prior to the *Wards Cove* decision. The comparable worth cases we review here were decided before *Wards Cove*. Therefore, the precedents should not be affected by that case or the Civil Rights Act of 1991.

The first post-*Gunther* comparable worth case to reach a decision at trial was *AFSCME v. State of Washington* (578 F. Supp. 846 [W.D. Wash. 1983]), the subject of the case study reported in Chapter 6. It was the only victory for the plaintiffs among all comparable worth cases, and it too was overruled by the court of appeals. The trial court opinion held in favor of the plaintiffs on both disparate treatment and disparate impact theories of Title VII liability. Thus the trial court opinion articulates how plaintiffs have pursued both theories of pay discrimination. Similarly, the reversal by the Ninth Circuit Court of Appeals exemplifies how the courts have reacted to these theories in pay cases.

District court judge Tanner was persuaded that the plaintiffs had made out a prima facie case of a disparate impact theory because: "Several comparable worth studies, since 1974, found a 20% disparity in salary between predominantly male and predominantly female jobs which require an equivalent or lesser composite of skill, effort, responsibility, and working conditions as reflected by an equal number of job evaluation points" (578 F. Supp. 846, p. 863). He also found that the state had not produced evidence of a legitimate, overriding business justification for such differentials. The judge found evidence of the discriminatory intent required to make out a disparate treatment case in part based on the fact that state officials had publicly acknowledged the meaning of the job evaluation studies and yet were continuing the present wage system.

Judge Tanner's formulation, if it had prevailed, would have given plaintiffs very powerful tools to challenge employer wage systems in which job evaluation studies had revealed unexplained wage differences. First, it would treat the unexplained, gender-based wage differences in job evaluation studies as valid evidence of disparate impact. Employers would then have to justify their wage-setting policies based on business justifications. Second, failure to act on job evaluation results showing unexplained gender differences would be construed as intentional discrimination. Such a doctrine would have turned lead into gold for classes of female workers. Job evaluation studies consistently yield an unexplained gender gap in pay. Under Judge Tanner's approach, this gap would be transformed into evidence of discrimination to which employers would have to respond.

No other court has embraced the kind of "pure" comparable worth theory Judge Tanner adopted in the *AFSCME* case, however. The court of appeals directly rejected those principles most clearly associated with comparable worth. First, it rejected the application of a disparate impact theory to the State of Washington's "practice of taking prevailing market rates into account in setting wages."[7] According to the court, disparate

---

7   *AFSCME v. State of Washington*, 770 F.2d 1401, 1405 (1985).

impact analysis was to be limited to cases challenging "a specific, clearly delineated employment practice applied at a single point in the job selection process" (ibid). Citing another Ninth Circuit case, the court ruled that "the decision to base compensation on the competitive market, rather than on a theory of comparable worth, involves the assessment of a number of complex factors not easily ascertainable, an assessment too multifaceted to be appropriate for disparate impact analysis. *Spaulding v. University of Washington*, 740 F.2d 686 (9th cir. 1984)" (p. 1406). The complexity of the practices at issue were to be controlled by a disparate treatment theory.

Second, the court dismissed the notion that job evaluation studies and comparable worth statistics by themselves would be enough to establish the requisite proof of discriminatory intent (p. 1407). Third, it rejected the contention that having commissioned the job evaluation study, the State of Washington was required to implement the study. The court reasoned that employers should be able to treat job evaluation as one diagnostic tool among others. If employers were bound by law to incorporate such studies, it would simply discourage employers from engaging in such analyses.

In addition to rejecting the "pure" comparable worth theory of the plaintiffs, the Ninth Circuit indicated that it was not otherwise persuaded by the evidence that the State of Washington had intentionally discriminated against workers in predominantly female jobs. Historical patterns of sex segregation of jobs were not enough to support such an inference. And the court singled out the fact that none of the named plaintiffs testified regarding specific incidents of discrimination (p. 1408).

Much of the appellate court's opinion in *AFSCME* can be read as a specific response to the district court's comparable worth theory, that is, refusing to find liability solely based on job evaluation results or for attempting to follow market rates. Yet at several points the language of the opinion takes for granted that the gender differentials resulted from the state following a market rate system.[8] What the court of appeals takes for granted is the focus of the empirical analysis in Chapter 6.

AFSCME, Spaulding, and other cases seem to have clearly repudiated the application of the disparate impact theory to broad-based attacks on market rate systems. More focused pay practices might still be subject to such a theory, however. The Ninth Circuit entertained a disparate impact theory when a female employee challenged her employer's "head

---

8   See, e.g., ibid., p. 1406. "A compensation system that is responsive to supply and demand and other market forces is not the type of specific, clearly delineated employment policy contemplated by *Dothard* and *Griggs*; such a compensation system, the result of a complex of market forces, does not constitute a single practice that suffices to support a claim under disparate impact theory."

of household" rule for medical and dental coverage.[9] More recently, a federal district court allowed women faculty members to bring a disparate impact claim against a university for establishing different schedules for minimum salaries for different groups (or tiers) of academic departments. See *Donnelly v. Rhode Island Board of Governors for Higher Education*, 929 F. Supp. 583 (D. Rhode Island 1996). The defendant university prevailed because plaintiffs could not establish that the practice actually injured women faculty, and the court was persuaded that the practice was justified by business necessity. Yet, as this case suggests, the courts might be amenable to cases where plaintiffs question specific rules or practices that have a discernible impact on the pay of female workers.[10]

Other Title VII Theories: Posner on the Legal Possibility and Economic Paradox of Between-Job Discrimination

The defeat of comparable worth theories had a significant effect on the pattern of sex-based pay discrimination claims brought in federal court. As we discuss in the next section, plaintiffs virtually stopped bringing large-scale, between-job cases by the late 1980s. Almost immediately after *AFSCME*, plaintiffs went to lengths to distance themselves from the label "comparable worth" in their complaints and briefs. Judges often were not sympathetic and applied the term, despite the plaintiffs' protestations.[11]

The failure of pure comparable worth theories does not preclude Title VII challenges to between-job, sex-based pay differentials. Plaintiffs still have the opportunity to make out a case of intentional discrimination. But the case law makes clear that they will need to rely on more than job evaluation studies. And any allegation that between-job differences

---

9   *Wambheim v. J.C. Penney*, 705 F.2d 1492 (9th Cir. 1983).
10 McCann (1994) concludes his review of the federal law by speculating that the fate of pay equity in the courts currently rests on the effect of the Civil Rights Act of 1991 on disparate impact theories of wage discrimination. McCann's supposition is that the statutory restoration of disparate impact theories may breathe new life into pay equity litigation by putting the burden on employers to explain the business reasons that justify paying female work less than male work. Given our reading of the decisional law prior to *Ward's Cove*, which largely rejected disparate impact approaches in pay discrimination cases, we doubt that the 1991 act will have this kind of effect. The 1991 act may be more influential in other ways, however. By expanding the right to jury trial and allowing compensatory and punitive damages in cases alleging intentional discrimination, it may spur additional filings of lawsuits (see *New York Times*, Jan. 29, 1997, pp. 1, 10).
11 See, e.g., *American Nurses' Association v. State of Illinois*, 606 F. Supp. 1313 (N.D. Ill. 1985); *International Union, UAW v. State of Michigan*, 673 F. Supp. 893 (E.D. Mich. 1987).

in pay are the product of gender discrimination will confront the question of whether the pay differences reflect market rates or are otherwise justified by efficiency principles. Judge Richard Posner's opinion in *American Nurses' Association v. State of Illinois*, 783 F.2d 716 (1986), vividly illustrates both the possibility of such legal claims within Title VII, as well as the skepticism of the dominant discourse on gender inequality and the law toward such claims.

Richard Posner, the father of the law and economics movement, former law professor at the University of Chicago, and judge on the Seventh Circuit Court of Appeals, can be cited as an articulate source of the dominant view. In a paragraph of *dicta* to an opinion granting the American Nurses' Association a chance to make out a case of pay discrimination against the State of Illinois, he surmises:

> Economists have conducted studies which show that virtually the entire difference in the average hourly wage of men and women, including that due to the fact that men and women tend to be concentrated in different types of jobs, can be explained by the fact that most women take time out of the labor force in order to take care of their children. As a result they tend to invest less in their "human capital" (earning capacity); since part of any wage is a return on human capital, they tend therefore to be found in jobs that pay less. (p. 719)

Posner's holding in *American Nurses's Association* lucidly lays out how the plaintiffs – a class of nurses and other workers in predominantly female jobs – can establish a case of between-job wage discrimination under Title VII. One way is to prove that the employer paid male jobs more than female jobs because they are populated by men, not women, and *not* because the employer is following market wage rates for all jobs. Posner's skepticism of this empirical possibility is revealed in his analysis of the adequacy of the plaintiffs' complaint. Posner asserts that the idea that Illinois would pay men more might be silly, but that does not make the complaint defective.

> If Illinois is overpaying men relative to women, this must mean – unless the market model is entirely inapplicable to labor markets – that it is paying women at least their market wage (and therefore men more), for women wouldn't work for less than they could get in the market; and if so the state must also be refusing to hire women in the men's jobs, for above-market wages in those jobs would be a magnet drawing the women from their lower-paying jobs. (p. 727)

Using the forum of an appellate court opinion, Posner gives authority to a conception of markets, employers, and gender inequality that explains the wage gap as the legitimate product of the choices of male and female workers and rational employers. Deviations from market rates in favor of male workers are portrayed as rare oddities that would require the erection of barriers to keep women from seeking better-paying jobs. Such blatant efforts to segregate jobs by sex presumably could be readily detected and remedied. Comparable worth is rejected as damaging to the very group of women it purports to help.

> Upsetting the market equilibrium by imposing [comparable worth] would have costly consequences, some of which might undercut the ultimate goals of the comparable worth movement. If the movement should cause wages in traditionally men's jobs to be depressed below their market level and wages in traditionally women's jobs to be jacked above their market level, women will have less incentive to enter traditionally men's fields and more to enter traditionally women's fields. . . . Labor will be allocated less efficiently; men and women alike may be made worse off. (pp. 719–20)

By reversing the trial court dismissal of the plaintiffs' case, Posner gives the plaintiffs a generous outcome. By invoking one particular empirical model of labor markets and employers as though it is the only plausible model, however, Posner constructs a harsh reality for workers in predominantly female jobs. The question we have is whether the empirical data support the dominant discourse's conception of pristine markets, rational employers, and informed, mobile workers.

Overall Trends in Sex-Based Pay Discrimination Cases after *Gunther*

To understand better the significance of the rejection of pure comparable worth theories and the doctrinal possibilities left in their wake, as well as the general disposition of the federal courts to gender-based pay discrimination, we must look at other theories of sex-based pay discrimination in the post-*Gunther* period. Pay discrimination cases can be thought of on a continuum that runs from conventional Equal Pay Act cases (which compare the pay of male and female workers in identical jobs) to cases that involve similar but arguably different jobs to comparable worth cases (which allege discrimination in pay among workers in very different jobs based on the results of job evaluation studies). These legal theories vary in the risk that courts will reject them on doctrinal grounds: All courts recognize conventional Equal Pay Act cases. In that sense, they are low risks for plaintiffs. Courts are more wary of cases involving only similar kinds of jobs, for they fall in a gray area between the Equal Pay Act and Title VII theories. And courts consistently have rejected pure comparable worth cases. Comparable worth is a very risky, indeed now unrealistic, theory to bring in federal court. Because the same fact situation can be characterized in different ways, plaintiffs often can choose which type of theory they will press in litigation. Thus the theory of discrimination brought by a plaintiff is not strictly determined by the nature of the gender inequality that exists in a particular organization.

The degree of acceptability of a theory of discrimination is not the only element in the calculations of plaintiffs about which legal theory (or theories) they pursue. Plaintiffs sometimes cannot make their facts fit a low-risk theory of discrimination and are forced to pursue high-risk legal theories that better match the facts. Plaintiffs may assert that male and female workers are doing substantially the same job and therefore should be paid the same. But if they cannot convincingly persuade a judge that the jobs are the same, plaintiffs might concede the jobs are different for men and women and contend that the evidence shows the employer is intentionally discriminating in how they pay women. Plaintiffs may have other motives in choosing their legal strategy (see Goldstein 1995). The plaintiffs who pressed comparable worth, clearly a high-risk legal strategy, were motivated by an interest in rapidly achieving major social change.

We generally know from the literature on comparable worth that *Gunther* led to a series of comparable worth lawsuits (see McCann 1994, 48–91), but we do not know how these cases differed from other cases in the post-*Gunther* era. What sorts of success rates did plaintiffs enjoy in such cases? How did courts' views on markets and efficiency considerations enter into those cases, compared with comparable worth lawsuits? Can we detect any decisive movement from one set of cases to the others, as plaintiffs alter their litigation strategies in response to the outcomes of other cases?

We attempted to perform a comprehensive census of post-*Gunther* sex discrimination cases with published opinions. Published opinions provide only a partial view of the total set of discrimination complaints and filings, for many complaints do not lead to lawsuits, and lawsuits only rarely proceed to trial (generally see Galanter 1983; Siegelman and Donohue 1990). Yet published cases proved the only readily available public data on pay discrimination litigation. And while it would be desirable to have data on the entire complex of discrimination filings, trends in the published opinions are interesting in their own right. They make up the precedents that shape future litigation in the field. Written opin-

Table 2.1. *Plaintiffs' Success Rates in Sex-Based Pay Discrimination Cases by Type of Legal Theory (Federal District Courts, 1982–1996)*

Year	Equal Work (Same Job)	Equal Work (Predecessor)	Similar Work	Comparable Work	Comparable Worth	Total
1982–88	41% (22)	57% (7)	32% (22)	36% (22)	17% (6)	37% (79)
1989–95[a]	60% (15)	75% (4)	20% (10)	0% (2)	0% (2)	42% (33)
1995–96[b]	47% (17)	29% (7)	50% (6)	0% (1)	— (0)	42% (31)
Total	48% (54)	50% (18)	38% (38)	32% (25)	10% (10)	39% (145)

[a] Through July 1995.
[b] August 1995 through January 1997.

ions articulate the legal and social grounds on which courts entertain or reject pay discrimination claims.

Our effort was informed by an article by Yong Lee, who classified district court and appellate court gender-based pay discrimination cases for the period 1982–88 (Lee 1989). The gist of Lee's argument was that too much attention had been given in the literature on discrimination to the concept of comparable worth. A less radical legal theory involving comparisons of male and female compensation – what he termed "comparable work" cases – enjoyed higher levels of plaintiff success than either comparable worth or more traditional Equal Pay Act cases. According to our tabulations from Lee's classification of district court cases, plaintiffs won only 1 in 5 comparable worth cases (20 percent) and 5 of 19 equal work cases (26 percent), but won 5 of 13 comparable work cases, for a 39 percent success rate. Lee's results were provocative. It suggested that even though comparable worth was largely dead as a legal theory, another legal theory that attacked between-job pay differentials was enjoying a relatively high success rate. If Lee's analysis were correct, it would make our empirical analyses of between-job pay differentials relevant to a viable legal theory of discrimination.

We reviewed Lee's analysis and updated his findings to the current time.[12] The results of this investigation are reported in Tables 2.1 and 2.2. The cases included in these tables were found through a computerized search of all cases that cited the cases listed by Lee, as well as all additional cases produced by that search. (This process is known as Sheppardizing cases.) Theoretically, such a search procedure will yield virtually every appropriate case. No doubt we missed some cases due to irregularities in reporting practices and our own mistakes. With that

---

12 We wish to thank Mark Dubnoff and Elizabeth Warren for superb research assistance in identifying, reading, and interpreting these cases.

Table 2.2. *Plaintiffs' Success Rates in Sex-Based Pay Discrimination Cases by Type of Legal Theory (Federal Appellate Courts, 1982–1996)*

Year	Equal Work (Same Job)	Equal Work (Predecessor)	Similar Work	Comparable Work	Comparable Worth	Total
1982–88	44% (16)	100% (4)	33% (15)	50% (12)	0% (3)	44% (50)
1989–95[a]	78% (9)	50% (2)	67% (6)	100% (2)	0% (1)	70% (20)
1995–96[b]	0% (5)	0% (1)	40% (5)	— (0)	— (0)	18% (11)
Total	47% (30)	71% (7)	42% (26)	57% (14)	0% (4)	46% (81)

Note: Cases are coded once at each level of courts based on the outcome in the most advanced stage of the litigation.
[a] Through July 1995.
[b] August 1995 through January 1997.

caveat in mind, the tables reflect a relatively complete survey of reported cases.[13]

Our reading of the cases convinced us that it was necessary to create our own scheme for classifying cases that departed from Lee's system. We settled on five categories, rather than the three Lee employed. We defined equal work cases as those in which plaintiffs asserted that the males and females who were compared worked in the same job. We noticed two distinct types within this group: cases in which the workers held the same job at the same time and predecessor-successor cases, in which men and women held the same job, but before or after each other. Our third category of cases also involves Equal Pay Act claims, but the jobs that are compared are less clearly identical than in the equal work cases. The plaintiffs in these cases argue that the jobs at issue are "substantially equal," making the employer liable under the Equal Pay Act. But often judges are not persuaded. As a consequence, this category of cases has the lowest success rate by plaintiffs of all but the comparable worth cases. The fourth category of cases involves comparable work. That is, the plaintiffs were not claiming that men and women were doing the same job, but they were arguing that the similarity of the work, combined with other evidence, established that the employer was engaging in pay discrimination. The last category is comparable worth cases – cases in which plaintiffs relied in part on job evaluation results to establish pay discrimination.

Our classification scheme produced results that differed from Lee's. The reason is transparent. Lee coded cases purely based on legal theory:

13 A large proportion of the cases concern pretrial motions. Cases were coded as victories for plaintiffs if at least one wage discrimination claim survived the court's decision. Of course, "victory" at the motion phase does not guarantee a final disposition for the plaintiffs.

If plaintiffs filed an Equal Pay Act claim, the case was coded under equal work. If plaintiffs urged a Title VII claim without arguing the work was substantially equal, and without relying primarily on job evaluation results to establish discrimination, the case was coded as comparable work. Lee's approach thus included more tenuous Equal Pay Act cases under the equal work heading. We preferred a more detailed breakdown of Equal Pay Act claims that differentiated according to the apparent similarity in jobs. Consider the results in Table 2.1. When cases involving "similar" work are removed from the equal work categories, the plaintiff success rate goes up dramatically for equal work cases. In our scheme, the two equal work categories yield the highest success rates for plaintiffs (48 percent and 50 percent, respectively). Our subset of comparable work cases has roughly the same success rate as we calculate from Lee's tables (32 percent), but it is appreciably lower than the success rate for equal work cases. Comparable worth cases record the lowest success rate for plaintiffs in both Lee's and our tables (10 percent).

Tables 2.1 and 2.2 disclose patterns that are clear, if not surprising. We do indeed find a continuum of plaintiff success among different types of cases. The two types of equal work cases are quite likely to succeed. Equal Pay Act claims for jobs that are only similar succeed less than four times in ten. Comparable work claims post a lower, but respectable win rate (32 percent). Comparable worth cases appear as rarities that almost universally meet defeat. They virtually disappear within six years after *Gunther*. Our results correct Lee's impression that comparable work cases were more likely to produce plaintiff victories than equal work cases. With the right kind of equal work case, plaintiffs stand an even chance of winning. Still, Lee is right to underscore the relatively high success rate for comparable work cases, compared with the failure of comparable worth claims.

The tables demonstrate a sharp decline in the number of opinions from the 1982–88 period to the period after 1988, but then a sharp rebound in the final one and one-half years. Indeed, the results for the most recent period took us by surprise. We extended the computer search for this period merely to update and verify our analysis of the case law. It confirmed the finding that the two "higher-risk" categories of comparable work and comparable worth claims had declined. The disappearance of comparable worth cases is understandable. Such cases were losers. The decline in comparable work cases is not so readily explained, for plaintiffs won a third of these cases in the earlier period. Yet it appears that there has been a surge in litigation activity in the three more straightforward forms of pay discrimination claims.

These data indicate that some seven years after *Gunther*, pay discrimination cases largely retreated from more ambitious between-job legal theories. Equal Pay Act cases made up more than two-thirds of the opinions after 1988, compared with only one-third in the earlier period. Comparable work and comparable worth cases made up less than 10 percent of the district court opinions in the later period, whereas they had made up 35 percent in the earlier years. It also is clear that plaintiffs did not simply shift strategies and pursue lower-risk legal theories. If this had been the case we would expect to see some kind of cumulative growth in the numbers of comparable work and similar work cases. Instead there is a sharp drop in these two categories. Plaintiffs largely abandoned theories of between-job pay discrimination after 1988.

The appellate court cases largely track the same pattern, but with smaller numbers. Here we also see the virtual disappearance of comparable work and comparable worth cases after 1988. Low frequencies make these figures subject to instability. Yet plaintiffs look to have enjoyed higher win rates in the 1988–95 period, followed by a major decline in success rates in the 1995–96 period.

These data suggest that the dissent to *Gunther* has, in practical terms, carried the day. Although the courts recognize the possibility of between-job pay discrimination cases, plaintiffs only rarely pursue them. The effective triumph of the Equal Pay Act model means that courts and employers have it both ways. Title VII's prohibition of between-job pay discrimination continues on the books. It thus supports the image that law and the courts stand ready to redress invidious gender-based pay discrimination, even when located between jobs. Yet it is a principle with little practical bite. Plaintiffs now accept, or at least no longer challenge, the pronouncements of the dominant discourse that between-job wage inequality is largely the product of the labor market or of valid business judgments. In the current legal regime, such wage differentials may be unfair in some broad historical perspective, but they are not treated as the responsibility of employers.

What is somewhat surprising, perhaps, is the resilience of more straightforward equal work and similar work cases in recent years. Most of these cases involved individual claims rather than class actions. This rise in cases may reflect the impact of the 1991 Civil Rights Act, which offers jury trials and punitive damages in lawsuits alleging intentional acts of discrimination (see *New York Times*, Jan. 12, 1997). Given the limitations of using reported cases, the increase in numbers of decisions must be interpreted cautiously. Nonetheless, it is a shift that merits further investigation.

The Market Justification: Ideology or Analysis?

The case studies in Part II of this book probe the link between labor market conditions and male-female wage differentials in four defendant organizations. As a predicate to that analysis we consider how courts in other cases have dealt with the issue. Such a review is necessary to appreciate the similarities and differences between our cases and others. The analysis also adds to the sociological understanding of how courts deal with these issues. Our reading of these cases suggests that courts typically assume that defendant employers are following the market, with little or no empirical analysis. The courts often appear to be expressing an ideological position rather than conducting an empirical inquiry. Sometimes a court's ideological stance is transparent in the language of an opinion. Sometimes this ideology is revealed indirectly in the kinds of data, analyses, or expert opinion the court cites as authority.

For analytic purposes we focus on five post-*Gunther* cases from among a dozen or so between-job cases. We selected these five because they contain more detailed discussions of the market justification than the other cases. The remaining cases either do not confront factual questions about the market or offer only extremely truncated analyses of the market issue.

Briggs v. City of Madison, *536 F. Supp. 435 (W.D. Wis. 1982). Briggs* contains one of the most thorough analyses of the market justification. Chief Judge Crabb, a woman, found that the defendant city had a legitimate reason for paying male "sanitarians" more than female "public health nurses." Citing defendant's evidence that sanitarians received higher pay from the state and the county, and that the health director had had difficulty recruiting a sanitarian in the past, Judge Crabb ruled that the city's "perception that the retention of sanitarians required raising their salary ranges . . . rebutted the presumption raised by plaintiffs' prima facie case" (p. 708). *Briggs* is the exception that proves the argument we are trying to make. It compares the salaries employers pay the "male" position and it considers evidence of actual hiring difficulties. Thus, while it credits the perception of the market by the employer as a legitimate source of pay differences, it also looks at actual market conditions.

Spaulding v. University of Washington, *740 F.2d 686 (9th cir. 1984).* The nursing faculty alleged it was discriminated against in pay compared with the faculties of other schools due to its gender composition. The appellate court rejected the plaintiffs' data as nonsystematic and noted a relatively damaging fact from the standpoint of a market analysis: The nursing school's salaries lag behind the pay of nursing schools at other institutions at about the same rate that other schools in the university lag behind their respective competitors. A substantial portion of the opinion is devoted to rejecting the application of a disparate impact analysis of market-based pay systems (p. 708).

As with *Briggs*, there is some meaningful analysis of the relative market position of the nursing school and other schools that permits the inference that the university is playing fair with the market among the various schools. Unlike *Briggs*, there is less analysis of any actual labor market experiences across these schools.

California State Employees' Association v. State of California, *724 F. Supp. 717 (N.D. Cal. 1989)*. Plaintiffs asserted that the state had not corrected gender-based wage disparities that originated in the 1930s between predominantly male jobs and female jobs. Judge Patel, also a female jurist, rejected the plaintiffs' theory. She was impressed by defendants' proof that in the 1930s predominantly female clerical jobs were paid about the same in public and private sectors, whereas predominantly male professional and technical groups in government lagged significantly behind their counterparts in the private sector (pp. 725–26). But such sector by gender differences might be explained by several factors, such as differences in hours worked or academic credentials or job security. It might not be appropriate to infer, as does Judge Patel, that the state was generous to women and stingy with men vis-à-vis market rates.

Because Judge Patel did not disclose the evidence that proved that the state was following the market, we cannot determine how much of her conclusion was based on supposition.

International UAW v. State of Michigan, *673 F. Supp. 893 (E.D. Mich. 1987); aff'd 886 F.2d 766 (6th cir. 1989)*. The UAW sued Michigan for sex discrimination in its pay system, which was based on eleven separate occupational groups, each of which established its own set of point ratings of jobs. The court of appeals affirmed the district court opinion in favor of the state. At several points the appellate court asserted the legitimacy of the state's pay system as though there were no doubt that the state was following the market (see, e.g. 886 F.2d 766, pp. 769, 770). The district court opinion stayed closer to actual evidence, although not much. It concluded that the shift from five more gender-mixed occupational groups to eleven more gender-segregated occupational groups "reflect[ed] legitimate labor market occupational groupings" (673 F. Supp. 893, p. 899). The basis for this conclusion was not disclosed. The court also cited expert testimony that the "wage disparities between predominantly male and female groups do exist in the labor market" (p. 900). This is a most general characterization of the external labor market, without any explication of the kind of external market that was being discussed or its relationship to the disparities in the Michigan system. Finally, the court asserted that the state was following the market, one indication being the use of salary surveys by state pay officials (pp. 901, 903).

The mere fact that the state does salary surveys is relatively empty evidence that it actually follows the market. The plaintiffs' posttrial brief cited testimony by the director of the survey that he had advocated abolishing the survey due to its methodological defects (Plaintiffs' Post-Trial Brief, p. 37). The plaintiffs asserted that the survey bore little relationship to actual wage levels. Most salary increases were made across-the-board (pp. 37–38). These factual assertions were never mentioned in the district court opinion.

AFSCME v. County of Nassau, *799 F. Supp. 1370 (E.D.N.Y. 1992).* Perhaps the most detailed judicial examination of the market justification for wage disparities between predominantly male and predominantly female jobs appears in the *County of Nassau* case. Individual plaintiffs and unions alleged that Nassau County engaged in intentional pay discrimination, both generally against predominantly female jobs and against particular female jobs. The case also is an object lesson for social scientists who work as expert witnesses, for the court was mercilessly blunt in finding fault with the plaintiffs' experts.

The plaintiffs presented an array of statistical, documentary, and testimonial evidence to show that "defendants engaged in intentional discrimination by systematically giving to predominantly female job titles lower salary grades than they would have received if they were not female-dominated" (p. 1378). The plaintiffs' evidence included (1) statistical analyses attempting to demonstrate that the initial job classification system adopted in 1967 had, in the last instance, raised the salary grades of predominantly male jobs by one and one-half grades, while it had not raised female job grades; (2) that upgrades were denied female-dominated jobs with demonstrated recruitment and retention problems, while they were granted for male-dominated jobs; and (3) that a statistical analysis of salaries in 1983 and 1986, which controlled for attributes of individuals and attempted to code aspects of job descriptions, found an unexplained wage difference between female- and male-dominated jobs of $2,473 in 1983 and $3,298 in 1986. The judge attacked the preparation of these analyses as relying on subjective decisions that could not be replicated by other social scientists. The most central problem with the plaintiffs' proof, however, was its failure to include variables to examine the impact of collective bargaining and market forces on the disparate outcomes and salaries.

While the judge said there was no evidence to indicate that the pay system as it was initially set up in 1967 had actually been based on market data, the judge held that there was abundant evidence that the county and the plaintiff union relied on market data in salary adjustments after the system was in place. The judge found credible a set of analyses by defendant's experts that including market data in regression equations tended to eliminate significant gender disparities in wages, that the county paid female-dominated jobs somewhat more than the national average while they paid male-dominated jobs below the national average, and that jobs that had seen significant increases in percent female had received larger than average pay increases in recent years.

> The market has animated every aspect of the County compensation system since 1967. Thus, to this extent – and to the extent demonstrated by [defendant's expert] in her report – the court finds that the plaintiffs have failed to demonstrate current Title VII sex discrimination by the County. (p. 1414)

The judge in *County of Nassau* asks many of the right questions from our standpoint, among them, Is the employer actually following the market? Much of the analysis is suspect, however. Without examining the same data that the experts possessed in the case, we can offer only tentative complaints. But we are aware from our more in-depth inquiries in the case studies contained in Part II of this book that some of the defendant's analyses may prove less definitive on the market issue than the court recognizes. For example, controlling market rates for jobs in which they are available may well diminish the gender disparities between jobs, but it pertains to a small number of jobs (some 101 here) out of a large number of jobs (some 1,500 here). Gender disparities may well be greater in jobs that are not directly compared with the market, precisely because management may have more discretion to determine salary levels for such jobs. Also, salary survey data may well play a role in the negotiations between labor and management over salary upgrades and raises, but how does it affect actual salary decisions? The court was skeptical about the impact of salary data at the initiation of the county's pay system but then rather uncritically accepted assertions about the importance of the data after 1967.

Another unanswered question is whether the market data were employed primarily to set across-the-board raises or were they used differentially by job category? If they were used differently across jobs, were they applied uniformly across male- and female-dominated jobs? As we observed in the *California State Employees* case, the recitation of the relative market standing of historically male and female jobs says relatively little about whether the salaries paid those jobs were necessary. Female-dominated jobs may do relatively better compared with the overall market for the same jobs than male-dominated jobs for a variety of reasons. It is too simplistic to answer a charge of disparate treatment in one specific organization and labor market context by making aggregate comparisons to national labor markets. The relationship of the county's salary levels to surrounding employers is more meaningful. But unlike the court in *Briggs*, the *County of Nassau* judge cited expert opinion to establish the correspondence rather than to provide some actual comparisons.

This review of cases indicates that courts have varied in the analytic approaches they have taken to the market issue. It is no simple matter to untangle valid judgments based on appropriate data from over-reaching factual pronouncements. A more satisfactory understanding of this problem requires the kind of in-depth analysis we present in the next part of this book. But even this preliminary foray into some of the leading cases on the question suggests that the courts have glossed over some critical dimensions of whether the market has been the main determinant of wage differences between male and female jobs.

Continuing Tensions: Markets, Efficiency, and Antidiscrimination Principles in Other Pay Discrimination Cases

When one considers the broad sweep of pay discrimination cases, it appears that the courts are struggling to reconcile a tension between deference to markets and efficiency considerations by employers and the antidiscrimination principle. We can see this conflict not only in more novel, between-job cases but also in conventional Equal Pay Act cases. In cases where a male succeeds a woman and receives more money than his predecessor, the courts sometimes have accepted the employer's justification that the male successor had more training and was more competent.[14] Although the courts may not use the terminology of market rates or efficiency principles in such cases, it is clear that they are persuaded that these factors rather than gender bias explained the pay differentials. The reason for a wage differential need not be economically rational, so long as the defendant persuades the court that it was not motivated by an animus toward women.[15]

Some commentators argue that the fourth exception to the Equal Pay Act – "factors other than sex" – should be broadly interpreted to immu-

---

14 See *Wear v. Webb*, 572 F. Supp. 1257 (D. Minn. 1983).
15 In one case a court rejected the claim of a client service manager that she was paid less than the boss's son, even though she had responsibilities that equaled or exceeded his. The court ruled that the pay differential reflected nepotism rather than sex discrimination as such. *Green v. Bettinger Co.*, 608 F. Supp. 35 (1984).

nize employers for pay practices that rely on market prices (including individually bargained wage agreements) or are based on efficiency considerations (Freed and Polsby 1984). Yet there is a long line of Equal Pay Act cases that hold that market wage rates do not justify pay differentials for the same work.[16]

Courts have been skeptical of other claims that employers have invoked to justify male-female wage differences in equal work cases. Extra credentials not necessary for job performance and pay differentials that are not commensurate with differences in duties performed have not protected employers from liability under the Equal Pay Act.[17] It also is clear from a set of cases on insurance benefits that market principles do not automatically trump other considerations in antidiscrimination law. *In Los Angeles Dept. of Water & Power v. Manhart*, 435 U.S. 702 (1978), the Supreme Court ruled that employers could not charge women employees more for pension coverage, even though insurers could charge different rates in the market based on gender-based actuarial tables. The courts sometimes accept employer justifications for male-female wage differences in Equal Pay Act cases. But, as we reported in Tables 2.1 and 2.2, plaintiffs won the majority of published equal work cases decided between 1982 and 1995.

Why should the courts take a fundamentally different approach to market issues in Equal Pay Act cases than in Title VII cases concerning comparisons between workers in different jobs? The *dicta* and the dissent to *Gunther* suggest the answer. Rehnquist's dissent voiced the worry that if courts entertained claims of between-job wage discrimination, it would lead courts into the analytic quagmire of trying to determine what male and female workers in various jobs should be paid (452 U.S. 161, pp. 188, 203). Brennan responded that *Gunther* presented no such problems. Given that the employer had conducted job evaluations and market surveys and had consciously set the pay of female matrons at a lower percentage of those results than the rate set for men, there was a clear standard for assessing remedies (pp. 180–81).

Both Title VII pay discrimination cases and Equal Pay Act cases present the courts with a dilemma of how to resolve conflicting values. The courts have been more willing to intervene in Equal Pay Act cases because they are limited to claims about particular jobs. The Equal Pay Act cases thus pose less difficult questions about how to assess damages

16 See, e.g., *Corning Glass Works v. Brennan*, 417 U.S. 188, 204.5 (1974); *Strecker v. Grand Forks County Social Services Board*, 640 F.2d 96, 99, n. 1 (8th Cir. 1980); *Brennan v. Victoria Bank & Trust Co.*, 593 F.2d 896, 898 (5th Cir. 1974).

17 *Kouba v. Allstate Insurance Co.*, 691 F.2d 873, 377–79 (9th Cir. 1982); *Peltier v. City of Fargo*, 533 F.2d 374, 377–79 (8th Cir. 1976); *United States v. City of Milwaukee*, 441 F. Supp. 1371 (E.D. Wisc. 1977); *Hodgson v. Brookhaven General Hospital*, 436 F.2d 719, 725 (5th Cir. 1970); 29 C.F.R. Section 1620.8 (1983).

and correct invidious pay policies than do Title VII cases, where the remedy might entail wholesale revisions in pay policies. Such difficulties may well have led to result-oriented decisions in Title VII cases. One way out of the dilemma is to rule that Title VII plaintiffs did not make their case.

Implications for Empirical Study

This review of the post-*Gunther* pay discrimination decisions yields several observations that are important to the social-scientific analyses that follow. First, the outcomes of between-job lawsuits brought under Title VII often hinge on an empirical judgment about evidence of intentional discrimination. With a few arguable exceptions, employers have not been rescued from liability by merely citing the possibility of market or efficiency factors as a rationale for wage differences. Rather, it has been the judicial finding that employers actually were following market and efficiency principles that proved fatal to the plaintiffs' contention. Thus the empirical question of why there is a wage differential between male and female jobs in a particular organization remains pivotal within the current law.

Second, comparable worth cases are a small portion of all cases and virtually disappear after 1990. Almost all comparable worth cases have been brought against public sector organizations, whereas private employers have only been subjected to equal work and comparable work cases. We discuss why in Chapter 4.

A third, related observation is that comparable worth claims could have been raised against private sector firms, but were not. Differences in the legal formulation of Title VII claims between public and private sector firms do not necessarily represent differences in the nature of inequality systems in the two sectors. The two private sector cases in our set, those against Sears and Coastal Bank, could have been brought as comparable worth cases but were not.

Three Paradigms of Law, Labor Markets, and Between-Job Gender Inequality in Organizations

The debate about sex-based wage differences within legal and policy circles revolves around conflicting conceptions of law, employing organizations, and labor markets. It is possible to summarize the differences under three paradigms: the free market model, the comparable worth model, and the organizational inequality model. We present these paradigms in Figure 2.1. After explaining each paradigm, we address its role in our analysis.

Law

Employing
Organizations ———————— Labor
Markets

Paradigm	Employing Organizations	Labor Markets	Law
Free Market	1) Rational price takers; deviants punished by law and markets. 2) Efficiency wage version: premiums based on higher productivity, etc.	Competitive; culture (gender stereotypes) shapes supply/demand, but not devaluation of female work.	Equal Pay Act; T7 Applied to extreme versions of intentional between-job wage discrimination.
Comparable Worth	1) Internalize market-based discrimination and society-wide devaluation of female work. 2) Organization-specific sex discrimination and devaluation of female work. Employers benefit from paying women less.	Noncompetitive and/or suffused with invidious gender effects. "Crowding" women into "female" jobs to depress female pay.	Comparable Worth: applying disparate impact standard to pay practices; adoption of "cleansed" job evaluation systems.
Organizational Inequality	1) Organization-specific sex discrimination and devaluation of female work. 2) Partially rational: internal politics, historical pay practices, and cultural principles mediate market rates and generate male-female pay differentials. Form and magnitude of gender inequality vary by organization. Employers may not benefit from gender differentials.	Vary in competitiveness. Culture (gender stereotypes) will affect supply/demand of workers; market rates affected by aggregation of employer practices. But no assumption of "crowding" or society-wide devaluation of female jobs. Market processes may raise female pay rates.	Regulated markets and organizations: expand definition of intentional discrimination and disparate treatment; scrutiny of market defense; mandated pay equity reviews and "best practice" models of pay systems.

Figure 2.1. Paradigms of sex-based pay discrimination.

The Free Market Paradigm

Orthodox labor economics typically interprets the wage differences between male and female jobs as the product of market forces. In this view, employers are price takers who pay workers according to going market rates. Efficiency wage theory attempts to explain some obvious departures from market rates (Akerlof 1984). These departures (premiums above the market) are offered to elicit high levels of performance or commitment to the organization and are, therefore, efficient.

Because this paradigm sees employers as rational price takers, it posits that between-job pay disparities will rarely reflect invidious preferences. Such behavior is thought to be costly to the employer and will be punished in the product market. In the long run, therefore, the market will purge itself of discrimination (Becker 1971).

The market paradigm is consistent with at least two theories of antidiscrimination law, both of which are less interventionist than the comparable worth or organizational inequality paradigms. The most extreme free market version is articulated by Richard Epstein (1992). Epstein rejects legal intervention on normative and policy grounds, except in narrow circumstances where the state itself fostered discriminatory conditions or where markets clearly do not operate in ways that allow workers a variety of choices of employment setting. Epstein argues that employers should be allowed to discriminate. They will only do so when it is efficient (for otherwise they face market extinction). Other employers will gladly hire disfavored workers to take advantage of labor savings. Attempts at legal regulation of pay levels is repugnant to Epstein because it violates principles of free contract. And Epstein proposes that it is almost never cost-efficient because it burdens employers without significantly expanding the employment opportunities of female workers.

The more centrist market-based view is expressed by Fischel and Lazear (1986). While they acknowledge the possibility of discrimination, and implicitly endorse attempts to reduce its prevalence, they argue that comparable worth is never an appropriate remedy. They assert that the law should only go so far as to insure that there are no gender-based barriers to job mobility within firms and that the Equal Pay Act should be enforced. To adopt comparable worth remedies would be a cure worse than the disease, because it would lead to inefficient reallocations of labor costs, would harm female workers by reducing the demand for their preferred jobs (due to the higher labor cost for predominantly female jobs), and would not necessarily compensate the injured (see also Killingsworth 1985).

In Figure 2.1 we identify the market view with a legal regime that relies on the Equal Pay Act and would find liability based on between-job disparities only in the most extreme versions of directly proved, intentional discrimination.

The Comparable Worth Paradigm

The comparable worth paradigm is based on a very different diagnosis of the sources of between-job gender inequality and the most effective legal approach to the problem. This paradigm has two versions of the market-organization relationship. Perhaps the most prominent conception is expressed by England (1992), who asserts that the market contains sex bias due to society-wide devaluation of female work. In this version employing organizations are largely price takers: they internalize gender-biased market wage rates. Another version, espoused by Steinberg (1992), locates the devaluation of female work within employing organizations. The mechanisms Steinberg emphasizes are very similar to those cited by England – that is, sexist cultural typing – but they operate to create unique inequalities in particular organizations. Both versions do not see a corrective potential in the labor market: England sees the market as the source of the problem; Steinberg sees organizational pay systems as relatively detached from market processes. The two versions concur in their recommendations for a remedy. They advocate realignments of pay systems based on job evaluation systems that are adjusted for (cleansed of) between-job gender bias.

The comparable worth paradigm dictates an interventionist legal approach. The paradigm rests on a faith that job evaluation studies can detect gender discrimination, even in circumstances where employers are following the market. It follows that employers would be legally obliged to adopt corrected job evaluation results. This is akin to a broad disparate impact formulation. Nothing more than job evaluation results would be required to establish employer liability. There would be no need to establish intentional, disparate treatment of employees in female job categories.

Weiler (1986) proposes a modest version of comparable worth policy. He suggests that the president should issue an executive order mandating comparable worth by federal government agencies. Such a policy shift would immediately benefit large numbers of female federal employees, set a standard to be emulated by other large organizations, and begin to alter the market conditions for predominantly male and female jobs.

The Organizational Inequality Paradigm

The last paradigm is our own invention. It poses an alternative theoretical model of the relationship between labor markets, organizations, and discrimination, and the legal and policy prescriptions that follow from such a conception. The organizational inequality paradigm is premised on the view that a significant portion of the wage gap between male and female jobs arises inside or is perpetuated by employing organizations and is not dictated by market or efficiency principles. The degree to which this is true will vary by organization and market context.

This paradigm implies the need for an antidiscrimination regulatory regime that investigates the dynamics of gender inequality within organizations and encourages employers to eliminate pay practices that disadvantage female workers, unless they are justified by market necessity or genuine efficiency considerations. Our paradigm does not call for the rejection of market processes in organizations. Indeed, pay equity may be advanced by opening organizational pay systems to market dynamics. But given the intractability of gender-based hierarchies in many organizations, we think some kind of broad interventionist approach will be necessary to significantly redress invidious pay disparities between predominantly male and predominantly female jobs. A more interventionist approach is possible within the existing framework of Title VII jurisprudence, if litigants and courts more effectively analyze data on gender inequality in organizations. The courts have been largely unwilling to entertain such analyses to date. Legislative or executive branch mandates for increased scrutiny of gender-based pay differentials may, therefore, be necessary.

The three paradigms capture different positions in the debate over unequal pay for women, but none of them fully corresponds to the current state of the law. As our review of the federal cases demonstrated, the courts clearly have rejected the comparable worth view and the extreme version of the free market paradigm. Our assertion is that while the courts theoretically could entertain claims of between-job pay discrimination, as allowed under *Gunther*, the empirical conceptions of markets and employers they have embraced in the cases is much closer to the free market conception than the organizational inequality view. In the empirical analyses that follow, we test the validity of these conceptions in the context of adjudicated cases.

Conclusion: The Questions to Be Addressed

The basic pattern of the cases on gender-based pay discrimination is clear. With *Gunther* the courts opened the door for plaintiffs to challenge wage differences between predominantly male and predominantly female jobs. They thus created the possibility of using Title VII to mount broad-based attacks on gender inequality in organizational pay systems. The courts quickly limited the practical effect of the doctrine, however, first by rejecting pure comparable worth theories of discrimination, and then by consistently finding that market forces and efficiency considerations explained between-job wage differences. The consequences of the decisions were apparent in the pattern of cases reaching decisions in the federal courts. By the end of the 1980s plaintiffs largely had abandoned general attacks on employer wage systems in favor of more focused, conventional legal theories involving Equal Pay Act violations or Title VII theories that were closely akin to Equal Pay Act claims.

The remainder of this book seeks to answer three questions that are raised by these legal developments. The first goes to the empirical issues that are crucial to decisions in the pay discrimination cases. Which theory of the relationship between organizations and labor markets best explains the wage differences between male and female jobs? Second, if we find that the courts were not justified in reaching the empirical conclusions they did about the sources of unequal pay for men and women, how do we explain their decisions? Third, if the courts were "wrong" in these cases, what are the implications for future policies on male-female wage inequality?

The next chapter introduces the social-scientific literature that has framed the debate over unequal pay thus far and lays out the theoretical position we seek to test in the case studies. Chapter 4 talks about the methodological strengths and weaknesses of our case study approach.

3

Toward an Organizational Theory of Gender Inequality in Pay

The influence of organizations on men's and women's wages is surrounded by practical and theoretical concerns. From a policy standpoint, whether anything needs to be done to redress earnings differences that exist inside organizations depends in part on the size and durability of the gender "wage gap" in society at large. If women's earnings are about to converge on those of their male counterparts, there is little practical benefit from understanding the nuances of where those wage differences came from. Indeed, even if the wage gap is significant and persistent, if existing market-based or cultural theories adequately explain the phenomenon, there would be little point in developing a new organization-level theory.

In this chapter we argue that neither is true. Despite some significant shrinking of the gender wage gap, substantial wage disparities continue, with no guarantee of a steady trend to wage parity. A significant portion of gender-based wage inequality exists between predominantly male and predominantly female jobs. And there are indications that organizations are the locus of a considerable segment of gender inequality in pay. We are warranted, therefore, in proposing a new organizational theory of gender-based wage inequality.

This chapter critically synthesizes the existing social scientific literature on the dimensions of and explanations for the earnings differences between men and women. It then proposes an organizational approach. In the first section we consider the size of the pay gap in both the United States and in other countries and how it has changed over time. In the second section, we turn our attention to the link between the wage gap and the structure of jobs in the contemporary labor force. This discussion lays the necessary groundwork for the third section, which reviews "market-based" theories for the existence of disparity in pay between predominantly male and predominantly female jobs. The fourth section of the chapter makes our case for bringing employing organizations into this theoretical picture. In the fifth section we assess how well the empirical literature addresses the issues raised by the market theories and those raised by our concern with organizational matters.

The sixth and culminating section of the chapter lays out elements of an organizational theory of between-job wage differences. One could of course accept a position that denies any distinctive role to organizations in pay determination. For example, one might hold the economic view that societal- and organizational-level patterns of wages are both merely derivative of individual economic decisions. Or one might take the conventional "structuralist" position that societal-level patterns are simple aggregations of the wages that organizations "assign" to jobs and individuals. But if one chooses neither of these positions, it is necessary at least to sketch the outlines of an alternative middle-range theory.

Empirical Dimensions of the Pay Gap

Do women as a group still earn less than men? If so, how much? While the first question can still be answered affirmatively, responding to the second question obliges one to enter a methodological and statistical thicket. At the core, the issues can be stated simply: On average, women engage in less paid work than men and any comparison of relative earnings needs to take this fact into account. Matters get more complex when we begin to define what we mean by "less paid work," for this phrase subsumes several related facts: (1) women are more likely to work part-time schedules than men are; (2) women are less likely to work overtime schedules than men are; (3) women are less likely to be employed year-round than men are; (4) women are likely to have less work experience or likely to have worked a smaller proportion of their adult lives than men are; and (5) women are less likely to be in the labor force at all than men are. How one takes these differences into account has a large effect on how one measures the wage gap and changes in the wage gap over time.

One conventional approach is to restrict the comparison of male and female earnings to an inspection of the incomes of those who worked full-time and year-round. In Table 3.1, trends are shown in the median earnings of full-time, year-round male and female workers in five-year intervals from 1955 onward.[1] The same data are shown graphically in Figure 3.1, where the median incomes are plotted on a logarithmic scale

1   Note that before 1985, the values shown are for the incomes of year-round, full-time workers and include a small portion of unearned income. Official published data are more readily accessible in earlier years on income than earnings. Comparing the trends within and between the sexes since 1985 for income and earnings data shows that there is no bias in using the income data as a substitute for earnings data for this special population.

Table 3.1. *Earnings and Female/Male Earnings Ratios for Full-Time/Year-Round Workers by Sex, 1955–1996*

| | Median Earnings[a] | | Female/Male Ratios |
	Males	Females	
1955[b]	22,801	14,704	0.645
1960[c]	26,156	15,870	0.607
1965[c]	29,306	17,562	0.599
1970[c]	34,062	20,222	0.594
1975[c]	35,618	20,950	0.588
1980[c]	35,483	21,346	0.602
1985[c]	35,281	22,783	0.646
1990[c]	33,226	23,795	0.716
1996[c]	32,144	23,710	0.738

[a] Earnings are presented in constant dollars, 1996 = 100.
[b] Values for 1955 only are yearly income of full-time/year-round workers. Source: U.S. Department of Commerce, Bureau of the Census. 1982. *Money Income of Households, Families and Persons in the United States: 1980*. Current Population Report Series P60 (132), p. 135.
[c] Source: U.S. Department of Commerce, Bureau of the Census. Historical Income Tables – Persons. Table P31. "Year-Round, Full-Time Workers – Persons (All Races) 15 Years Old and Over Median Earnings by Sex, 1960 to 1996" (downloaded Feb. 5, 1998, from http://www.census.gov/hhes/income/histinc/P31.html).

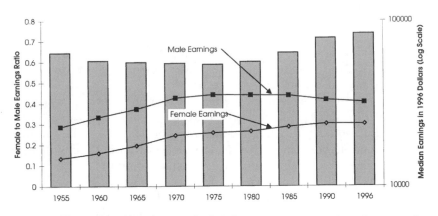

Figure 3.1. Trends in male-female earnings, 1955–1996. Data are for full-time, year-round workers; values for 1955 are incomes, all others are earnings.

so that (1) equal slopes represent equal rates of change in income and (2) the distance between the male and female lines is proportional to the female-to-male ratios (which are also represented by the height of the vertical bars). When the data are presented in this fashion, one is able to see the trend in relative female earnings in a different light. For males, the period from 1955 onward is essentially composed of two trends: rising real earnings from 1955 to 1970 followed by stagnant or declining earnings from 1970 to 1996. For females, the story is a bit more complicated with rising earnings from 1955 to 1970 (although at a slightly lower overall rate of increase than for males), stagnant earnings from 1970 to 1980, and then slowly rising earnings again from 1980 onward. When the male and female trends are taken together, it is clear that the period of rising male earnings that ended in 1970 was associated, until the late 1960s, with an increase in the "gender gap." Since then, the gender gap has shrunk as a result of both slightly declining real male earnings and slightly increasing female earnings.

These ratios are subject to a variety of quibbles, including differences in the number of hours worked by men and women who are nominally "full-time" (see Horrigan and Markey 1990), and differences that arise from comparing the median *weekly* earnings of male and female full-time earners. If all these recent trends and caveats are taken into account together, it would be reasonable to conclude the following: (1) the gender gap in earnings has probably narrowed to the point where females who work a similar number of hours as males earn at least 75 percent of male earnings and maybe somewhat more; (2) additional narrowing of this gap probably will be as much a function of weak increases in real earnings for males as it is of increasing earnings for females. In general, at recent rates, it seems unlikely that the gender differential in earnings will disappear anytime in the next decade or two.

Another slant on the issue of the relative size of the gender wage gap is obtained by making comparisons between the United States and other countries. Absolute parity, defined as a ratio of female-to-male earnings equal to one, is both an easy-to-understand and an appealing goal; it becomes a more compelling goal if it is a state of affairs that has actually been realized in other societies. Table 3.2 presents a comparison of ratios of female to male *wages* for several different categories of countries at two points, a date in the early 1980s and a date in the early 1990s. The data reported for countries other than the United States and Canada are taken from the *1993 Yearbook of Labour Statistics* published by the International Labour Office. In most instances the earnings listed are described as average earnings taken from surveys of employing establishments. The values shown for the United States are not strictly comparable insofar as they are derived from the Current Population Survey

Table 3.2. *Female to Male Earnings Ratios by Country in 1983 and 1992*

	1983			1992			
	M	F	Ratio	M	F	Ratio	Year
Less developed countries							
Cyprus	59.74	34.73	0.58	113.92	70.06	0.61	
Paraguay	40,646	3,322	0.81	403,197	281,293	0.70	
Costa Rica	7,046	4,519	0.64	39,146	30,344	0.78	
Egypt				39	31	0.79	87
Kenya	1,753.2	1,508	0.86	3,513.5	2,976.6	0.85	91
Turkey[a]	1,310.6	1,274.4	0.97	56,310	50,924	0.90	91
Sri Lanka	33.94	24.75	0.73	102.99	91.47	0.89	91
Asia							
Japan	325,537	183,989	0.57	465,720	236,505	0.51	91
Korea	340,960	159,050	0.47	1,005	562	0.56	
Hong Kong	95.9	73.7	0.77	280	190.1	0.68	
Europe							
Luxembourg	293.8	191.7	0.65	373	243	0.65	90
Switzerland	17.36	11.66	0.67	24.44	16.21	0.66	91
Czech Republic	3,272	2,238	0.68	4,391	3,099	0.71	91
Belgium	287.09	213.82	0.74	381.91	287.71	0.75	91
Germany	16.23	11.71	0.72	22.66	17.51	0.77	
Netherlands	16.89	12.97	0.77	19.9	15.41	0.77	91
France	34.73	28	0.81	47.23	38.14	0.81	90
Denmark	79.37	66.96	0.84	121.36	101.05	0.83	91
English-speaking							
United Kingdom[b]	3.7	2.57	0.69	6.09	4.28	0.70	
Canada			0.64			0.72	
United States[c]	378	252	0.67	514	395	0.77	93
New Zealand	8.18	6.41	0.78	16.33	13.21	0.81	
Australia	9.3	7.77	0.84	15.17	13.79	0.91	

Note: Earnings values are in local currency units, generally on a per-hour basis.
[a] Data for earlier period are from 1984.
[b] Data for earlier period are from 1985.
[c] U.S. data are weekly earnings.

household survey.[2] At the same time, if used with appropriate caution, the comparisons are still informative.

In general, the earnings ratios tend to be lowest in the East Asian societies for which data are available. Beyond the large absolute earnings disparities found between men and women in these countries, it is also doubtful that they made much progress in closing the gender gap during

2 A second issue is whether the "averages" shown for most countries are medians or means. For the U.S. data, the relative earnings of females decline considerably when earnings ratios are calculated *for individuals* on the basis of means rather than medians. It is not clear, however, whether the same pattern would emerge for establishment data that probably underreports the earnings of high-level executives and officials.

the decade in question. The situation in the less developed societies mirrors their geographic locations – they are all over the map. Although one is well advised to be especially careful in making generalizations when the quality of the data may be suspect, the ratios in these Third World countries are perhaps higher than one would expect initially. In part, this pattern may reflect the relatively low levels of female labor force participation in the Islamic countries represented here, Egypt and Turkey.

In the European countries the earnings ratios also exhibit a wide range. The values shown here may be unrepresentative due to the un-availability of data from most Scandanavian countries and Italy, places that previous studies have shown to have low gender earnings gaps (Blau and Kahn 1994). However, in general, the ratios are higher than in the Asian countries. Perhaps the most remarkable feature of the data shown for these societies is their virtual stability during the decade in question. Only in Germany was there evidence of a meaningful narrowing of the gender gap in earnings. The English-speaking countries displayed in the final panel tend, on average, to have even smaller earnings gaps. More-over, in three of the five countries shown, there was a substantial improvement in the ratio of female to male earnings during the late 1980s.

Against this backdrop, the U.S. picture is somewhat easier to decipher. As in the other English-speaking countries, the earnings gap narrowed in the United States over the decade. At the beginning of the period, only six of the countries listed had lower earnings ratios; by the end, eleven did, putting the United States squarely in the middle of the pack. This performance is significant, for it calls into question the premise of a recent report about the relative size of earnings gaps in the United States and other countries. Blau and Kahn (1992) note that "observed" U.S. earnings ratios tended to be relatively low but that this pattern could be explained by the overall larger level of inequality in the United States compared with that in other countries. Their argument does not take into account the kind of progress documented in Table 3.2. While it is possible that the United States earnings gap might have shrunk even further had overall inequality not increased in the United States during the 1980s, it is important to recognize that the United States can now be seen as fairly typical of industrial democracies rather than as a laggard.

Given stagnation in the closing of the earnings gap in many European countries, it is also appropriate to revisit the question of what makes for relatively large or small earnings differences between the sexes across societies. Blau and Kahn argue strongly that the overall level of earnings inequality in the United States is the primary culprit, a pattern they attribute to its decentralized system of earnings determination. "Specifically, centralized wage-setting institutions which tend to reduce interfirm and interindustry wage variation and are often associated with conscious policies to raise the relative pay of low-wage workers regardless of gender may indirectly reduce the gender pay gap" (1992, 533). Given the changes in the most recent period, we would offer an alternative conjecture: Reduction of the earnings disparity between men and women may be responsive to political action that creates favorable legislation, as in Canada and Australia, or a climate that is favorable to the enforcement of existing legislation, as in the United States. We would also raise the possibility that nationally centralized, administered pay systems may contain their own barriers to the complete elimination of male-female earnings disparities – a topic we will return to both theoretically and empirically.

The Link between Gender Inequality and Jobs: A Formal Analysis of a Complex Phenomenon

It is not only, or even primarily, the absolute size of the wage gap that has fueled interest in the pay equity movement in recent years. Were it not for the fact that *jobs* are the link between individuals and earnings, the entire concept of comparable worth would never have emerged. It is crucial to be clear about several issues that arise when the link between gender, jobs, and earnings is brought to center stage. First, we will consider what it means to say that inequality between men and women can be "within job" or "between job" in character. Second, we will address the topic of what a job is and how different definitions have different implications for the choice of remedial measures. Finally, we comment on the relationship between the occurence of within-firm, invidious differences in pay between predominantly male and predominantly female jobs in general, and pay differences that would be specifically targeted under a pay equity or comparable worth program.

The Difficulty of Untangling Within-Job Inequality and Between-Job Inequality

In discussing within- and between-job inequalities, it is best to begin simply. Thus, we start by assuming either that all individuals are equally able and qualified for the jobs in which they work or that any differences in ability or qualifications have been statistically removed, realizing, of course, that statistical adjustments when actually applied can never function in such a straightforward, clinical fashion. We also assume that the definition of jobs is unproblematic.

First consider a pay system in which gender inequality in pay is entirely the product of within-job pay differences between men and women. Men and women would be represented in equal proportions across jobs, meaning that there is no occupational segregation by gender. The overall wage gap between men and women in such a hypothetical system would reflect women's diminished earnings within each job. The relationship between the overall wage gap and the wage gap within each job can be shown to be the following:

$$\overline{Y}_{m} \cdot - \overline{Y}_{f} \cdot = \sum_{i=1}^{I} \left(\frac{n_{fi}}{N_f} \times (\overline{Y}_{mi} - \overline{Y}_{fi}) \right)$$

where

$\overline{Y}_{mi}$ = Mean male earnings in job i
$\overline{Y}_{fi}$ = Mean female earnings in job i
n_{fi} = Number of females in job i
N_f = Total number of females.

In words, the overall pay gap is the weighted average of the within-job pay gaps where the weights are given by the proportion of female workers in each job.[3] This pattern of inequality – of pure within-job earnings differences – reflects the kind of economic problem that the Equal Pay Act was designed to remedy.

Next consider a pay system in which gender inequality is solely produced between jobs, that is, where men and women earn the same wage within jobs, but a greater proportion of men hold higher-paying jobs. In this instance the wage gap would be completely untouched by legislation of the Equal Pay Act variety, since the within-job earnings differences are all zero. As before, the overall pay gap between males and females can be expressed as a sum of weighted algebraic components:

$$\overline{Y}_{m} \cdot - \overline{Y}_{f} \cdot = \sum_{i=1}^{I} \left[\left(\frac{n_{mi}}{N_m} \right) - \left(\frac{f_{mi}}{N_f} \right) \right] \times \left(\frac{\sum Y_{fi}}{n_{fi}} \right).$$

In this case, the overall gap comprises a weighted average of within-job female earnings means where the weights are defined as the difference

3   In this example, identical results would be obtained if the weights were defined as the proportion of males or the proportion of all workers in each job rather than as the proportion of females. This constancy does not obtain when the proportion of males and females differs across jobs as in the next two examples. As a result, an element of arbitrariness is introduced into the decomposition depending on which population is chosen as a reference point.

between the proportion of male workers in the job and the proportion of female workers.[4] This is a pattern of labor market inequality that comparable worth advocates allege would exist even if there were universal compliance with the terms of the Equal Pay Act. Note that job segregation per se is not sufficient to cause an inequality in pay; job segregation must be coupled with an overrepresentation, on average, of male workers in better-paying jobs. In other words, there is the possibility of a noninvidious version of between-job wage differences in which men and women work in different jobs but in which the sex composition of a job is unrelated to its level of earnings.

Finally, consider the most complex, and perhaps most realistic kind of pay regime, in which gender inequality in pay is the product of both within-job gender differences and between-job gender differences. The formulas just presented can be used to model the within and between components of the gender earnings differences. Significantly, however, the sum of the two components from these calculations does not necessarily equal the overall level of male-female earnings difference. The reason for this is that there is an interaction component of the wage difference related to the size of the within-job wage difference in jobs in which males or females are overrepresented. This interaction component (assuming that female weights are used as in the preceding formulas) can be written as follows:

$$\sum_{i=1}^{I}\left[\left(\frac{n_{mi}}{N_m}\right)-\left(\frac{f_{mi}}{N_f}\right)\right]\times(\overline{Y}_{mi}-\overline{Y}_{fi}).$$

The consequence of this is that when both features of inequality – disproportionate representation and within-job earnings differences – are present, any decomposition of the overall wage gap into a "within-" and a "between-" job component is doubly arbitrary. In the first instance, the calculation of components is arbitrary because there is no reason to prefer female weights over male weights or "gender-averaged" weights. In the second instance, arbitrariness arises because the interaction component could be reasonably allocated to either the "between" or the "within" portion of the earnings gap. Thus, the lack of an unambiguous calculus of decompostion is one reason that attempts to specify the gains from adopting a comparable worth policy is an elusive and perhaps futile task.

4 Again, the first component might have been defined as the mean earnings of males within each job and identical results would have been obtained in this example when male and female earnings within jobs are presumed to be equal. As before, this identity breaks down when both types of earnings inequality are present, as in the next example.

But it is not the only difficulty. A second problem stems from the assumption that the between-job differences are entirely attributable to invidious treatment based on the sex composition of the jobs in question. Even if one assumes, as we have, that the abilities and qualifications of workers are not responsible for the differences in between-job wages, one still needs to rule out differences in external market wage rates as a cause of the disparities. Thus, the standard neo-classical critique that labor supply differences might produce the kind of between-job wage rate patterns shown in our second formula needs to be acknowledged.

Defining a "Job"

A further complication in assessing the amount of the gender gap attributable to between-job differences in general, and pay equity violations in particular, is the matter of defining what a "job" is. There are two problems. In a crude job defintion scheme, "head" or "lead" checkout clerks in a supermarket might be classified in the same job category as regular checkout clerks despite having slightly different job responsibilities and pay. Or job definitions might blur the distinction between the context in which work is done, if, for example, the checkout personnel in a food retailer's convenience store division were put into the same classification as the checkout personnel in its supermarket division.

A number of earlier studies (Treiman and Hartmann 1981; Bielby and Baron 1986) concluded that the amount of job segregation, and presumably the size of the between-job earnings gap component, increases systematically as the definition of jobs becomes increasingly fine-grained. The inference is sometimes made, incorrectly, we argue, that if the most detailed job categories used by large employers were the basis of this calculation, the degree of job segregation between men and women would be nearly complete. (Of course, this becomes tautologically true if a job is defined as the task an individual does for *her* employer. We consider this an extreme interpretation.) This proposition also implies that the proportion of the wage gap attributable to between-job effects would be extremely large if one were able to make calculations based on the most detailed job classifications being used by employers.

The claim of near total job segregation needs to be scrutinized carefully. First, as the formula presented here shows, the "between-job" component of pay differences depends not only on the degree of segregation but also on the pay levels of jobs that are disproportionately male and female. As one moves to more microscopic analyses of employment distributions, segregation may increase but the correlation with pay levels might not increase or might even decrease. Second, the assertion of near total segregation needs to be examined with data on many more employment systems than have previously been studied. This is a task that will be taken up in the ensuing case studies.

A final issue related to the definition of jobs is that many pay equity studies do not use job data at all but instead rely on quasi job categories such as the U.S. Census three-digit occupational classification scheme. Even where the designation of task bundles is relatively narrow in a census occupation category – for example, "post-secondary social work teachers" – the designation of employers is not. That is, some of the wage gap exists because (1) even within jobs and occupations women tend to work for "lower-wage" employers than men; and (2) "women's" occupations might be disproportionately located among these low-wage employers. For example, community-based child care centers and large manufacturing firms with on-site child care facilities both employ janitors and child care workers, but the ratio of child care workers to janitors is probably much higher in the generally low-wage community centers than in a business such as Ford Motor Company. Although a pay equity regime might equalize the janitors' and the child care workers' pay within each setting, it would still leave an aggregate pattern of child care workers being paid less than janitors. In general, then there remains the possibility that occupations that are disproportionately female are also occupations that are disproportionately found among low-wage employers, making the isolation of a pure "between-job" component – that is, one purged of employer effects – an even more daunting task.

How Consequential Is Between-Job Wage Inequality?

These and similar considerations have prompted some analysts to assert that even full-blown comparable worth policies would have inconsequential effects on the overall pay gap. Weiler, for example, concludes after surveying recent literature:

> [T]he significance of the "percent female" variables evaporates, leaving it to explain only a small fraction of the wage gap. Thus, even if a comparable worth strategy were entirely successful in eliminating the effect of this suspect factor upon the pay of female-dominated jobs, the total gender gap in earnings would drop by only two or three percentage points. (1986, 1790–91)

The validity of Weiler's estimate of the size of the reduction in the earnings gap is suspect. Note how he implicitly conflates gains from comparable worth with the significance of the [residual] effect of the "percent female" variable. In doing so, he embraces what has become an almost standard definition of the need for comparable worth: the coefficient in a linear regression equation relating percentage female in an occupation to the earnings of workers in the occupation, where separate predictions are calculated for average male and average female salaries. (Technically speaking, in the contextual approach the dependent variable is the individual's earnings adjusted for other determinants of earnings.) This practice has been repeated so often that this measure of a pay equity violation has become the definition not only of a "comparable" worth violation but also of the existence of invidious, gender-based, between-job pay differences of any kind (see, e.g., England 1992). For several reasons, however, this correlation should not be taken as the only embodiment of invidious between-job pay differences.

First, the aggregate percent female is only one possible indicator of the dominance of a job by male or female workers. Studies of other social problems have demonstrated the importance of "tipping-point" phenomena – situations in which the aggregate percentage only has an effect on individual behavior in the vicinity of certain threshold values – as when the proportion of high-status residents in a neighborhood approaches and then dips below 5 percent (Crane 1991). The use of a continuous predictor, the percent female, risks misattributing income variance due to other sources that occur well away from the threshold to gender bias. This is particularly troubling when there is disagreement in specifying and measuring other nondiscriminatory sources of between-job differences and these other variables are not properly taken into account. Moreover, if male-female between-job differences present themselves in a highly discontinuous fashion, any corrective measures implemented on the basis of an incorrectly specified continuous model will introduce their own biases. Those women working in jobs nearer the threshold are likely to receive too little in the way of compensation adjustments and those working in completely segregated jobs would receive too much. (The converse holds for those working in male jobs. Too much of the costs would be imposed on those at the extremes of the distribution of percent female in the job.)

Second, using the percent female-income correlation as the definition of pay equity tends to confuse competing explanations. As a thought experiment, imagine a world in which occupations differ in contributions to productivity, where women tend to be discriminatorily excluded from high-productivity occupations, but where wages reflect productivity without any further "cultural" discrimination. In an aggregate study with separate equations for the sexes, if no controls for job productivity characteristics are included, it is easy to see that the percent female-wage correlation overestimates the amount of gender bias in the wage structure per se. Some of the differences in pay stem from the higher-productivity requirements in the male job sector. If differences in all relevant occupational-level skill and productivity factors could then be controlled, the correlation of percent female and income would be reduced to zero, because the discrimination would be in occupational entry, not in occupational rewarding. But if all aggregate job characteristics could not be properly taken into account, a correlation between percent female and occupational wage would remain but would very easily be misattributed to pay discrimination rather than entry discrimination.[5] Although this situation is somewhat unavoidable, it further points out the necessity of viewing percent female coefficients in OLS regressions as a potentially flawed indicator, rather than as a defining criterion, of pay inequity between jobs.

Taking all this into account, we draw a different conclusion from Weiler's concerning the size and nature of between-job gender inequality in pay. Rather than characterizing the gains from eliminating unjustified between-job male-female wage differences as being small or nearly insignificant, we think that the evidence could just as easily be used to describe the effects as positive but indeterminate in size. That is, the narrowing of the income gap could exceed Weiler's estimate of a 2 to 3 percentage point effect if more detailed job categories were examined or if the overrepresentation of female jobs in low-wage firms were not as important as some now believe it to be. (See, e.g., Sorensen 1994 and Petersen and Morgan 1995, discussed later in this chapter.) At the same time, it is clear that justification for legal attention to between-job differences has to rest on more than vague speculation about purported gains that it will produce in the overall economic position of women in American society. Pay equity legislation or any other policies aimed at "between-job" inequality are not likely to eliminate female poverty, eradicate on-the-job harrassment, or shatter glass ceilings. But none of the issues we have considered so far would lead to the conclusion that differences in earnings between men and women who work for the same employer but in different jobs should be exempted from legal or empirical scrutiny.

Market Theories of Between-Job Wage Differences

This is the conclusion, however, of many neoclassical economic analysts who premise their argument primarily on theoretical rather than empir-

---

5   In actual studies the situation is even more complex because aggregated measures of **individual** qualifications are often used instead of direct measures of job skills.

ical grounds. They assert that between-job differences are first and foremost a result of free market processes. Any comprehensive analysis of between-job disparities must entertain such arguments alongside the plausible alternative of organizational causation.

Curiously, comparable worth scholar-advocates also often minimize the distinctive contribution of organizations to pay determination. In their view, cultural biases in job evaluation are so widely diffused that employers can still discriminate in favor of predominantly male jobs over a very long period of time while each of them is rigorously "following the market." That is, any tendency for the market to correct itself will be lost if the behavior in question is something that "everybody does." Such interemployer conformity in establishing lower female wage rates would be more plausible if there are only a small number of actors involved or if national wage guidelines prevailed, as in Australia. But wage determination in the United States is extremely decentralized. The sheer number and variety of employers alone suggests the necessity of analyzing how employers vary in their treatment of male and female employees, particularly in setting wage rates for jobs of various types.

Characterizing wage determination in the United States as *decentralized* is a bit like describing pebbles on the beach as "nonsquare" – the descriptor is accurate but using it allows one to ignore great variation in the subject. Yet the complexity that results when pay decisions are made in thousands of different local contexts can be a source of clarification as well as confusion for the social analyst.[6] The underlying premise of our argument is that wage levels are the outcome of the interaction of distinct social forces, which can be grouped, at least initially, into three main categories: market, organization, and culture. Because these basic forces are spread unevenly over the terrain of the American employment system, comparisons of wage setting across different contexts is a revealing exercise. In more centralized systems, it can be quite difficult to see how these forces operate or interact when they are congealed in a unitary decision process. For example, market supply and demand pressures do not go out of existence when a national wage structure is put in place, but their operation may be both transformed and rendered less visible compared with some wage-setting arenas in a decentralized milieu.

In the next section, we consider theories of between-job wage inequal-

6 "Local" is used here to mean the opposite of global and is not meant to imply a widespread tendency toward geographic particularization. The fact that the U.S. government imposes a unified wage structure on its employees is, thus, a confirmation of local determination, not a refutation of it. (This is true because the federal government practices represent only one of many ways in which pay scales are set.)

ity in which market forces play a central role. Our discussion begins with conventional market models that deemphasize employment discrimination and other invidious labor market processes. We then turn to an examination of what can be called "tainted" market models, which allow for the introduction of various discriminatory distortions into the market process but that, at the same time, rely on market mechanisms as a proximate cause of between-job wage differences.

Market Models

Conventional Models. In explaining between-job gender differences in pay, market-based theories rely on the same fundamental principles that they use to explain wage differences in general. On the demand side, individual employers each confront a marginal revenue product schedule for their output and are willing to pay different labor inputs – people in different jobs or occupations – differing amounts depending on their contribution to that revenue product. The market aggregates these various preferences into a marketwide demand schedule for each kind of labor. For example, if public preferences shift toward taking more exercise under the tutelage of aerobic instructors and personal trainers, the demand curves for these occupations will, other things equal, move to the right as health clubs and other facilities shift their production more in this direction. On the supply side, individual decisions also weigh heavily as workers of various types gauge the advantages and disadvantages of various bundles of work activities (occupations) and decide how much money they would need to work a given amount in a given job. If more individuals, of any type, find a given bundle of activities more attractive – or at least less onerous – the supply curve to that occupation will shift to the right as well. The wage rate for a given occupation will be determined by the intersection of these curves and will, when the system works smoothly, mostly reflect the relative preferences of consumers and workers.[7]

An integral element of this theory is that at any given time, both those interested in buying labor – employers – and those selling it – employees – will confront market prices for occupations as a fixed reality. Whatever discretion they exercise in the short run will be directed toward questions of quantity. Thus, employing organizations are portrayed as price takers, and our hypothetical health club will decide how many hours it can schedule of aerobics instruction at a given wage rate but

---

7   We should add that the demand for workers also depends on the technology that relates occupational performances to the output produced by each firm.

will have little individual influence on the going rate for employees in this occupation.

Applying these principles to the explanation of differing wage rates for predominantly male and female types of work appears to be a straightforward endeavor. Perhaps the most essential modification necessary is to account for the existence of occupations that depart so dramatically from a balanced mix of male and female workers. Aside from the possibility of employer discrimination, an issue we will address shortly, the concentration of women in some jobs and men in others could be based on choice – a proposition that market theories wholeheartedly endorse. There are at least two plausible accounts of how men and women make different occupational choices.

First, the duties and performances involved in the work of some occupations might be more attractive to women and less attractive to men (or vice versa). For example, more women than men may be drawn to lines of work that require one to give care to or to nurture others. For our purposes, there is no need to debate whether this attraction results from any number of biological causes or from the way in which most boys and girls are socialized by parents and schools. In either case, to the extent that there is a "problem" to be solved in this area, it is hard to envision how it is a problem that devolves onto employers to rectify.

Second, the organization of work typical of an occupation, but not its intrinsic duties, might be better suited to the other social roles occupied more frequently by women. The best-known hypothesis of this sort is the "skill depreciation – career interruption" conjecture put forward by Solomon Polachek and others. The basic idea is that in some occupations one's skills atrophy at a faster rate during periods of inactivity or withdrawal from the labor force. At the same time, the working population is thought to be segmented into two groups with very different chances of interrupting their careers to pursue other activities, specifically child bearing and child rearing. If so, it would be logical to expect women to gravitate toward those occupations in which the penalty for episodic departures from the labor force was relatively small (Polachek 1981). As logically compelling as such a link might seem, support for it has been quite scarce in the empirical literature. Marini (1989) cites several studies that among other things show that: (1) "women in predominantly female occupations do not experience lower wage depreciation than women in predominantly male occupations" (see England 1982, 1984b); (2) "women with continuous labor force participation are no less likely to be in predominantly female occupations than are women who have experienced labor force interruptions" (see England 1982; Corcoran, Duncan, and Ponza 1984); and (3) "women's anticipated labor force participation in adolescence and early adulthood has no significant effect on the sex type of the occupation in which they are later employed" (see Lehrer and Stokes 1985).

In sum, the pure market-based theory of between-job wage differences of men and women rests ultimately on a hybrid account that draws on both economic and noneconomic reasoning. Occupations are paid what the market will bear based on supply and demand, but the most convincing account of why men and women choose different occupations involves some combination of presumed innate inclination and the powerful shaping influence of differential socialization. However, once the door is opened to the influence of socialization and cultural factors generally, it becomes difficult to argue that they do not also influence the "market process" itself. Thus, we now turn our attention to a second group of theories that we identify as "tainted market models."

Tainted Market Models. This variant of the market approach raises the possibility that between-job, male-female earnings differences result in part from marketwide tendencies to discriminate against women. Tainted market models share the assumption that supply and demand forces are still important in wage determination and continue, for the most part, to see individual employers as "price takers." Or, stated differently, one would find unexplained "pay gaps" between those working in predominantly male and female jobs even among nondiscriminatory employers. These theories contend, however, that there are external, invidious factors that intervene in the market process to the detriment of those working in predominantly female jobs.

Crowding theory is one explanation of this type. The essence of this model is that there is persistent discrimination against women that prevents or strongly discourages them from entering traditionally male jobs. As a result, women are restricted to a limited subset of jobs in which the market has too many job seekers chasing too few offers (i.e., it is "overcrowded"), and wage rates decline as the labor supply curve shifts to the right (Sorensen 1994, 38; England 1992, 72; Bergmann 1974). Although there are other variants of the crowding idea, in this particular version it is not necessary to assume that there are any preexisting wage differences between "male" and "female" jobs. Discrimination in hiring and job assignment is sufficient to produce the observed result of depressed female sector wages.

Nonetheless, this theory raises some difficult issues. First, why is the net flow of women out of male jobs that is produced by discrimination not counterbalanced by an influx of male "refugees" from the depressed wages that appear in the "nondiscriminatory" sector? This counterflow of male workers would be in the interests of "male sector" employers who would confront a looser labor market and lower wage rates. If it did occur, it would also tend to reestablish higher wage rates in the female sector that these males were deserting. In a similar vein, Baron and Newman note that "men were no less concentrated in male-dominated jobs than were women in female-dominated jobs" (1990, 156). In reply, it might be argued that the jobs that women are excluded from also contain entry barriers against other workers as well – as in the construction trades, for example – that would prevent such counter-movements from taking place. But once this argument is made, one can no longer presume that the wage rates of the two types of jobs would be equal in the absence of gender discrimination. Thus a different model is called for.[8]

Killingsworth (1985, 89–91) does offer a model that combines discrimination against women in hiring with preexisting wage differences between various occupations. (In his model, however, the preexisting wage differences are due to normal, and justifiable, economic forces such as differences in productivity and/or differences in nonpecuniary aspects of the jobs in question, and are not monopoly rents that arise from other kinds of barriers to entry.) His model holds that employers of labor in high-wage occupations prefer to hire men and will pay them a wage premium and will try to avoid hiring women. Or if they cannot avoid women completely, they will not pay them the wage premium. The end result is that (1) men are overrepresented in high-paying occupations and women are overrepresented in low-paying occupations and (2) the original wage difference between the two types of occupations – the econonomically rational part – is widened; (3) there is a within-occupation wage difference in the high-paying sector that favors males.

It is curious that Killingsworth adds the stipulation that women are paid lower wages when they are hired into male sector jobs. A widening of the between-job wage differences would occur even without this added measure of invidious treatment. Furthermore, it raises two additional problems to be explained. The first, and perhaps lesser of the two (although the only one Killingsworth addresses), is the argument that normal competitive forces should lead rational employers to undercut the within-job wage differences by bidding up the price of the services of the equally productive, but undervalued, female workers. The second is that this kind of discrimination flies directly in the face of the least controversial and longest-standing piece of antidiscriminatory federal legislation, the 1963 Equal Pay Act. (If the theoretical problem is to

8   We are deferring discussion of whether this or any other type of market "taint" would be eroded by competitive market pressures over the long run. These are important issues, but they appear with regard to almost all kinds of discrimination, not just for the simple crowding model.

account for a residual within-occupation difference, an alternative, and more plausible, explanation would involve examining the possibility that women in high-wage occupations are more likely than men to work for low-wage firms.) A modified discrimination model, one without Equal Pay Act violations, can be offered, however. Under this model, employers do prefer to hire males in high-wage occupations, do systematically exclude women from such positions, but do pay the few female exceptions who are hired the same wage premium.

It is worth pausing briefly to examine the implications this model has for the kind of wage discrimination that would appear in conventional statistical analyses. Under this model, male occupations and female occupations would be observed to earn different wages even if the qualifications of incumbents (education, training, experience, etc.) were taken into account. However, once *job* and *occupational* characteristics were taken into consideration, whether these were productivity related or "rent" related, the wage difference between predominantly male and female occupations should disappear. That is, the primary mechanism in this model is a differential access or hiring mechanism. If the hiring discrimination nut were to be cracked, there would be no need for any additional steps to be taken to redress the between-job differences between men and women.

Not surprisingly, comparable worth advocates feel the need to offer an alternative account of the source of between-job, male-female pay differences. That is, only if the sex composition of jobs itself is implicated as a direct cause of reduced earnings is a remedy required that goes beyond ensuring equal opportunity in the hiring/job placement process. To this end, a theory is adduced that is another variation on the theme of tainted markets. In contrast to those considered so far, it blends a broader array of causes into the bitter mix that poisons the market process. First, and most central to the explanation, is the idea of cultural devaluation. Not only women as a gender but most things feminine, including female skills, traits, and tasks, are undervalued by society and male decision makers. Second is the proposition that this devaluation insinuates itself into the wage determination process by affecting the kinds of judgments that are made in the job evaluation schemes found among major employers. England (1992), a leading proponent of this viewpoint – which she sees as cultural capital theory applied to gender – makes these arguments explicitly:

> Feminist critics of current job evaluation practices charge that the choice of factors and weights is biased in favor of men. . . . The contention is that the skills or tasks that typify female jobs will receive lower positive or even negative returns

(weights) in comparison to skills and tasks typical to men's jobs. (1992, 104–5)

Among the female task traits that are alleged to be devalued in this way are verbal skills, small-motor manual dexterity, and facility in "nurturant" human interaction.

A third point, although one that is more implicit than explicit in this approach, is that the diminished wages that accompany cultural devaluation become a marketwide phenomenon. Thus, the position that defendant organizations in pay equity litigation often adopt, what we have labeled the "market defense," is held by comparable worth theorists to be no defense at all. This is the fundamental contribution that follows from arguing that the discrimination in question flows from cultural sources. As elements of a cultural system, the beliefs involved can be seen both as pervasive and as unconsciously held. Because they are socialized into these belief systems as children, adult decision makers of either gender may put them into play without even realizing that they are doing so. From this point of view, it is logically consistent to assert simultaneously that employers are price takers and that the market is "wrong." The market wage only seems untainted, and might appear so even to a female employer, because it is based on beliefs that everyone takes for granted.

If one accepts this portrait of the labor market, the case for comparable worth takes on renewed luster, at least initially. If the market is populated by cultural automata, little remediation can be expected from the forces of competition. Moreover, by increasing wage rates for jobs that are predominantly female, comparable worth mandates kill two birds with one stone. In the short run, they diminish the wage gap between women and men, and in the long run, they lead to a recalibration of the cultural yardsticks that measure female work unfairly. The assumed logic here is that if librarians make as much as fire hydrant inspectors, they must be doing something that is pretty important[9] (see England 1992, 118; Sunstein 1991).

Before moving on, however, it is appropriate to ask whether the premise of this argument is as plausible as it seems at first glance. First, not every employment sector is dominated by organizations that use job evaluation systems and pay matrices. In some sectors, it may be quite reasonable to assume that wage rates are influenced by "derived" demand – the amount that each type of work contributes to the value of the final product. Under these circumstances, there will be a powerful

---

9   The example of librarians and fire hydrant inspectors comes from the City of Chicago in the mid-1980s in which the pay grade of the former was considerably beneath that of the latter.

incentive for an employer who is spending too little on workers in predominantly female jobs to increase the rate of pay and hire more productive individuals up to the point at which the marginal increase in pay matches the marginal increase in contribution to the final product. In situations in which an occupational market is composed of both kinds of employers (i.e., those subject to competitive forces and those relatively immune from them), it is reasonable to ask whether the market-driven segment might set the terms for the administered-pay segment, as well as the reverse. After all, as we shall see in subsequent chapters, market surveys are a routine part of the salary-setting process in almost all bureaucratic pay systems. In short, the cultural capital version of the tainted market theory shares with its more orthodox counterpart a tendency to make global assumptions about aspects of market functioning that might better be addressed through attention to market contexts per se.

When tainted market theories are explicitly introduced into comparable worth lawsuits, however, they are seen as having very different implications than more orthodox market concepts. Specifically, federal court rulings have consistently refused to hold individual employers liable for gender differences in pay that result from them paying market-determined wage rates. Underlying the courts' reasoning are neoclassical economic principles, tenets that would require that **all** of the market difference in rates be removed before a comparable worth claim could be supported. Thus, the battle lines are drawn in a debate over market functioning. Unfortunately, the debate has taken a somewhat abstract and philosophical turn. For their part, the neoclassically minded assert that cultural bias, like other forms of taste discrimination, is costly in markets and will tend to be driven out by the forces of competition. In the terms of rational choice theory, maintenance of gender bias in pay among a group of employers is a "collective" good that requires some unidentified mechanism that constrains individual employers from acting in their own self-interest, which in this case would be to hire away high-quality female workers from their competitors by paying them fairly. To this argument, cultural bias theorists have responded that there are other considerations that would allow such a bias to persist. (One possibility is monopsony; another is that the wage difference might be the result of male employers' altruistic bias in favor of male workers. On monopsony, see Madden 1973; on male altruism, see England 1992.)

This debate has not proved fruitful, primarily because the ideological issues are only thinly buried beneath the surface of assertion and counterassertion. A better starting point, in our view, is to recognize the existence of both pervasive cultural bias and competitive markets but to challenge the causal primacy of either influence. With this background in mind, we now address some structural features of the labor market that require us to pay more explicit attention to the organizational context in which between-job wage differences are found.

Organizations and Labor Markets

There are two related aspects of the growth in size of employing organizations that have tempered the influence of competitive labor market conditions on the nature of employment relationships. The first has been the spread of the so-called internal labor market, and the second the emergence and proliferation of bureaucratic personnel systems. (Other studies refer to this second element in various terms: Burawoy [1979] describes the rise of the "internal state," Edwards [1979] and Baron et al. [1988] discuss the spread of "bureaucratic control systems," while Bridges and Villemez [1994] investigate the nature of "bureaucratic personnel management.")[10] From the point of view of organizational influences on wage determination and possible discrimination, both pat-

---

10   Some readers may question our omission of two other related literatures that each demonstrate how both wage levels and the correlates of wages differ depending on the industry and firm for whom one works. The first is that group of studies concerned with specifying the effects of "sectoral" location or position in the "segmented labor market" on various groups of workers. (See the numerous studies reviewed in Baron and Bielby 1980 and Hodson 1984.) For present purposes, this body of literature is of only marginal significance since its primary concern with markets is the position of the employing organization in its product markets (monopolist, oligopolist, competitor), a circumstance that has been shown to be only loosely correlated with its position in the factor market for labor (Zucker and Rosenstein 1981). To be sure, monopoly profits may be associated with higher than average levels of unionization, which is one type of labor market "imperfection," but the question whether firms in the "core" of the economy exercise greater power in the labor market per se has not been dealt with extensively. (It would be a strange exercise of this power if it always led those firms to pay higher wages for workers of comparable quality.)
    Of somewhat greater relevance are those studies that concern themselves with the effect of the size of the employing organization on the wages paid to its workers. Stolzenberg (1978), who finds not only higher wages but higher wage returns to education in larger employing establishments, is a case in point. Inevitably studies of this type direct attention toward the determinants of wage differences within firms, rather than toward differences between types of firms or industries as in the sectoral studies, and point to influences on wages and wage structures that reflect organizational exigencies as opposed to market-derived prices. For example, Jacobs (1981, 700) asserts that "in positions where an exemplary individual accomplishment does not add much to organizational performance, organizations will have flat pay scales and emphasize punishments as the predominant way to control their employees." The common thread running through studies of organizational influences on social stratification is that large employing organizations must be seen as more than an unrelated collection of individual occupational markets in which the employer acts as a "price taker." Instead large organizations comprise related systems of pay and nonpecuniary compensation.

terns embody a similar logic. Each represents the institutionalization of nonmarket, organizational influences, which tend to interfere with pure market determination of wage rates, and in this sense, both increase managerial discretion. Precisely because both represent *institutionalized* systems, however, managerial discretion is not unlimited and is, in fact, channeled in predictable ways by these practices. Together we refer to these institutions as the administered labor system.

Internal Labor Markets

Among the most important developments that affect the legal resolution of wage disparities between men and women is the creation of internal labor markets (ILMs). In the context of our analysis, the definition of an internal labor market is particularly crucial. Following Kerr (1954), some scholars take a broad view that recognizes almost all closed or restricted labor markets as "internal" and includes craft labor markets under the same general rubric as firm-specific employment systems. Because we are interested in developing an organizational theory of gender inequality, we must necessarily adopt a narrower definition. An employer that hired only from craft (internal) labor markets and paid the "going rate" in all instances would seem to be in an ideal position to justify any resulting gender wage disparities as both a genuine business exigency and a reasonable response to market forces. Organizational intermediation would not play a role in such a wage system. Thus, the internal labor markets of interest here are those that some have called "firm internal labor markets" (see Althauser and Kalleberg 1981).

Although definitions vary, a central element in most representations of firm internal labor markets is the recognition of two classes of jobs. The first are idiosyncratic and are defined only in terms of a division of labor that is specific to a given enterprise or employer; the second are those which are standardized and defined with reference to an external occupational system (see Williamson 1975; Bridges and Villemez 1991). Partially overlapping this distinction is another that distinguishes between jobs that employers fill from within the firm and those that are filled by hiring from the external market. In practice, these two dimensions tend to converge, but, for a variety of reasons, employers may choose to establish promotion sequences and "job clusters" that protect the standardized jobs as well as the idiosyncratic ones. When such systems are well institutionalized, with hiring restricted to certain "ports of entry" and labor allocation determined by administrative rules, an internal labor market can be said to exist (Gitelman 1966; Doeringer 1967; Doeringer and Piore 1971; Althauser and Kalleberg 1981; Finlay 1983; Jacoby 1984; Pfeffer and Cohen 1984; Osterman 1984; Baron,

Davis-Blake, and Bielby 1986; Althauser 1989; Bridges and Villemez 1991, 1994)

The existence of internal labor markets has important implications for the legal analysis of between-job wage disparities. If the competitive market is operative only in establishing wage rates for entry-level jobs, much of the invidious effect of occupational gender segregation will lie sheltered from the competitive discipline of the market. Treiman and Hartmann recognize these tendencies explicitly:

> Only for entry-level jobs are wage rates strongly influenced by the competitive forces of supply and demand. The major supply for the jobs higher on the ladder are those workers already in the firm, and the only effective demand for those particular workers is that of their current employers. Some of the jobs have few, if any analogues in the external labor market and no established market wage rates; rather it is the employer, and possibly workers, who determine appropriate wage rates for the jobs. (1981, 47)

Nevertheless, the role of internal labor markets in sustaining between-job gender disparities in pay has been given only passing attention. One of the most comprehensive treatments of pay equity to date, Paula England's *Comparable Worth* (1992), devotes only a few scant paragraphs to the topic, essentially arguing that the major importance of ILMs is to retard any closing of the pay gap that might be achieved through open and discrimination-free market competition (p. 282). Sorensen (1994) offers a stronger argument linking internal labor markets to between-job gender differences in pay under the rubric of an "institutional model of discrimination." Her rendition of this linkage is that internal markets are the cause of pay equity violations.

> [F]irms with internal labor markets are more likely to discriminate than other firms. Since they use occupations as their unit of decision to establish pay and promotional opportunities, individuals within these occupations are treated similarly. Hence, it is to the firm's advantage to make sure that workers within each job are as similar as possible. (1994, 47)

While internal labor markets might conceivably take the form of parallel but unequal job ladders for men and women (and on occasion have taken this form), there is nothing inherent in the construction of ILMs to require racial, ethnic, gender, or class-origin homogeneity in their staffing. To the contrary, ILMs closely resemble the promotion hierarchies that are one of the essential features of the Weberian model of rational bureaucracies and, by analogy, might be expected to operate on universalistic and achieved criteria rather than particularistic and ascriptive ones.

Our belief about the role that ILMs play in between-job gender inequality lies somewhere between these two positions. In contrast to England, we want to emphasize that ILMs have some bearing on the *origin* of gender differences in pay. But unlike Sorensen, we would not argue that ILMs *require* such inequality. Instead, internal labor markets are a critical feature of many organizations that allow them to maintain invidious pay differences in the face of countervailing pressures that might otherwise tend to reduce such differences. This role of ILMs is particularly significant when taken in conjunction with other elements of bureaucratic personnel management.

There is also evidence that ILMs have become a widespread feature of the organizational landscape in the twentieth century. Baron, Dobbin, and Devereaux-Jennings (1986) provide data on the diffusion of "promotion and transfer systems" between 1927 and 1935. Their sample, drawn from National Industrial Conference Board files, is somewhat skewed in favor of larger establishments. Across all industries and among firms with more than 250 employees, these systems were found in 24 percent of establishments in 1927 and in 17 percent in 1935 (1986, 357). By 1980, Bridges and Villemez found that among a random sample of Chicago employees, 49 percent of workers were employed in jobs their employers reported as being part of promotion ladders – regardless of the size of the employing organization (Bridges and Villemez 1994, 62). Data from the General Social Survey for 1989, a representative national sample, show patterns that are consistent with these trends. In that survey, employers reported that they used formal procedures to promote employees in 49 percent of the jobs studied – either to a higher level within the current job classification or to a higher job classification (Kalleberg and Van Buren 1996).[11]

In the past ten years, there has been increasing concern about the future of long-term employment relationships and other aspects of internal labor markets. Fuel for this fire has come from a series of studies discussing and documenting the expansion of the "contingent labor market" (Pfeffer and Baron 1988; Dickens and Lang 1987; Applebaum 1987; Lozano 1989; duRivage 1992; Harrison 1994; Osterman, 1988; Tilly 1992; Abraham 1990; Bernhardt 1995). Although it is clear that part-time, temporary, and other forms of low-commitment employment have increased, it is less certain what this means for internal labor

11 Data based on the 727 CORE and the 727 GSS jobs that were studied by the General Social Survey researchers. We excluded from these recalculations data on the matching sample of managers, because they would have tended to add an upward bias to these estimates.

markets. Unless one assumes that all workers in the early 1980s were part of ILMs, growth in these alternative, contingent work arrangements might have come primarily at the expense of workers who were involved in other non-ILM kinds of employment relationships with their employers.

To date, evidence on the survival of ILMs in the face of contingent employment growth is fragmentary and inconclusive. In an analysis of changes in job mobility patterns between 1983 and 1991, Bridges (1995) found some evidence that internal labor market arrangements were weakening. Jobs that were more well entrenched in ILMs in 1981, as measured by the mobility patterns of their incumbents, had increases in the level of "unstable" market movement between 1981 and 1993. But, at the same time, DiPrete (1993) found that ILMs continued to play a buffering role in the face of corporate restructuring in the late 1980s. Gardner's analysis of job displacement in the period between the early 1980s and the early 1990s found that the overall rate of displacement of workers from their jobs had remained stable at 3.8 percent (1995, 45). Even researchers who examine identical data sources have produced conflicting reports on the possibility of declining job stability. Using Current Population Survey data from 1979 through 1991, Swinnerton and Wial concluded that, "if the pattern of the 1980's persists, workers who have stable, long-term jobs will make up an increasingly exclusive club" (1995, 304). However, a reanalysis of the same data by Diebold et al., who corrected inconsistent coding in the earlier analysis, led to the conclusion that "there appears to have been no case for concluding there have been wholesale declines in job stability" (1996, 348). Given this ambiguous empirical record, it is premature to announce the end of internal labor market relationships.

Bureaucratic Personnel Systems

Modern personnel administration with its embedded notions of due process and industrial justice is empirically related to, but analytically distinct from, the establishment of internal labor markets. Observers of these systems have long recognized the implications that rule-ordered internal "states" have for the experience of industrial work as a system of social control (Selznick 1969; Burawoy 1979; Halaby 1986). Equally important but perhaps not as widely appreciated is the influence that modern personnel practices have had on the determination of wages in large, contemporary organizations. However, some like Baron et al. (1986) have recognized this connection. In discussing the spread of modern personnel practices during the 1940s, they make the following observation about a 1947 job evaluation plan in the steel industry: "Labor viewed the new system as consistent with their aim of eradicating capricious wage differentials, while steel companies saw the chance of systematizing and streamlining employment practices" (1986, 372).

The thrust of our argument is that rationally designed compensation schemes involving job evaluation and sometimes external wage surveys need to be considered as integral elements of quasi-legal governance systems that arise in some large bureaucratic work organizations. Compensation schemes, just like systematic grievance procedures, lead to a structure in which "normative beliefs establish a prescriptive baseline that workers use to grade the employer's exercise of authority, and thereby set their level of attachment" (Halaby 1986, 635). That is, personnel systems grounded in rational-legal norms provide an important legitimating function for contemporary management. Thus, employees come to expect fairness and due process in the allocation of rewards as well as punishments in these settings. In short, it is no accident that employers often depart from strict adherence to a price (wage) schedule set by supply and demand in the external market; it is a structural exigency of organizational life.

It would be a mistake, however, to describe these systems as if they completely ignored the market. To the contrary, as has been recognized for many years, "scientifically" based compensation systems purport to follow the market by incorporating information on prevailing rates in an area for what are sometimes referred to as "key" or "driver" jobs (Hildebrand 1963; Dunlop 1957). Two points are of immediate importance.

The first is that even if one assumes real market determination of the wage rates for these "key" jobs, the linkage of other wage rates to these key rates must of necessity involve the exercise of managerial discretion. This is true because there are a host of competing principles that must be taken into account in maintaining internal equity: honoring the "natural" social comparisons employees make with those around them (see Gartrell 1982); maintaining wage differentials that are large enough to encourage labor supply from "feeder" to "receiver" jobs; and providing wage differentials that are not too far out of line with differences in skill, effort, training, and responsibility.

The second point is that it is never entirely clear whether wage rates in the "key" jobs are established through actual market testing and individual bargaining with prospective workers (and prospective quitters) or the wage surveys carried out for such positions are merely a way of justifying decisions that have already been made. Thus, a key issue in our analysis of the four case studies is how wage surveys were conducted and utilized by the defendant organizations in their compensation systems.

Considerable data exist showing that structured pay plans or compensation schemes are a widespread feature of American corporate and organizational life. In a 1976 survey of corporations in six industries (consumer goods manufacturing, industrial goods manufacturing, banking, insurance, public utilities, and retail trade), the Conference Board elicited information on the use of job evaluation for various types of positions. Among nonexempt salaried workers (largely lower-level office and clerical personnel), the percentage of firms using job evaluation ranged from 50 percent in retail trade to 88 percent in banking. In each of these industries the system used in well over half the cases was the "Hay" system or another formalized "point factor" technique (Weeks 1976, 46). In their historical study, Baron et al. (1986) report that among companies with more than 250 employees, the percentage of those companies doing job evaluations increased from 18 percent in 1935 to 61 percent in 1946.

To conclude this section, we observe that contemporary managerial practice in both profit- and nonprofit-making organizations often collides with the dictum that economic efficiency requires these organizations to act as mere price takers in the market for labor. Considerations related to both the "internal labor market" and "bureaucratic personnel systems" suggest that managers in large formal organizations are often able to exercise considerable discretion in establishing wage rates for various kinds of jobs. While compensation schemes that incorporate data from external wage surveys can be described as "market sensitive," they can hardly be characterized as market determined and involve multiple layers of discretionary judgments. What remains to be seen, however, is whether this discretionary power is used systematically to the detriment of those who work in predominantly female job classifications. Thus a key question is addressed in our empirical studies: Under what circumstances in the system of personnel relations does the necessary combination of discretionary opportunity and discriminatory motive arise to produce invidious between-job wage discrimination? Weiler (1986), in perhaps the most comprehensive treatment of comparable worth to date, offers a diagnosis that is in much the same spirit.

> As illustrated by *Lemons*, real world labor markets leave a good deal of leeway for countless managerial judgements about how to classify, value, and pay certain jobs in comparison to others. The exercise of such discretion makes possible, although not inevitable, the exercise of sex discrimination. . . . This is not to deny that real competition obtains in different labor and product markets, which does place definite economic constraints upon the ability of firms to engage in discriminatory employment practices, not only in

this new area of comparable worth, but also in the area long governed by Title VII and the Equal Pay Act. But the issue of whether sex discrimination has a sufficiently depressive effect upon the wages paid for female work, thus warranting a public policy response, is a matter to be resolved only by detailed empirical investigation and not by a priori judgements about what a "market" must entail. (1986, 1762–63)

Empirical Studies of Between-Job Wage Inequality

There are a multitude of studies in the pay equity literature that attempt either to demonstrate the "need" for a comparable worth policy or to estimate the gains that those working in predominantly female jobs would reap if the policy were widely implemented. Before reviewing these studies, we will recapitulate the most important empirical issues involved in the debate over reducing between-job male-female pay inequality. In our view, the central questions concern (1) within-employer versus labor-force-wide patterns of inequality; (2) the role of other sources of earnings inequality; (3) the extent of gender segregation across occupations and jobs; and (4) exogenous prices derived from external competitive markets versus administered prices set in internal labor markets.

In the U.S. economy, where there is no centralized determination of occupational wage rates, comparable worth "violations" are of necessity outcomes that result from individual employers' behavior. Similarly, any corrective measures would have to be implemented on an employer-by-employer basis. As Sorensen (1994, 21) states, "Such [comparable worth] policies are designed to eliminate the underpayment of 'women's work' *within firms*" (emphasis added). Even if one subscribes to the view that between-job wage inequality of males and females results from a pervasive cultural devaluation of things feminine, the necessary locus for observing this discounting would be in the wage-setting practices of individual firms and other employing organizations.

The pay equity literature categorizes the issue of job placement as a separate form of discrimination about which separate claims (hiring bias, promotion bias) can be made and for which separate remedies can be sought. Our view is that the more employment is characterized by internal labor markets and by firm-specific divisions of labor, the more important it is to specify the locus of job segregation. Under these circumstances, many jobs exist that have no clear counterparts in the broader occupational world. The sex composition of these jobs is necessarily affected by a welter of competing influences – the practices and prejudices of employers, the interests of unions, and the ideologies of personnel bureaucrats – to name only some. In this internal sphere, decisions about job assignments that produce sex-segregated work forces are a necessary condition for invidious pay practices. Although invidious between-job pay differences might arise independently from an employer's job assignment practices, the same social forces that produce disparities in pay might be expected to produce disparities in job assignments.

A final, but more arguable, proposition is that empirical studies ought to try to isolate the portion of the between-job wage difference that can be attributed to employers' attempts to "follow the market." On this score, if one's theory identifies general cultural devaluation as the reason for diminished earnings in predominantly female occupations, adjusting out or removing the effects of market wage rates is utterly illogical. By doing so, one would be removing from consideration the very institutional mechanism that allows gender inequality to persist. We reject the logic of this argument and assert that it is essential to consider that some of the between-job portion of the sex gap may be due to market forces.

It is desirable to attempt to identify this portion of the wage gap precisely because the market is not a legally "suspect" institution. But recognition must be given to the fact that wage setting does take place in the confines of large, bureaucratic work organizations. In their practices, these organizations filter aspects of their environments (including external labor markets and cultural values) and add numerous institutional complications (internally defined divisions of labor and associated job ladders, organizationally specific constellations of political power, and elements of their own unique belief systems, e.g., concerns for "internal equity" in pay rates). To understand why women's jobs are underpaid, one needs to consider all these factors and to examine as much as possible empirically how various kinds of organizations interact with external markets. In this context, it would be surprising if market wage rates were either completely ignored or mechanically adopted by employers. Having reviewed the requirements for a comprehensive, empirical study of between-job pay inequality, we now turn to the extant literature.

Empirical Studies

The most influential group of studies have been those that utilize data from the U.S. census and other representative samples of the entire labor force. These studies typically analyze data that have been aggregated to the occupational level, relying almost always on the most detailed three-digit occupations reported by the U.S. Census Bureau.

Our first question is, How well have these various labor force/demographic studies done in taking employer-by-employer variations into account? The answer, unsurprisingly, is not as well as one would like. Only one labor force study explicitly recognizes that employers are the primary locus of comparable worth reforms (Sorensen 1994), and one other speculates that national labor force data might overestimate the amount of the wage gap attributable to pay equity problems (Aldrich and Buchele 1986, 128). In the former case, the concession that is made to the need for employer-specific data is to adjust income differences by industry by including forty-two dummy variables for specific industries in an OLS regression equation. The effects of industry – a crude proxy for firm – are as follows:

> [W]ithout industry controls, women earn 20 to 25 percent less in an all-female job rather than an all-male one. Men earn 29 to 33 percent less under similar circumstances. Once detailed industry control variables are added to the earnings equation, the wage penalty associated with "women's work" declines somewhat. In this model, women earn 15 to 23 percent less in an exclusively female occupation rather than an exclusively male one. Men earn 24 to 25 percent less in similar circumstances. (Sorensen 1994, 37)

These findings are completely consistent with our argument. Labor force patterns ought not to be confused with organizational ones.

One additional study does address the question of how much "employer segregation" might be contributing to the male-female wage gap. Petersen and Morgan (1995) carry out an innovative analysis of data collected by the Bureau of Labor Statistics at the establishment level. This source includes reports from sixteen industries and contains a record of individual pay rates by sex by occupation by establishment within each industry. Applying a decomposition technique that is slightly different from the method shown in section II, they discover several noteworthy results. First, within-establishment, within-job wage differences (i.e., those that could be construed as Equal Pay Act violations) are small relative to the total male-female wage gaps – on the order of one-tenth of the total difference. Second, within each industry, a larger proportion of the male-female wage difference is due to the disproportionate employment of women in low-wage establishments. Third, a still larger proportion of the gap results from occupational segregation of women in lower-wage occupations.

Unfortunately, because of the methodology used, it is not possible to use their data to give a definitive answer to the question raised here: How much would the wage gap be reduced if between-job, within-employer differences were eliminated? Petersen and Morgan do demonstrate, however, that across industries, the average within-establishment ratio of male to female earnings is 85 percent – an improvement on the 81 percent ratio found in the aggregate. Within firms, some of the remaining 15 percent exists between jobs and some within. They estimate that only about 2 percent is within jobs. Of the remaining 13 percent gap, some is due to skill differences and some is due to invidious differences related to sex composition. Therefore, a generous estimate of how much difference comparable worth might make could be obtained by reducing the 13 percent figure by an additional 3 percent to about 10 percent of the remaining gap. In round numbers then, full implementation of comparable worth might reduce the pay gap by 10 percentage points. The lack of control variables measuring job characteristics or individual qualifications in this study makes it impossible to offer a more precise estimate.

The cupboard is equally bare when one searches this literature for studies that include market wage differences, with two exceptions. Parcel (1989) includes controls for "factors that **could** be expected to influence levels of supply and demand." When her model is applied to 1980 Census Bureau earnings data aggregated into more than four hundred occupational categories, the results are empirically puzzling. The sign of a "reserve labor pool" variable is generally positive, which is opposite of what was expected. In equations where female and male annualized earnings are separately predicted, the percent female coefficient is significantly negative only in the male equation. However, the lack of significance for percent female in the female equation does not seem to have resulted from the inclusion of the "supply and demand influencing" factors because they either have signs opposite of what was predicted or the effects are not statistically significant. Nevertheless, the lack of clearly interpretable effects of market-related variables should not be taken as decisive in this instance, if for no other reason than the fact that national data may not be the most appropriate place to look for supply and demand effects.

Sorensen's (1994) analysis of Current Population Survey and Panel Study of Income Dynamics data from the 1980s, already noted, is the other study to attempt a control for market wages. This study is based on the contextual analysis of individual-level data from these two large national surveys. Percent female in the detailed occupation is included in models that also include controls for a wide variety of individual level earnings predictors. To test the effect of external market rates, Sorensen adds the average female wage in each occupation. In four of the eight tests she carries out, the coefficient for percent female is reduced below the level of statistical significance. In two others, the coefficient becomes nearly insignificant. The only equations in which the percent female coefficient remains large are equations for male workers in the public sector. That the males' coefficients are less affected is probably explained by intraoccupational segregation. Within the census occupation categories, the suboccupations of men will probably differ from the suboccupations of women. If so, female average wages are a very poor proxy for male market rates in many occupations, and the controls for the weaker proxies are relatively ineffective in explaining the percent female correlation. Here, too, national averages of wages across occupations are a weak substitute for market pressures that individual employers might be subjected to. In general, then, the demographic/labor force studies have been no more successful in dealing with the market issue than they have been in dealing with firm-level effects.

The next task is to evaluate how well studies do in controlling for "nonrelevant" factors in the assessment of pay equity violations. Our conclusions are twofold: (1) The demographic/labor force studies were initially not very credible in this regard, but have become increasingly robust, and (2) there is still considerable disagreement over which factors are relevant and which are "nonrelevant."

Three trends can be observed in the record left by these comparable worth studies. First, studies with fewer control variables have been supplanted by studies with more control variables. Second, studies of occupational aggregates have been yielding to studies that add the percent female in the occupation as a contextual variable. Third, conventional cross-sectional controls for individual characteristics have given way to innovative methods of controlling individual differences using longitudinal data. To appreciate the first trend, consider two aggregate studies of occupations – one by Ferber and Lowry published in 1976 and one by Filer published in 1989. In the former, the effect of percent female was estimated across 520 occupations controlling for a single variable, education, and its interactions with percent female. In the latter, the effect of percent female was estimated across 430 occupations controlling for up to "225 available job characteristics," although the basic results hold for a restricted analysis using 66 of the job characteristics in question. Comparing the results of these two studies yields a predictable result: Lowry and Ferber find a large negative impact of percent female in each occupation, while Filer finds no statistically signficant impact.

Because the latter uses more control variables, are Filer's findings or the findings of others with large numbers of predictors to be given more weight? Not necessarily. Many of the "predictors" that his analysis includes are incorporated under the logic that they are alternative "rewards" from employment that workers trade off against higher income – a theory familiar to economists under the rubric of compensating differentials. As others have pointed out, the results of this sort of exercise require there to be some plausibility or face validity to the factors that are proposed as alternative rewards. Thus, Filer includes a measure of workers' "lack of interest in power." Is being able to relax and not scramble for the top a condition of work that workers would be willing to pay for? Or, alternatively, is lack of *interest in power* among those working in a job tanatamount to a *lack of power* and autonomy – a negative trait that would have to be compensated by higher wages? Unless one can make a strong a priori case in one direction or the other, it is difficult to know whether the proposed "reward" ought to be adjusted out of employees' incomes or not. In addition, the lack of a clear a priori relationship means that one may be adjusting for the effects of income rather than for its causes. Thus, higher occupational income is probably associated with higher satisfaction, which in turn may be associated with general satisfaction and a lack of concern for "power" per se. For many of the variables that Filer includes, there is no clear before-the-fact prediction, and no way to rule out such alternative interpretations.

It is, of course, possible to have too few control variables as well as too many. As mentioned earlier, the question turns on specifying which sources of between-job wage inequality are legitimate and which are not and including a set of control variables that will only adjust for income differences that are legitimate. On some matters there is consensus. Income-enhancing traits like education and previous work experience that individuals bring with them to jobs are widely viewed as legitimate sources of between-job earnings differences. There is also rough agreement that job requirements such as certain levels of skill, effort, and responsibility also should be statistically controlled before examining income differences associated with gender composition.

There may be real disagreement about other kinds of factors, though. As an example, consider labor union membership. (A multitude of other variables could be cited here.) On one hand, representation by unions is clearly a "factor other than sex" and would constitute a legitimate source of earnings difference under Title VII. However, the gains that incumbents in a job realize from bargaining depend, in large part, on employers' as well as employees' behavior. Not only can management choose to resist the wage claims of some groups more than others, but it can also choose to resist the organizing efforts of some groups more vigorously. Thus, while union membership may be a factor other than sex, it is possibly a factor strongly influenced by employers' differential treatment of the sexes. One of the liabilities of the aggregate studies is that they contain no contextual information that could be used to resolve questions about which control variables are properly included and which are not.

One additional development in this group of studies has been the application of a "fixed-effects" methodology that in essence controls for all unchanging aspects of a person that might influence his or her salary. Thus, Kilbourne et al. (1994) reanalyze panel survey data from the National Longitudinal Survey in which individual employees are followed over a sixteen-year period. In effect, by treating each person as his or her own control group, aspects of a person such as years of completed education, parental background, and even difficult-to-measure factors such as implicit preferences are removed as confounding causes of current income level. The results of this exercise are informative insofar as they demonstrate that even with stringent controls for these latent influences, a significant salary disadvantage accrues to those working in jobs with a higher proportion of female employees.

Finally, and unsurprisingly, the aggregate labor-force studies take the nature and degree of occupational segregation largely as a given. England (1992, 285), for example, is willing to see enforcement of equal opportunity in hiring and job access as a reform that is complementary to pay equity reform but views job segregation as a related but separate problem. When the data at hand obscure the identity of employers, it is hard to imagine how one could proceed any differently.

All in all, much of the empirical literature, like the theoretical literature, assumes a rather detached stance toward the practices and behavior of employing organizations. Its view of employers' relationship with external markets parallels its views of the sources of occupational segregation. In each instance, employers are portrayed at worst as pawns of cultural stereotypes and at best as passive transmitters of disadvantages that have their origins in the broader society. However, a number of studies of between-job pay inequality have used organization-level data. As a prelude to the development of our organization theory of between-job gender inequality, we review the more important of these studies.

Organizational Theories of Between-Job Wage Differences

Although extant literature has not completely ignored the possibility that organization-level factors interact with the market to cause between-job wage differences, attention to the subject has been widely scattered. In this section, we review those approaches that do recognize the possibility of organization-to-organization variability in between-job wage inequality, and we offer two alternative models that approach the subject from a slightly different perspective.

Perhaps no group of researchers has done more to probe the organizational sources of gender inequality (or to identify the organizational characteristics that might allow its remediation) than James Baron and his colleagues. In a recent series of studies of the California state personnel system, they examine how a wide range of organizational features affect levels of job segregation and male-female, between-job differences in pay (Baron and Newman 1989, 1990; Strang and Baron 1990; Baron, Mittman, and Newman 1991) Drawing eclectically from the current catalog of organizational theories, among them resource dependence, population ecology, neo-institutional theory, Baron and colleagues' basic insight is to see levels of organizational gender inequality as covarying with an organization's sensitivity to environmental influences. Thus, organizational age (or time of founding) matters because organizations tend to be imprinted with the external conditions prevalent at their time of birth. Organizational size matters because smaller organizational units are less ossified and more responsive to their external surroundings. Larger and more standardized job categories have more gender inequality because they are most connected and most sensitive to external market pressures. To the extent that features internal to an organization (percent female, rates of hiring, promotion, etc.) have an effect in this theory, it is because they can be construed as providing resources that are used to respond to pressures for equality arising from outside the organization.[12]

There is some risk of overstating the "resource-environment" slant to this very complex body of work, as it does take into account a large number of variables and does stress the importance of factors such as representation by activist unions that are only marginal features of the environment. There is less ambiguity about another aspect of these studies, though – the portrayal of the external market as an invidious, but varying, influence on the wages paid in predominantly female jobs. For example, in explaining why large, standardized job classifications might be associated with greater gender disparities in pay, Baron and Newman state:

12 Two examples provide a sense of this analytic stance. In commenting on the finding that disproportionately female jobs suffer a lower wage penalty in expanding jobs the researchers write: "For instance, the entry of women and nonwhites produces less devaluation in growing jobs, where the 'pie' presumably is expanding enough to reduce the perceived threat by those favoring the status quo" (Baron and Newman 1990, 173). And, in explaining why subunits with female executive officers might have work forces that are more integrated by gender, Baron et al. suggest that it is because "the personal characteristics of the organizational leader can have important *symbolic* effects on organizations . . . the *visibility* of top-level females within an organization facilitates integration" (Baron, Mittman, and Newman 1991, 1368; emphasis added).

[L]arge job classifications that cut across diverse
organizational settings are likely to be subject to the strongest
labor market pressures. . . . Accordingly, one might expect
greater penalties in these positions, because these generic jobs
(e.g. secretary) are most likely to embody societal race and sex
stereotypes, or to display the oversupply emphasized by
economists. (1990, 159)

While this is reminiscent of the tainted market model, it adds two sub-
tleties of its own: (1) bureaucracies, even state bureaucracies, may not
merely "passively discriminate" by following the market but can add
their own overlay of invidious treatment, and (2) different organizational
locations may be more or less beyond the reach of the market's generally negative influence. As Baron and Newman (1990, 172) summarize
the matter, "On balance, then, our findings suggest that observed relationships between demographic composition and prescribed pay rates
cannot be traced solely to inexorable market forces confronting state
government agencies."

This is sensible, but does not go far enough. Any model of the joint
role of market and organizational forces in creating and sustaining
between-job gender inequality in pay must take account of the possibility that *both* markets and organizations contain forces that lead to wage
discrimination against predominantly female jobs but also that *both*
contain forces that tend to counteract those discriminatory influences.
On the market side, the models discussed previously are quite explicit
about the role of market competition as a potential egalitarian influence
(in the orthodox model) and the role of crowding and cultural stereotyping as potential invidious influences (in the tainted market models).
What is needed is a more thorough accounting of the social processes
operating in organizations as they interact with their market environments in creating more or less between-job inequality in their own work
forces.

Toward an Organizational Theory of Between-Job Gender Differences in Pay

There are five organizational processes/principles that bear further investigation as mechanisms that mediate external market influence. The first
is technical efficiency. Levels of pay in differing job roles must be high
enough to induce individuals of differing skills and abilities to enter these
roles and to perform at a minimally acceptable level after they are hired.
Where organizations share similar technologies, similar product markets,
and similar working conditions, these technical considerations will tend
to produce rates of pay for jobs that are closely associated with a par-

allel structure of market wage rates – unless, of course, one or more of the other four considerations plays an important role. The second is "internal equity." As has been noted before, many organizations spawn internal normative orders that define relative rates of pay between various positions as being appropriate or fair irrespective of any possible points of comparison in external markets (Smith 1990; Bridges and Nelson 1989). It can by hypothesized that these equity concerns may carry increased weight in true internal labor markets that comprise firm-specific jobs and in situations where a given job structure has been in place for a relatively long period of time and has acquired a kind of "traditional" legitimacy.

A third organizational consideration entails relationships of patronage, sponsorship, and other forms of personalism. It has been repeatedly documented that American business, despite its endorsement of universalistic reward criteria, has never extinguished the embers of personal favoritism. Dalton, for example, provides ample evidence of the role that "connections" played in departures from the official salary structure in one of the plants he studied (1959, 173–78; see also Jackall 1988). In the following chapters, we consider the role of particularism not only in a narrow sense, as when a manager takes care of a favored subordinate, but also more generally, when an entire salary structure might be shaped by the successful efforts of a division leader to look after "his people."

A fourth set of market-mediating influences on rates of pay can be subsumed under the heading of "organizational culture." Organizational ideologies and belief systems can have an influence on the overall position of the firm's or unit's salary structure as when some organizations deliberately stake out a position at the upper end of a salary curve in a local labor market. But, at the same time, an internal culture can also have a differential impact on predominantly male and predominantly female jobs. For example, if a particular organization maintains an internal self-image as a traditional, hierarchical organization, being highly competitive in the market may be defined as taking care of the predominantly male senior officers and allowing the salaries of the predominantly female lower ranks to stagnate.

Yet another influence on the size of between-job, male-female salary differentials will be an organization's need for external legitimacy. These considerations form the cornerstone of so-called neo-institutional theory. According to this theory, there are a number of factors that make organizations more and less sensitive to environmental pressures for social approval. For example, organizations that produce vaguely defined outputs may feel they need to do more to justify their existence than organizations producing more palpable social and physical goods. In any event, organizations with this need are apt to respond in a procedural vein, adopting the symbolic trappings of culturally approved and valued practices, regardless of their contributions to internal efficiency. Thus, Edelman (1990) demonstrates how more vulnerable organizations speeded up their adoption of due process grievance machinery compared with their less vulnerable counterparts. While formalized pay systems are themselves another example of an assumed "legitimacy-enhancing" symbolic structure, it cannot be assumed that the adoption of such systems automatically diminishes between-job pay gender differences in pay (but see Anderson and Tomaskovic-Devey 1995). Other organizational innovations, however, including the adoption of various affirmative action plans, may have a more direct effect on reducing between-job gender inequality.

Stating a list of organizational processes and principles that may either reduce or enhance earnings inequality falls short of providing a comprehensive account of how organizations interact with markets in this sphere. As a beginning step in this endeavor, we offer two alternative models of this interaction, each of which draws somewhat unevenly on several of the five principles just considered. These models are the administered efficiency model, and an organizational inequality model that emphasizes two dimensions of organizational life as significant sources of gender inequality: (1) organizational or bureaucratic politics, and (2) the organizational reproduction of cultural advantage.

The administered efficiency model is characteristic of those branches of economics that recognize that organizational influences might derail pure market determination of wage rates. Most recently, for example, "efficiency-wage theorists" have argued that organizational effectiveness might be enhanced if some workers are paid more than their marginal products (Akerlof 1984).[13] More relevant to present concerns are an earlier generation of institutional economists who addressed the problem of systematic differences among wage rates within firms (Dunlop 1957; Livernash 1957).

The most sophisticated statement on the issue remains that provided by Hildebrand, who worried that "the notion of a range of indeterminacy [in organizational wage rates] can be pushed too far, at the cost of

---

13 The gist of these arguments is that the wage system as a whole may be efficient in the long run, despite the fact that its constituent parts are unfettered by short-run marginal productivity constraints. We find this theory problematic in two principal regards: (a) by moving the problem of market convergence to the long run, it does not eliminate the need to specify the mechanisms through which this long-run adjustment takes place; and (b) it tends toward a functionalist logic that whatever pay structure exists has survived the test of competitive pressures. Much of the evidence we present here suggests that these competitive pressures can be extremely weak in certain contexts.

losing all the economics of wage determination" (1963, 297). We can use Hildebrand's analysis to identify the key elements of the administered efficiency model. The first element is a tight linkage between the development of an internal job structure and an internal wage structure. Conceptually, these are different aspects of a firm's internal makeup, and it is likely that some factors that exert a major influence on the job structure (e.g., technology) exert only a minor or indirect influence on the wage structure. Without the existence of a "firm-specific" division of labor, however, wage rates would be set almost completely by external supply and demand. Second, the pay structure is anchored to the external labor market through the establishment of "key jobs," positions that are closely tied to similar jobs in the outside market. Of crucial importance is the fact that wage determination in the key jobs is assumed to proceed through the simple mechanism of supply and demand.[14] While wage surveys are both feasible and often used for jobs of this type, these formal methods can be regarded as a means of convenience, and identical results with perhaps longer time lags could be accomplished by a process of trial and error in making wage offers to prospective applicants and quitters.

The third, and final, aspect of the administered efficiency model concerns the nature of the wage relationships it identifies between "key" and "nonkey" jobs. Although almost all statements in the "institutionalist" paradigm leave room for the operation of factors such as custom and equity, these influences are never regarded as fully legitimate, and the prime consideration in establishing within-job-cluster differentials is the efficient allocation of labor among jobs differing in their contribution to economic output. Although never analyzed with complete precision, there are two assumptions about what efficiency means in organizational practice.

The first is that rate differentials are closely tied to differences in labor productivity associated with differences in skill, effort, or responsibility. Here, too, the operation of formal methods (i.e., job evaluation) is recognized, but these are seen again as a matter of convenience where "real markets" are not readily available. Second is the principle of homogeneity of interest within management and labor and their opposition to each

14 Writes Hildebrand (1963, 274–75, 276): "The labor market exerts its main force upon internal wage rates through 'market-oriented' jobs, that is, jobs that are fairly uniform in duties and vocational requirements as among firms in the local area. . . . Such jobs will be particularly sensitive to the market, which manifests itself through the number and quality of new applicants and through the voluntary quit rate. . . . Thus, they [market-oriented jobs] represent one kind of key job, with a key rate in the structure. They do so because the work is comparable, the employers compete for this kind of labor, and mobility is greater among such workers. Accordingly, the rate for a market-oriented key job must be adequate to hold the quantity of labor sought, in the numbers desired" (ibid., p. 276).

other. Workers, particularly when organized, are seen as creatures of habit favoring the maintenance of the status quo in relative wage rates. Management, by contrast, is unequivocally on the side of efficiency, preferring change over stasis when confronted with altered conditions requiring changing organizational solutions to the problem of efficiency.[15]

The administered efficiency model is silent on the question of whether the external labor market is tainted with sex discrimination, leading to the invidious undervaluation of women's work. Because the model portrays the internal wage structure as mirroring the effects of supply and demand in the external market, it would not be inconsistent with the model to find gender-based wage differentials inside organizations similar in size to those found in the outside world. The model implies, however, that the internal wage structure would not exacerbate such gender differences. For, to the extent rate differentials in the internal system are not directly linked to the external market, the model suggests they will be determined by differences in skill, effort, responsibility, and working conditions.

Although the administered efficiency approach does bring organizational considerations to bear on our understanding of the wage determination process, it ignores many of the normative, cultural, and institutional forces operating in work organizations. Specifically, its portrayal of organization management as a unitary and efficiency-seeking group fails to capture important forces that are rooted in the quasi-legal systems that govern work rules, employee discipline, pay, and other personnel matters in large bureaucracies (Selznick 1969). Sometimes labeled "internal states" (Burawoy 1979), these governance mechanisms create an arena in which normative and political considerations exert substantial influence over wage policies. Thus, the types of compensation schemes we analyze in this book do not exist in isolation from other elements of these governance systems, and employees come to expect fairness in the allocation of both rewards and punishments in these settings, for example, internal equity (Halaby 1986, 635). Furthermore, the centralization of pay decisions in a well-defined organizational subunit creates a focal point for the expression of competing claims on the size and distribution of the payroll budget.

---

15 Again, Hildebrand's (1963) treatment is revealing. "Even without unionism, the key job and its associated cluster are natural units from which the design of the internal wage structure must proceed. Where management is free to act alone, it usually will rank its jobs by effort and skill, tying dependent job rates to key rates" (p. 288). "Second, they [internal wage differentials] should furnish adequate incentives for high worker efficiency throughout the organization. In purport, job evaluation seeks to achieve these objectives in systematic fashion – if you wish, by substituting technical standards and uniform procedures for the results that otherwise would be provided by an effectively competitive labor market, if one were available" (p. 290).

Our theory of organizational inequality more explicitly incorporates these normative and political dimensions and considers their consequences for gender-based wage inequality. We will refer to one important set of these factors under the rubric of "bureaucratic politics." The key insight of this approach is that noneconomic influences on pay levels are neither random nor minor deviations from market- or productivity-based considerations but are systematically linked to the interests of organizational constituencies and are important sources of wage differences. The idea of bureaucratic politics is quite consistent with principles set forth in the literature on "power in organizations." The interest of organizational power theorists in explaining budget allocations directly parallels our concern with understanding salary determination (in fact, in many public sector contexts, salaries are the major portion of the budget). A concern for bureaucratic politics, like the organizational power theories, is the assumption of homogeneous goals within organizations (see, e.g., Pfeffer 1981; Pondy 1970). Furthermore, both theories recognize that outcomes reflect the level of resources, broadly defined, available to different groups and constituencies (Fligstein 1987; Perrow 1970).

From our standpoint, the bureaucratic politics dimension of pay determination is perhaps best seen as a special case of organizational power theory in which several points are emphasized. First, while it is traditional to see power as lodged in formally defined organizational sub-units, such as corporate functional groups or academic departments (Miner 1987; Pfeffer and Moore 1980), our notion of bureaucratic politics recognizes other kinds of actors as potentially influential participants in salary setting. For example, the main actors in many large organizations would include staff officials within personnel departments, line officials in various departments, senior management, employee unions, and other activist groups. Second, we emphasize more heavily the significance of bureaucratic rules (as opposed to bureaucratic sub-units) than is typical of most of the literature. Rules governing salary determination are important not only as an object of bureaucratic political struggle (Pondy 1970) but also because they literally create some of the participants in the system, they specify the issues on which various groups can claim to have a legitimate interest, and they determine the kinds of political resources that can be brought to bear on the decision-making process.[16] A third set of concerns in our approach is the nature of the decision-making principles that govern the system (such as

16   For example in the public sector, some states allow union representation but do not permit collective bargaining over wage rates. In other states labor relations rules may permit both. We expect that the latter will exhibit constellations of political influence that are unlike those of the former.

the prevailing rate standard or the organization's market "positioning" wage policy) and how these formal principles are translated into organizational practice (e.g., through the implementation of a wage survey).

The conception of salary determination in large organizations as a system of bureaucratic politics has very different implications about the sources of between-job gender inequality than does the administered efficiency model. Rather than viewing gender differentials as the organizationally internalized product of market or efficiency considerations, the bureaucratic politics model provides more room for the operation of other organizational factors that produce between-job gender inequality. For example, in this model "internal equity" is not simply a free-floating subjective value but is a principle that in some contexts is institutionalized in the practices and beliefs of the bureaucrats who administer the organization's pay system. Likewise, concern for external legitimacy becomes a tool that can be wielded by various employee interest groups intent on rewiring an organization's compensation circuit boards. In yet other situations, the combination of parochial organizational climates with traditions of sponsorship and patronage produces a system of personal politics that can have dramatic implications for the shape of reward systems. What each of these considerations has in common, though, is that it suggests that the imbalance of political resources between the incumbents of predominantly male and predominantly female jobs can, in various organizational contexts, generate economic inequality between men and women.

The second organizational dimension of between-job inequality we consider is the organizational reproduction of cultural (i.e., male) advantage. Like some versions of the tainted market model, it is based on the premise that women occupy a cultural position that devalues their economic contributions.[17] It differs from those versions, however, in asserting that the general cultural disparagement of things feminine has its most pronounced influence on pay disparities in *interaction with the culture and structure of employing organizations*. In other words, a presumed deficit in cultural capital is not a handicap that uniformly diminishes the rates of pay associated with women or with jobs that have "feminine" traits. Instead, it diminishes rewards differentially depending on other normative and structural aspects of the organization's environment.

There are some scattered precedents in the sociological and popular

---

17 In many contexts, however, the economic devaluation of women does not necessarily consign them to a ubiquitous dishonorable status. To the contrary, economic disparagement can often be combined with rather inflated notions of female virtue and honor.

literature for looking at organizational employment patterns as repro-
ductive of communally based status differences. In some instances the
explicit emphasis is on the work organization as a nearly passive receptacle for status patterns found in the local community. Thus, Mack
(1954) describes how a midwestern industrial concern maintains an
internal labor force that is completely segregated by ethnicity in the same
manner as the local community.[18] Dalton's (1959) depiction of another
midwestern site contains a compelling portrait of how for the past several
decades an internal spoils system has operated in favor of members of
the local Masonic order at the expense of Catholics:

> [I]f we drop the Catholics from our calculation, because as a
> group they considered themselves to be ineligible, we see that
> nearly 80 per cent of the eligible managers were Masons. This
> is a highly significant difference and suggests, with the other
> data, that Masonic membership was usually an unofficial
> requirement for getting up – and for remaining there. (1959,
> 191)

Although one might see this as an added example of how internal status
patterns directly replicate external ones, other considerations temper this
conclusion. First, Dalton also cites a much earlier era at the factory when
a reverse pattern of dominance existed (Catholics were on top); second,
although Dalton studied three other industrial and commercial sites in
the same locale, he makes no mention of the Masonic-Catholic status
split in those institutions.[19] Significantly, he does mention several
instances in which mobility-oriented employees put aside their preexisting reluctance and affiliated with the Masonic order in a highly
calculated manner. In other words, the institutionalization of a communally based status characteristic inside the factory produced a kind
of feedback loop in which the significance of the external split was
reinforced.

There have been several studies of organizational gender inequality
that are broadly consistent with our concept of the organizational reproduction of male cultural advantage. Ruth Milkman's (1987) study of job
segregation by sex in the twentieth-century automobile industry and electrical industry is relevant to this discussion in two major aspects. First,
her research convincingly demonstrates that gender-related patterns in

18   The factory is a railroad repair shop in which the Italians work at the lighter, less
     intensive patchwork jobs and the Swedes and Finns specialize in the heavier complete
     rebuilding of badly damaged cars. Interestingly, this division of labor is supported by
     a set of opposed cultural representations that allow each group to see the work of the
     other as consistent with a derogatory group stereotype. For example, the Italians
     regard the heavy rebuilding work as well suited to the alleged stolid and slow-witted
     nature of the Swedes.
19   It is difficult to discern whether this silence is due to a lack of comprehensive data on
     the other sites or the absence of the structural split.

job assignment and wage levels were quite variable across different employment contexts. She gives primary emphasis to variability between the two industries themselves, particularly their different histories and technologies. Because work in the electrical industry was controlled through piece rates rather than with high-speed assembly lines, and was also in general somewhat "lighter," the electrical industry employed a much higher proportion of women than did automobile manufacturing. At the same time, even though both industries practiced widespread job segregation and explicitly recognized "men's" and "women's" jobs, gender boundaries were less rigid in the electrical industry.

> This [the risk of female unemployment in the depression] was facilitated by the relative flexibility of the sexual division of labor in electrical manufacturing. Women and men worked in similar jobs far more frequently than they did in auto: Women did "light" coil and armature winding, men did "heavy" winding, women worked on "small" drill presses, men worked on "large" ones and so on. (Milkman 1987, 30–31)

Milkman also provides numerous accounts of variability in gender employment patterns at the plant level within industries. She provides an example from the wartime auto industry of two plants making similar products (aircraft motors) but varying in their proportion of female workers by a range of 25 percent (2 percent in one factory, 27 percent in another). In the electrical industry, plants making similar products employed, respectively, 16 percent, 27 percent, 39 percent, and 56 percent female workers depending on which of four cities they were located in. Unfortunately, while noting the importance of this variability, Milkman fails to offer much explanation of it and instead presents it as an argument for the arbitrariness of gender segregation in general.

The second major contribution that Milkman makes is to recognize the influence of the wider culture on gender employment patterns in particular factories. Management in each industry was not driven by a simple calculus of short-run profit maximization, which, for example, would have led it to engage in widespread substitution of female for male labor during the Great Depression. Equally important is her appreciation of the mediating role of industrial organization with regard to elements of the broader culture that are brought into the production sphere. She accomplishes this by referring to the varying "idioms" of sex typing – the specific ideological constructions that are used to explain and justify gender segregation somewhat differently in different industries:

> In the manufacturing sector, sex-typing speaks a different language, rooted not in women's family role, but in their real or imagined physical characteristics and capacities. No one

pretends that being nurturant or knowing how to make a
good cup of coffee are important qualities for factory jobs.
Here the idiom centers on such qualities as manual dexterity,
attention to detail, ability to tolerate monotony, and, above
all, women's relative lack of physical strength. (1987, 15–16)

A second set of studies that illustrates the importance of culture as it
is reproduced in organizational pay practices has been carried out by the
comparable worth scholar-activist Ronnie Steinberg (Steinberg 1992;
Steinberg and Walter 1992; Steinberg and Jacobs 1994). In her account,
the primary organizational loci in which male cultural advantages have
become congealed are the various job evaluation and pay systems
adopted by employers in the past fifty years. Included here are the well-
known Hay Point Factor System but also other systems such as the
SKEW (Stevenson, Kellogg, Ernst, and Whinney) plan. The central criticism of these systems is that they explicitly reward job complexity but
implicitly define job complexity as an attribute that corresponds to level
in a bureaucratic or supervisory hierarchy. In defining complexity in this
way, other kinds of job complexity that are more likely to be found in
lower-level positions go unrecognized and unrewarded. Since women and
predominantly female jobs are less likely to be located anywhere except
at the bottom or first level of authority in organizations, these systems
inevitably short-change them. A second fault that she detects in most job
evaluation and pay plans is that they promote inertia in the relative pay
levels of various jobs. Given that many systems have been in place since
the early 1950s, a time when pay differences between men and women
even in the same job were accepted, using a system that perpetuates this
pattern is obviously discriminatory.

The empirical examples that Steinberg offers in support of these observations are drawn from a protracted legal battle between nurses in the
Province of Ontario, Canada, and the various hospitals that employed
them. The provincial pay tribunal endorsed the plaintiff's argument that
these systems did not fully recognize the amount of complexity in nurses'
jobs. Modest wage adjustments and back pay were eventually obtained.
Less apparent in the accounts of these cases is how individual employing organizations may have participated in the reproduction of males'
cultural advantage other than by adopting or not adopting a particular
pay and job evaluation plan. Some hints that individual organizations
may have played a more active role in the devaluation process can be
found, however. In discussing the implementation of the pay plan at one
hospital Steinberg writes:

[I]n unilaterally carrying out the actual evaluation of jobs at
North York Hospital, only managerial employees were

> involved. Ironically, but not surprisingly, management rated its own jobs higher than did the consultant who rated the same jobs. Management also rated the nursing jobs consistently lower than the consultants did. (Steinberg and Jacobs 1994, 108)

While she is silent about whether this was a common practice at other hospitals, actions of this sort are clearly examples of the organizational mediation of broader cultural advantages and disadvantages.

An example that applies this model more directly to the case of gender stratification in organizations can be found in recent press accounts of discrimination charges brought against a stock brokerage[20] (Antilla 1995). The specific complaints involve bias in hiring, promotions, and demotions, not equal pay for jobs of equal value, but the case neatly illustrates the organizationally contingent nature of sexism that is central to this model. The three female complainants allege that despite their outstanding records as top-producing bond brokers, they were demoted and transferred and unfairly had their salaries cut. As evidence of discriminatory treatment they cite numerous statements made to them by male managers in the company. When one was demoted she was told: "You need to be closer to home to spend more time with your daughter. . . . The 25-year-old guys have goals. . . . They want to drive fancy sports cars so they can pick up the girls and get out of mommy and daddy's house and get married" (Antilla 1995, C1). Another female employee was selected to attend a conference but was told after her attendance to look for a new job. Subsequently she was transferred, had her salary cut by 25 percent, and had the value of her accounts reduced from twenty to three million dollars. The newspaper account states that she

> said in a complaint filed with the National Association of Securities Dealers in February that Mr. Olde (the founder and owner) had harassed her publicly at meetings of brokers. "He asked her what sexual overtures she would engage in to close a sale with a reluctant securities purchaser," stated the complaint. (Antilla 1995, C3)

Although it is tempting to view these reports as simply the latest outcropping of latent male patriarchy that permeates the entire economy, other facts of the case put the matter in a slightly different perspective. For one, as little as five years earlier women had held a much better position in the company than was now true, dropping from 15 percent of

---

20 The charges in question took the form of a formal complaint filed with the Equal Employment Opportunity Commission.

Olde's nationwide sales force in 1990 to 7.5 percent by 1993. For another, even though "the securities business has long been considered a bastion of white men, Olde stands out to Ms. Friedman, the lawyer, as an unusually hostile place for women and blacks" (ibid., C3). Significantly, the company made a recent transition from conducting business as a pure discount broker to instituting an internal reward system that distributes "handsome commissions to be more like a full-service firm" (ibid.).

Our interpretation of this case, if the asserted facts are valid, is that it clearly shows the interaction of societal sexism, corporate culture, and institutional features of the environment. While the wider male culture provides the rhetoric, and perhaps some part of the motivation, for the invidious treatment of female employees, the highly entrepreneurial, highly aggressive culture of this particular firm provided a necessary ingredient for the discriminatory compound to be created. Moreover, two other elements may have been necessary catalysts. First, there is the change to an even more results-oriented compensation plan, and second, there is the fact that in the securities industry there is a mandatory "industry-run arbitration panel that handles all grievances in private" (ibid). The latter factor, of course, would serve to insulate a firm of this size from the normal institutional pressures associated with its visibility and position in the market as the third largest discount brokerage.

Thus, despite several empirical demonstrations of organizationally produced gender inequality, lack of systematic theorizing has limited the development of a more comprehensive understanding of the phenomenon, including its variety, pervasiveness, and operating mechanisms. The four case studies reported in the next section are the beginning of a more comprehensive approach. We probe data on organizational pay systems to evaluate the applicability of the market and organizational models we have outlined. With the possible exception of the neoclassical model, most of the models considered are not mutually exclusive. It is possible that elements of bureaucratic politics might exist alongside a market for some kinds of work that are tainted by a general cultural prejudice. Our expectation, though, is that these inequality principles will not be randomly distributed throughout the population of employing organizations. In fact, a primary goal of the detailed investigation of cases is to produce an empirical assessment that weeds out those models that have the least evidence in their favor, but also one that formulates grounded hypotheses about the conditions under which the other models are more and less applicable.

4

Methodological Approach: Law Cases, Case Studies, and Critical Empiricism

Cases typically mean very different things for lawyers and social scientists. For lawyers and judges, cases are decided one at a time. Indeed the particularity of cases has an exalted status in the law. The Constitution limits the jurisdiction of federal courts to "cases and controversies," meaning that federal courts are not to be a forum for dispensing legal advice in the abstract. Rather, federal courts are intended to resolve specific contests among here and now opposing parties. As such, law cases require authoritative resolution. Someone wins; someone loses. Judges do not have the luxury of calling for more research or saying it may be this or it may be that. They must decide the case before them.

There is something akin to the process of generalization in legal reasoning. Lawyers and judges argue about the general principles in the case law or code law that should govern a legal outcome. And there is a strong norm (precedent or stare decisis) that "similar" cases should be decided the same way. Yet the individual case has a recognized significance of its own. Judges will never admit to deciding an individual case unfairly in order to preserve the pristine quality of a general principle.[1]

For social scientists, in contrast, cases are the stuff from which generalizations are developed. The theory of probability, which informs much social scientific thinking, is based on repeated trials and random samples. The outcome of each unit sampled is not important in itself. The universe is assumed to contain individual variation. The nature of that variation is best captured through repeated trials and samplings, which will reveal both the best estimate of the value of the variable of interest and the range of uncertainty that brackets the true parameter. While social science only rarely engages in actual replication, social scientists typically

---

1 The nature of judicial decision making is the subject of a vast literature in jurisprudence and political science. The introductory text offered to law students to gain a glimpse of the internal logic of legal reasoning in the American context is Levi (1949). For an analysis of the prototype of judicial decision making in a comparative perspective, see Shapiro (1981). Dworkin (1977) provides a useful analysis of the "professional model" of legal reasoning and jurisprudential debates about the principles underlying law.

interpret their cases inferentially. That is, they treat the cases as instantiating broader processes or phenomena rather than as an end in themselves. Unlike lawyers and judges, social scientists have the luxury of making probabilistic statements, of calling for further research before they commit to one position or another in a scholarly debate.[2]

This book is based on social-scientific reanalyses of decided law cases. We use the materials generated by litigation to study organizational pay systems. Our case study design thus does not comfortably fit either the legal or the social-scientific paradigm. We are seeking a more authoritative treatment (from a social-scientific perspective) of a small set of cases, some of which are important in the legal doctrine on pay discrimination. Each case study is unique and important in itself, for each organization contains a system of gender inequality that reflects its own particular history and the influences of its environment. While we think it necessary for sociology and for law to take account of the unique aspects of organizational inequality systems, we also are interested in these cases as representatives of a broader universe of organizational and market contexts. We selected our cases in part to capture some of that variation. The most important difference we incorporated into our design was the distinction between public and private sector organizations.

Our approach represents a departure from many case studies of lawsuits. Case studies of law cases typically are motivated by one of three concerns: First, many ask whether the courts got the social science right (see generally Saks and Baron 1980; Finkelstein and Levin 1990; Saks 1990). Did the judges read the literature on jury size or the death penalty or the meaning of a word correctly? (See, e.g., Baldus, Woodworth, and Pulaski 1990; Cunningham et al. 1994; Cunningham and Fillmore 1995.) Did they employ the right test of statistical significance? Second, legal historians, anthropologists, linguists, and others often seek to interpret what the judges, lawyers, and litigants are doing in the case at hand. That is, they look at the legal process to draw inferences about how the legal and social context affected the behavior, language, and decisions of the actors involved (Freyer 1984; Mertz 1990; Gooding 1994; Grossberg 1994). Third, scholars look to law cases for what they reveal about a society in a given historical period (see, e.g., McEvoy 1995; Tomlins 1994; Horwitz 1977). All three types of scholarship give priority to explaining a legal phenomenon or the function of law within society.

We also are interested in these questions. We look at how well liti-

---

2   King, Keohane, and Verba (1994, chap. 2) articulate the strong version of this tendency by asserting that inference is the defining quality of social scientific research. Many sociologists and anthropologists reject such a perspective. For a discussion of different perspectives, see Ragin (1992).

gants and courts in these cases dealt with empirical questions. We consider the role that litigation played in the organizations studied. But our most pressing concern in the examination of these cases is the fundamental theoretical question of what produces the kind of gender-based wage inequality that is a persistent, if variable, aspect of organizational life. Law cases are a rare and valuable window into organizational processes. As sociologists of organizations and inequality, we are taking this unusual opportunity to look into organizational pay systems.

It would be impossible and uninteresting to stop with an analysis of inequality in organizations and ignore the legal dimensions of the cases. The law is not only a window into organizations: It is a prism. It magnifies and distorts, focuses and blurs aspects of organizational life. Some understanding of litigation and the discovery process is essential to interpreting the data. More important theoretically, these cases offer a unique vantage point on law and inequality. Each case represents an instance in which law confronts organizational practice. As plaintiffs and defendants construct alternative accounts of male-female wage differences, they call attention to the role that legal rules and justice claims play within each organization's employment system. Moreover, the cases reveal the interaction between law as an external power and the internal workings of these organizations. The outcomes of these cases are the most concrete manifestation of that interaction. As we compare our empirical results with the opinions of the courts, we are examining the role that the courts have played in redressing or legitimating organizational pay practices that affect the economic standing of male and female workers. In these ways we approach the cases as sociologists of law.

This chapter addresses methodological concerns that are particularly important for our approach. We first state the rationale for a case study of litigated cases, describe how we selected our cases, and summarize salient characteristics of the case studies. We then examine perhaps the most serious problem with our research design. To what extent are these defendant organizations representative of the broader universe of employers? Or by looking only at the targets of extended litigation, have we committed the fatal mistake of selecting on the basis of the dependent variable? We then turn to a basic dilemma of sociolegal research of the sort we present here. The problem is the authority of social-scientific research in the context of litigation. How can social scientists adjudicate between competing theoretical explanations of issues presented through litigation when they do not control the process and may not gain access to data that would allow for a more definitive test of their theory, and yet their results may shape the course of future litigation or policy judgments?

The Rationale for a Case Study Approach

The previous chapter described the current state of research on labor markets, organizations, and gender inequality. We found that although there has been considerable interest in the organizational dimensions of inequality, much of the work remains at the aggregate level. Research has mapped the diffusion of equal employment opportunity structures by economic sector, size, and other organizational variables (Edelman 1990, 1992). Scholars have examined the pervasiveness of internal labor markets and bureaucratic personnel systems in organizations, and the effects of these structures on job mobility, pay, and other characteristics of employment (Baron, Davis-Blake, and Bielby 1986; Bridges and Villemez 1994; Knoke and Kalleberg 1994). Other studies have analyzed the scope and organizational determinants of gender-based job segregation (Bielby and Baron 1986; Baron and Bielby 1980; Baron, Mittman, and Newman 1991).

Only rarely have researchers probed the dynamics of inequality in a specific organizational context. Those who have do not address how organizational pay systems interact with market forces in setting the pay levels of predominantly male and female jobs.

We decided to attack the issue through a small number of case studies selected on theoretical and practical grounds. An important premise of our theoretical argument (the organizational inequality model) is that market and organizational context are crucial determinants of the nature of gender inequality in the workplace. We felt it was more important to understand the relationship between markets and particular organizational pay systems than it was to attempt to survey a broad population of organizations. Such detailed studies of organizational pay processes would give us confidence that we understood the mechanisms that produced gender inequality in these organizations. These results might suggest how future research should investigate whether the patterns in these organizations were present elsewhere. We could not see how the process might have worked in reverse; that is, we could not see how aggregate-level studies of organizations could sensibly examine the interface between markets and gender inequality in pay, given the current state of the literature.

Our strategy has been vindicated by what we have found in the four organizations studied. Although we selected the organizations according to specific criteria, and from a range of available cases, the most interesting aspects of our findings could not have been anticipated in advance. It is only by in-depth inquiry that we could have come to understand the gendered dimensions of these pay systems. We expect that similar mechanisms are operating in many large organizations. But it remains to be seen whether broader surveys of organizations can meaningfully measure such phenomena.

Perhaps the most common mode of data collection for organization-level research on employment issues is to rely on the responses of an organizational informant (sometimes paired with a worker in the organization; see, e.g., Bridges and Villemez 1994; Kalleberg, Knoke, and Marsden, and Spaeth 1994). This approach may work well for getting at basic descriptive data, like the existence of an EEO office, how a particular job is filled (whether by advertising, internal promotion, etc.), or even estimates of expenditures on job training. But how does one assess the operation of gender bias in the collection and processing of market wage data or job evaluation results? The analysis of such complex and crucial factual issues cannot rest on the observations of an organizational informant. Rather, they require a range of kinds of data and perhaps the recorded observations of a set of differently situated informants.

That leads to the next practical consideration. How can sociologists gain access to such sensitive and potentially damaging information from organizations? For the most part, the answer has been that they cannot. We have taken advantage of situations in which organizations have been legally compelled to produce such information. The use of law cases as case studies raises some unique methodological considerations. After describing the cases we selected, we discuss these concerns.

Overview of Case Characteristics

Table 4.1 summarizes key analytic and empirical characteristics of the four case studies. We present it here as a guide for some of the comparisons we make throughout the book, as well as to demonstrate the organizational and legal variations we have captured in these case studies.

All defendant organizations are relatively large, although there is a huge gulf in size between the two smaller organizations, the University of Northern Iowa and Coastal Bank, and the two larger ones, an entire state employment system and the nation's largest retailer. The *Sears* case contains the most focused pay discrimination claims, in that it is limited to comparisons of males and females within each of fifty-one "checklist" (exempt or professional employee) job titles. The other three cases concern allegations of pay discrimination across a wide range of jobs. *Christensen* and *AFSCME* explicitly mount theories of between-job pay discrimination (comparable worth claims). *Coastal Bank* involves allegations of several kinds of placement, promotion, and pay discrimina-

Table 4.1. *Characteristics of Cases Examined for This Research*

	Defendant Organization	Plaintiff Class	Male Comparison Group	No. of Jobs Involved	No. of Employees	Types of Discrimination Alleged	Used Job Evaluation Data as Evidence?	Testimony by Victims?	Legal Outcome[a]	Job-Level Data?	Individual-Level Data?	Supplementary Interviews?
Public sector												
Christensen v. Iowa (1977)	State university	Female clerical workers	Male physical plant workers	147	848	Promotion, pay discrimination (both comparable worth and disparate treatment)	Yes	Yes	Trial: d.v. App.: Upheld	Yes	Yes	Yes
AFSCME v. State of Washington (1985)	State government	Workers in predominantly female jobs	Workers in predominantly male jobs	1,652	33,515	Pay discrimination (both comparable worth and disparate treatment)	Yes	No	Trial: p.v. App.: Rev'd Settled pending further appeal	Yes	Limited (from census)	Yes
Private sector												
EEOC v. Sears (1988)	Largest national retailer	Female workers in 51 professional jobs	Male workers in same 51 jobs	513	5,169	Hiring, promotion, and pay (disparate treatment within job titles)	Yes	No	Trial: d.v. App.: Upheld	Yes	No	Limited
Glass v. Coastal Bank (1986)	Large money center bank	Women and minority employees	White, male employees	666[b]	2,738[c]	Initial placement, promotion, and pay (disparate treatment)	No	Yes	Trial: p.v. settled before further appeal	Yes	Yes	Limited

[a] Definitions: d.v. = defendant verdict; p.v. = plaintiff verdict; App. = result on appeal.
[b] 580 nonofficers and 86 officers.
[c] 2,328 nonofficers and 410 officers.

tion, but stops short of questioning pay disparities between predominantly male and predominantly female jobs. The four cases meet our criterion of containing sufficient numbers of workers and jobs to allow meaningful statistical analyses of the determinants of male-female wage differences within and across jobs.

All four defendant organizations employed job evaluation and market surveys as part of the process by which they set wages. The nature of these results, the extent to which results are linked to specific jobs and individuals, and the role that such data played in the litigation vary by case. Job evaluation results are used to prove discrimination in *Christensen* and *AFSCME* (by showing income differences between male and female jobs after controlling for evaluation points); they are used to establish job equality or comparability in *Sears* (by showing salary differences between men and women in the same job with the same evaluation points), and they are not used in the litigation against Coastal. Even so, we have included job evaluation points in some of our analyses on the Coastal work force. The presence of job evaluation data in some form in all four cases allows us to examine how the organizations created and used these data, how well evaluation points correlated with income levels, and the impact of job evaluation results on the legal outcome.

We possess very different kinds of data on the four defendant organizations. We have adapted our treatment of theoretical issues based on the kinds of data available in each case. One important difference indicated in Table 4.1 is whether we have data on the actual pay of individual workers, as well as on the jobs in which they work. We know job-level data (like starting salary or midpoint salary) for the jobs at issue in all four cases. Individual-level data are available as well in *Christensen* and *Coastal Bank*. These data allow us to decompose earnings functions into pay that is attributable to individual characteristics (within-job pay variation) and to job characteristics (between-job variation). Such multilevel analyses allow us to address a number of important questions about the nature of income determination in these organizations, including whether public and private organizations behave differently in paying "the person" or "the job."

The last feature of the cases we comment on here is variation in legal outcome. The *Coastal* case represents the only instance of a final legal victory for the plaintiffs. There the plaintiffs agreed to a substantial settlement in the wake of a favorable trial court decision. The *AFSCME* case also produced a settlement, but the plaintiffs had lost at the appellate court level and were awaiting a decision on a petition to rehear the case en banc. Political and fiscal pressures encouraged a rather substantial settlement. Yet the lasting legal outcome was a clear loss for the plaintiffs and the pay equity movement as a whole. We made no effort to select the cases based on whether the plaintiffs won or lost in court. Nonetheless, given that we studied the cases in depth, we can offer some suggestions about why the plaintiffs won and lost the cases they did.

In short, we gained rich sets of data on each of four very different types of organizations in four different market contexts. While the cases contained different legal theories, different kinds of evidence, and different legal outcomes, they all yielded data on the patterns and dynamics of gender inequality in organizations that sociologists rarely come to possess for scholarly purposes. Four case studies will not provide a definitive resolution of all the issues raised here. Yet, if our theoretical framework explains these four cases, it will be a respectable beginning.

The Selection of Cases

We attempted to select cases to represent important variations in the relationship between markets and organizational wage determination systems. We limited ourselves to organizations that were large enough (1) to contain a range of occupations, (2) to employ a sufficient number of employees to allow meaningful statistical analysis of wage differences between male and female jobs, and (3) to have a sufficiently differentiated set of job positions to create at least the possibility of the sorts of internal promotion systems and firm-specific jobs associated with internal labor markets and bureaucratic personnel systems. Within these parameters we were interested in organizations that varied on two dimensions: public sector versus private sector and the proportion of the work force in firm-specific versus marketwide jobs.

The public-private distinction is widely thought to be crucial to labor-management relations in organizations generally and wage administration in particular. First, management in public sector organizations is not driven by profit motives. There is some speculation, therefore, that public sector management may be able to indulge discriminatory preferences without facing the same kinds of economic costs that private management does. Indeed, Sorensen's (1994) analysis of census data suggests that the male-female earnings gap is larger in the public sector than in private industry. Second, public sector organizations tend to have more rigid pay systems, whereby wages are more strictly determined by job grade and rank within grade, than in the private sector, in which there is more managerial discretion in setting wage levels, at least within grade. Thus a larger proportion of gender inequality in public sector pay systems may reside in differences between jobs rather than in differences between males and females. Third, public pay systems may have a more explicitly political character than private wage systems. Not only is the pay of state workers an item in the state budget, and thus open to scrutiny and debate, but the pay of workers and job categories is often a matter of public record. It is possible for one group of workers to learn what other workers are paid. Such information is closely guarded in private firms, perhaps in part to prevent comparisons and contention among workers.

As we noted in Chapter 2, the public-private distinction also tracks a very significant difference in pay discrimination litigation. With minor exceptions, comparable worth litigation, comparable worth legislation, and collectively bargained pay equity adjustments have been confined to the public sector. The absence of pay equity activity in the private sphere may be explained by the factors mentioned earlier. In-depth case comparisons of the magnitude of gender disparities, the degree to which the disparities are attributable to between-job wage differences, and the political and legal climates of the organizations are necessary to develop a fuller explanation for the concentration of pay equity in the public sector.

The proportion of the work force in firm-specific jobs is of interest in assessing (1) the degree to which the wages for certain jobs are set independent of external labor markets and (2) whether such positions appear to be a significant source of exaggerated male-female wage differences.

Although we encountered some difficulties, we ultimately arranged access to documents and labor force data in four cases that largely satisfied our theoretical criteria. As reported in Table 4.1, two cases are public sector cases and two are private sector cases. What is less clear is whether we successfully captured significant variation on the internal labor market variable. The work force analyzed in the *Christensen* case has the fewest indications of an internal labor market: most vacancies are filled from outside applications. Although the remaining three organizations engage in considerable outside hiring, they also contain many career ladders that entry-level workers climb to occupy positions that are relatively unique to the organization. None of the organizations possesses the kind of highly idiosyncratic production functions that create large numbers of workers with completely firm-specific skill sets. The fact that our sample does not include a classic internal labor market in some ways presents an analytic advantage. For if we find that these organizations mediate between market forces and pay levels, we can expect even more pronounced organizational effects in the more extreme case of an internal labor market.

Our selection of cases was in part constrained by practical problems in gaining access. We had no difficulty gaining the agreement of lawyers and parties to turn over records and documents for the two public sector lawsuits. We encountered obstacles in the suits against private defendants, however. Initially we planned to use *IUE v. Westinghouse* (see Chapter 2) as one of our case studies. The case had settled before going to trial, after a court of appeals ruling in favor of the plaintiffs. Our examination of the case files indicated that discovery had not produced enough material about the employer's pay practices to support an empirical analysis of the theoretical issues in which we were interested. In two other cases we obtained permission from plaintiffs' lawyers to go through case documents, only to find the existence of protective orders from the court barring use of pay system data for purposes other than the litigation.

Given these frustrations, we turned to the *Sears* case. The lengthy trial in *Sears* created a public record that contained a very rich set of reports and exhibits about Sears' employment and pay practices. We were able to copy and analyze these documents because they already were public. When we were examining the documents for the second private sector case, *Coastal Bank*, we discovered that some, but not all, of the documents were covered by a protective order. After discussing the situation with the lawyers who had given us initial access to the case materials, we collected and copied relevant documents that were not protected by court order and decided not to reveal the identity of the defendant organization. Throughout our analyses we refer to the defendant by the pseudonym Coastal Bank and have altered some of our descriptions of the organization to cloak its identity.

Protective orders are a major barrier to the use of court records for organizational analyses. We expended considerable time and money locating private sector cases that were not sealed from external examination. We were fortunate to find two cases where interesting materials were not excluded from public, scholarly analysis. This difficulty obviously shaped our case selection, as well as the kind of data we obtained in each case. Yet the constraints probably did not skew the results of case selection. The defendant organizations in these cases are notable within their respective industries, but they do not appear to deviate from other large organizations in how they determine the pay of jobs held by men and women.

Law Cases as Organizational Case Studies: Advantages and Disadvantages

Lawsuits that accuse employers of discrimination can make compelling case studies of organizational inequality. Some reasons are obvious. The cases we study here are significant legal precedents. As a result, our analyses have direct legal implications. Moreover, by applying empirical scrutiny to issues decided by litigation, we can gain insights into important legal processes. How well does the litigation process handle the complexities of claims about the determinants of gender inequality? What does the disposition of these cases suggest about judicial approaches to gender inequality in American society?

Other advantages of litigated cases may be less obvious. We have found case records to be a rich source of information that sociologists rarely gain about organizations. Discovery in these cases yielded vast amounts of data about the origins and operating procedures of organizational pay systems, as well as the actual compensation levels of job categories and individuals. Sociologists do not often have the benefit of sworn testimony by organization officials and their accusers. While it is true that we were not there to formulate the questions put during cross-examination, the lawyers and experts often got to what we considered key issues. Litigation also can be a valuable focal point for additional interviews with organizational informants. We found that lawyers and litigants were not at all reluctant to talk about past cases and their participation in them. These post hoc interviews often proved very valuable as a means of tying up loose ends on empirical issues or providing direct evidence in support of specific analytic interpretations.

As we noted before, lawsuits are a unique lens through which to peer into organizations. Yet the lens of litigation can distort as well as bring into focus organizational phenomena that are seldom observed. The distortion may occur both in individual cases and through bias in the selection of cases that are litigated.

Litigation involves strategic efforts by competing parties to depict the facts in a way that support their legal theory. One of the standard canards of law school civil procedure and evidence classes is that litigation is not a truth-seeking enterprise but a mechanism for resolving disputes. Social scientists thus must be wary of what litigation produces. Although it is possible for analysts to reconstruct the nature of discovery requests and responses, the documents and transcripts generated by discovery do not come with a definitive guide. The credibility, accuracy, and comprehensiveness of documents and testimony must be evaluated by the researcher, and uncertainties about its probative value should be noted. Some documents appear relatively unproblematic. A consultant's report on a pay system can be examined for what it is. But even such reports are not beyond question. Is it the final draft, for example? Are the changes from preliminary to final draft noteworthy? We very often faced such problems of interpretation when wading through documents. We have attempted throughout to report possible sources of error in the sources we employ. Overall, we have been impressed by the quality of data the cases have yielded.

Selection bias is a particularly acute problem facing our design. The most pressing issue is whether we selected our cases on the dependent variable. That is, because the four organizations studied here were sued for gender discrimination, does that mean that they differ systematically from other employing organizations that have not been sued in the same way? There is the danger that the nature of gender inequality in these organizations is more extreme than in organizations more generally. As a result, our conclusions may not generalize to other organizations.

In evaluating the risk of selection bias, it is important to define the conceptual universe about which we want to make inferences. Our primary interest is the universe of large employing organizations. Unlike other studies of employment discrimination litigation (see, e.g., Culp 1985; Burstein 1989), we are not interested in whether our cases are representative of the population of litigated cases or even potential grievances. If we were, we would be on very shaky ground. In their comparison of unpublished and published cases in the employment discrimination field, Siegelman and Donohue (1990, 1150–56) found that published cases were longer, more complicated, more likely to pose unusual doctrinal issues, contained larger classes of plaintiffs, and had outcomes that differed from those of unpublished cases. Chapter 2 revealed that our cases are unusual, even among reported cases. In contrast to most pay discrimination opinions, our cases involve large classes of plaintiffs, large numbers of jobs, comparisons among men and women in different jobs, and the more legally ambitious theories of pay discrimination under Title VII, rather than more straightforward Equal Pay Act claims. Thus, the four cases are an unusual subset of an unusual subset.

Our sample is far more defensible for the purpose of analyzing pay systems in large organizations. Available statistics indicate that large public and private sector organizations commonly are confronted with claims of sex discrimination. Dunworth and Rogers (1996, 532, 566) report that there were some 122,771 job-related, civil rights suits filed between 1971 and 1991, and such lawsuits appear quite broadly distributed among Fortune 2,000 corporations. Thus the mere fact that our defendant organizations were sued does not set them apart from other large companies.

It also does not appear to be the case that these organizations were sexist outliers. The two public sector cases come from states that have been at the forefront of addressing pay equity issues. Both Washington and Iowa adopted some form of pay equity legislation in the 1980s

(McCann 1994). Progressive legislative politics does not necessarily correspond to progressive pay policies within the public bodies of these states. Yet it seems less likely that state employers in progressive states would have more sexist pay policies than employers elsewhere.

We have the greatest concern about selection bias in the Coastal case. The plaintiffs' lawyers and some plaintiff informants suggested that Coastal was unusually backward on matters of gender equality compared with other financial institutions in the same city. Coastal is the one defendant organization in our sample that lost its case before settling. Our analysis of Coastal emphasizes the masculinist tendencies of the organization. Yet we are not convinced that the patterns of gender inequality at Coastal are that different from other financial institutions. Statistics we compiled on the presence of women at various ranks in Coastal and in other financials in the same locale indicate that Coastal was, if anything, more willing to hire and promote women (see Tables 8.2, 8.3).

Other considerations support the choice of these organizations for intensive analysis. These firms employ job evaluation and market surveys and have centralized rules to govern pay decisions – all practices that are widespread among large employers.[3] Indeed the employers in these cases defended themselves in part based on the assertion that they were following common practices in the industry. Consulting firms played a role in designing and revising the pay systems of all four organizations. Because consultants sell their systems to many large organizations and explicitly compare the practices of these particular organizations to those of other organizations in the environment, we know that the formal features of these organizations' pay systems will be similar to other large organizations.

We make no pretense of our ability to generalize to a complex universe of employers and labor market contexts from a sample of four organizations. To a certain extent, this is an inescapable trade-off between depth and breadth. We have chosen depth. But there is analytic leverage in these case studies. As we discussed in the previous section, the four organizations met our specifications for testing questions about the relative force of market and organizational factors in determining gender-based salary differences. Moreover, these cases are more interesting because of their judicial pedigree. In three of the four cases studied, the courts held that male-female wage differences were the product of employer responses to market forces and legitimate efficiency consider-

---

3 Baron, Dobbin, and Jennings (1986) reported that as early as 1946 some 61 percent of companies with twenty or more employees used job evaluation procedures. For a discussion of contemporary patterns of bureaucratic personnel practices, see Bridges and Villemez (1994, 60–64).

ations. If we find evidence of serious departures from competitive market processes and efficiency principles in these cases, it will drive home the need to scrutinize assumptions about the impact of labor markets on male-female wage differences.

Authority in Law or Authority in Social Science? Critical Empiricism and Sociolegal Studies

We close this chapter with observations on how our approach fits into current debates about theory and method in sociolegal studies and in studies of gender inequality.

This is a time of great ferment in the legal and social-scientific academy. On the one hand, critics of positivist social science – post-modern theorists, feminists, critical legal scholars – have raised fundamental questions about the nature of truth claims made by empirical sociolegal scholars (Trubek 1984; Silbey and Sarat 1987; Trubek and Esser 1989). They attack the supposed value neutrality of empirical research as disingenuous or confused and insist that empirical research is never without implicit value positions. Feminists attack the pretense of a universalistic scientific community and assert that "universal" scientific methods are in fact discourses of power that were developed by and still are controlled by white males (Smith 1990). They advocate replacing the image of science as a unitary method or process with an explicit recognition of the subjective position of the researcher and the partial nature of the knowledge that different subjective positions can produce (Harding 1986). Critical legal scholars have advanced parallel concerns about orthodox legal scholarship. They challenge the view that the law can be studied as a unified, logical system and insist instead that both law and legal scholarship must take account of the standpoint of different social groups (see Delgado 1984; Fineman 1991; Matsuda 1988; Minow 1990; Williams 1991). It follows that a crucial aspect of feminist sociolegal scholarship is to "ask the woman question" in fields of inquiry that previously were silent on issues of gender (Bartlett 1990, 837–49).

On the other hand, this also is a period in which law and the social sciences are increasingly dominated by economic and rational actor models of social action. The study of law and economics has become a major intellectual influence in American law schools and in judicial decision making. Economic analyses of law and legal behavior represent the antithesis of critical epistemologies. They make the imperial claim to explain the behavior of workers and employers in terms of a wage-price calculus. Indeed, it is the discourse of markets and efficiency considerations that has controlled the debate over the extension of antidiscrimination law to between-job gender inequality. That discourse has rejected suggestions for expanded legal intervention into gender-based pay disparities on the grounds of a deeply held empirical conception: that the disparities reflect market processes and efficiency concerns and any attempt to adjust these processes would lead to significant economic harm to society.

The disjuncture between the epistemologies of feminist and critical legal scholars, on the one hand, and orthodox economists, on the other, puts us in a bind. We bring to the debate over the sources of gender disparities in pay a set of critical theories that question the orthodox economic view. In many respects we favor an interpretive, social constructionist view of the process by which wages are determined, including our sense that "markets" have arbitrary boundaries, bear an uncertain relationship to the value of various jobs within an organization, and thus are very much subject to manipulation according to the distribution of power in organizations. But we also believe in the effort to formulate and test social theories of social action. And we rely on a standard set of quantitative and qualitative social scientific techniques to gather and test the evidence in support of such theories.

There is the danger, of course, that we please no one with our project. Critical feminist and legal scholars may dismiss us because of our conventional methodological approach. Economists will reject the theoretical conclusion, even if they embrace certain aspects of our methods and conceptual approach. These are dangers with which we are prepared to live. We think our kind of critical empiricism has the potential for raising empirical issues that orthodox economists and the courts and policy makers who follow their lead cannot easily ignore. In the current political and academic climate, we think it is no small advantage to employ standard social scientific approaches to question the received wisdom about the sources of between-job gender inequality and to reopen the question about whether the law should be employed to attack these differentials.

Our attempt to employ data produced by litigation to develop a more comprehensive, theoretically sophisticated analysis of the relationship between labor markets and organizational pay systems as they relate to gender inequality in pay confronts a fundamental epistemological problem. In what sense can our reanalysis of the same kinds of data available to the courts be taken as authoritative, when we obtain the data secondhand, without the same kind of direct control over the proceedings exercised by the courts? While we are at a disadvantage with respect to the courts in some ways, we have several advantages as well. We have the benefit of time, of a more complex theoretical framework, and of the ability to frankly discuss the uncertainties and limits of the available data. The courts also might state their views on the level of uncertainty in the facts before them, and resolve the case based on where the burden of proof lies among the parties. In the opinions we have read for this project, courts rarely take such a position. Instead, they develop an overall assessment of the facts and draw legal conclusions from this deterministic reading of the evidence.

In our case studies we often criticize the empirical analyses offered by the courts and the parties. Our primary goal in what follows, however, is not to retry these cases according to the same legal standards the courts invoked. Instead, it is to use the data provided by these cases to test competing conceptions of the wage determination process in organizations. Our conclusions have legal and policy implications. But we do not presume to take the place of the judge or other policy makers in assessing the appropriate response to our empirical results. Rather we appeal to standards of social scientific analysis. The ultimate authority of our findings rests on the canons of social-scientific inference. With these standards in mind, we turn to the empirical analysis of the cases.

Part II

The Case Studies

A. Public Sector Organizations

5

Paternalism and Politics in a University Pay System: Christensen v. State of Iowa

We begin with the beginning. In 1974 representatives of female clerical workers at the University of Northern Iowa filed suit claiming that they were the victims of pay discrimination under Title VII of the Civil Rights Act of 1964. The university paid predominantly male physical plant workers higher wages, even though many male and female jobs had been assigned identical pay grades based on the results of an internal job evaluation study. After the plaintiffs lost at the trial level, the Eighth Circuit Court of Appeals rejected their appeal.

> Appellants have failed to demonstrate that the difference in wages paid to clerical and plant employees rested upon sex discrimination and not some other legitimate reason. The evidence shows that UNI paid higher wages to plant workers because wages for similar jobs in the local labor market were higher than the wages established under the Hayes System. . . . We find nothing in the text and history of Title VII suggesting that Congress intended to abrogate the laws of supply and demand or other economic principles that determine wage rates for various kinds of work. We do not interpret Title VII as requiring an employer to ignore the market in setting wage rates for genuinely different work classifications. (*Christensen v. State of Iowa*, 563 F.2d 353 at 355–56 [8th cir. 1977])

Before the term became fashionable, *Christensen* was the first case to present "comparable worth" as a theory of wage discrimination under Title VII. The distinguishing feature of the plaintiffs' theory was that pay discrimination under Title VII, unlike discrimination defined by the Equal Pay Act, did not require a finding that the men and women being compared held the same job. Indeed the *Christensen* case posed what has become the stereotypical description of a comparable worth lawsuit: the comparison of wages of predominantly female clerical workers, such as secretaries, and predominantly male blue-collar workers, such as truck drivers. *Christensen* also became the first case in which the market

119

defense proved fatal to a comparable worth claim. As the passage from the appeals court just quoted indicates, if employers persuasively assert that they are following the market in paying male and female jobs differently, despite indications from job evaluation studies that the jobs are of equal value, they will not be held liable for discrimination. (See also *AFSCME v. State of Washington* 770 F.2d 1401 [9th cir. 1985]; *American Nurses' Association v. State of Illinois*, 606 F. Supp. 1313 [N.D. Ill. 1985]; *Lemons v. City and County of Denver*, 620 F.2d 288 [10th cir. 1980].) *Christensen* is, therefore, an important legal precedent.

Christensen is a sociologically interesting case as well, and a logical beginning in the set of organizational case studies we will consider. It offers perhaps the best opportunity to examine whether the wage inequities were the product of market forces or organizational factors. Unlike the other defendant organizations we examine, the University of Northern Iowa has one location. This circumstance allows us to place its wage practices in the context of a particular labor market. That labor market itself is of modest and knowable proportions. It can be analyzed through census data and Bureau of Labor statistics, as well as through the wage surveys the university collected. We were fortunate in this case to obtain both individual-level income data and documentary information on the pay system. We are, therefore, in a position to analyze the origins and consequences of specific organizational wage practices and to consider whether certain practices can be justified by principles of market necessity or economic efficiency.

Christensen poses a stringent test for the model of organizational inequality we offered in Chapter 3. According to that model, the bureaucratic politics of organizations mediate between gender inequality in the labor market and gender inequality inside organizations. One of the conditions that will increase the effect of organizational politics on organizational inequality is the degree to which the labor force is made up of internal labor markets, that is, relatively well ordered ladders of work force positions that are accessible only through entry-level positions. In a sense, the further one moves away from the entry port for a job ladder, the further one moves away from the influence of the external labor market. Presumably this phenomenon increases the zone of discretion exercised by the internal pay system. The university notably lacks such job ladders. The jobs that make up its nonprofessional work force are commonly found across numerous types of employers and firms. There are very few firm-specific job titles that would prevent comparisons with other employers. In theory then, administrators could rely quite directly on market comparisons in setting wage levels. This ability in turn should limit the effect of bureaucratic politics on organizational wage setting.

In this and other respects, the university may reflect the characteristics of moderately large employers who are undergoing the transition from relatively less formal, more paternalistic systems of employment relations toward a fully bureaucratic personnel structure. The university's total work force numbered about 1,500 from 1973 to 1975, the period in contention. It became clear during our fieldwork that the university administration in general, and its personnel function in particular, did not fit the model of bureaucratic impersonality. A small cast of characters ran the university pay system, and a small cast of characters challenged it in court. Although individuals enter our case narrative according to their official titles, official position does not figure prominently in how informants describe the actions and intentions of various participants. They refer to others by name (frequently first name), not by position. And they most often attribute behavior to personal style and interpersonal relationships, rather than to policies or to formally defined organizational duties. From the standpoint of the analyst, this feature gives us confidence that we were able to speak to most of the central actors in the organization and the lawsuit. From the standpoint of generalizing beyond this case, the moderate size of the organization and its history must be kept in mind.

The relatively small scale of this case allows us to see how the dynamics of litigation can affect the treatment of empirical questions. One of the striking features of *Christensen* is how badly both the judges and the parties dealt with the empirical issue of whether the university's pay practices were justified by market necessity. We will attempt to explain why.

We begin by summarizing the litigation itself. Of particular interest is how the parties and courts depicted whether the university was following the market by paying physical plant workers more than clerical workers. Next we lay the groundwork for our analysis of that question. We describe the context of the university's pay system: the community, the university as an organization, and the local labor market. After providing a history of the evolution of the university's pay system until the time of the lawsuit, we present quantitative analyses of patterns of gender inequality in the university work force in the two years before and after adoption of the contested pay system. The quantitative analysis is followed by a look at the market defense through sets of focused empirical analyses and the examination of qualitative data concerning the university's pay system. We conclude that university wage policies favoring jobs held predominantly by men did not simply reflect local labor market conditions but instead reflected the superior political position of male workers relative to female workers within the university.

The Litigation

Our usual image of a class action discrimination lawsuit includes a grass-roots organization of alleged victims, which works in concert with the attorneys who prepare the legal arguments. Nothing could be further from the truth in *Christensen*. Although the lawsuit was brought as a class action on behalf of all female clerical employees at UNI, there were only two named plaintiffs: Pauline Christensen and Phyllis Gohman. The lawsuit was waged as a kind of personal campaign by the two women, aided by their attorneys and two expert witnesses. No other women took the stand to say they had been discriminated against. As one informant said, "Iowa is a polite place. There was not much support for them" (personal interview, June 23, 1986).

Christensen and Gohman were inspired to pursue their claims at a meeting of women faculty members who were organizing to complain about sex discrimination in faculty salaries. The group was addressed by David Dutton, a lawyer who was prominent in local Democratic Party politics and who later became district attorney. Dutton had successfully represented women workers in a series of Equal Pay Act cases against local meatpacking companies. He and his younger associate, Thomas Staack, agreed to represent Christensen and Gohman in their lawsuit, as well as the women faculty members in a separate suit against the university.

In their complaint, the plaintiffs charged that the university discriminated against women in hiring, promotion, and pay. They initially sued under both the Equal Pay Act and Title VII but dropped the Equal Pay Act claim by the time of the trial. At trial Christensen and Gohman testified that they had applied for but, because of their sex, had been denied promotions to positions previously held by men. The plaintiffs relied on statistical testimony by a psychology professor at the university that showed that after seniority had been taken into account, female employees earned some $1,700 less per year than male employees. (At the mean wage in the pay system this amount equals a 23 percent difference.) They also drew heavily on the report of a job evaluation study commissioned by the State Board of Regents.

In fiscal year 1974–75 the Board of Regents retained a compensation consulting firm, Hayes-Hill Inc., to establish a new statewide compensation plan for the five institutions under its jurisdiction. Basing its recommendations on the results of job evaluation studies, the new system placed many predominantly female jobs in the same job grades as predominantly male physical plant jobs, with the result that many male and female jobs would have received similar compensation. Nonetheless, university officials expressed concern that under the new plan, physical plant jobs would not be paid well enough to attract and retain qualified workers. In response, the Hayes firm conducted special surveys about starting wages for several jobs. Eventually the starting pay for all physical plant jobs was set at a higher step within their respective pay grades, effectively reestablishing the previous wage difference between male and female positions.

The plaintiffs characterized as discrimination the university's decision to raise the pay of physical plant jobs above that called for in the pay matrix initially recommended by Hayes. They seized on language in the Hayes report concerning sex discrimination.

> This approach [using wage survey data only to set a gradient for the results of job evaluation] has the advantage of eliminating discriminatory pay practices, particularly as applied to female employees. It appears that the entire job market tends to discriminate against positions which are predominantly occupied by women. Since each classification is assigned to a salary grade on the basis of its responsibilities and impact, the approach treats predominantly female classifications on the same equity basis as other classifications. The approach rewards individual classifications on the basis of their contribution to the operation of the institution, not strictly on market values. As a practical matter, this means that some classifications may be paid slightly above or slightly below market levels. (Hayes and Associates Report, Nov. 1974, p. 25)

For its defense the university called the two pay consultants who had devised the university's previous and current versions of the pay system. They testified that the compensation plans operated in gender-neutral fashion, that is, that predominantly male and predominantly female jobs were treated in the same way. Personnel officials from the State Board of Regents and from the university took the stand to describe how the pay systems had evolved and how the university attempted to offer equal employment opportunities to women and minorities. The university officials answered the plaintiffs' charges about the physical plant jobs the women had applied for, indicating that in some instances women declined openings, and in other cases women had been hired for the positions in question. All defense witnesses testified that the salary curve at the university had been established based on market surveys and that the departures from the original pay matrix were part of an effort to follow the market in setting wage levels (Tr. Trans., Aug. 18–19, 1976, pp. 363–596; for abbreviations used for citations in the text, see the appendix on court documents and case materials).

Plaintiffs' counsel then pulled a surprise. They called another UNI professor, industrial psychologist David Whitsett, as an expert rebuttal witness. Whitsett's testimony included three main assertions. First, he asserted that the market discriminates against women and therefore, to the extent the university was following the market, it too discriminated against women. Second, he stated that several physical plant jobs had been given additional job evaluation points after the regular process of assigning points by job evaluation committees had been completed. He suggested that this was a departure from proper professional practice and that it produced evaluation results biased against clerical jobs. Third, reviewing local employment availability statistics, he testified that there was no scarcity of labor for physical plant jobs in the Waterloo–Cedar Falls area. He expressed doubt that higher wages were necessary to recruit physical plant workers (Tr. Trans., Aug. 19, 1976, pp. 597–652).

Despite references to market surveys by defense witnesses, the market issue was not prominent in the university's defense. In the pretrial conference, the defendants asserted "that if there be such comparable positions [to establish pay discrimination], that the Plaintiffs' pay is based upon the market for their services in the Cedar Falls–Waterloo area compared with others performing substantially similar services and work at UNI" (Order on Final Pretr. Conf., May 13, 1976). But the university's trial court brief did not discuss the market. It was only in a proposed finding of fact that defense counsel asserted that the university was following the market in setting wage levels. The defense brief emphasized two facts: the jobs involved were different, and the plaintiffs had not demonstrated conclusively that there were barriers preventing women from applying for physical plant jobs. From these facts the university's counsel first argued that the Equal Pay Act did not apply, because the jobs were not the same. Second, they argued for an interpretation of Title VII (later rejected by the Supreme Court in *Gunther*) that would have limited Title VII wage discrimination claims to cases involving men and women performing the same job.[1]

The trial court largely adopted the university's legal and factual positions. It concluded that a plaintiff seeking to establish a sex discrimination claim under Title VII must show equal work. Finding that the

---

1 In *County of Washington, Oregon v. Gunther*, (452 U.S. 161 [1981]) the Supreme Court opened the door for comparable worth lawsuits by holding that the "equal work" requirement of the Equal Pay Act did not apply to Title VII pay discrimination cases. Thus, even if male and female workers held different jobs, a court might find that an employer engaged in sex discrimination in pay.

clerical and physical plant jobs were not substantially equal, it held that the plaintiffs had not made out a prima facie case of wage discrimination. The court also found that the university compensated its employees according to a bona fide merit system. In a lengthy footnote to this finding, it described how the various compensation systems employed by the university over the years all had relied on market data to set wage levels. It attributed the departures from the initial Hayes pay matrix for physical plant jobs to market necessity. "The result of the survey was that several physical plant jobs were given 'step increases' in order that the university might compete with the local labor market in attracting competent people for certain physical plant jobs" (Tr. Ct. Opin., Nov. 11, 1976, N.D. Iowa, p. 2, n. 3). The court went on to find that women workers were free to apply for jobs held predominantly by men and that women were not locked into clerical positions by university policies.

The plaintiffs and the university argued the facts and issues in much the same way before the Eighth Circuit Court of Appeals: The plaintiffs asserted that the university had discriminated by following the market rather than the initial Hayes pay matrix; the university contended that the plaintiffs had failed to establish discrimination because the jobs were not the same and because women were free to apply for any position. A somewhat more sophisticated approach to the market issue was presented in the amicus brief supporting the plaintiffs filed by the Equal Employment Opportunity Commission. The EEOC brief argued that the university, contrary to its consultant's advice, had preserved the traditional hierarchy among male and female earnings by placing physical plant jobs in steps that were high enough to maintain prior wage levels. The EEOC questioned the economic necessity for doing so.

> Apparently the university made no attempt to determine whether, under the prevailing market conditions, it was, in fact, unable to recruit qualified persons for the jobs at the step-one wage level contemplated in the system. (See App. 83–90)

> Testimony at trial, however, revealed that there was, in fact, no scarcity of available people in the Waterloo–Cedar Falls area for those male jobs which defendants had accorded advance-step starting salaries (App. 241). To the contrary, the Iowa Employment Security Commission's 1975 Manpower Information Report for the Waterloo–Cedar Falls Area (SMSA) shows that there is a surplus of unemployed experienced laborers and craftsmen in the local labor market (App. 99, 100). Thus, with respect to new employees, also, the manner in which the university implemented the Hayes System

> tends to preserve, without apparent justification, the
> previously existing disparities between the wages paid to men
> and those paid to women performing jobs which its own
> experts have concluded are of equal value. (EEOC Brief, pp.
> 20–21)

The court of appeals took a different tack from the trial court, one that gave more emphasis to the market issue. Rather than address the legal issue of whether Title VII wage discrimination claims required proof of equal work, the appeals court held that job evaluation studies alone would not sustain a prima facie case of wage discrimination. Given that the university had not erected barriers to the hiring or promotion of women and that it had followed the market in granting higher wages to physical plant workers, the university was not guilty of sex discrimination. In a footnote the court announced that a more serious case would be presented "if the record had established that the university relied upon prevailing community wage rates in setting pay scales for male-dominated jobs but paid less than community wages for jobs primarily staffed by women" (*Christensen*, p. 355, n. 5). The court saw no such complexities in the case before it. It proclaimed, in language that has been quoted in numerous cases decided after *Christensen*, that the plaintiffs' "theory ignores economic realities. . . . We do not interpret Title VII as requiring an employer to ignore the market in setting wage rates for genuinely different work classifications" (*Christensen*, p. 356).

What the court of appeals confidently assumed is, from our perspective, the central question. Did the university in fact ignore the market in according physical plant employees step increases not given other employees? And, if so, why? This issue was never fully addressed in the trial testimony of either the university officials or their consultants. Nor did the plaintiffs' expert witnesses attack the issue directly. Plaintiffs' counsel never questioned whether the university was following the market in an inconsistent fashion for male and female workers. Indeed, counsel pursued the opposite strategy of trying to indict the university for following a discriminatory market. Although the EEOC tried to argue that the university's departure from its consultant's recommendations was not supported by economic necessity, the court of appeals chose not to give the argument serious consideration.

We turn then to the empirical analysis of the university's compensation system. To appreciate the relationship between the university's internal employment system and the labor market, it is first necessary to gain a better understanding of the community and organizational context in which the university employment system operated.

The Context: Changes in the Community, the University, and the Labor Market

The Community

Few things about Cedar Falls, Iowa, evoke an image of a traditional "college town." Although the university campus contains a respectable number of classroom buildings and dormitories, it is on the fringe of the community and is bordered on its western flank by the fertile soil and sprouting corn that covers the entire region. Even within the town, the campus appears not to dominate the commercial life of the village. To be sure, there is a small cluster of pizza parlors, bars, and a bookstore adjoining the campus, but it is overshadowed by a nearby highway "strip," which, with its franchised restaurants and discount merchandise stores, could be found in any of a thousand suburbs.

Cedar Falls is part of the metropolitan area anchored by the larger city of Waterloo. The area experienced gradual population growth between 1970 and 1980, increasing in size by 4 percent. By 1980, the population of Cedar Falls reached some 36,000. Another 102,000 persons resided in the rest of the metropolitan area (as defined by the Census Bureau in 1980), the majority of whom (76,000) lived in Waterloo. There is a modest-sized minority population in the metropolitan area: blacks make up about 6 percent of the total population and other minorities about 1 percent.

The symbolic standing of the campus in the community is diminished by the historical strength of the area's manufacturing base. Despite recent reductions in force, the John Deere farm equipment corporation ("Deere's" in the local vernacular) remains the premier employer, both in numbers and in the relative generosity of the wages and fringe benefits it offers. Nor is it alone. In 1973, when the lawsuits against the university were in their formative stages, the Census Bureau reported the presence of several other large business establishments. Six other private employers (two hospitals, one meatpacking plant, one ordnance manufacturer, one pump manufacturer, and one metal fabricator) each employed over 500 persons, and several governmental or quasi-governmental units were also in this size range (the county government, the City of Waterloo, and the two public school districts).

A prolonged agricultural slump brought dramatic changes by the mid-1980s. The Rath Packing Corporation closed its doors, eliminating nearly 4,000 jobs, and John Deere reduced its work force by at least the same amount. Although these changes have affected the university's labor market position, both their recency and the fact that conditions have stabilized mean that the town's self-concept remains the same. Today, as then, people think of their community as a town built around workers, even if fewer are working today than in the past. The presence of the university has added some balance to this conception, but the industrial ethos of the town has permeated the campus as much as, if not more than, the academic culture has affected the community.

The University

UNI still bears the marks of its origins as a teacher-training institution. By the early 1970s, however, growing enrollments and organizational differentiation had transformed many aspects of the institution, including its personnel system, into a bureaucracy. Although UNI has the multicollege structure associated with university status, the colleges number only five – natural sciences, business, social sciences, education, and humanities – fine arts. Until 1909, the campus operated as the Iowa State Normal School. At that time, the name was changed to the Iowa State Teachers College, and it became an entity under the State Board of Regents, joining the University of Iowa and Iowa State. From that date until 1961, the only degrees awarded were Bachelors of Arts in Education. Once again, however, the institution was renamed – it became the State College of Iowa – to reflect expanded offerings and degrees in the liberal arts. Finally, in 1967, the campus acquired its current name and status as the University of Northern Iowa.

Despite the fact of its equal formal status within the Board of Regents system, there is widespread sentiment that UNI remains a "poor relative" of the two older and larger institutions. In addition to the stigma associated with its prior incarnation as a "teachers' college," UNI has neither the research presence, the reputation, nor the degree offerings to compare itself with the other schools. By 1979, advanced degree offerings were quite limited, with one doctoral-level and six masters-level programs in place. Our informants also alluded to the Board of Regents' use of UNI as a proving ground for changes in organizational policy, such as collective bargaining strategies.

From the late 1960s through the 1970s, the campus grew considerably in physical size and enrollment. In 1965, the student body numbered 5,147; by the fall of 1979, on-campus student enrollment was slightly greater than 10,000. Over the same period, the university grew from 34 to 44 campus buildings (*College Blue Book* 1965, 1975, 1981). An equally significant change has occurred in the administration and bureaucratization of the campus. In fifteen years, the number of administrators had nearly quadrupled while the student body was doubling.

Employment was also increasing in the nonadministrative component of the university. Comparable figures are difficult to obtain for the various types of positions (i.e., faculty and nonacademic positions), but the general trends are clear. In 1965, there were 350 faculty members; by 1980 the faculty had grown to 694. Data describing employees who are neither administrators nor faculty are available for a more limited period in this time span. Curiously, between the 1970–71 academic year and the 1974–75 academic year, the number of "merit system" employees dropped from 879 to 837 (Master Report). Nevertheless a considerable number of merit system vacancies were filled during this period. University Affirmative Action reports show that 111 positions were filled in 1973–74 (92 of them by outside hiring) and 147 were filled in 1974–75 (130 by outside hiring). Thus the university was not immune from turnover during these years. If total merit system employment figures were available for a broader time span, an increase in total employment would surely be revealed.

The bureaucratization of employment relations was also reflected in the observations of informants. The director of the personnel office during the period reported to us that on his arrival in 1966, there was hardly a personnel structure in place at all. Hiring was largely decentralized, with unit managers recruiting and training their own staffs. Before the change to a more formalized personnel system, recruiting, especially for physical plant positions, was described as very informal. Openings often were filled through word-of-mouth advertising and particularistic ties, with friends bringing in friends, and relatives bringing in relatives (telephone interview, July 17, 1986).

Before 1976 the university apparently operated on the basis of job seniority rather than "university-wide" seniority. In a job seniority regime, employees who change job classes sacrifice any accumulated "length of service" points and start again at the bottom of seniority lists. Such a system tends to discourage workers from changing job classes, and may, therefore, preserve patterns of gender-based job segregation. For example, a secretary who applied for a physical plant position would lose service points in her clerical job and might face greater risks of being laid off during a staff cutback. One of our informants claimed that job seniority was the governing principle in the early 1970s. Defense counsel conceded this point in their trial brief in response to trial testimony by Phyllis Gohman, but contended that it was of no legal significance because men faced the same situation in applying for a new job (Tr. Brief, p. 5).

If job seniority controlled in earlier years, it no longer did by the mid-1970s. The 1976 edition of the *Rules of the Regents Merit System* makes no mention of job seniority and describes seniority provisions in terms virtually identical to those currently in effect. According to the current personnel director, length of service now operates most directly with regard to layoffs. Employees with longer tenure have "bumping" rights to jobs held by those with shorter tenure, provided the job is in a job class in which they previously worked (personal interview, June 23, 1986).

The merit system rules have less to say about the use of seniority in qualifying for promotions or transfers in nonlayoff situations. Where movement from one position to another requires passage of a competitive examination, the rules call for existing employees to receive a bonus of five points, although the grading scale for such exams is not specified. Another section states with regard to selection for promotion "as far as practical and feasible, all vacancies will be filled by the promotion of qualified permanent employees, based on individual performance and examination results with due consideration for length of service and capacity for the new position" (Iowa Board of Regents 1976). But as Affirmative Action reports reveal, this provision did not establish a formal system of internal movement within the university. For example, in the 1974–75 fiscal year, of the sixty-five nonclerical, merit system positions filled in the university, only 3 percent involved the transfer or promotion of an existing employee. The figure among clerical workers was higher, 18 percent, but still more than four out of every five vacancies were filled from outside the university. (Aff. Action Plan, July 18, 1975, p. 74, Jt. App.) Supervisory or higher-ranked positions might well be filled internally, but these make up only a small number of vacancies in a given year. Most hiring has been done from the external labor market.

These patterns suggest that the university grew larger and more bureaucratic without creating a clearly established internal labor market. A longtime clerical worker drew a clear distinction between the "old days" when there was considerable flexibility and employees were given personal consideration, and the more rule-oriented regime that replaced it. In describing the more relaxed atmosphere of the past, she indicated that it was possible to leave work for a few hours in the middle of the day to take children to doctors and dentists without proceeding through official channels (personal interview, June 23, 1986).

Unionization was another process that began to transform university employment relations during the late 1960s and 1970s. According to several accounts, the earliest union activity was centered in the physical plant department and started in the latter half of the 1960s. To a large extent, active unionism was imported into the university when it hired a small group of male workers who had left the Rath Packing Corporation during one of its periodic contractions. The influence of their former union association was apparently so strong among these rank-and-file workers that they continued to use the name of their old organization, the United Packing Workers of America (UPWA), albeit informally. Although these men had not occupied major leadership positions in the meatpackers union, many of them became leading figures in the union at the university.

This early labor activity apparently confused and upset campus administrators. Until it began, the managerial climate of the university exhibited an ethos of "personalism" and informality that paralleled the leadership style of the longtime president, J. W. Maucker. One embodiment of this ethic of cooperation was the establishment of several "employee relations" committees composed of both labor and management. The administration found that the clerical workers' committee operated harmoniously and, in their eyes, beneficially to the clerical employees' interest, but the physical plant committee was another story. Not only were the blue-collar workers demanding and confrontational, but some administrators found them also to be uncommitted to the spirit of the committees themselves. That is, if they were unable to win on the committee front, the activists would then carry their grievances through union channels as well. As one administrator put it, "They had a sweetheart arrangement. If they didn't get what they wanted through one approach, they would try the other. . . . they had two chances at everything" (telephone interview, July 30, 1986). Worse yet, in the view of some administrators, was that the union men were enjoying their ability to make management respond to their constant sniping. Less involved observers described the situation with slightly different emphases. Neither the administration nor the union activists understood what responsible unionism was supposed to involve, and each side had an excessively confrontational view of the larger process.

Not surprisingly, this rancor materialized quite early in the form of an illegal strike that lasted for five days in 1969. The issues involved recognition of the union, the establishment of more formal conditions of employment, and greater input of the workers into the evaluation of their job requirements. This action was confined almost completely to the physical plant department. The dormitories and food service operations continued operating as usual. Although they were reluctant to do so immediately, the administrators sought and obtained a restraining order forcing the men back to their jobs.

There was no collective bargaining law for public employees in the State of Iowa until 1974. One university official suggested that the strike itself might have contributed to the passage of collective bargaining legislation. The new law provided for organized representation of state workers, but denied employees or their organizations the right "to induce, instigate, encourage, authorize, ratify, or participate in a strike against any public employer" (1974 Iowa Acts [65 G.A.] ch. 1095, §12; now Iowa Code Ann. §20.12 [West 1995]). The law failed to grant "union shop" provisions and protected the rights of individual employees not to join or pay dues to unions. Operating under the provisions of this legislation, Council 61 of the American Federation of State, County, and Municipal Employees (AFSCME) soon became the recognized bargaining agent for university physical plant employees. Shortly thereafter, the AFSCME local also began to represent food service workers. It was not until the early 1980s, after a change in rules governing representation elections (from requiring a majority vote within a unit to requiring a majority vote across all units), that clerical workers were represented by AFSCME in contract negotiations. The UNI faculty is represented by a local union that is unaffiliated with any national groups. Like the physical plant workers, its members sought and won recognition shortly after the enabling legislation went into effect.

The Labor Market

Because *Christensen* turned on questions about the position of the university in the local labor market, it is crucial to understand the general contours of the Waterloo–Cedar Falls labor market. The issues that motivate our discussion are the complexity of the local occupational wage structure, the relative availability of workers for different kinds of jobs, and the nature of variations in the male-female wage gap across industrial sectors.

Table 5.1 displays employment trends for selected industries in the Waterloo–Cedar Falls SMSA (which is coterminous with Black Hawk County, Iowa). Although the university was experiencing rapid growth at this time, other employers also were growing rapidly. The number of persons employed as nonagricultural wage and salary workers in the area increased by 27 percent from 1970 to 1978, to 63,300. Throughout the period, employment in manufacturing industries was relatively high despite the fact that it decreased from 36.6 to 33.8 percent. (The U.S. average in 1973 was 26.1 percent. U.S. Bureau of Census 1974, Table 563.)

Within manufacturing some sharply divergent trends are apparent, however. Employment in machinery manufacturing and in food and kindred products reflects almost entirely the experiences of two firms, John Deere farm equipment and Rath Packing, respectively. During this period, employment growth at Deere was extremely robust and outdistanced the labor market as a whole. At the same time, the beginning of the end, which finally came in 1981, had begun to manifest itself at Rath Packing. Employment at Rath had been periodically de-

Table 5.1. *Employment Trends in Selected Industries in Waterloo-Cedar Falls SMSA, 1970–1978 (Establishment-Level Data)*

	1970	1974	1978
All nonagricultural wage and salary workers	49,700	58,000	63,300
Machinery	9,400	13,000	14,800
Food and kindred	4,300	3,500	2,300
Retail trade	8,300	9,700	10,300
Service	7,400	8,600	10,200
Government	8,200	9,500	11,100
Unemployment rate	6.1%	3.0%	4.3%
Percent employed in manufacturing	36.6%	36.9%	33.8%

Source: Iowa Employment Security Commission, *Area Employment Developments*, June 1970; June 1974; *Labor Area Summary*, June 1978.

creasing since the early 1960s, when it stood at 7,200. Rath's bad luck in the 1970s set it apart from the rest of the local economy. Thus, with the exception of laid-off packing house workers, there was no readily available pool to support the university's expansion during the period in question. Durable goods manufacturing, retail trade, government, and other services were all growing and competing with the university for labor. Competition from the largest employer in town, John Deere, was especially keen.

Although these figures provide an aggregate view of the local labor market at various points, it is important to remember that the university interacted with several different occupational markets. Since the early 1970s the university operated with an internal classification scheme that identified five groups of nonacademic employees: administrative occupations; professional and scientific occupations, including, for example, lab technicians; clerical occupations; physical plant occupations; and dormitory and food service occupations. Of these, the broadest class is physical plant. It includes boiler operators, security officers, craft occupations, groundskeepers, custodians of classroom buildings, and most other blue-collar jobs performed outside of dining halls or dormitories. Clerical workers are defined somewhat more narrowly than in some other schemes, including only office clerical workers and excluding nonoffice clerical workers such as mail clerks, who are categorized as physical plant workers by this system.

Historical data on these occupational groups in the external market are not readily available, yet data from the 1980 census of population can be manipulated to provide some interesting estimates of market con-

Table 5.2. *Employment and Unemployment by Occupation in Waterloo–Cedar Falls SMSA, 1979*

	Occupation Group				
	Mgr. & Admin.	Prof. & Scien.	Clerical	Physical Plant	Service
Estimated number with work experience in past 5 years	6,050	5,282	10,600	35,300	10,900
Out of labor force	11.6%	12.6%	20.3%	19.5%	33.5%
In labor force	88.4%	87.4%	79.7%	80.5%	66.5%
Unemployment rate	2.5%	1.1%	3.4%	6.9%	9.7%
Percent of total with unemployment in past year	7.2%	10.1%	15.4%	18.6%	25.1%
Mean weeks of unemployment in 1979 for those unemployed	9.8	11.9	12.3	12.9	11.6
Percent of nonemployed looking for work	20.0%	18.6%	20.5%	33.5%	24.9%
Percent of total who worked in 1975	85.7%	72.6%	65.1%	69.9%	40.5%
Weeks worked in 1975	44.8	41.9	37.0	38.3	27.2

Source: "A" and "B" Public Use Samples, U.S. Census of Population, 1980.

ditions for these categories.[2] Table 5.2 presents employment data for what is usually referred to as the experienced civilian labor force.[3] Examining this population allows us to draw inferences not only about the supply of workers in various occupation groups at this time but also the potential supply of such persons.

One distinct impression conveyed by Table 5.2 is that clerical occupations were not decidedly "oversupplied" relative to some other occu-

2 The specific sources used were the A and B Public Use Samples from the 1980 census. Taken together, these samples present individual-level data on 6 percent of the SMSA population that can be aggregated into the university's occupation scheme. The estimates shown in Table 5.2 have been weighted to provide estimates of the total population in the area. The 1970 census data were not available at this level of density and, therefore, could not be used to provide comparable figures.
3 Included are all persons sixteen years and older who have held any kind of job in the past five years. Some of these were not currently in the market, meaning that they were neither employed nor officially unemployed. (That is, they had not actively sought work in the past month.) For those who were not currently employed, the occupation they were classified into was that of the job they last held.

pation groups in the community. For unemployment, whether measured by the percentage of the labor force currently unemployed by the official standard, or looking for work (whether or not officially unemployed), or having experienced any unemployment in the previous calendar year, the story is the same. Clerical workers had middling amounts of unemployment. Their rates exceeded those of administrative and professional workers, but in general were lower than those in "physical plant" types of work. In fact, the group with the most dismal employment picture was the service worker category. Their official unemployment rate was nearly 10 percent, a total of 25 percent were unemployed at some point in 1979, and those who were unemployed averaged 11.6 weeks of joblessness.

The Bureau of Labor Statistics, in the Area Wage Survey series, periodically publishes data on wage levels for selected metropolitan areas, including Cedar Falls–Waterloo. Table 5.3 presents a reaggregation of some wage-level data for the November 1973 reporting period. (The data are from responses to BLS surveys of selected business establishments in the area.) In this table, wages are shown separately for three groups of predominantly female occupations and for two groups of predominantly male occupations. The latter do not include wage levels for skilled craft occupations because too few of this group were employed in nonmanufacturing establishments to allow for meaningful comparisons. In each instance, the number of cases refers to the number of workers covered in the surveys, not the number of establishments.

It is readily apparent that clerical wage levels were considerably below those in low-skilled manual occupations. This was particularly true when we compared the percentage of a group that had low earnings, defined as less than $3.60 per hour or about $7,200 per annum. Several other trends can be seen in this table. First, there were substantial differences in earnings within the clerical category based on skill level and sector of employment (manufacturing or nonmanufacturing). These factors were not purely additive in their combined influence, however. That is, if we restrict attention to clerical workers in manufacturing, there is a steady improvement in the wage picture from group A to group C. This was not the case in nonmanufacturing, where the most skilled category of clerical workers has relatively low earnings.

Among the manual occupations shown, there are also differences based on skill, differences that are especially pronounced among nonmanufacturing workers. The most menial plant occupations in nonmanufacturing have the worst wage profile of all the groups compared, including the lowest-paid clerical workers. Except for that group, however, wage levels in the predominantly male occupations surpass those in nearly all of the female-dominated clerical categories.

Table 5.3. *Wage Levels for Selected Occupations in Waterloo–Cedar Falls SMSA, November 1973 (BLS Data)*

| | Wage Levels (%) | | | | |
	Low[a]	Medium[b]	High[c]	Total	N
Clerical occupations					
Group A: Bookkeeping mach. operators, class B typists, accounting clerks, receptionists, switchboard operators					
Total	68	32	1	101	173
Manufacturing	64	35	1	100	88
Nonmanufacturing	97	3	0	100	29
Not Specified	59	41	0	100	56
Group B: Payroll clerks, class D secretaries, gen'l stenographers					
Total	42	40	18	100	144
Manufacturing	41	40	19	100	125
Nonmanufacturing	53	37	11	101	19
Group C: Class A accounting clerks, class A, B, & C secretaries, class A typists, senior stenographers					
Total	40	38	22	100	124
Manufacturing	28	43	29	100	89
Nonmanufacturing	71	26	3	100	35
Custodial and material movement occupations					
Group A: Janitors, warehouseman, laborers					
Total	9	82	9	100	907
Manufacturing	4	86	10	100	851
Nonmanufacturing	71	29	0	100	56
Group B: Plant guards, truck drivers, order fillers					
Total	3	67	30	100	266
Manufacturing	3	68	30	101	239
Nonmanufacturing	4	63	33	100	27

[a] Under $140 per week (clerical) or $3.60 per hour (other).
[b] $140–$199 per week (clerical) or $3.60–$5.00 per hour (other).
[c] $200 or more per week (clerical) or $5.00 or more per hour (other).
Source: Bureau or Labor Statistics, Nov. 1973.

We can draw several tentative conclusions about the labor market as a whole from these data. There are some significant wage disparities between clerical and low-skilled plant work. Yet an employer inspecting these figures in an effort to select the proper wage for a given occupational category would confront considerable variability. He or she would need to exercise some discretion in the choice of rates for particular jobs. As we noted earlier, one large employer in town, John Deere, stood alone in offering very high wage levels. It is possible that much of the variation in Table 5.3, especially that between manufacturing and nonmanufacturing, reflects the skewing influence of this single employer. With this in mind, an employer may have had less trouble choosing an appropriate wage level.

We pursued this possibility by analyzing data on income levels for selected occupations from the 1980 census of population. Although these values reflect the state of the labor market in 1979, five years after the period of interest, they have the advantage of allowing for more detailed breakdowns by the type of employer than is possible in BLS data or the 1970 census. Table 5.4 gives results for two groups of industrial employers – farm equipment manufacturing (almost entirely John Deere) and all other manufacturing – and for two groups of nonmanufacturers and service employers – public administration and schools and all others (hospitals, stores, etc.). Data are shown both in "raw" form and after adjustment for worker quality and hours worked. In assessing the position of a group of employers in the local market, the adjusted data are perhaps a better standard of comparison.

Three patterns in the table interest us. First and most salient, industry category very significantly affects the mean earnings of the incumbents of various occupational groups. Employees of John Deere (farm equipment manufacturing) have the highest earnings within each occupation category. Although some of this advantage is due to worker quality differences, after adjustment the most poorly paid farm equipment manufacturing employees – secretaries – have higher earnings than all but two other categories: craft workers in the utilities and other manufacturing sector, and nonoffice clericals in the utilities and other manufacturing sector.[4]

Second, although the high earnings of Deere employees clearly stand out in this analysis, there is substantial variation in occupational earnings levels across the remaining sectors, even after controlling for worker quality. A hypothetical employer would still be left to choose which sector to use as a reference group in setting earnings levels. Third, and most important substantively, male-female occupational earnings patterns vary by industrial sector. The lower panel of Table 5.4 shows the adjusted earnings of selected occupational groups. Secretaries lag behind craft workers and nonoffice clericals in every industrial context, but

4 Specifically, the earnings data were adjusted as follows: At the individual level, earnings were predicted from a model that included, in addition to sex, education and implied experience. To this model, dummy variables were added for the main effects of the industry categories, the occupation categories, and the interactions between them. The coefficients for these categorical effects form the basis for the estimates in Table 5.4.

Table 5.4. *Wage Levels for Selected Occupations by Industry Type in Waterloo–Cedar Falls SMSA, 1979 (Census Data)*

	Util. & Other Manuf.	Farm Equip. Manuf.	Public Admin. & Schools	Other Nonmanuf.	All Groups	N
Part I: Unadjusted mean salaries						
Secretary	$9,150[a]	$15,570[a]	$6,530	$6,390	$7,525	141
Other office clerical	10,360	16,170	7,330	7,260	9,050	346
Craft	16,470	23,870	12,640[a]	12,120	17,040	494
Nonoffice clerical	14,250[a]	17,820	13,210	8,990[a]	14,240	79
Janitors and laborers	12,720	15,410	6,660[a]	5,950	9,000	300
Protective service & operatives	12,630	18,560	12,720	12,440	15,490	674
Other service[b]	—	—	2,910	3,790	—	405
Part II: Mean salaries adjusted for experience, education, hours worked						
Secretary	$9,071[a]	$14,150[a]	$6,757	$7,158	$9,034	141
Other office clerical	9,585	15,574	9,574	7,859	10,398	346
Craft	14,901	21,899	13,493[a]	11,516	15,452	494
Nonoffice clerical	14,675[a]	15,733	12,955	8,447[a]	12,952	79
Janitors and laborers	12,628	14,971	8,696[a]	8,657	11,238	300
Protective service & operatives	12,134	17,311	11,509	11,972	13,231	674
Other service[b]	—	—	6,606	7,133	—	405

[a] Mean based on number of cases less than 20.
[b] Mean not shown where number of cases is less than 10.

they lag much further behind proportionally in the public sector and utilities/other manufacturing. (Only in these settings is the difference between secretaries and nonoffice clericals statistically significant.) Office clericals fare somewhat better, but they too are particularly underpaid relative to nonoffice clericals in the public sector and other manufacturing. Seen somewhat differently, what is out of the ordinary are the relatively high earnings of craft and nonoffice clerical workers in the public sector and the utility/other manufacturing sector.

Such varying levels of wage inequality across industrial sectors pose a paradox for economic theories of labor markets. Conventional economic theory suggests that public administration and other nonmanufacturing (services) ought to be operating in the same labor markets. But the results are not hospitable to that interpretation. Unionization no doubt affects wage levels but does not provide a ready explanation. Whereas farm equipment manufacturing is heavily unionized, nonmanufacturing is not, and utilities/other manufacturing and the public sector are partially unionized. Rather, there seems to be something unusual about labor relations in the public sector and the utility/other manufacturing sector that works to the disadvantage of female occupations. Although we cannot completely or definitively explain these trends, close investigation of the university pay system that was at issue in *Christensen* reveals how this pattern emerged in one public sector setting.

The Evolution of the University's Compensation System

The Hayes system was the third compensation system employed by UNI since the late 1960s. The first comprehensive compensation structure, devised by the management consulting firm of A. T. Kearney Company, was instituted in 1967 and remained in effect through fiscal year 1972–73. The State Board of Regents developed its own plan, which was employed for only one year, 1973–74. The Hayes system was adopted in 1974–75. Both the Kearney and the Board of Regents plans made an explicit distinction between physical plant and clerical jobs. The Kearney plan actually contained separate pay schedules for blue-collar and clerical jobs and was based on separate wage surveys for the two occupational groups. The Board of Regents effectively did the same. Although all jobs were listed in the same matrix of pay grades, many physical plant jobs were treated as "short-range" jobs, meaning that they started at a higher step within pay grades than other, mostly clerical jobs. The latter were placed at the starting step for pay grades and, therefore, were a "long-range" away from the maximum wage in their pay grade.

The system initially proposed by Hayes and Associates represented a significant departure from the earlier pay plan. Unlike A. T. Kearney Company, the Hayes firm was not selected by UNI but was retained by the State Board of Regents to revise and unify the pay systems of all the institutions under the Regents' jurisdiction. Hayes initially had consulted with the University of Iowa on its compensation structure, and its engagement with the Board of Regents grew out of that contact. Under the Hayes system each job in the five regents' institutions was rated by a committee of management and workers to determine how many points the job should receive for skill, effort, responsibility, and working conditions. Those ratings determined the pay grade a job was assigned to. Wage levels for pay grades were set according to a salary curve that established a relationship between pay grades and wages. The salary curve was based on wage surveys conducted with employers of the same jobs within a fifty-mile radius of the Board of Regents institutions. A single pay matrix was established for all five regents' institutions, but local exceptions were allowed if the pay levels in the matrix fell substantially below local wage rates. Within each pay grade, the rule of thumb was that there should be a 40 percent spread between starting and maximum pay, which would be divided into sixteen steps. Employees typically would move up two steps for each year of meritorious service.

The Hayes system was, therefore, less oriented to the market than its predecessors. To be sure, it employed market surveys to set salary gradients, but it gave far greater emphasis to internal equity considerations based on job evaluations. The lead Hayes consultant on the project openly expressed distrust in the market as a measure of what workers should be paid:

> We generally feel that the market is really difficult to use to try to determine pay for individual jobs, just because individual jobs vary a lot and it's very hard to define the market. Therefore, we use the market in terms of getting an overall perspective [on] where the whole salary level ought to be, but we primarily concentrate on the internal equity question and internal evaluation. (Dep. of JAH, Aug. 3, 1976, p. 92)

And later in the same deposition:

> [I]n general any system that says they base everything on outside salaries, that generally just can't be done, because you generally don't survey all the jobs or find matches for all jobs, and in that case, the markets are defined differently for

different jobs. So if you just base it solely on just external
salaries or job markets, we think it's sort of a difficult thing
to document, just because of . . . the fact that the markets
can be defined so differently. (Dep. of JAH, Aug. 3, 1976,
p. 113)

The Hayes consultant thus identified two fundamental problems in
using market data to set salary levels in virtually any organization: (1)
"[I]ndividual jobs vary a lot" and you can't find matches between surveyed jobs and inside jobs, and (2) "markets can be defined so differently" that market comparisons become arbitrary. In the Hayes approach, indeed in most organizational compensation systems, external
markets set parameters on organizational pay levels. Occasionally the
organization finds it cannot recruit and retain workers at existing internal rates, and it is forced to raise at least some rates. Far more prominent in the Hayes system was the rational justification of internal wage
differences provided by a job evaluation scheme.

According to the Hayes consultant, the chief failing of the prior
system's use of higher, "short-range" starting pay for physical plant jobs
was a failure to document why they were justified.

[I]n our evaluation of the system, we were unable to document
why classifications had been assigned to different pay ranges,
other than the explanation given where the jobs were assigned
based on an outside market and internal relationships. But
the internal relationships were never really documented. And
they probably existed in the eyes and minds of the people
that implemented the system, but they were never really put
down and documented, so that we didn't know what they
were. We couldn't really trace back and say why is this job
here and why is this job here, other than the fact that it
depends on market and internal relationships. And it could
very well have existed. We just didn't know what they were,
and the people in the system [the employees] had difficulty
understanding what they were. (Dep. of JAH, Aug. 3, 1976,
p. 122)

The Hayes consultants recognized the principle of raising wages above
the general salary curve, but insisted that it should be done only when
demanded by specific market experience. "[To] the degree you had to
pay more money to attract people in, then you ought to be able to do
it, but it ought to be based on what it actually takes to do that" (ibid).
Moreover, such exceptions should be reviewed every year to insure they
were necessary.

> What our rule is in a system we set up, if the incumbents are
> presently earning this higher rate, and in addition that's what
> the market tends to pay – that is, you can't get people for less
> – if it meets those two tests, then we recommend that since the
> other consideration is being able to staff the institution with
> that salary range, that adjustments be made to hire the people
> in that range, but that it be identified as a market – a
> particular market consideration, and that it be reviewed every
> year. (Dep. of JAH, Aug. 3, 1976, p. 118)

Consistent with these comments, Hayes recommended that if surveys
of starting salaries indicated that there might be difficulty in hiring or
retaining workers at the established pay grades, and if the university in
fact encountered such difficulties, starting salaries should be set four
steps above the minimum. The university should wait to see whether it
could successfully hire workers at the new level. The university did not
follow the recommendation, but instead raised the starting pay levels for
all physical plant jobs, even those it did not include in wage surveys.
Hayes also suggested a variety of other steps to rationalize the compensation system, including the hiring of professional compensation analysts
and the periodic preparation of reports concerning turnover and application rates for each job in the system (Hayes and Associates Report,
July 23, 1974, p. 24; Dec. 1974, pp. 30–36).

It is ironic, given the testimony of the Hayes consultants, that the court
of appeals upheld the pay system on the grounds that the university was
following the market. It also is telling that the Hayes consultants could
not find any documentation that satisfied them that the higher starting
salaries for many plant jobs, the so-called short-range jobs in the earlier
system, were necessary to meet market conditions. As we will see, the
prior pay levels exerted a significant influence on wage rates after adoption of the Hayes system.

Quantitative Analyses of Pay Inequality before and after the Hayes Plan

Work force data collected in connection with the lawsuit allow us to
examine how patterns of gender inequality changed as a result of the
installation of the Hayes system in 1974–75. We begin with an overview
of the characteristics of employees who worked in merit system jobs (i.e.,
nonfaculty, nonadministrative positions) during the two fiscal years for
which we have data, 1973–74 and 1974–75 (see Table 5.5). The total
size of the work force and the proportion of men and women it com-

Table 5.5. *Characteristics of Individuals in Two Pay Systems*

	All Employees	Female	Male
Employees in 1973–74 (Board of Regents pay system)			
No. of employees	848.00	574.00	274.00
Mean grade	10.04	8.76	12.72
Mean tenure (days)	2,111.48	2,135.63	2,060.88
Mean earnings ($)	6,474.31	5,873.49	7,716.00
Proportion leaving	0.25	0.24	0.28
Proportion in jobs with starting salary exceptions	0.44	0.29	0.77
Employees in 1974–75 (Hayes pay system)			
No. of employees	837.00	576.00	261.00
Mean grade	104.67	103.96	106.24
Mean tenure (days)	2,257.99	2,267.40	2,237.25
Mean earnings ($)	7,246.97	6,618.55	8,627.02
Proportion hired	0.24	0.24	0.24
Proportion in jobs with starting salary exceptions	0.11	0.01	0.32
Proportion in jobs included in market survey	0.57	0.55	0.61
Employees in 1973–75 (both pay systems)			
No. of employees	635.00	437.00	198.00
Mean grade			
1973–74	10.37	9.11	13.18
1974–75	104.90	104.19	106.46
Mean tenure			
1973–74	2,453.44	2,456.27	2,447.19
1974–75	2,818.44	2,821.27	2,812.19
Mean earnings			
1973–74	6,748.23	6,075.30	8,213.05
1974–75	7,601.34	6,900.22	9,132.35
Proportion in jobs with starting salary exceptions			
1973–74	0.47	0.32	0.79
1974–75	0.12	0.01	0.35
Proportion in jobs included in market survey 1974–75 (only)	0.56	0.55	0.58

Source: UNI payroll documents, 1973–74; 1974–75.

prised were virtually unchanged. Turnover was quite extensive, with about one-fourth of employees leaving and nearly as many being replaced in a one-year span. At the individual level a slightly higher proportion of men than women left the university, and men had a correspondingly lower level of tenure – although the difference between men's and women's average tenure was less than two months on a base of about six years.

The most dramatic difference between the sexes was in grade and salary levels. In each of the two years, men were in jobs that were more highly rated and were earning salaries that were about 30 percent higher than those of women at the university. It is important to bear in mind that earnings are a function of two factors: the pay range that corresponds to the grade level of the job and the worker's position within this pay range. In the Board of Regents Merit Pay System, many jobs were explicitly defined as short-range jobs, meaning that employees in those jobs had starting salaries set considerably above the minimum step for that pay range. As the table clearly shows, men were considerably more likely than women to be found in short-range jobs.

Another feature of the division of labor that underlies the various pay plans at UNI is the extent to which jobs at the university are similar, at least in their formal designations, to jobs found elsewhere. The market survey the Hayes firm conducted in conjunction with its revamping of the pay plan gathered comparative data on about thirty of the occupations found at UNI. Significantly, nearly 60 percent of the UNI workers were employed in occupations that were found in enough other employers' work forces that meaningful surveys could be carried out. Furthermore, although this fact does not appear in our quantitative tables, many other workers were in jobs that also had meaningful external referents. These other job titles include positions such as baker, cook, groundskeeper, boiler operator, and security officer. This organization does not contain many "idiosyncratic" jobs.

Table 5.6 presents data on the jobs found in each pay system. The first panel presents data on all jobs that were included in the Board of Regents Merit System Pay Plan in 1973–74, the second panel presents a parallel analysis for all jobs incorporated in the Hayes classification and pay system, and the third panel presents comparative data on jobs that were common to the two somewhat different systems.

Table 5.6 illustrates several ways in which the pay system at UNI changed. First, there is evidence of some rationalization of the system as the new scheme was originally implemented. The total number of job categories was reduced from 147 to 118 and the mean job size increased by a little more than 1 person per job. (Job size refers to how many persons hold a job with a particular description.) In large part, this consolidation resulted from the elimination of a number of jobs that had only one incumbent (hereafter "single-incumbent" jobs). (Note that the increase in average job size was about half as large for jobs that were found in both systems.) That this simplification resulted from job elimination is also evident when we note the high proportion of 1974–75 employees (815 out of 838 – 97 percent) who worked in jobs that existed in both job classification plans. In other words, only

Table 5.6. *Characteristics of Jobs in Two Pay Systems*

	By Percent Male			
	All Jobs	10% or Less Male	11%–89% Male	90% or More Male
Jobs in Iowa merit pay system, 1973–74				
No. of jobs	147.00	74.00	7.00	66.00
Mean grade	12.00	9.28	11.00	15.15
Mean tenure (days)	2,344.01	2,180.31	2,728.69	2,486.74
Mean earnings ($)	7,096.32	5,917.58	6,997.01	8,392.76
Mean size (persons)	5.77	6.65	24.43	2.80
Mean turnover rate	0.36	0.39	0.27	0.33
Proportion of jobs with starting				
salary exceptions	0.41	0.22	0.48	0.60
Jobs in Hayes pay system, 1974–75				
No. of jobs	118.00	54.00	8.00	56.00
Mean grade	106.81	105.00	105.12	108.84
Mean tenure (days)	2,913.80	2,795.40	2,595.48	3,073.44
Mean earnings ($)	8,421.77	7,035.63	7,449.87	9,902.30
Mean size (persons)	7.09	8.87	24.75	2.86
Mean turnover rate	0.23	0.23	0.28	0.22
Proportion of jobs with starting				
salary exceptions	0.12	0.00	0.13	0.23
Jobs in both pay systems				
No. of jobs	100.00	50.00	6.00	44.00
Mean grade				
1973–74	12.38	9.80	11.17	15.48
1974–75	106.48	104.90	105.50	108.39
Mean tenure				
1973–74	2,842.02	2,674.98	2,938.15	3,018.73
1974–75	2,989.55	2,802.92	3,232.90	3,168.46
Mean earnings				
1973–74	7,407.73	6,213.65	7,033.25	8,788.57
1974–75	8,310.70	7,018.33	7,933.23	9,801.40
Mean job size				
1973–74	7.52	8.72	26.00	3.64
1974–75	8.15	9.52	33.17	3.18
Mean turnover/hiring rates				
1973–74(turnover)	0.14	0.14	0.17	0.13
1974–75(hiring)	0.15	0.17	0.11	0.14
Proportion of jobs with starting				
salary exceptions				
1973–74	0.42	0.21	0.39	0.66
1974–75	0.13	0.00	0.17	0.27

3 percent of the second year's work force was employed in newly labeled or created jobs.

The newly introduced system was also simplified because many fewer jobs had starting salaries set above the minimums for their pay grades. The older system explicitly incorporated these exceptions under the rubric of short-range versus long-range jobs, with the former typically involving starting salaries eight or nine salary steps above the minimum levels. In 1973–74, 40 percent of all jobs had starting step exceptions. In the new system this proportion was reduced to 12 percent of all jobs. The reduction is consistent with the outside consultants' general orientation to market surveys as a device for anchoring the entire pay matrix rather than as a device for setting the actual pay rates of specific jobs.

A third difference can be seen in how gender-related job patterns were altered over the period. Obviously, the job structure was highly segregated by sex in both years with over 90 percent of the jobs being either predominantly female or predominantly male (defined as occupied by 90 percent or more of one sex). There was a slight increase in mixed-sex jobs, from 4.7 percent of all jobs in fiscal year 1973 to 6.8 percent under the new classification plan. Nevertheless, the most dramatic difference in the new system was a narrowing of the pay grade differential between predominantly male and female jobs. In 1973–74, predominantly male jobs averaged six pay grades higher than predominantly female jobs. Under the new system this differential was reduced to three pay grades. Although this partly reflects a reduction in the number of pay grades, from twenty-five to fifteen, we shall see that this change was associated with some relative upgrading of female jobs under the Hayes plan. When the ratio of earnings in predominantly male to predominantly female jobs is examined, however, the limits of this upgrading become clearer. For example, if one calculated the ratio of "male job" to "female job" earnings in the last panel of the table, the "constant occupation" subset if you will, it declines only from 1.41 to 1.39 – hardly a dramatic decrease.

Another relative constant in the two plans is the fact that predominantly male jobs average considerably fewer workers than either mixed-sex or predominantly female jobs. Thus, although the new pay and classification plan appeared to have eliminated many single-incumbent jobs, this elimination occurred much less often in the male job segment of the work force. Finally, these data are interesting because they reveal that predominantly male jobs were not beset by any higher instance of turnover than female jobs. Although, as we have seen, male workers left at slightly higher rates, their departures were more likely to have occurred in the larger job classifications, lowering the net turnover rates for male jobs qua jobs.

The earnings difference between men and women in the two pay systems can be subjected to more rigorous quantitative scrutiny (see Appendix 5.1 for complete details).

There are several interesting findings that emerge from this analysis. The first is that the aggregate amount of gender inequality changed very little in the two pay systems. With or without controls for various factors, women's earnings were about the same percentage lower than men's in the two years under scrutiny. What changed, however, was the mechanism through which this inequality occurred. In the first year, wages were unequal largely because women were in jobs with lower pay grades than men were. Once women's overrepresentation in short-range jobs is taken into account, all the remaining wage disparity is attributable to the grade component.

Second, as we have suggested, the Hayes system seems to have resulted in some meaningful revisions of the grade differentials between the sexes. Compared with statistics for the previous year, the grade component of gender-based wage inequality (after controls) has been reduced by half. What happened, however, was that the within-grade difference component increased substantially, nearly wiping out the strides that women had taken toward "grade" parity.[5]

Third, the results indicate that there is substantial gender inequality that cannot be explained by some very basic measures that we associate with the value of workers and jobs. After controlling for tenure, salary basis, and market salary levels, women earn some 17 percent less than their male counterparts. The market salary data decrease the gender differential by a mere six-tenths of 1 percent. Our analysis adds other characteristics associated with pay differentials, such as job family, rank in a job series (the "level" variable), or being a single incumbent (which may denote some special skill or position in the organization). Some of these variables are not indisputably measures of the value of a job. Job family, for example, may reflect negative or positive biases based on the gender or race of incumbents. And single-incumbent jobs may reflect organizational patronage instead of responsibility. But if we make the conservative assumption that these variables tap meaningful distinctions in the

---

5   Market salary survey data were not available for 1973–74. Market salary levels were computed as the average of salaries reported for Waterloo, Cedar Falls, and Marshalltown, the three cities in UNI's local market. Model B3, which controls for the market values of salary captured in the November 1974 survey, shows that the within-grade differences became a more important source of wage inequality than the between-grade differences. Hayes Report, June 29, 1974, pp. 25–43.

value of positions, we still find significant gender differentials after controlling for these variables. With this full complement of controls, women earned some 16 percent less than men in 1973–74 and some 11 percent less than men in 1974–75.

We lack data on some fundamental measures of job qualification, such as education level and work experience. These might help to explain the wage gap we observe. It was possible to create a small sample of UNI employees from 1980 census data (it is the only institution of higher education in the public sector in the Waterloo–Cedar Falls SMSA) that contains more such variables. In regressions on three occupational subgroups within UNI, those in occupations that were not subject to wage surveys by Hayes and Associates ($n = 38$), those that were ($n = 35$), and managerial and professional workers ($n = 58$, most of whom are not present in the nonprofessional work force analyzed here). After controlling for work force experience, total hours worked, years of education, the presence of a disability, and marital status, we found that sex had a statistically significant effect in the two nonprofessional groups but not in the professional and managerial subgroup. It is also interesting that education did *not* have a statistically significant effect on the earnings of the UNI workers – except among the professionals and managers. Because of the small sample size, these analyses can hardly be considered definitive. Yet they are consistent with a pattern of unexplained gender differences in earnings levels at the university.

The result that may be the most difficult to explain with market or efficiency models is the gender differential within pay grades. Differences across pay grades can be justified on the basis that jobs within grades have equal numbers of job evaluation points. But why should we find differences within pay grades after controls have been introduced for tenure, starting step exceptions (which supposedly reflect market necessity), and market salary levels? If these are residual deviations from efficiency norms left over from earlier pay systems, we would have expected them to have been so identified by the Hayes pay consultants. But there is no explicit record to that effect, except a reference in a Hayes and Associates report to the number of jobs receiving pay above the maximum set for that job's pay grade. One would have to invent tortured logic to argue that the sorts of differentials shown in these models can be attributed to unmeasured productivity. Such unmeasured productivity would have to escape detection in job evaluation techniques and not be reflected in job rank or in explicit measures of market value and market necessity. It seems quite plausible that the unexplained differentials within pay grades are a product of gender bias.

Two specific features of wage inequality apparent in the cross-sectional data on the nonprofessional work force lend further credence to this view. First, male workers obtain substantial returns from jobs in which they are the sole incumbent. In a regression in which the reference group is women working in multiple-incumbent jobs, after controlling pay basis and seniority we find that women working in single-incumbent jobs earn some $186 more than the reference category. Males in multiple-incumbent jobs earn an average of $1,150 more than their female counterparts. And men in single-incumbent jobs receive an average of $2,300 more than females in multiple-incumbent positions.

Again we lack data on educational credentials and preuniversity working experience necessary to assess systematically whether the large premium men receive for single-incumbent jobs can be explained as a reflection of human capital or marginal productivity. We can gain some limited understanding of the organizational importance of single-incumbent jobs by inspecting the titles of jobs held by single-incumbent males and females. Some of the male jobs imply considerable skill and responsibility, such as architectural assistant, various assistant foreman positions in the crafts, and electronics technician. Yet the male jobs also include seemingly lesser positions, such as mail carrier, golf attendant, recreation specialist, and ticket seller. Among the female jobs are some obviously lower-status positions, such as mail clerk, key entry operator, and telephone operator. But the female jobs also include a graphics specialist, various office coordinators, and recreation director. The job titles do not on their face reveal that single-incumbent males are clearly more deserving of higher compensation than female workers in one-incumbent jobs.

Second, we also found that a much larger proportion of males received above maximum salary in 1974–75 than was true for women and that the average differential above the pay grade maximum received by men was almost double that received by women. By inspection of the pay matrix and the salaries received by pay grade, we determined that nineteen women and forty-one men received above maximum pay in 1974–75. Those women made up 3.3 percent of the female nonprofessional work force and received on average $263 above the maximum allowed in their pay grade. Those men made up 15.7 percent of the male nonprofessional workforce and received an average of $467 more than the maximum set for their pay grade.

The absence of complete statistical controls for characteristics of workers and jobs requires that both patterns be interpreted cautiously. Yet it is clear that men in the university's nonprofessional work force gained far more than women by obtaining relatively unusual and well-paying positions in the organizational hierarchy. Because such jobs hold few incumbents, they escape the scrutiny lavished on populous clerical or even skilled labor positions. Baron (1991) reports several studies documenting the tendency for white males to be overrepresented in sole-occupant positions in organizations, which are higher in status and salary than when similar positions are held by women and minorities (pp. 116–22). Although the reason men obtain much higher rewards from such positions is not clear, it may well reflect subtle, unconscious processes of discrimination in favor of males.

As Baron suggests,

> The tendency . . . for men and whites to monopolize one-person organizational job titles illustrates these processes. White men typically have preeminent influence in most organizations, and they enjoy a privileged position within the larger social order. Accordingly, it seems plausible that white men have a more elaborate and differentiated schema of the work they do than they do of "women's work," which has become institutionalized within the formal structure of organizations. (1991, 118)

Explaining the Departure from the Initial Hayes Plan: Market Necessity or Organizational Politics?

Both the trial court and the court of appeals gave substantial weight in their opinions to the notion that the university departed from the Hayes scheme to pay male workers higher wages because it was a market necessity. Judge McManus wrote a lengthy footnote in his trial court judgment citing wage survey results that indicated that certain male jobs commanded higher market wages than certain female jobs. As we look back on the *Christensen* opinion, it seems that the empirical question of whether the university was following the market should have been pivotal to the outcome.

Yet the market issue was not subjected to close analysis in the course of the litigation. In their trial testimony, various officials of the university and the State Board of Regents referred to market circumstances as an acceptable basis for granting higher starting salaries (D. Walton, Tr. Trans., pp. 449–50; D. Volm, Tr. Trans., pp. 503–6). But their statements were quite abstract. They never specifically indicated that the university was having difficulty filling physical plant jobs. James Hughes, the Hayes firm consultant, when asked to comment on the suggestion of the plaintiffs' expert that the university could have tried to hire workers before raising starting salaries, offered only a halfhearted rebuttal.

Q: Another alternative was to set all the rates at Step 1 and just hire whomever you can get.

A: Right. I guess that is a possibility.

Q: Is it realistic?

A: I can't really say that for sure. But there did seem to be enough of a differential that that would be difficult. Although I think the intent is to hire as close to Step 1 as possible, to that sense I would certainly agree.

The plaintiffs' attorneys did not mount a consistent challenge to the assumption that the university was forced to raise the starting wages of predominantly male jobs. They did not cross-examine university officials about whether they were experiencing high levels of turnover in male jobs or whether they had encountered difficulties hiring applicants for physical plant jobs. They did not interrogate the Hayes consultants or university officials about how the wage surveys were done or whether they constituted convincing evidence that male jobs required higher starting pay. Indeed, given the plaintiffs' strategy of accusing the university of discriminating by following a discriminatory market, plaintiffs' counsel sometimes seemed eager to prove that the university based its wage structure on the market (see, e.g., Tr. Trans., p. 496).

The only direct attack on market necessity came in the rebuttal testimony of the plaintiffs' expert, David Whitsett. Expert witnesses who are called to rebut assertions made by the other side in a lawsuit are not subject to stringent requirements to disclose reports and the bases for their expert opinions, as are witnesses called to support the case in chief. Defense counsel objected to Whitsett's testimony on grounds of unfair surprise, but Judge McManus allowed the testimony into evidence. The plaintiffs' gambit may have allowed Whitsett's assertions to go unchallenged by other experts, but it also may have diminished the effect of his testimony. Because the testimony came at the end of the trial and was admitted under a somewhat questionable technicality, it may not have had as much authority as if it had been presented as integral to the plaintiffs' case and had been open to serious examination by defense counsel and its experts.

Whitsett testified that higher wages were not necessary to hire physical plant workers. He cited unemployment statistics that tended to establish that there was no scarcity of labor for the physical plant jobs (Tr. Trans., pp. 632–35). Whitsett's discussion of market necessity may have been weakened by the next topic he addressed. Responding to questions by plaintiffs' counsel, he cited a Department of Labor report indicating that within the same occupational categories and the same industries male workers generally were paid higher wages than female workers (Tr. Trans., pp. 636–38). The point of the testimony was to document the existence of sex discrimination in the market. But the court may have interpreted the data to show that gender differences of the sort found at the university were typical in the labor market generally.

A telling indication that the plaintiffs had not effectively attacked the market necessity question was that the university's attorneys did not remember such an argument by the plaintiffs.

> Q: Did the plaintiffs hit you for not following the market?
> *Attorney One*: No.
> *Attorney Two*: No. The university was following the market and the plaintiffs thought the university was.
> *Attorney One*: It was following the market in relative positions vis-à-vis the market [i.e., it underpaid equally across jobs].
>
> (Personal interview, June 24, 1986)

Moreover, the plaintiffs' own expert, David Whitsett, indicated to us that he had "no recollection of asserting that the university was discriminating with respect to the market" (personal interview, June 23, 1986).

Although neither the parties nor the judges in the litigation seriously inquired into whether market conditions justified the university's decision to give advanced pay levels to physical plant jobs, there is much in the court records and in our interviews with university officials that addresses the issue. We now turn to these data to consider how well the departures from the regular pay schedule are explained by market factors.

Three arguments can be adduced to support the interpretation that the advanced pay levels for physical plant jobs were dictated, not by market requirements, but by overriding principles of organizational pay systems. These are, first, that the salary survey data assembled by the Hayes consultants indicated that predominantly male jobs were paid substantially more than female jobs; second, that university officials sincerely believed that such wage levels were necessary to hire and retain qualified physical plant workers, whereas clerical pay levels were adequate; and, third, that physical plant jobs had been paid higher levels in the past and that to reduce their wage levels or raise the pay of clerical workers without raising physical plant wages would have led to intolerable strife within the work force.

The Evidence from Wage Surveys

To assess whether the data from wage surveys showed a market necessity for higher physical plant wages, we start by examining how the trial

court incorporated results from wage surveys into its opinion. Court
records include two sets of wage survey results, one based on a May
1974 survey and one based on a survey done in November 1974. Judge
McManus quoted results from the latter of these in his judgment.

> [T]he second round local community salary survey, however,
> showed laborers receiving an average annual salary of
> $9,983.00 while a clerk II was receiving only $6,728.00.
> Accordingly, the recommended starting salary at the university
> for a laborer was grade 103 step 10 or $6,756.00 while a
> clerk II started at grade 103 step 1 or $5,544.00. A similar
> contrast is found by comparing a painter surveyed at
> $11,703.00 and starting at grade 108 step 9 or $8,484.00
> with a secretary III surveyed at $7,513.00 and starting at
> grade 108 step 1 or $7,572.00. (Judgment, Nov. 11, 1976,
> p. 2)

By choosing these examples, Judge McManus projected an image of a
simple factual situation in which market data deviated from the initial
Hayes pay matrix for physical plant jobs. The impression given was that
physical plant jobs grouped in the same job grade as clerical jobs were
paid substantially more in the market (according to salary survey data).
After the physical plant jobs were given advanced-step pay, they still
received substantially less than market values, whereas clerical jobs were
paid just slightly below or even slightly above the surveyed value.

But this is a somewhat distorted and oversimplified representation.
First, the judge did not acknowledge that the initial pay matrix was based
on market data that related job evaluation points to average pay levels
for jobs with similar numbers of points. Second, the figures the judge
cited were for Waterloo only. The university considered salary data from
two other localities as well, and indeed it is located in Cedar Falls, not
Waterloo. The survey showed that laborers and painters received substantially less in the other two communities (for laborers, $7,942 in
Cedar Falls–Waverly and $8,823 in Marshalltown; for painters, $8,609
in Cedar Falls–Waverly and $11,211 in Marshalltown). Clerk IIs and
secretary IIIs, by contrast, received substantially higher pay in at least
some of the other communities, according to the survey (for clerk IIs,
$6,051 in Cedar Falls–Waverly, $7,704 in Marshalltown; for secretary
IIIs, $8,227 in Cedar Falls–Waverly; $10,135 in Marshalltown) (Hayes
and Associates Report, Dec. 1974, pp. 17–18). Not only did the judge
choose the one locale that maximized the market differentials, he chose
two predominantly male occupations that appeared underpaid compared
with the market data and two female occupations that appeared to be
paid very close to the market. Not all comparisons of male and female
jobs would have yielded the same impression. A more fundamental

problem with the judge's treatment of the survey data is that it did not acknowledge that the market values varied quite dramatically across locales and from the results of the survey taken six months before. The wide variation and instability of survey results should have given pause in using the surveys to define the going rate for clerical and physical plant jobs.

It is possible to review more systematically which jobs were granted starting pay exceptions based on market data. The same Hayes and Associates Report cited by Judge McManus contains a listing of jobs that were considered for higher starting pay. It included entries for grade, job title, whether the jobs had "competitive starting salaries . . . at or below step four" of the grade (denoted "yes" or "no"), recommended step within grade, and recommended starting salary (which is a direct function of grade and step). Twenty-six of these jobs were unambiguously present within the UNI work force. For jobs that were surveyed, we analyzed each job to determine how far above or below the market average it fell. (We divided the step 1 pay level for each job's assigned grade by the average of the three communities' wage levels reported in the wage survey results. The wage survey results for each community are based on employer responses, weighted by the number of workers they employ in a particular job (Hayes and Associates Report, Dec. 1974, pp. 17–23). We then cross-classified the jobs depending on whether they were granted a higher starting step (and thus a higher starting salary), the extent to which they were below the market wage, and sex composition. (Once again, male jobs are defined as 90 percent or more male, female jobs are 90 percent or more female, and mixed jobs fall in between these proportions.)

Table 5.7 reports the results. Sex composition has a very striking effect that is only partly explained by wage survey data. Eleven of thirteen predominantly male jobs received higher starting salaries, compared with twelve of twenty-six jobs overall, one of two jobs of mixed gender makeup, and none of eleven female jobs. The table suggests that the market data support six of the eleven exceptions given male jobs, in that they would have fallen below 85 percent of the market average. Five of the male jobs given exceptions, however, were not surveyed at all. And one mixed job and three predominantly female jobs that also fell below 85 percent of the market average were not granted higher starting pay. The table does support the general assertion that, as measured by these survey data, female jobs at the university were better compensated vis-à-vis the market than predominantly male jobs. Yet the university did not follow a consistent principle in giving higher starting steps to all jobs below the market. It gave exceptions to five of six male jobs that were not surveyed, while denying an exception to the female job that was not

Table 5.7. *Cross-Tabulation of Jobs Granted Starting Pay Exception by Sex Composition and Market Salary*

Ratio of Starting Salary to Market Salary[a]	Granted Exception			Not Granted Exception			Total
	Male	Mixed	Female	Male	Mixed	Female	
Below 85%	6	1	0	0	1	3	11
Above 85%	0	0	0	1	0	7	8
Not surveyed	5	0	0	1	0	1	7
Total	11	1	0	2	1	11	26

[a] If paid at step 1 of grade. Divided by mean of weighted averages for Waterloo, Cedar Falls, and Marshalltown.
Source: Hayes Report, Dec. 1974, 17–23, 30–33.

surveyed. And it denied exceptions to the mixed and female jobs that fell below 85 percent of the market average. If one takes the wage survey data seriously, they provide only weak support for the market necessity position.

Indeed, there may be good reason not to accept the survey data as an accurate measure of the market value for predominantly male and female jobs. The Hayes reports and the testimony given by the Hayes consultants at trial and in depositions provide little documentation of how the surveys were conducted. (Apparently all organizations within a fifty-mile radius of the university, in towns of 20,000 population or more, that employed 200 or more employees were contacted; see Hayes and Associates Report, July 1974, p. 1.) In the next chapter we illustrate how wage surveys can become highly politicized processes in which various groups lobby for changes in procedures that will benefit their interests. Although the documents in *Christensen* do not allow us to examine the dynamics of the wage survey in similar detail, there is at least one suggestion that the wage surveys undertaken by the Hayes firm were subject to political pressures of some kind.

The description of the outside survey contained in the December 1974 Hayes and Associates Report includes a new paragraph not contained in similar reports prepared in July and November 1974. After describing which classifications and which employers had been surveyed, it states: "In addition, the wage rates published by Master Builders of Iowa for carpenters, electricians, painters, and pipefitters were incorporated into the survey" (Hayes and Associates Report, Dec. 1974, p. 6). One suspects that these wage rates increase the surveyed rate of the craft occupations and were included at the request of craft workers, who are

overwhelmingly male. The former president of the union local that eventually was established at the university, when asked how wages were set
in the years covered by the lawsuit, understood the importance of how
wage comparisons were made. He said,

> [Wages] were supposed to be compared to local wages. . . .
> We got federal wage/hour reports. The university always paid
> a lot less. We always wondered how the university lowered the
> average [in wage surveys]. They paid about two-thirds of what
> Rath and Deere paid. Now we are in a much better position
> than Rath, which has closed, and where workers have had to
> make give backs, etc. All kinds of employment has its ups and
> downs, but university work is stable. It's pretty much
> permanent. (Telephone interview, June 9, 1986)

What we cannot know is whether other occupational groups, particularly those in which a larger proportion of members are women, such
as nurses, lab technicians, or secretaries, might have been able to formulate similar proposals to have favorable data "incorporated into the
survey" if they had been better organized. How wage surveys are conducted can very significantly affect estimated differentials between predominantly male and predominantly female positions. If wages paid to
seasonal male workers are used to define annual earnings, this choice
will inflate the estimate of the market wage. Just as the union local president described, physical plant workers may accept much lower wages
at a university because the job is stable and the working conditions more
pleasant than those in factory or construction work. Similar discounting
takes place for predominantly female clerical jobs at universities. Clearly
there are high-earning clerical workers, such as legal secretaries or executive secretaries. But perhaps because these positions are so exceptional
and are relatively hidden from view, they do not bootstrap wages in the
occupation generally. There is no equivalent to the "prevailing wage"
rate within construction work (really the unionized wage rate) for
clerical workers.

Perceptions of University Officials

The wage survey data may have been inconclusive on the issue of market
necessity. The two university officials most directly involved in hiring and
wage setting, the director of personnel and the vice president for administration, long after the conclusion of the lawsuit, however, entertained
no such uncertainty. When we asked what would have happened if the
university had gone with the first set of Hayes recommendations, the

former personnel director replied, "[T]here would have been no way at all to hire anybody" (telephone interview, July 17, 1986). The former vice president gave a similar response to the same inquiry. Describing the hypothetical situation of an advanced clerical worker and a plumber being placed in the same job grade under the Hayes pay matrix, he said "you couldn't hire a plumber for that" (telephone interview, July 30, 1986).

Given the frankness these informants showed in other portions of the retrospective interviews and the fact that both had long since left employment at the university, we take these statements as highly credible. What is far more problematic is the basis for their perceptions. Was their belief in the need for higher physical plant wages based on actual experiences in hiring and retaining workers at different wage levels? Or was it based on other factors, such as the political pressures they felt from male workers, or culturally established patterns of valuing "male" work above "female" work? Other passages from the interviews with these respondents are revealing, if not dispositive.

During its period of expansion in the late 1960s and early 1970s, the university significantly increased hiring of faculty and staff. It faced a shortage of qualified candidates with Ph.D.s for faculty positions but apparently had a ready supply of workers for physical plant jobs.

> Q: How did you go about hiring those people?
> *Vice president*: We just advertised and they applied. It was easy to hire them. [W]e drew on the whole metropolitan area, and also to some extent on the surrounding rural communities. The university was seen as a desirable place to work. People did respond to the security of the employment, the fact that it was year round. Even at a lower wage a carpenter could make more working for the university year round than for a construction company.
> (Telephone interview, July 30, 1986)

At various times, for various occupational groups, the university struggled to compete with John Deere, the major industrial employer in the area. The concrete instances of direct conflicts with Deere recalled by these informants concerned clerical positions and data processing, not physical plant workers (what the personnel director referred to as "skilled" people).

> Q: Given the high wages at Deere, was turnover a problem?
> *Personnel director*: To a greater degree in clerical than for skilled people. We might lose a custodian. But hell, people

from Rath [a reference to physical plant workers previously employed by Rath Packing] could have gone, but they never did. Good clerical people could and did.

(Telephone interview, July 17, 1986)

And from the vice president:

Q: What about [hiring] the clerical people?
Vice president: They were also easy to hire. There was a time after the lawsuit you asked about, when it was difficult. That was when Deere was expanding again. We were competing with John Deere and losing a lot of our trained people to them. We took an informal policy at the time, that if anybody left us to go to John Deere, we wouldn't hire them back if they were laid off over there. It was kind of a dirty trick, but we had to do it. It only took one case when we had to do it, then the word got around. The quality of our clerical people was dropping. We had an agreement with John Deere for a while not to hire our clerical people from us, but that only lasted about 6 months.
Q: You actually went out there?
Vice president: Yes.

(Telephone interview, July 30, 1986)

The last quotation refers to a period after the *Christensen* lawsuit, but may be relevant to how the university dealt with issues of pay and hiring for clericals in the earlier period. It would appear that rather than attempting to compete in price, which would have required raising wages, university officials engaged in anticompetitive behavior. They threatened employees that if they took competing offers, they would foreclose future opportunities. And they attempted to restrain the offers competitors made to their clerical work force. Note that the university's pay policies were constrained under the Board of Regents' statewide salary system. Local exceptions were allowed only in certain cases. As the personnel director commented, "The whole thing was political. We were a small institution. Here there were much higher wage rates [than other cities in the state]. But we couldn't get our wages up" (telephone interview, July 17, 1986). The statement is not quite accurate. The state pay plan allowed the university to grant starting step exceptions to physical plant jobs. During the early 1970s, the university did not make similar attempts to grant exceptions for clerical positions, either locally or statewide.

The relatively limited quantitative data on turnover also do not clearly

---

Table 5.8. *Turnover Rates by Job Family and Salary Level Relative to Market, University of Northern Iowa, 1974–1975*

Job Family	At or Below 95% of Market Salary		Above 95% of Market Salary		Market Salary Not Surveyed		Total	
	Turnover Rate	N of Cases	Turnover Rate	N of Cases	Turnover Rate	N of Cases	Turnover Rate	N of Cases
Clerical	0.280	175	0.093	54	0.303	162	0.263	391
Dormitory and food service	0.333	72	0.104	96	0.114	70	0.177	238
Physical plant	0.139	36	0.077	13	0.324	105	0.260	154
Total	0.276	283	0.098	163	0.270	337	0.256	783

support the official view that higher salaries for male jobs were necessary. As reported in Tables 5.5 and 5.6, although a slightly larger proportion of male workers (28 percent) than female workers (24 percent) left the university between 1973–74 and 1974–75, when we look at jobs, predominantly female jobs experienced higher rates of turnover (39 percent) than predominantly male jobs (33 percent) or mixed-gender jobs (27 percent). We can further refine the analysis of turnover to look at differences among job families and the effect of differences between actual pay and market salary. Table 5.8 presents this breakdown. Where a worker's salary stood vis-à-vis the external market rate for his or her job was determined by comparing an employee's salary for the earlier year (1973–74) with the mean salary rate for his or her occupation category according to the November 1974 survey.[6] The cutoff point used for the data in Table 5.8 was 95 percent; workers were judged to be below market rates only if they fell below 95 percent of the surveyed value. Of course, many employees were in occupations that were not included in the November market survey.

Several interesting features of UNI's situation are revealed here. Overall, turnover rates were about the same for physical plant and clerical employees, whereas food service and dormitory workers had relatively lower rates of transition. The pattern of turnover was very different for these job families when employees' market positions are taken into

6   The list of job families contained in this table is not exhaustive. In addition to those listed, forty-three UNI employees were employed in other job families such as "Laboratory and Technical" or "Communications." Also included in this group was a small number of workers whose job family could not be ascertained.

consideration.[7] As expected, those who are below market rates have higher turnover than those at or above them. What is interesting, however, is that the "below market" turnover rate for physical plant workers is as small as it is. That is, of those workers who are below their surveyed rates, the lowest turnover rates belong to the physical plant employees, not the clerical or food service employees.

It is understandable that university officials, had they been aware of these turnover relationships, might have concluded that something needed to be done to enhance the retention of employees whose salaries were lagging behind the market. What is inconsistent with the results shown here is the diagnosis that the most acute turnover problem was with physical plant employees who were below the market. If anything, these data suggest that a higher priority should have been given to the retention of poorly paid clerical and food service/dormitory workers or to clerical and physical plant workers in jobs that were not surveyed. It may be that different levels of turnover are tolerable for different families of jobs. Turnover among clerical staff may do less damage than turnover among the boiler operators during frigid Iowa winters, for example. If this were the case at UNI, none of our informants mentioned it.

Thus there is an unexplained leap in the perceptions of university officials that they had to pay physical plant workers higher wages. Their statements with respect to actual experience and the snapshot of turnover data we possess indicate that clerical workers, as much as physical plant workers, posed problems of retention and worker quality. The wage survey data reviewed in the previous section could be interpreted to show that physical plant jobs were more severely underpaid with respect to the market than clerical positions. But the university officials did not speak of the wage surveys as significant to their thinking. Nor did they use the wage surveys in a consistent fashion to determine which jobs should be given starting pay exceptions. It is far more likely that the perceptions of university officials were rooted in historical wage patterns within the organization, patterns that consistently paid physical plant jobs at higher levels than clerical workers.

The Organizational Imperative to Maintain Continuity in Wages

At several points in the trial testimony it is established that workers were paid in the new Hayes system at least as much as they earned in

---

7   The log-linear statistical test for the null hypothesis of no three-factor interaction was rejected. The likelihood ratio chi-square was 16.10 with four degrees of freedom. This indicates that the relationship between turnover and market situation differs according to which job family one is in.

the prior year, plus the approved across-the-board pay increase given the workforce.

> Q: Is it true, Mr. Hughes, that for incumbents, they were basically just taking their salary, what they made the year before, given their normal increase or seven and a half percent increase and then placed on your schedule? . . . In other words, their salary then was basically based on what they made in prior years?
>
> A: Yes. This is not an unusual procedure. Normally when you do these kinds of studies the first assurance that management gives to their employees is that nobody's salary will be reduced in implementing any kind of a new plan.
>
> (Tr. Trans., pp. 574–75)

Indeed it appears that the prior wage levels, rather than market conditions, may have led the university to raise starting steps. When defendant's counsel questioned the lead Hayes consultant about the number of salary surveys that had been conducted, he gave this testimony:

> *Mr. Hughes*: In developing the pay plan for 73–74, . . . we did do a salary survey. . . . The purpose of that survey was to develop where the entire curve should be placed for the entire matrix. Once this was done, and the system was implemented, it was brought to our attention there were certain jobs where the going rate that had been paid people, and also the market rate, was above what would be Step 1 in the new salary grade that they were assigned in.
>
> (Tr. Trans., p. 559)

In the first instance the witness speaks about prior pay levels. He then quickly mentioned "market rate," even though no specific "market rate" sources are described. From that point on in the testimony, the witness referred to his firm's recommendations for dealing with such "market problems." The consultants basically suggested that the university should test the market at the lower wage rate to see if it encountered hiring problems. Instead the university raised all the physical plant jobs to higher steps within grade, even jobs that were not surveyed.

The former vice president for administration quite directly admitted in an interview with us that previous pay levels were a decisive consideration in not following the initial set of Hayes recommendations. After he discussed the relative pay of a plumber and a secretary, and how it would have been impossible to hire a plumber for what one pays a secretary, we asked:

Q: So you were looking at what the lowest salary you already paid was, and you felt you couldn't bring people in below that? [The vice president for administration agreed.]

(Telephone interview, July 30, 1986)

Trial testimony by a Board of Regents official revealed that the 1973–74 Board of Regents pay plan followed the same principle. Employees were kept at the same pay levels they had received under the prior (Kearney) system, plus across-the-board raises (Tr. Trans., pp. 490–92).

It might be argued that even if the university were departing from the market as the ultimate test of what starting wages were necessary, equity demanded such a result. As the preceding testimony indicates, organizations are virtually obliged not to cut salaries of current employees when revising the pay system. Reducing actual pay levels would generate enormous conflict and dissatisfaction within an organization. Yet one must not confuse the policy of preserving the salaries of current employees when a new system is implemented with the decision the university made here to increase permanently the starting salaries of several jobs beyond the levels recommended by an initial salary survey. The consultants had devised a mechanism for coping with overpaid employees. They were to be "redcircled," that is, their current salaries frozen (subject only to base rate increases) until the salary matrix eventually caught up with them. The university was unwilling to take the position that some physical plant jobs had been overpaid compared with clerical jobs. It thus preserved differentials between predominantly male and predominantly female jobs, including differentials in the starting pay of future employees.

Organizational Politics at UNI

The arguments that the university's wage policies can be explained by market necessity, perceived market necessity, or widely accepted norms about organizational pay practices suffer some serious limitations. A more complete account must examine how organizational politics shaped the perceptions and practices of university officials. Interviews with the participants make it abundantly clear that male and female workers were organized very differently.

The physical plant workers, known informally as the "meatpackers" because of their identification with unionized workers at the now-defunct Rath Company, engaged in self-conscious collective activity. The clerical workers, in contrast, were content to participate in amicable "committee" meetings with university officials, in which they discussed matters like attendance at the university Christmas party. When the lawsuit was filed, not one other woman came forward to join the two named plaintiffs. When collective bargaining for public employees became legal in the state, the clerical workers were the last group to vote for union representation, several years after physical plant workers and the college faculty had done so.

The predictable result of these differences was that university officials gave higher pay to predominantly male positions, all else being equal, than they gave to predominantly female positions. It was a tendency consistent with past practice that could be justified by the selective use of wage survey data. At the very least, it maintained historical levels of pay inequality in the face of credible indications that the pay differentials were not justified by job evaluation or hiring and retention needs.

The personnel director recalled the contentious character of labor relations with the physical plant employees.

> *Personnel Director*: One set of meetings I will remember as long as I live. These were Wednesday afternoon meetings with representatives of the physical plant group to discuss conditions of employment. Although not very specific, these meetings became confrontational and argumentative in character. The university was surprised by this because they had established these sounding-board-type meetings in all three areas [physical plant, clerical, and food service/ dormitory workers] after having had very good experience with similar meetings with people in the clerical area. The secretaries were easier to deal with because they were more attuned to the administration.
> (Telephone interview, July 17, 1986)

Note the contrast between the confrontational interactions between male workers and male administrators and the apparently polite exchanges between the female clerical committee members and male administrators. In a separate interview, the vice president for administration at the time elaborated on the difference between plant workers and clerical employees.

> *Q*: Were the clerical employees more satisfied than the other employees?
> *Vice president*: [He mentioned the different employee relations committees and drew an explicit comparison between the good relations with the clerical committee and the poorer relations with the physical plant committee. With the

physical plant group] there were four- to five-hour meetings every week. Another difference in attitude was that the physical plant committee wanted only themselves represented, but the clerical workers wanted to have an administrator, which they elected, present at their meetings.
. . .

Q: What kind of things did they [clerical workers] want?
Vice president: Well, hard to remember. Things like the Christmas party. Actually they wanted to be able to take off from work to do their shopping instead of going to the Christmas party. We told them either you work at your desk or you come to the Christmas party, but no time off. So that was one they didn't win. But there were other things we helped them with. Like the health insurance policy . . . , life insurance, there was also discussion about a clerical lounge. Things like that, nothing big.

There was a big difference between the physical plant and the clerical workers. The physical plant people work on teams, so they're used to doing things together. The clericals are spread all over campus and they identified more with their supervisors and units. I would say it is sort of a dispersion thing.

(Telephone interview, July 30, 1986)

The description of the two committees evokes the contrast between labor-management struggle by male workers versus the polite participation of female clerical workers in a paternalistic system. In some sense the women workers did not even dare to speak for themselves. They preferred instead to elect male representatives to act as liaison with university leaders. At least according to the account of the male administrators they dealt with, female workers did not make demands, they had "problems" that officials "helped" them with. The problems concerned the amenities of employment, such as issues surrounding the Christmas party and a clerical lounge; they were "nothing big."

Moreover, the everyday working lives of physical plant and clerical workers molded the structure of their political organization. It was no great leap for the physical plant workers to take collective action. They worked in teams and were used to "doing things together." Whereas plant employees probably punched the same clock and ate together, clerical workers were "spread all over campus" and identified with supervisors and their departments. This was hardly the basis for group formation and mobilization.

Two events epitomize the force of male physical plant cohesiveness and the absence of clerical worker solidarity: the successful strike by physical plant workers and the failed class action led by Pauline Christensen and Phyllis Gohmann.

The president of the union local at the time of the strike told us that plant workers had organized informally in 1968 and carried out the illegal strike in 1969. "We never negotiated formally, but due to the strike we got fifty classes [job classifications] changed. We shut down the campus for five days, then they got an injunction. Fifty classes got more pay" (telephone interview, June 9, 1986). To the personnel director the strike was a culmination of ongoing strife. A few people in the dormitory system struck, but the dormitories "continued to function relatively normally." He indicated:

> [T]he strike ended after several days when they got a court injunction forcing the workers back. He didn't really want to do this, but there was feeling that the university had to get back to business as usual. It might have been better if the strike had gone on for a few more days. (Telephone interview, July 17, 1986)

The personnel director had wanted to fight it out with his antagonists, the meatpackers, but he did not prevail within the university administration. Other officials believed it was necessary to return to business as usual. And as a result of the strike, fifty presumably male-dominated jobs were given pay raises. Clerical jobs were not mentioned in any informant narratives about the strike and presumably were unaffected in pay raises after the strike.

Class action litigation can be a form of collective action, for instance when it is brought by a social movement organization or when it grows out of grass-roots efforts within a particular locale. But the two plaintiffs in this case were not supported by other clerical workers.

> Q: Why did no other women get involved in the lawsuit?
> A: [Pauline and Phyllis were not leaders among the women; they were not especially popular or anything.] They were standing out there alone. Also clerical workers were not given to that type of activity. If you track things down to the present, you probably will find that clerical workers are still not represented by [a union].
> (Interview with clerical worker 1986)

In the eyes of one of the plaintiffs' attorneys, the lack of broader support weakened the chances for victory. The university settled a sex discrimination case brought by female faculty members at roughly the same time as the *Christensen* case. We asked the lawyer who had represented the plaintiffs in both cases why there was a different outcome. He responded that the faculty case was stronger legally, because faculty positions looked more like the same job. In the *Christensen* case the jobs held by men and women were clearly different. He continued:

> And it could be the fact that we had a great deal of faculty support. It could be that to offend them as a group meant problems down the road. And I think you also have to consider that faculty males were more supportive of their [the faculty women's] position than were the counterparts of the clerical people. (Personal interview, June 24, 1986)

Because the female plaintiffs were "out there alone," the political costs to the university of fighting the lawsuit were low. There was no prospect that university life would be disrupted by busloads of clerical workers going to court. Just such a danger prompted a settlement in the faculty case, even though the defense attorneys claimed that the settlement was so small that "We thought we had done nothing but win that case" (personal interview, June 24, 1986).

It is no surprise, then, that university officials were, in the words of one informant, "worried about the union guys, but not the women" (personal interview, June 23, 1986). Every decision the university made concerning the conditions of physical plant employment was subject to intense scrutiny and challenge. As the president of the union local indicated, the plant employees were constantly arguing that they were not being paid fairly according to published labor statistics or according to what they knew about union rates at the major industrial employer in the area. In the aftermath of a strike and in the face of continuing agitation, university officials immediately dismissed the lower pay levels proposed for plant jobs in the initial Hayes recommendations. No parallel collective activity was undertaken by clerical workers, even though they too might have argued that they were underpaid compared with at least some segments of the labor market. The market did not compel the university's decision. Organizational politics compelled the university to give selective attention to the demands of workers in predominantly male jobs.

Conclusion

The Hayes system recommendations would have significantly reduced between-job gender inequality at the University of Northern Iowa. That

quiet reform was undone by entrenched interests within the organization. University officials were so conditioned by the militance of male
physical plant workers that they rejected the recommendations that
would have tended to close the gender gap in wages.

Perhaps the most unfortunate aspect of the lawsuit was that the pivotal
empirical issue was dealt with only in the most superficial and stylized
way. The university was excused from liability because it was deemed to
be following the market in departing from the recommended pay matrix.
We now think that is a highly questionable conclusion. If the trial court
had come to the same interpretation of the events that we offer, it does
not necessarily follow that the plaintiffs would have prevailed. The
opinion of the court of appeals contains language that might treat the
political effectiveness of various groups of workers as a valid basis for
paying them different wages. "The value of the job to the employer represents but one factor affecting wages. Other factors may include the
supply of workers willing to do the job and *the ability of the workers
to band together to bargain collectively for higher wages*" (*Christensen
v. State of Iowa*, 563 F.2d 353, at 355–56, 8th cir. 1977; emphasis
added). How far the courts would be willing to go to excuse male-female
wage differentials based on organizational politics is an open question.
But given the wariness of courts to allow discrimination based on the
preferences of customers, one suspects that if such an exception were
granted, it would be narrowly circumscribed.

Moreover, if we read the case from the perspective of legal realists, it
was unlikely, given the circumstances of this litigation, that the plaintiffs
would have won. The plaintiffs' lawyer acknowledged in retrospect that
the case decision may have been based on the potentially far-reaching
consequences of a ruling in favor of the plaintiffs.

> Well, this is not in either of the opinions. It's just my opinion.
> I think that the case turned on the enormity of the
> repercussions of ruling that [this was discrimination] and
> recognizing that in order to award damages or give relief, it
> would be necessary to actually pay them based on the factors
> of skill, work, responsibility, etc., which would have been a
> very substantial financial burden on the university and the
> State of Iowa. (Personal interview, June 24, 1986)

We are willing to recognize these political realities, but we are not persuaded that the *Christensen* case is either good law or good sociology.
According to our analysis, the opinion in *Christensen* misrepresents and
oversimplifies the dynamics of gender inequality in the organizational
pay system under investigation. The entire set of participants in the case
failed to come to grips with the forces that shaped patterns of gender

inequality in the university pay system. By attributing differentials to the market, the opinion does nothing to encourage female workers to organize politically, nor even to attend to the details through which pay decisions are made. Even legal realists would hope that courts might do a better job of getting the facts right. Even if the plaintiffs did not make an adequate case for establishing discrimination, they at least deserved a careful analysis of where their evidence fell short, rather than the kind of overreaching interpretation of the facts handed down by the trial court and the appellate court.

In various ways, courts provide authoritative interpretations of social life. Although these interpretations may have the largest effect on the conceptions of lay audiences, they may begin to reshape the conceptions of the social world held by social scientists as well. As courts define what is a "realistic claim," this may lead ineluctably to changed definitions of reality even among sophisticated audiences. Decisions such as *Christensen* may do the disservice of polarizing opinion by pushing advocates of pay equity to reject market-based pay systems altogether, and by reconfirming the article of faith on which economic conservatives base their opposition to any legal scrutiny of between-job wage differentials. Our analysis of *Christensen* suggests that social scientists and serious policy analysts would do well to seek their own counsel in examining the sources of gender inequality in organizational pay systems, rather than rely uncritically on the characterizations offered in judicial opinions.

Appendix 5.1

There are three dependent variables in Appendix Table 5.A1. The first is the natural log of the dollar earnings values reported in Tables 5.5 and 5.6. The coefficients of the gender variable reported in this table are for a dummy variable representing males and are approximately equal to the percentage differences of male and female earnings.[8] The second and third variables analyzed here are two components of this logarithmic wage variable. The first component is the log of the starting salary that corresponds to the particular grade for that worker's job. The second component is the log of the ratio of each person's

---

8   Technically, the relative effect of gender on wage is given by $\exp(c)$ minus 1, where c is the coefficient of the dummy variable at issue. For values of the magnitude shown in Table 5.7, below 0.25, the transformed coefficients are virtually equivalent to those shown (Halvorsen and Palmquist 1980).

Appendix Table 5.A1. *Gender Effects on Individual Earnings in Two Pay Systems, University of Northern Iowa*

	Board of Regents Merit Pay System 1973–74 (N = 825)			Hayes Pay System 1974–75 (N = 814)		
	Log Salary	Log Starting Salary	Log Difference[a]	Log Salary	Log Starting Salary	Log Difference[a]
Means	8.744	8.616	0.129	8.857	8.716	0.141
Gender effect						
A. Unadjusted	0.252	0.160	0.077	0.250	0.150	0.100
B. Adjusted for:						
1. Tenure, salary basis	0.212	0.160	0.052	0.216	0.123	0.094
2. Tenure, salary basis, starting salary exception	0.204	0.191	0.013[b]	0.177	0.094	0.083
3. Tenure, salary basis, market salary	—	—	—	0.171	0.076	0.095
R^2 (Model B2 or B3)	0.570	0.434	0.351	0.637	0.433	0.373
4. Tenure, salary basis, starting salary exception, job family, level, single incumbent, single incumbent male	0.155	0.072	0.083	0.109	0.044	0.065
R^2 (Model B4)	0.636	0.703	0.409	0.694	0.665	0.447

[a] Log of ratio of actual salary to starting salary for pay grade.
[b] t statistic not significant.

actual earnings and the starting salary at the first level of his or her pay grade. Because these two components add to the log of the person's own earnings (the first dependent variable), the coefficients for each predictor also add to the coefficients for the first dependent variable. This mode of presentation allows us to decompose the wage-gender relationship into a "grade" component – that due to the fact that men are in more highly graded jobs – and a "difference" component – that due to the fact that men tend to be further above their range minimums than women. Some models include controls for a set of variables called "salary basis." Specifically, these are dummy variables that represent those who are on part-time status, those who are on full-year contracts, and those who are on nine-month contracts. Other models include variables indicating whether a worker holds a job given a starting exception, the market salary for the job according to the Hayes salary survey reports (1974–75 only), in which of the five job families used by the university their job falls, whether he or she holds a single-incumbent job, and an interaction term for sex by single-incumbent job. Note that all salaries have already been converted to the full-year equivalents of hourly pay rates.[9]

9 Full regression equations are available on request. We report the results in simplified form because no inconsistent or otherwise noteworthy patterns appear in the coefficients for the control variables.

6

Bureaucratic Politics and Gender Inequality in a State Pay System: AFSCME v. State of Washington

In 1985, a three-judge panel from the U.S. Ninth Circuit Court of Appeals overruled a lower-court decision that the State of Washington had unlawfully discriminated in pay against employees working in predominantly female jobs. At the district court level, the case had been argued in part according to the logic of comparable worth. Prior to the appellate court's decision, the plaintiffs, the American Federation of State, County, and Municipal Employees (AFSCME), and their attorneys and supporters were optimistic that the district court's ruling would set the stage for a succession of cases that would establish the principle of equal pay for work of equal value under Title VII of the Civil Rights Act. In its reversal of the lower court, the appellate court lowered the curtain on this impending legal drama before the end of the first act. A subsequent settlement of $100 million provided some relief for the affected state employees, but did nothing to revive the effort to expand legal theories of pay discrimination against women. This case, which in retrospect was a turning point for pay equity in the federal courts, is the basis for this chapter's investigation of pay inequality in a state pay system.

In many ways, *AFSCME v. State of Washington* provides a sharp contrast to the *Christensen* case that we analyzed in the preceding chapter. *AFSCME* reflects how much the social environment was different in Washington State in the 1980s than in midwestern Iowa in the 1970s. First, at least superficially, the role of the public employee union involved in each case was considerably different. While the two named plaintiffs in *Christensen* received little more than lip service from a local union, AFSCME was at center stage legally and financially in the suit against the State of Washington.

Second, the defendant organizations were quite dissimilar. Although both were public sector organizations, the size, geographic dispersion, complexity, and even the culture of the State of Washington personnel system set it apart from the University of Northern Iowa. As pointed out in the preceding chapter, the administrative component of UNI had undergone fairly rapid change in the years just prior to the lawsuit. In important respects, however, employee relations were still tinged by personalism, and bureaucratic rationalization, although always present in latent form in the rules and procedures of the State Personnel Board, was just beginning to catch hold at UNI. During an interview with one of the more "modern" personnel officials, we were told that some of the trouble connected to the *Christensen* suit might have been explained by the sexism of a departed university vice president. By contrast, bureaucratization had proceeded much further in the personnel system in Washington. The number of job titles alone ran into the thousands, and exceeded the number of actual employees at UNI. And while the modus operandi fell short of total universalism, control over the Washington bureaucracy was beyond the reach of any single individual.

The Washington case is also dissimilar from the action against UNI because the doctrine of comparable worth itself had matured considerably in the intervening years. Although *Christensen* was litigated under a clear theory of comparable worth, that jobs of equal evaluated worth ought to be paid equal wages, the terms "comparable worth" and "pay equity" were never used during the course of the protracted litigation. The *AFSCME* litigation was the product of a self-conscious pay equity movement at the state and national level.

In *Christensen*, one encounters all the actors involved, plaintiffs, attorneys, and defendants, as strangers in relatively unfamiliar territory. They believed they were navigating this terrain with conceptual tools that were untested, thoroughly rational, but, above all, completely novel. For example, one of the plaintiffs' lead attorneys described the idea that wages set through market processes possessed an inherent presumption of reasonableness and fairness as "old fashioned thinking." By way of contrast, in Washington all parties concerned were not only familiar with the doctrine of comparable worth but either, in the case of the defendants, partially endorsed it or, in the case of the plaintiffs, fully embraced it. Although the positions of the litigants moved toward opposite poles as the case proceeded, it was clear to all involved that comparable worth was the primary issue on the docket. What was less obvious at the beginning of the case, but became increasingly apparent as events moved forward, was the central role that an appeal to free market forces would play in the state's defense.

Because the market issue became so crucial to the outcome of the case, the Washington case is a valuable resource to those studying market and organizational influences on pay determination. Although the case records did not contain data on the earnings or characteristics of individual employees, they did provide exceptionally detailed information at the level of jobs, particularly concerning the linkages of jobs to each other in the pay system itself. In addition, because the plaintiffs' attorneys were sensitized to the possibility of a "market defense," during the depositions of key personnel officials they asked many cogent questions related to the putative influence of the market on wage rates in the system. After reviewing the development of the lawsuit itself, we will use these data to explore how market and organizational forces interacted to affect the pattern of between-job earnings differences between the sexes in this setting. (For abbreviations used for citations, see the appendix on court documents and case materials.)

The Lawsuit

In 1973 after complaints by the executive director of the Washington Federation of State Employees (the state affiliate of AFSCME, hereafter referred to as WFSE), Governor Dan Evans ordered the state director of personnel to investigate charges of wage disparities suffered by those working in predominantly female jobs compared with those working in predominantly male jobs (578 F. Supp. at 860 [1983]). A pilot report from the Higher Educational Personnel Board and the Department of Personnel (DOP) indicated that wage disparities of this sort did exist and that they were not due to lower job worth in the more heavily female classifications (578 F. Supp. at 861 [1983]); Plaintiffs' Appellate Brief, p. 14). Evans responded in 1974 with the hiring of Norman Willis, an independent consultant, who was given the mandate to conduct a "more comprehensive look at the situation" (Plaintiffs' Appellate Brief, p. 15). Later that year, Willis tendered his report, which found that "the tendency is for women's job classes to be paid less than men's classes, for comparable job worth." As a corrective to this disparity, the report suggested moving salaries in the predominantly female jobs up to the level established by the male "salary practice line" (Plaintiffs' Appellate Brief, p. 16). This initial recommendation was not implemented but was followed up by a second study that was conducted in 1976 to update the earlier findings. It, too, found the same pattern of between-job differences as the earlier report.

Before Evans left office at the end of 1976, he issued a proposed budget that included a $7 million appropriation to implement Willis's recommendations. However, his successor, Dixie Lee Ray, did not include these remedial funds in her own budget request. Nevertheless, "the State legislature amended the civil service law to require the submission of a biennial 'supplemental salary schedule to the legislature . . . which indicates those cases where the board determines that prevailing rates do not provide similar salaries for positions which require or impose similar

responsibilities, judgment, knowledge, skills and working conditions'"
(Plaintiffs' Appellate Brief, p. 19). Even though another job evaluation
study was carried out in 1980 using the Willis methodology, no action
was taken to implement the study's results or any of the supplemental budget recommendations. Subsequently, on September 16, 1981,
AFSCME filed a formal complaint with the Equal Employment Opportunity Commission (578 F. Supp. at 850–51, 861–62 [1983]).

The EEOC took no action on the complaint. In April 1982, the U.S.
Department of Justice issued a right-to-sue letter. In July 1982, AFSCME
and the WFSE filed a federal lawsuit on behalf of 15,500 workers in
jobs held primarily by women. The case went to trial on liability issues
in August 1983. The injunctive relief and backpay issues were tried in
November and December. The presentation of evidence and argument in
all phases at the district court level took no more than sixteen days. Judge
Tanner issued his opinion on December 14, 1983 (578 F. Supp. 851
[1983]). In little more than one year, the lawsuit had produced a judgment for backpay and pay raises at an estimated cost of $400 million
dollars and injunctive relief ordering the State of Washington to change
pay practices that resulted in the underpayment of employees in predominantly female jobs as measured by the evaluated worth of those
jobs. The pace at which the case was litigated and decided was breath-
taking. Both sides to the case indicated in interviews that they had to
scramble to meet the court's trial schedule. Both felt they did not have
as much time for preparation that the complexity of the issues demanded
(personal interviews 1988).

In Chapter 2 we summarized the opinion of Judge Tanner and the
court of appeals decision that reversed it sixteen months later. Judge
Tanner concluded that the plaintiffs had demonstrated sex-based pay discrimination, in part through the public acknowledgment of state officials,
and in part through direct evidence based on job evaluation studies, statistical evidence concerning the correlation between percent female in
jobs and lower pay, and evidence on historical patterns of sex segregation. Judge Tanner did not directly address the degree to which the wage
disparities were attributable to market processes outside the state pay
system. The market issue was pivotal to Judge Kennedy's opinion reversing Judge Tanner's. Kennedy did not simply reject the "pure" comparable worth elements of the lower-court opinion that would have based
liability on job evaluation results alone. He built several of his legal conclusions on the empirical assumption that the state was in fact following the market in paying men's and women's jobs. "Title VII does not
obligate [the state] to eliminate an economic inequality that it did not
create" (770 F.2d at 1407 [1985]).

Following the decision of the appellate panel, the plaintiffs petitioned for a review of the opinion by the full court of appeals. While the petition was pending, the state offered to settle the lawsuit for a cost of $100 million. State officials preferred to settle so as not to alienate an important constituency, female state employees, and to end the uncertainty over the state's possible legal exposure, which was damaging its bond rating (personal interview, 1988). The plaintiffs' lead counsel throughout the litigation until that time, Winn Newman, advised against settlement. Newman was by all accounts the leading entrepreneur seeking to establish a Title VII basis for comparable worth (see McCann 1994, 61). He wanted to press the case to gain a favorable legal precedent. AFSCME decided to accept the settlement. Newman resigned from the case (personal interview, 1988). The plaintiffs were left with a legal defeat but with what appeared on paper to be a substantial monetary settlement.

Research Design and Data

We are examining the relative explanatory power of market, efficiency, and organizational inequality models in the context of the compensation plan enacted in the Department of Personnel in the State of Washington in the mid-1970s. There are several reasons to be confident that this particular case is not an isolated and atypical personnel system. First, like other personnel bureaucracies, this one was not designed out of whole cloth but developed in part in response to reports and recommendations obtained from outside consultants who were playing similar roles in other organizations, both public and private, in the same time period. The State of Washington defended itself in this case by claiming that it behaved no differently from other employers. Second, the State of Washington is not the only state government to be sued for alleged pay equity violations. Similar actions have been brought against the states of Michigan and California. Eight other states have adopted some form of comparable worth pay program, and pay equity studies have been undertaken in at least ten others (Congressional Research Service 1985; Bureau of National Affairs 1986). Many other public sector employers have dealt with similar allegations (see, e.g., the settlement between AFSCME and the City of Los Angeles; Bureau of National Affairs 1985). Third, where it is possible to make quantitative comparisons between the Washington State system and others, it does not appear to be more rampantly sexist or egalitarian than they are.

The sources we employ here include statistical data on jobs, census data, legal documents, documents on the operation of the pay system, and some twenty in-depth interviews that the authors conducted between

1986 and 1988 with DOP officials, personnel officials in state agencies, union representatives, legislators and staff, and lawyers and experts involved in the lawsuit itself.

Salary Determination in the DOP

The major outlines of the DOP wage determination system conform quite closely to the conceptual scheme embodied in the administered efficiency model, which emphasizes the degree to which between-job pay differences are based solely on objective, technical criteria (see Chapter 3). A crucial principle of job classification inherent in the DOP system relates to the set of jobs that are pegged to a common external salary referent. As in many large personnel systems, the DOP conducts periodic salary surveys of wages in "external" occupations that are comparable with some of the jobs in the state's internal classification structure. The jobs for which surveys are conducted are referred to as "benchmark jobs," and in 1982 there were ninety-six such jobs. In principle, all other jobs in the system are linked, or "indexed," to one of the benchmark jobs (or "key jobs," in the administered efficiency schema).

Salary determination for most jobs is the result of a multielement process. For benchmark jobs, the results of the external survey have to be translated into an internal job range. For example, a decision was made that the benchmark job "warehouse worker 1" should be assigned to salary range "31," equivalent to a starting salary of $1,208 per month. In theory, the pay rate for the benchmark job reflects a "pure" market evaluation. In practice, it embodies several decision rules that lie outside the operation of the market per se, such as whether to compare each benchmark individually with the market or whether to average several benchmarks together (see subsequent discussion). A second element of the wage determination process is deciding which benchmark jobs should be used as referents for each nonbenchmark job. In some cases, the decision appears straightforward, as when "warehouse supervisor 3" is indexed to "warehouse worker 1." Indexing relationships frequently cut across job family lines, however.[1] The job "central supply technician,"

---

1   Job families are groups of loosely related jobs (denoted by sequential code numbers) that are similar to each other in the functional responsibilities of the jobs or their institutional settings. For example, jobs in the "general clerical" family include "messenger-clerks," "receptionists," "clerks," and "clerical supervisors," among others. A second level of job grouping is created by the establishment of "job series." For example, within the job family titled, "Highway, Bridge, Engineering, and Related," there is a five-position series beginning with "Cartographer 1" and ending with "Cartographer 5." Not all DOP jobs are part of these job series, however. In total, there are 412 distinct job series, which account for 1,206 of all jobs identified in the records available to us.

for example, a member of the same job family as "warehouse worker 1," is indexed to the job "attendant counselor 1," which is in the "nursing institutions" job family. Thus, indexing takes account of job family membership but only partly so. A third element of the wage determination process involves deciding how far above or below the benchmark salary the salary for a particular job should lie. In 1982, the position "warehouse supervisor 3" was ascertained to be fourteen ranges above "warehouse worker 1," its benchmark, and its starting salary was set at $1,707. (A difference of one range corresponds to a salary difference of 2.5 percent.) As the example illustrates, beyond whatever discretion exists in the establishment of salary ranges for benchmark jobs, nonbenchmark job salaries involve two additional discretionary components: (1) a decision about which job each should be indexed to and (2) a decision about what the salary should be relative to that index point.

The establishment of these relationships among jobs allows us to incorporate some additional variables in our statistical models of pay levels. One group of variables identifies the properties of the benchmark job to which each nonbenchmark job is indexed. Included here are measures of the percent female in the benchmark jobs, the total number of employees in the benchmark jobs, and the similarity of the jobs to their benchmarks (i.e., whether they are in the same job family or job series). A second set of variables indicates whether a job is or is not part of a job series (e.g., cartographer 1, cartographer 2, etc.) (see note 1), where it lies in its series (its series position), and if it is part of such a series, whether the series includes a benchmark job or not.

Third, many of the state's job titles contain designations indicating that the job is that of a "supervisor" or "manager." From these key words, we derive two dummy variables, one indicating that the job is "supervisory," the other that it is "managerial." Finally, the state publishes a list of entry-level "jobs which require high school education but not experience" and classifies the level of education needed as "high school," "business school," "college," or "graduate." Dummy variables are included to capture these distinctions as follows: One dummy variable, "entry-level job," indicates which jobs "require education but no experience," regardless of the level of education needed. Three other dummy variables are included that index whether the specific job requires (1) business school, (2) college, or (3) graduate-level credentials.

As should be obvious at this point, the wage determination plan enacted for the DOP manifests the characteristics of the administered efficiency model. If we assume for now that wage rates for the benchmark jobs follow relatively closely wage rates that prevail for their counterpart jobs in the external market, there are two implications for wage gaps between male and female jobs. First, the salary survey process should reproduce in the benchmark jobs the same size and pattern of salary differences found in the external market. Predominantly female benchmark jobs will differ from predominantly male benchmark jobs by amounts that reflect the differences in counterpart jobs in the external economy. We would not expect to find that the "gender gap" for non-benchmark, that is, nonmarket, jobs would exceed that found in the benchmark jobs. To the extent that the pay gap for nonbenchmark jobs is larger, it should be reduced to comparable size (i.e., comparable with the gap in the benchmark job set) once relevant productivity factors are taken into account statistically. Second, the administered efficiency model implies that the correlation between "femaleness" and pay rate in the nonbenchmark jobs themselves will disappear when controls are put in place for legitimate sources of earnings differences. In Washington, these legitimate sources include the nature of the duties of the job and its institutional context (these are captured in our model by the job family, job series, and managerial responsibility variables), and also the place of jobs in the internal mobility system (these are captured by our "entry-level" variable and the "series position" variable). As the later analysis demonstrates, these factors constitute a comprehensive set of controls that predict a substantial proportion of the variation in between-job pay rates.

Results of Statistical Analysis of Pay System

Job Classification Plan

We begin the analysis of the DOP system with a descriptive overview of job, wage, and gender distributions. In Table 6.1, three categories of jobs are defined according to their positions in the benchmark indexing system. The first is jobs that are themselves benchmarks. In principle, the wages for all jobs of this type are directly determined by reference to wage rates in similar jobs outside the DOP system. For some jobs, these external rates are ascertained by means of a survey of other public and private employers in the State of Washington; for others, the rates are derived by surveying wage rates for similar jobs out of state, for example, comparable positions in the state governments of Oregon, Idaho, and so on. In this table, jobs that are not benchmarks are further divided into those which are in the same series as benchmark jobs and those which are not. For example, "clerk typist 1" is in the same job series as "clerk typist 2," a benchmark job, and would thus be classified into the second row of Table 6.1. Nonseries jobs and jobs in series without benchmarks

Table 6.1. Distribution of Number of Jobs and Workers by Benchmark Status of Job, Department of Personnel, State of Washington, 1982

Benchmark Status of Job	Percent Female in Job				Job Incumbents (%)		
	All	0%–30%	31%–70%	71%–100%	All	Male	Female
Benchmark	5.8	4.5	10.4	5.9	36.6	32.8	40.6
Nonbenchmark							
Benchmark in series	12.5	11.3	15.9	13.4	22.3	17.1	27.8
Other	81.7	84.2	73.7	80.7	41.0	50.1	31.5
Total	100	100	100	100	99.9	100	99.9
N	(1,652)	(1,057)	(289)	(306)	(33,515)	(17,124)	(16,391)

Table 6.2. *Mean Size of Job and Deviation from Benchmark Job by Sex Composition of Job, Department of Personnel, State of Washington, 1983*

Percent Female in Job Class	No. of Jobs	Mean Size	Mean Percent Female in Benchmark	Mean Monthly Starting Wage
0	802	4.8	20.9	$2,129
1–10	63	66.3	17.3	1,878
11–20	114	19.0	26.6	1,859
21–30	92	23.9	34.0	1,858
31–50	192	20.5	43.4	1,806
51–70	102	62.4	51.6	1,540
71–80	57	39.4	63.6	1,422
81–90	44	69.9	69.4	1,297
91–99	32	139.5	82.2	1,212
100	181	5.7	53.4	1,567

appear in the third row of this table. The purpose of this classification is to provide a rough indication of how far removed jobs and their incumbents are from direct comparison with an external "going wage rate."

Table 6.1 demonstrates that benchmark jobs are a small minority – 6 percent – of all jobs in the DOP system, but because of their larger size, benchmark jobs employ nearly 37 percent of DOP employees. Breakdowns by sex type of job and gender of employee reveal an interesting pattern. Male jobs (defined as 30 percent female or less) are less likely to be benchmarks and are less likely to be in a job series containing a benchmark. While mixed-sex jobs are most likely to be benchmarks, the effect on employees of different genders is not a neutral one. The last two columns of the table show that a much higher percentage of men (50 percent vs. 32 percent) are in positions that are least exposed to external comparisons and a higher percentage of women than men are employed in benchmark jobs per se. Whether this contributes to overall wage inequality will be examined later.

Table 6.2 summarizes information about job size and wages for jobs with different gender compositions. The fourth column of Table 6.2 provides some preliminary impressions of the character of the benchmark indexing system described earlier. Here there is a trend, but an irregular one, for jobs with higher proportions of females to be indexed to benchmark jobs that are more heavily female. Thus, the benchmark job for the "average job" that is 91–99 percent female is itself 82 percent female.

At this level of detail, however, such comparisons are hardly surprising or profound. Given the system of job families and job series discussed earlier, there is a natural tendency for jobs that are in related families to have both similar gender compositions and similar or identical benchmark jobs. Table 6.2 also provides an impression of the gross differentials in salary levels between jobs with varying sex compositions. Although the salary levels more or less gradually decrease as jobs become more female, predominantly male jobs have salaries that are roughly 50 percent higher than predominantly female jobs. It is important to keep in mind that these salary figures are the minimum salary level for each job's pay range and thus are unaffected by different levels of employee tenure in different types of jobs.

Earnings Differences

Benchmark versus Indexed Jobs. To put our investigation of the pay structure in its proper context, we first consider how position in the system (i.e., being in a benchmark vs. indexed job) affects the salaries of individual employees. In Table 6.3 we present our analysis of the determinants of individuals' earnings as reported in the 1980 census.[2] Earnings functions were estimated separately for DOP employees in two types of occupations – those containing benchmark jobs and those containing only "indexed" jobs (see panel A). The former, we have argued, are more closely linked to external prevailing wage rates than the latter under the terms of the DOP pay plan. Obviously, the decennial census does not classify individual respondents explicitly on this attribute of their jobs. However, incumbency in a benchmark job classification can be estimated on the basis of the individual's detailed occupation category. Using the job descriptions provided in the state's salary survey plan, we coded the ninety-six benchmark jobs into detailed census categories. The DOP respondents who reported an occupation included on this list (the

2 These selection criteria produced an analysis sample totaling 87,020 respondents: 3 percent of these were classified as state DOP employees, 1.9 percent as state higher education system (HEPB) employees, and 95.1 percent as nonstate employees. The variables used in the subsequent statistical analysis include income ("wage or salary in 1979"), completed years of schooling, race (blacks coded "1," others "0"), sex (females coded "1," males "0"), Spanish origin (Mexican, Puerto Rican, Cuban, and other Spanish coded "1," others "0"), English language facility from (speaks only English, coded "0," to speaks no English, coded "4"), marital status (currently married coded "1," others coded "0"), hours worked in 1979 (computed from weeks worked times number of hours worked per week), experience and experience squared (computed from age minus imputed age of school leaving [education plus six years]); and disability status (with a work disability coded "0," no work disability coded "1").

Table 6.3. *Comparison of Earnings Functions in Benchmark and Nonbenchmark Occupations in Selected Industry Categories, 1980 Census of Population Data*

	Nonbenchmark Jobs		Benchmark Jobs	
	Unstandardized	Standardized	Unstandardized	Standardized
A. State DOP sample				
Intercept	−7,449.3*	—	−11,561.9*	—
Hours worked yearly	4.51*	0.359	5.07*	0.381
English-language problems	−825.64	−0.038	−393.09	−0.019
Race	−2,564.34*	−0.061	−167.23	−0.003
Spanish origin	−1,475.34	−0.029	−962.42	−0.017
Years of school completed	537.49*	0.176	723.34*	0.232
Experience	392.61*	0.672	420.45*	0.686
Experience squared	−6.31*	−0.539	−6.34*	−0.491
Marital status	1,584.41*	0.093	716.22*	0.042
Female	−5,406.86*	−0.322	−4,076.46*	−0.250
No work disability	1,752.58*	0.051	1,614.21*	0.049
R^2 (adj.)		0.519		0.470
No. of observations		901		1,627
Mean income		$13,142		$13,682
Ratio of predicted incomes (female/male)		0.650		0.742
B. Aerospace sample				
Intercept	−6,648.74*	—	−14,647.69*	—
Hours worked yearly	4.13*	0.226	7.32*	0.271
English-language problems	−1,074.49*	−0.034	−856.09	−0.020
Race	−1,106.21	−0.017	1,086.67	0.016
Spanish origin	−6,961.69*	−0.076	−877.54	−0.010
Years of school completed	667.57*	0.166	964.52*	0.208
Experience	661.54*	0.979	550.44*	0.565
Experience squared	−10.22*	−0.715	−6.63*	−0.310
Marital status	2,254.08*	0.121	1,228.46*	0.048
Female	−6,238.94*	−0.334	−9,820.47*	−0.414
No work disability	2,121.56*	0.050	4,070.13*	0.062
R^2 (adj.)		0.430		0.578
No. of observations		1,975		926
Mean income		$19,730		$20,180
Ratio of predicted incomes (female/male)		0.711		0.613
C. Other industry sample				
Intercept	−5,339.12*	—	−9,879.18*	—
Hours worked yearly	4.27*	0.307	4.87*	0.310
English-language problems	−912.10*	−0.038	−605.83*	−0.019
Race	−397.85	−0.005	−1,383.40*	−0.018

Table 6.3. *(cont.)*

	Nonbenchmark Jobs		Benchmark Jobs	
	Unstandardized	Standardized	Unstandardized	Standardized
Spanish origin	−186.38	−0.002	−115.64	−0.001
Years of school completed	502.62*	0.112	872.68*	0.186
Experience	414.38*	0.544	366.71*	0.437
Experience squared	−6.49*	−0.404	−5.42*	−0.315
Marital status	873.93*	0.040	951.71*	0.040
Female	−6,290.02*	−0.299	−6,792.94*	−0.285
No work disability	2,459.10*	0.050	2,229.05*	0.041
R^2 (adj.)		0.375		0.349
No. of observations		31,514		29,864
Mean income		$11,852		$12,140
Ratio of predicted incomes (female/male)		0.578		0.586

* Coefficient or difference significant $p < 0.05$.

implied benchmark list) were coded as benchmark job workers; the others were not.[3]

Income in both sets of occupations is strongly influenced by the usual proxy variables for investment in human capital – completed education, work experience, and good health. Furthermore, both groups are marked by residual earnings differences between men and women and blacks and whites (although the race differences are not statistically significant in

3   The procedure for generating the "implied list" of benchmark jobs was as follows: The job title of each Washington State benchmark job was referred to the 1980 Alphabetical Index of Occupations and Industries (U.S. Bureau of the Census 1980), and the corresponding three-digit occupation code number was added to the list. This resulted in a total of sixty-four census occupation codes' being used to represent ninety-six benchmark jobs. For example, the DOP classification "information officer 1" was linked to the 1980 census occupation "public relations specialist" (no. 332). The likely bias in this procedure is to classify too many census respondents into the benchmark job category. Comparison of the relative frequencies from the census and court records confirms that there is an overrepresentation in this direction. In the census sample of individuals, 65.7 percent are classified as working in benchmark positions. When the DOP sample of jobs is weighted by the number of incumbents in each, 36.6 percent of DOP workers are found to be in benchmark jobs. The classification procedure used for census respondents has probably produced a sample of nonbenchmark workers that is relatively clean; i.e., it does not include any of those in benchmark jobs, and a sample of benchmark workers that includes some who do not belong there. The two samples do resemble each other in one important respect, however. The census sample shows that benchmark jobs have a sex composition of 52 percent female and 48 percent male, while the nonbenchmark jobs are 43 percent female and 57 percent male. The DOP

the benchmark occupation group). Of greater interest, however, is the fact that the unexplained pay gap between men and women is significantly larger ($t = 2.60$) in the indexed jobs than in the benchmarks. (The race difference shows the same pattern, but barely misses statistical significance; t = 1.95.) Moreover, not only is the absolute gender earnings difference smaller among the benchmark occupations, but the ratio of female-to-male earnings (adjusted for other factors) is higher there (74 percent vs. 65 percent). Taken at face value, this result is inconsistent with the premises of the administered efficiency model.

This larger residual, however, is potentially the result of something unique about this set of nonbenchmark occupations that would dispose them to have higher earnings disparities in the world at large, not just in the State of Washington pay system. To evaluate this possibility, we have conducted a parallel analysis on the nonstate portion of the Washington public use micro sample. Because the State of Washington is a large employer, a type of organization that has repeatedly been shown to differ from small employers (Villemez and Bridges 1988; Hodson 1983; Kalleberg, Wallace, and Althauser 1981), we have subdivided the nonstate employees into two groups – workers in the aerospace industry and workers in all other industries. The former group is overwhelmingly employed in Washington State by a single large employer and provides an especially meaningful comparison in this context. Panels B and C of Table 6.3 present the regression results for these groups. To preserve maximum occupational comparability with the DOP work force, we weighted the nonstate samples with the relative occupational frequencies in the DOP labor force.

The crucial lesson to be learned about gender disparities from this table is that the difference between benchmark and nonbenchmark jobs in the state DOP is indeed unusual compared with two relevant external markets. The same occupations – the benchmarks – that have smaller relative gender coefficients within the DOP (as measured by comparing the absolute values of the unstandardized coefficient for the female dummy variable) have larger coefficients in the two external samples (i.e., in aerospace −$9,820 is larger than −$6,239, and in other industries −$6,792 is larger than −$6,290). Furthermore, the pay gap as measured by the adjusted income ratio between women and men also is peculiar in the DOP. The pay gap is larger in the nonbenchmark jobs than in the

records indicate a sex composition for benchmark jobs of 54 percent female and 46 percent male, and in nonbenchmark jobs of 46 percent female and 54 percent male. Thus, both samples show that benchmark jobs are disproportionately occupied by females and both agree about the relative size of the disproportion. Furthermore, once these proportions are weighted by the size of the benchmark jobs in each sample, they produce identical estimates of the overall proportion of DOP workers who are female, 49 percent.

benchmark, market-oriented jobs. In aerospace the opposite pattern prevails, and in other industries there is essentially no difference in the ratio. We conclude from Table 6.3 that the larger pay gap for indexed, non-benchmark jobs in the DOP does not result from occupational patterns that are prevalent in the entire economy.

Readers are strongly cautioned against overinterpreting the data shown in Table 6.3. Comparisons with external employers have been made solely for the purpose of ruling out "marketwide" occupational patterns as a competing explanation for the difference between benchmark and nonbenchmark jobs. In particular, comparisons of dummy-variable coefficients for gender across employers are especially treacherous since the mean incomes are so different. In fact, we suggest that the pattern of income ratios shown in this table should give pause to anyone attempting simplistic generalizations about whether state and other governmental employers discriminate more or less than other employers. At a minimum, this depends on specifying which other employers one is referring to.

Pay Differences in Nonbenchmark Jobs. Thus the census data run counter to expectations based on the administered efficiency model that male and female wage differences, after one controls for human capital characteristics, would be larger for benchmark (market-oriented) jobs than for nonbenchmark (nonmarket-oriented) jobs. Our qualitative examination of how the DOP calibrates wages for jobs does provide a plausible account for such a pattern, however. Efficiency considerations often compete with other powerful organizational principles in the determination of wage rates. Because the wage rates of indexed jobs are not directly compared against market referents in a wage survey process, and thus are determined by discretionary judgments about which benchmarks they should be indexed to and the number of deviations above or below the benchmark they should be indexed at, they may be more susceptible to the influence of these competing principles than are the wage levels of benchmark jobs. The loosening of efficiency constraints in the indexing process may well allow various invidious effects on pay decisions, including the introduction of gender bias. Two examples of principles that conflict with strict adherence to efficiency norms will illustrate.

There is a strong tendency for the DOP to honor the "equitable" or "customary" wage expectations of workers and managers. The manager of the wage survey reported traditional expectations of agencies and employee organizations are an important consideration in determining pay differentials among jobs (Dep. I, pp. 57–62). Several informants recounted instances indicating the sensitivity of employees to changes in job titles and pay levels that affected (or appeared to affect) their standing vis-à-vis other workers. Both management and workers have come to look at wage differentials among jobs as a kind of natural, normative order that should be observed even when there is no clear rationale. The effect of these norms is documented most clearly in cases where the DOP decided to maintain consistency with traditional alignments rather than change rates in the direction indicated by the wage survey. Some of these decisions can be interpreted as being consistent with differences in working conditions or job responsibility, such as when institutional cooks were given wage rates above those indicated in the survey because of the unique difficulties of having to work with prisoners and mental hospital inmates (Dep. I, pp. 53–56). Several other instances, however, appear to reflect mere deference to custom, as when adjustments were made to preserve internal alignments between reproduction technicians and clerical workers (Dep. III, p. 98), between lab technicians and medical technologists (Dep. V, p. 140), between food service aides and licensed practical nurses, laundry workers, and attendant counselors (Dep. III, p. 17), and between personnel officers, agency accounts officers, and other professional and administrative classes (Dep. IV, pp. 48–59). The force of custom, operating independently of efficiency principles, may well be a significant source of gender bias in decisions on the pay of nonbenchmark jobs.

The pay bureaucracy also is committed to the principle of maintaining continuity in relative wage rates over time (even if this produces departures from technically rational wage levels). This concern has become virtually an end in itself. The manager of the salary survey reported that relative wage relationships established in the first systematic pay plan developed in 1963 were relatively intact in the early 1970s (Dep. I, p. 120). When formal indexing was introduced in 1976, it merely codified twenty years of decisions on wage levels reached through informal consultations between the DOP staff, agencies, and employee organizations: "We had the same staff working on survey after survey, so usually there was continuity among personnel officers and employee representatives, so many of the decisions [from earlier years] were retained." The new system preserved the "informal understood relationship[s]" about relative pay levels (Dep. III, pp. 84–88), so that "[a] lot of the alignments we have now have been what you might consider traditional. They've been used over a long period of time and found to be workable" (Dep. I, p. 60). According to one of the inventors of the benchmark indexing system, the formalization of indexing froze relative wage levels and limited the degree to which indexing took account of changing technology and job content. In the view of this informant, the DOP departed from the original conception of indexing as an admittedly subjective, but fluid, tool for assessing the relative values of jobs. This implies that wage differentials among nonbenchmark jobs would be unlikely to mirror changes in their "marginal productivity."

Departures from efficiency criteria in pay decisions also occur by default or bureaucratic intransigence. In theory, the adequacy of wage levels can best be examined by analyzing the relationship between wage levels and patterns of recruitment or retention for specific jobs. Although agencies and employee organizations use turnover data when arguing for pay raises for particular jobs, the DOP does not collect centralized turnover data, does not require agencies to keep or present turnover data in standard fashion, has never studied the relationship between turnover and pay rates, and does not retain the turnover statistics that are presented from one year to the next (Dep. I, p. 125; Dep. III, pp. 8–10; Dep. IV, pp. 54, 60–61, 104–6). The inconsistent use of turnover statistics may well contribute to gender inequality. An agency official informed us that predominantly male craft jobs received special above-survey wage rates when experiencing less than 10 percent turnover, while nurses did not receive special pay until turnover rates exceeded 50 percent (personal interview, 1988).

This disruption of orderly efficiency by forces inherent in internal labor markets has been recognized by other scholars, most notably Doeringer and Piore (1971). In fact, their analysis suggests that both formal pay systems and the influence of social custom are permitted to operate by the looseness of competitive forces in internal labor markets. Moreover, they imply that custom and wage structures are required to operate in these settings to resolve the indeterminacy that would result from the application of neoclassical principles to the special circumstances of internal markets. While our data confirm that both custom and administrative regulation play central roles in the DOP, our findings also suggest that more is involved than either social inertia or long-run cost minimization. To present a more systematic account of the relative effect of administered efficiency considerations versus other organizational factors, we examine quantitative data on the pay system itself. Here we rely extensively on a job-level analysis of data that were presented to the court in *AFSCME*. In the *AFSCME* case, the plaintiffs submitted a large volume of documents, including job-level data for roughly sixteen hundred positions in the DOP job system. The reanalysis reported here is based on those jobs in the DOP system in 1982 for which completed information is available in tabular form in the various supplementary excerpts.

While the full details of this analysis are available elsewhere (Bridges and Nelson 1989), the key findings can be summarized rather easily. The starting salary rates for jobs that are predominantly female are lower for a variety of reasons, some consistent with economic efficiency arguments and some not. For example, jobs that require completion of a four-year college degree program have higher salaries in general than those that require only two years of post–high school "commercial" training. To the extent that jobs with more than their share of women have lower educational requirements they will be paid less. Or, to the extent that a job is at the top of a promotion sequence (e.g., cartographer 5 compared with cartographer 1), it will also be paid more generously. Jobs also differ according to the values assigned to them during the job evaluation process, and pay differences associated with these ratings are, by and large, economically rational.

However, the pay system itself introduces two additional influences on a job's pay rate that are not anticipated by conventional efficiency explanations. Jobs that are not themselves benchmarks have to be paired with benchmark jobs, a process that establishes a first-level approximation to the ultimate value of the job. Second, once these preliminary valuations are accomplished the precise value of the job in question is set by establishing its deviation from the benchmark job's salary range. Both of these processes are important because there are informal limits on how wide the deviation values are permitted to be. Thus, psychiatrists in state mental hospitals could be indexed many ranges above ward attendents, but they are not. Everything else equal, it is better to be indexed to a benchmark job that has a higher salary. And, of course, given which benchmark a job is linked to, it is better to be above rather than below that benchmark.

What our analysis reveals is that, after controlling for a plethora of "efficiency relevant" factors such as educational requirements and series position, jobs that are more heavily female have two distinct characteristics. First, they are more likely to be paired with benchmarks that are themselves disproportionately female. That is, despite the fact that a variety of other job family and job series relationships have been controlled, each 10 percent increase in the female composition of an indexed (i.e., nonbenchmark) job is associated with a 1 percent increase in the percent female in the benchmark. This indicates the strong possibility of residual sex stereotyping in the establishment of links between indexed jobs and their benchmarks. And, because female benchmarks have lower salaries than male benchmarks (for whatever reasons – discrimination, occupational crowding, choice-based oversupply), this stereotyping also lowers salaries in jobs with a higher proportion of females.

Furthermore, jobs with a higher proportion of female workers have consistently lower deviation values from their benchmark ranges than jobs with more male workers. According to this model, because of this effect alone, jobs that are 100 percent female would have salaries 13 percent (i.e., five ranges) lower than jobs that are 100 percent male. At the median of the sex distribution (15 percent female for the median male, 75 percent for the median female), the gap would be about 8 percent, or three ranges. Although one might argue that omitted variables account for this effect, it is instructive to note that an extremely high proportion of variance (between 68 percent and 95 percent) has been accounted for in each dependent variable. Furthermore, these results are completely consistent with the pattern revealed in the census analysis. If in jobs that are not directly related to external prevailing wage rates there is a tendency systematically to lower the pay range of predominantly female jobs relative to their benchmarks, or raise predominantly male jobs relative to their benchmarks, one would expect to find pay disparities between men and women within this internal segment that persist after the benchmark component has been controlled. Thus, both the qualitative and quantitative data we have analyzed imply that the state pay bureaucracy does not simply reflect patterns of gender inequality in the market but is itself a source of gender inequality.

Interest Representation and Its Effects on the Pay System

In this section we advance the argument that the deviations from the administered efficiency model that we have observed are not just random errors or the result of "sloppy efficiency" but reflect the operation of bureaucratic politics in the salary-setting system. After identifying the main actors in the pay system, we analyze the effect of their participation on various categories of jobs and workers and consider more generally the effect of bureaucratic politics on gender inequality in the system.

The Main Actors

Decisions on pay levels are made through ongoing interactions among a set of organizational actors, the most important being (1) the DOP itself (which consists of a politically appointed, part-time board and a large permanent staff), (2) the state agencies that employ various job categories, and (3) employee organizations (such as the Washington Federation of State Employees), which, in the absence of collective bargaining over state pay levels, consult with the DOP staff during the wage survey and bring the claims of various workers to the DOP board. Each actor brings a particular set of interests and resources to the wage-setting process.

The DOP. The DOP is the focal point of the activity of participants in the pay system but is not merely a passive receptacle of interest representation. The DOP created and controls the wage survey; it is the basis for much of the department's claim to status and resources in the state bureaucracy. As such, the DOP staff has attempted to accommodate pressures from various constituencies by operating the wage survey as a kind of pluralist technocracy; that is, the survey is organized and presented as a technical function but one that responds to appeals from various groups, even on low-visibility decisions about survey methods (see subsequent discussion). Ultimate decisions on pay are made by the DOP board after public hearings. The board generally defers to staff recommendations but occasionally overrules staff decisions on the basis of presentations by employee groups and agencies. To avoid criticism from agencies and employee organizations, the DOP staff has attempted to maintain stable relative wage levels; to maintain credibility with the fiscally conservative state legislature, it has minimized estimates of aggregate salary increases. Thus, for example, the survey manager reported that even though data on small employers were questionable on technical grounds and were "not cost efficient" to collect, they were used anyway: "Politically it goes a long way towards selling the credibility of the Survey, so we would not be inclined to make any modifications" (Dep. I, p. 212).

Notwithstanding its sensitivity to political context, the DOP staff pursues goals that are characteristic of bureaucratic organizations: It attempts to impose technical and procedural rationality in a system permeated with particularism and unpredictable events. Although the DOP is subject to ongoing appeals to reassign various jobs to different pay ranges, its staff has a strong preference for limiting such changes to the implementation of the biennial survey. More radical changes always run the risk of violating workers' sense of equity, which they equate with the existing regime of relative pay levels. This orientation also is embodied in its evaluation of the comparable worth settlement adopted in 1985, to which it objected not for substantive or value reasons but on the grounds that the settlement has infused the once orderly pay matrix with a welter of complicated irregularities.

State Agencies. State agencies participate in wage survey deliberations as part of their competition for state resources. The key actors in each agency are its personnel officials. As representatives of their agencies before the DOP, they actively screen requests for pay increases from the division heads and employee groups of their agencies to determine what claims the agencies will officially propose to the DOP. Without prompting from us, the agency officials interviewed consistently characterized the salary-setting system as "political" (personal interview, 1988). Their usage was not merely idiomatic. According to these informants, agencies with more political resources (such as the Department of Labor and Industries) commanded better wages for their employees than did agencies (such as the Department of Social and Health Services) that were politically unpopular because of the kinds of functions they performed. A personnel official said the same was true in his agency in that the political standing of subunits affected his decisions to present cases for pay increases. This informant recounted an instance when he had denied a unit manager's request that the personnel office lobby for a pay increase for a particular job category but had later helped the unit manager formulate a strategy for getting the job indexed to a different, higher-paying benchmark (personal interview, 1988).

Employee Organizations. Employee organizations pursue different strategies with respect to the pay system depending on the nature of the employees they represent and the kinds of political resources they control. Although other unions representing trade crafts or other specific occupational groups (such as retail clerks) have participated in DOP pay proceedings, by far the most important of these has been the state chapter of AFSCME, the WFSE. The federation's long-standing policy has been to oppose collective bargaining over wage levels. According to federation officials, it has preferred the wage survey over collective bargaining because it had an intrinsic appeal to politicians and voters: State workers were making neither more nor less than workers in the private sector (personal interview, 1988). Other informants were more skeptical of the federation's motives, suggesting that the federation saw the existing pay system as one it could more effectively manipulate by "walking across the street" to officials in the state capitol or through the disbursement of political action committee funds to office seekers (personal interview, 1988).

The federation has enjoyed an insider role in the pay system. A federation official described how in the 1960s and early 1970s, his organization's officials were involved in informal meetings after the formal meetings; in these "smoke-filled rooms" real negotiations on relative wage rates and overall pay increases were worked out with representatives of key agencies, legislators, and state budget officials (personal interview, 1988). This informant indicated that the formalization of the wage survey and budget planning had significantly "opened up" the process. Informants assert, nonetheless, that the federation remains influential in the current salary-setting process. As one state official suggested, "The federation always says that they are outside the system. But the unions have bargained and compromised the system into what it is today" (personal interview, 1988).

These observations by informants lend credibility to conceiving of DOP's salary determination process as a system of bureaucratic politics. Interviews with participants establish that they continually argue and negotiate about the very rules that define the wage-setting system – its jurisdictional structure, the use of a prevailing rate standard rather than collective bargaining, the inclusion of small employers in the wage survey, and so forth. Moreover, within the structure of these rules, groups continue to pursue strategies to advance their goals. Putatively technical questions become the arena for political contests. An informant described an instance in which he thought the DOP staff had intentionally underestimated the complexity of tasks associated with a particular job to undercut his recommendations for a pay raise. In response his organization hired and trained a job evaluation expert to participate in future job evaluations; the new employee was instructed to "insist on certain [results]" and justify them technically "one way or another." The informant went on to suggest that if the DOP staff remained recalcitrant, he would force a confrontation before the DOP board, which, he predicted, "would be a fight I would win" (personal interview, 1988).

The Underrepresentation of Female Workers

A particularly significant dimension of the configuration of employee organizations active in the pay system is the absence of groups that unambiguously lobby for women's interests. Groups that traditionally represented women, such as the Washington State Nurses Association, were consistently described as passive and ineffective on pay issues (personal interview, 1988). Only in the years since 1982 have there emerged union locals headed by women that have begun to represent predominantly female job classes more aggressively. Unlike the federation, however, these new groups have not focused on working within the existing pay decision process. Rather they have sought to supplant the current wage survey with collective bargaining. Informants from these organizations suggested that collective bargaining offered them a significantly improved position in the system, because "everyone would have a place at the bargaining table," even if their organizations did not have the largest memberships or the most financial resources (personal interview, 1988).

The lack of direct involvement by women's organizations in the pay process makes the role of the federation as a representative of women's interests all the more critical. Federation officials claim that they demonstrated their commitment to gender equality by sponsoring the AFSCME litigation. Yet other informants suggested that the federation was motivated in part by its concern that other more radically feminist unions might encroach on its turf, that some local leadership viewed the litigation as a "nuisance," and that the primary impetus for the lawsuit came from AFSCME's national office (personal interview, 1988). The federation's current membership is still roughly only half female, and, at the time of the filing of the lawsuit, women constituted a smaller proportion. Even now federation officials make clear that their efforts to advance comparable worth were never to be at the expense of male members. As one official said, the federation has never advocated "robbing Peter to pay Pauline" (personal interview, 1988). Indeed, the federation remains pragmatic in its approach to prevailing rates and comparable worth. An official openly stated that the federation's objective is simply "to get the most money for [its] members." To do so, it would give priority to obtaining the prevailing rates indicated in the wage survey and would then attempt to add comparable worth bonuses on top of that (personal interview, 1988). Despite its support for the *AFSCME* case, it is an open question whether the federation has been equally forceful in pressing the pay claims of predominantly male and predominantly female jobs.

It is doubtful that the other main advocates for pay raises in the system, agency personnel officers, have been equally active in representing the interests of predominantly male and predominantly female jobs. Inspection of the sex composition of top positions in state agencies reveals that they are overwhelmingly male. As noted earlier, the political status of subunits within agencies influences decisions about which claims to press before the DOP. Because women are less likely to occupy powerful positions in the agencies, agency officials are less likely to exert influence on behalf of women's claims. Moreover, it was apparent from our interviews with the leaders of the recently arrived women's unions that there were antagonistic relationships between these groups and some of the major agency personnel heads with whom they had to deal. Even though agency personnel officers are crucial as channels of influence on DOP pay decisions, these advocacy groups dismissed the possibility that agency officials would work with them in making proposals for pay increases for female job categories (personal interviews, 1988).

Some Effects of Interest Representation on Wage-Determination Outcomes

Having described the orientations of the main actors in the pay system, we now turn to the effects of their participation on wage setting generally and gender inequality in particular.

Pressures for Result-Oriented Decisions. The analysis to this point has emphasized our finding that pay decisions concerning nonbenchmark (indexed) jobs have been a significant source of gender disparities that cannot be explained by market or efficiency principles. We have tacitly assumed that the DOP's measurement of market rates for benchmark jobs is more directly controlled by a logic of administered efficiency and thus is less affected by countervailing norms and processes. While we continue to subscribe to the view that there is more discretion in setting wages for nonbenchmark jobs than for benchmark jobs, it is instructive to examine the degree to which the wage survey itself is affected by organizational politics. Drawing on the testimony of survey managers, Table 6.4 summarizes the major stages of the salary survey. It documents how employing agencies and employee organizations participate in virtually every stage of the indexing system and wage survey. The DOP consults with agencies and employee groups about what benchmark jobs to survey, whether to use in-state or out-of-state benchmarks for particular jobs, whether to use special surveys rather than the typical sampling approach, how to write job descriptions for comparisons with other employers' positions, what cases to drop as having insufficient data, what results to audit, and even what results to ignore in final wage recommendations. These exchanges affect a significant portion of survey result – between 10 and 20 percent in 1982, according to the survey manager (Dep. II, pp. 7–10).

Many of these consultations involve efforts by the agencies or employee groups to achieve particular results. The DOP staff will audit any survey result an agency questions (Dep. II, p. 19). Thus, one phase of the auditing of results is entirely nonrandom and is dictated by demands from agencies and employee groups. For example, in response to a request from the state patrol, the DOP was asked to check the survey results for communications technicians. After the first audit, the DOP increased the survey result by one pay range. According to the survey manager, "The agencies were [not] enthusiastic about the results, and they suggested that we make a reevaluation of some of the data, which we did. We . . . found some that probably were questionable, some of the data, and I think following this stage, the weighted average was increased . . . three range[s]" (Dep. II, p. 12). When asked how the data were questionable, the survey manager said that it appeared that some of the small employer results probably were not comparable; they were dropped from the sample, with the predictable effect of raising the weighted average (Dep. II, pp. 12–13). Informants suggested that there was at least some conscious manipulation of overall survey results as well. On one occasion the DOP survey results indicated a significantly lower percentage increase in pay levels than those offered for similar jobs

Table 6.4. *Major Stages of the Wage Survey, State of Washington, Department of Personnel*

Procedural Stage	Responsible Officials	Other Participants	Data Sources
Decisions on composition of "job families" and "job series"	DOP staff	Agencies, employee organizations	Dep. IV, p. 67
Indexing nonbenchmark jobs to benchmark jobs	DOP staff	Agencies, employee organizations	Dep. III, pp. 87, 96; Tr. Vol. III, p. 26
Plan for actual survey	DOP staff	Legislative budget committee, agencies, employee organizations	Dep. I, pp. 36–38; Dep. V, p. 75; Tr. Vol. III, p. 38
1. Selection of benchmarks	DOP staff	Legislative budget committee, agencies, employee organizations	Dep. I, pp. 43–45, 65; Dep. II, p. 51; Dep. IV, p. 11
2. Choice of in-state, out-of-state, or special survey	DOP staff	Legislative budget committee, agencies, employee organizations	Dep. I, p. 38; Dep. I, p. 147; Tr. Vol. III, pp. 59–60; Dep. II, pp. 1–7; Dep. I, p. 38; Dep. I, p. 178 et seq.
3. Decisions on sampling by employer size	DOP staff	Legislative budget committee, agencies, employee organizations	Dep. I, p. 37
Review of survey results before preliminary release[a]	DOP staff	Agencies, employee organizations	Dep. I, pp. 7–13; Tr. Vol. III, pp. 75–76
Consultations on preliminary survey report	DOP staff	Agencies, employee organizations	Dep. I, p. 65; Dep. V, p. 62
1. Dropping benchmarks	DOP staff	Agencies, employee organizations	Dep. II, pp. 51–53
2. Averaging benchmarks	DOP staff	Agencies, employee organizations	Dep. II, p. 54
3. Ignoring survey results	DOP staff	Agencies, employee organizations	Dep. III, pp. 96, 98
DOP staff recommendation to DOP board	DOP staff	Agencies, employee organizations	Tr. Vol. III, p. 26
Hearing on staff recommendation after 20-day notice	DOP board	Agencies, employee organizations	Dep. I, p. 166; Dep. III, p. 96; Tr. Vol. II, pp. 94–96
Board recommendations to legislature incorporating board's changes in staff recommendations	DOP board		Dep. III, p. 96; Dep. IV, p. 64

[a] Includes auditing results for particular jobs resulting from dropping some employers and dropping cases for low response rate, unexpected results, etc.

in the higher education personnel system. According to an informant, the divergence was created by DOP officials who "had their eyes" on what percentage increase the legislature would tolerate (personal interview, 1988).

These observations demonstrate that the definition of "market rates" is itself an organizational process that attracts the efforts of organizational actors to shape the results. The market is to some extent socially constructed by the employing organization. In sum, interest group politics is pervasive and affects pay decisions on both benchmark and nonbenchmark jobs.

Interest Representation and Salary Adjustments. Thus far, we have found high levels of interest group participation in a pay system that exhibits significant gender inequality. Is this mere coincidence or is there a direct link between patterns of interest group activity and specific decisions that disadvantage women relative to men? In the absence of "smoking gun" evidence of gender bias, the best one can do to address the question is to examine a set of specific pay decisions to determine the effect of interest representation on different categories of workers.

In the course of a lengthy deposition, the plaintiffs' lawyer questioned the manager of the wage survey about a definable set of actions taken in 1982, including decisions to drop, add, and average benchmarks; decisions to deviate from survey findings; the conduct of special surveys; and provisions for extra-pay assignments. Forty-eight job classes were covered in the questioning.[4] The job classes discussed were coded according to sex composition in 1982; whether there was any explicit reference to participation in the decision by an agency, an employee organization, or an employee group; and whether the effect of the decision on the job

---

4   It was possible to identify the lists of jobs the lawyer based his questioning on. Therefore, we know that the jobs were not systematically selected by the plaintiffs' lawyer to present his clients' case in a more favorable light. The only jobs discussed, however, were those affected by some kind of action taken. That is, no questions were asked about decisions that resulted in leaving the survey results or methods undisturbed. Also included is a small number of examples brought up by the witness himself. Those forty-eight "cases" represent only a small number of decisions made in the course of the wage survey. Because these decisions deal overwhelmingly with job classes that are benchmarks or for which other explicit documentation exists, they are far more visible than other survey judgments. While we can make no claim that these instances are representative of decisions made in the survey and indexing process generally, there is no reason a priori to suspect that they constitute a biased set for evaluating the extent to which agencies or employee groups participate in survey decisions or the extent to which their participation benefits jobs held predominantly by men or women. Indeed, given the relative visibility of decisions about these jobs, one might expect that the DOP would handle these decisions very carefully to avoid the appearance of undue influence or gender bias.

Table 6.5. *Favorability of Salary Adjustment Decisions by Role of Agency or Employee Organization by Sex Composition of Jobs, Department of Personnel, State of Washington, 1982*

| Agency/Union Role | Outcome | | | |
	Favorable	Unfavorable	Neutral/ Not Known	Total
A. *All jobs*				
Involvement mentioned	19	0	3	22
Involvement not mentioned	3	4	9	16
No discussion	—	—	10	10
Total	22	4	22	48
B. *Male jobs*				
Involvement mentioned	12	0	3	15
Involvement not mentioned	2	0	4	6
No discussion	—	—	10	10
Total	14	0	17	31
C. *Mixed or female jobs*				
Involvement mentioned	7	0	3	7
Involvement not mentioned	1	4	5	10
Total	8	4	5	17

class was favorable, unfavorable, or unknown. The results of this classification are shown in Table 6.5.[5]

Several patterns in the table are immediately obvious. In panel A, the extent of agency involvement is revealed by the fact that in the thirty-eight cases in which there is discussion of the reason for the adjustment, there is an explicit reference to the involvement of an agency or employee

---

5 We followed a conservative approach in our coding. If there was no clear reference to the participation of these groups, they were not classified as an instance of involvement. Thus groups may have participated in the decisions on some of the cases classified under "not mentioned" and "no discussion," but the record does not clearly disclose this. Many of the cases coded "no discussion" probably were affected by such involvement. In order to save time in the deposition, the lawyer established that the actions taken on five "no discussion" jobs were explained by the same types of reasons that held for the preceding cases. Although most of these had been identified as involving agencies or employee organizations, given the ambiguity of this umbrella characterization, we coded the five cases under "no discussion." Similarly, in determining whether the effects of an action were favorable or unfavorable, we required a clear indication from the record or from salary-survey documents. As a result we coded twenty-two cases as having "unknown/neutral" effects. In one-third of these twenty-two cases, jobs were changed to an average of other relatively well paid benchmarks, such as the trades or engineering groups. Again, we think these are probably favorable results, but without more specific information we coded the effects as unknown.

organization twenty-two times (see row 1). Significantly, there is an over-whelming tendency for these changes to raise salaries. And, if agencies or unions were involved, the results are universally favorable. The totals in panels B and C indicate that almost two-thirds of the actions (thirty-one out of forty-eight) are initiated for predominantly male jobs. The combination of these patterns – the prevalence of male jobs and the favorableness of the outcomes – necessarily dictates that many more male jobs than female or mixed jobs benefit from these adjustments. The second and third panels reveal an interesting sidelight to these patterns. When agencies and unions get involved in claims for female and mixed jobs, the results are just as good as they are for male jobs. Without this active intervention, however, the adjustments made to female and mixed jobs were favorable only one time in ten. This pattern suggests that people working in mixed or female jobs are disadvantaged by neglect (in the form of fewer agency or union claims on their behalf) rather than overt discrimination.

Within the limitations of these data, Table 6.5 provides support both for the prevalence of constituency involvement in salary setting and for the link between such involvement and the relative advantage of pre-dominantly male jobs. Agencies and employee groups occasionally advocate the interests of the incumbents of predominantly female jobs and, when they do, are successful. Far more often, however, they represent the interests of and win benefits for predominantly male jobs. For such a pattern to exist, it is not necessary that the DOP, the agencies, or employee organizations intentionally discriminate against women in the immediate context of these wage adjustment deliberations. However, such a pattern appears entirely consistent with the relatively weak posi-tion of women's organizations and predominantly female jobs in the configuration of the main actors in the pay system. Workers in predom-inantly female jobs have not enjoyed the same level of representation by agencies and unions as workers in predominantly male positions, with the result that decisions made in the course of the wage survey have con-tributed to gender inequality in pay.

The Preservation of Historical Disadvantage. The DOP has followed a set of practices that has tended to preserve historically based patterns of inequality in the pay system: It adopted a system of relative wages in the early 1960s, maintained "historical" and "traditional" pay alignments throughout the 1970s, never reduced wages for jobs even if survey results indicated such cuts (Dep I. pp. 99, 144–45), and granted several across-the-board pay increases that left the relative wage structure intact (Dep. IV, pp. 68–93). These tendencies were reinforced by the configuration of political interests in the pay system. The DOP has been reluctant to change relative wage levels because, in the words of a managing official, "anytime we tried to change it, we would hear from an agency or employee organization" (Dep. III, pp. 86–87).

This preservation of historical wage levels has most likely worked to the disadvantage of predominantly female jobs. An internal study by the DOP reported that in 1971, the ratio of female to male monthly salaries was 0.706 ($594/$841), and that 86.9 percent of women employees worked in "traditionally female positions." The study found that by 1976 there had been modest movement in these relative levels, with women earning 0.721 of average male earnings ($802/$1,112) and with 79.1 percent of female employees holding "traditionally female jobs." While the figures indicate a shrinking wage gap, the relevant consideration here is that patterns of gender inequality were more pronounced in an earlier period. In a market or organizational context in which the trend is to reduce the gender wage gap, policies that enhance continuity in relative wage levels will tend to retard reducing the wage differential.

The patterns that are so preserved are at least in part the product of the more explicitly gender-biased employment practices of an earlier era. The State of Washington, like many employers before the effective date of employment discrimination laws, followed employment policies that tended to segregate women in sex-stereotyped jobs. For example, the state advertised separately for at least some male and female jobs until 1973 (*AFSCME v. State of Washington*, 578 F. Supp. 846, at 860 [W.D. Wash. 1983]). Consistent with this fact, our own calculations reveal that the level of sex segregation among DOP jobs was higher in 1976 ($D = 69$) than in 1982 ($D = 63$; D = index of dissimilarity). These patterns concern job assignment rather than pay but certainly have implications for male-female wage differentials if the flow of applicants for positions is restricted along gender lines. Also if sex stereotyping was operating in job assignment during this earlier period, it is likely that it also was operating in decisions on pay levels in earlier years.

The model of administered efficiency, which conceives of management as a unitary, rational actor, cannot readily explain the patterns of interest representation that are pervasive in the Washington State pay system. Nor can it explain the significant departures from efficiency considerations that these organizational politics produce. We do not suggest that every deviation from the ideals of rational compensation systems should be read as the influence of bureaucratic politics. In systems such as this, however, where the principles and practices of salary setting can be traced to the interests and activities of key actors, sociological models of wage setting will be enriched by attending to the relationship between wage determination and organizational politics. In the present case the data suggest that the disadvantaged position of female workers in the bureaucratic politics of this system has both contributed to and tended to preserve inequality in pay between predominantly male and female jobs.

Conclusion

To understand gender inequality in systems like the State of Washington's, one must consider both market and organizational influences. Contrary to assumptions often made in sociological research on gender-based wage differences in large organizations, such organizations do interact with and are at least partially constrained by external labor market conditions. Substantial effort is devoted to monitoring the price of certain categories of labor, and the results of these inquiries are taken seriously by the officials of the system. To a considerable extent, they believe their pay-setting decisions reflect market conditions. And relative pay levels for male and female jobs in these large systems are often no more discrepant than for similar jobs in the external market.

Our quantitative assessment has shown that predominantly female jobs systematically pay less than predominantly male jobs even after we control for educational requirements, job family, rank in job series, indexing for job evaluation points, and the salaries of the market-oriented jobs themselves. Much of the gender inequality in the system is, therefore, the direct product of organizational decision making. The pattern we find runs directly counter to the conventional explanation of male-female wage differences, which holds that such differences result from market rather than organizational influences. Instead our results show that there is more inequality between predominantly male and predominantly female jobs for jobs that are removed from direct market comparisons than for those jobs that are market benchmarks.

The qualitative examination of the wage-setting process demonstrated how organizational processes can lead to this outcome. The wage survey that sets pay levels, first by establishing the prevailing rates for benchmark jobs and then by indexing the remaining jobs to the benchmarks, appears on the surface to be an objective, sex-neutral, almost scientific mechanism for measuring the market value of state jobs. Closer analysis indicates that the system is shot through with subjectivity, arbitrariness, and interest group politics, virtually from beginning to end. How the market is measured – the jobs that are surveyed, the firms or state governments used as reference points, what data are rejected as inaccurate – is very much subject to these pressures. The "market" is, to a significant degree, a social construction of the system. And while market rates may be an important consideration in determining pay levels, they are by no means the sole determinants. Equally powerful are considerations of political expedience, custom, and internal alignment. What looks at first to be a system based only on administered efficiency is in significant respects a system of bureaucratic politics. It appears that workers in predominantly female jobs have, until recently, been relatively powerless in the system. Their interests have not been as effectively represented by employee organizations or department heads as have the interests of male counterparts. The system's commitment to the preservation of historical patterns of pay differences among jobs also has locked predominantly female jobs into a relatively disadvantaged position.

There is a double irony to the political dimensions of this pay structure and the debate over comparable worth. The critics of comparable worth have suggested that proposals to pay jobs according to subjectively evaluated worth rather than market value should be seen as a garden variety form of rent seeking by a special interest (Fischel and Lazear 1986). Our analysis indicates that the wage-setting process in the State of Washington DOP has been a pervasively political, subjective process from its inception. The movement for pay equity in Washington, in the shape of both the *AFSCME* lawsuit and the legislation eventually adopting comparable worth to a limited extent, reflects female workers' collective efforts to deal with the state pay system on its own terms, that is, as a political system. They did not possess the resources to do so internally and therefore had to resort to a more fundamental, external attack on inequality in the system.

Our results in this chapter, as in Chapter 5, suggest that plaintiffs can find substantial evidence of disparate treatment of workers in predominantly female jobs without having to rely solely on job evaluation studies (what might be termed "pure comparable worth theories"). Now that we have examined organizational and market data in depth, we can better evaluate the empirical aspects of the appeals court opinion in *AFSCME*. Recall that when Judge Kennedy rejected the plaintiffs claims, he asserted, "Title VII does not obligate [the state] to eliminate an economic inequality it did not create" (*AFSCME*, p. 1407, n. 1). While it is outside the scope of this chapter to examine whether our results indicate "intentional" discrimination on the part of employers engaging in the kind of behavior we have observed, we are certain of one conclusion. It was not, as Justice Kennedy wrote, a simple reflection of market forces for which the employer was not responsible.

B. Private Sector Organizations

7

Corporate Politics, Rationalization, and Managerial Discretion: EEOC v. Sears, Roebuck & Co.

We now turn to patterns of gender inequality in pay in private sector organizations. The first case we consider is the massive litigation brought by the Equal Employment Opportunity Commission (EEOC) against Sears, Roebuck and Company, at that time the largest retailer of general merchandise in the United States.[1]

Sears employed some 380,000 workers in over 4,000 facilities in 1986 (*Sears* I, p. 1288; for abbreviations, see the appendix on court documents and case materials). A sophisticated personnel department had been in existence for several decades that ran training programs, regularly collected attitudinal and performance data about employees, and administered batteries of psychological tests used for hiring and promotion decisions. Yet Sears had been built on an ideology of decentralized management. Group, territorial, and store managers had largely unchecked authority in many organizational functions. Among the most significant was discretion in setting the salaries of more than 18,000 middle-level managers and supervisors who reported to them – a group known as "checklist" employees.

In the 1970s the highly decentralized character of Sears's personnel and compensation policies came under internal and external attack. Although Sears had adopted an affirmative action program in 1968, in 1973 the EEOC filed administrative charges of sex discrimination against the company. Perhaps in response to the threat of government sanction, top management made the program mandatory in 1974. Company officials ordered that one out of every two lower-level (known as time-card) positions be filled by women or minorities. The order was extended to upper-level, checklist jobs in 1979 (*Sears* I, pp. 1293–94). In 1975 external consultants retained by upper management reported that the compensation system was flawed by internal inequities, was not perceived as fair by employees, and resulted in Sears paying many em-

---

1   *EEOC v. Sears, Roebuck & Co.*, 628 F. Supp. 1264 (N.D.Ill. 1986) (hereafter *Sears* I); 839 F.2d 302 (7th Cir. 1988) (hereafter *Sears* II).

ployees more than what comparable positions commanded in the market (Hay Report May 1975, Jt. App., Vol. 14, p. 216 et seq.). As a consequence, in 1976 management adopted a centralized job evaluation-compensation program that sharply curtailed the discretion of store managers and other middle management in setting wages.

When the EEOC eventually sued Sears, one of the targets of the lawsuit was the gender differences in earnings for the checklist jobs for the period 1973–80.[2] Sears mounted an extremely vigorous defense to all aspects of the EEOC's complaint. The company attempted to portray itself as the victim of a plot between the EEOC and the National Organization for Women to make an example of the nation's largest retailer. With respect to the pay issues, Sears was in a potentially embarrassing position. The consultants it had retained had roundly criticized the checklist compensation policies as inefficient and decoupled from the market. In an apparent response to the consultants' suggestions, the company had initiated a fundamentally different compensation program in 1976, midway through the period covered in the government's complaint. Rather than back away from a defense of the earlier form of the checklist compensation system, Sears argued that whatever the system's faults, gender bias was not one of them.

Despite the presentation of apparently damning statistical evidence by the EEOC, Sears won at both the district court and appellate court levels. The opinions made clear that the EEOC had made a fatal mistake in presenting its case. It did not put one live victim of sex discrimination on the stand, choosing instead to rely exclusively on statistical data. Sears countered the statistical evidence with a welter of opposing expert accounts and criticisms. The trial court judge was persuaded that Sears had exercised business judgment rather than gender bias in how it constructed and operated its pay system. He characterized the early form of the compensation system as having "maximum flexibility . . . to respond to the surrounding markets" (*Sears* I, p. 1288). He similarly viewed several compensation practices that predictably disadvantaged female employees as reflecting reasonable business decisions.

The litigation against *Sears* illustrates the forces that shape gender inequality in large private sector organizations and thus allows us to test the explanatory power of market, efficiency, and inequality theories. The case brackets a period of considerable turmoil in the organization, when management was attempting to impose affirmative action and a uniform compensation system on an immense, highly decentralized enterprise. It

---

2   The lawsuit also asserted discrimination in hiring and promotion into commissioned sales jobs. We do not deal with that portion of the litigation. (For discussions of these more celebrated aspects of the case, see Schultz 1990; Scott 1988.)

seems clear that the compensation system that had developed prior to 1976 was not well disciplined by market or efficiency forces and had produced a considerable amount of gender inequality. It also seems clear, however, that the gender wage gap in checklist compensation was shrinking throughout the 1973–80 period. The crucial question we will attempt to address is why. Was it a response to a reinvigorated management quest for market rates or efficiency? If so, does this vindicate the administered efficiency theory of pay determination? Or are these changes better seen as part of a larger system of organizational inequality, in which organizational politics continues to mediate the pay-setting process in ways that systematically disadvantage female workers?

Historical Background

Any chief executive of Sears in the late 1960s and early 1970s faced something of an organizational anomaly. He was simultaneously the head of the nation's largest retailing enterprise and part of an extremely decentralized administrative apparatus. In the words of one observer, "The territories had gained so much control over company communications that corporate directives from Chicago were rewritten when they weren't thrown away" (Katz 1987, 17). Moreover, the belief in decentralization was so powerful that it seemed to many of the participants that this unique corporate structure had been part and parcel of the Sears style of operation from the very beginning, or at least since the ascendancy of General Robert Wood to the company presidency in 1928.

Like much of the ideational content of corporate cultures in general, the notion of a traditional legacy of decentralization at Sears was based as much on selective reconstruction of the past as on historical fact. Although Wood was a clear champion of "flat" organizational structures and a strong believer in individual responsibility and initiative, the history of the company during the 1930s and 1940s was marked by wide swings between central and regional control. In its first incarnation, the territorial system implemented by General Wood in the early 1930s failed to distribute much of the power outside of the central office. Territorial offices were limited to staffs no larger than three people and their direct activities were to be limited to personnel matters and to the allocation of merchandise to the various stores and mail-order facilities in their areas (Chandler 1962, 298ff.). When this incomplete decentralization proved unworkable, Wood quickly dismantled it in 1932 and established a more centralized structure with newly strengthened headquarters departments of personnel and retail administration.

By the end of the 1940s, however, decentralization and strong territorial offices had won out. Beginning in 1940, Wood and his top executives decided to make a second attempt at territorial organization. The nature and scope of the territorial offices was different this time around. The territorial offices were given much more autonomy and each contained a nearly complete line of functional departments, which had formerly existed only in headquarters. Thus, the Midwest Territory in 1948 contained staff responsible for real estate, display, inventory control, traffic, personnel, public relations, auditing, credit, and operations. Only merchandising, which was primarily responsible for purchasing, remained centralized in two locations in Chicago and New York. Significantly, each vice president in charge of a territory had complete responsibility and autonomy in managing the affairs of his operation. In fact, those headquarters units corresponding to strong functional departments in the field (e.g., personnel and operations) operated almost entirely on an advisory basis. Headquarters managers retained significant prerogatives primarily in two areas: financial control and merchandising.

This aside:

> In the spirit of decentralization, each vice-president in charge of one of the five sovereign territories had developed his own administrative procedures . . . . They could structure a staff around themselves in whatever way they liked, and even after the territories each employed over fifty thousand people, the territory kings preferred to dole out raises and bonuses personally to even the most junior executives. (Katz 1987, 17)

Nevertheless, the decision to keep the merchandising function as one centralized in the "Parent" had significant consequences for the company in its mature years in the 1970s and 1980s. Ever since the inception of the strong territorial system, a marked tension existed between the buyers in the New York and Chicago merchandising offices and the retail executives in the regional offices and stores. As Sears's market position deteriorated in the 1970s, a rift between the "Parent" and "Field" came to be a significant focal point in the corporate dynamics of the firm.[3] By the late 1970s, there was a clear battle for corporate ascendancy being waged between the "merchants" in Chicago and the "operators" in the field.

---

3   Katz (1987) provides an illuminating discussion of how pricing and sales promotion policies proved to be a continuing irritant between those in headquarters and those in the field. In fact, failure to resolve adequately the dilemma of control and financing of in-store sales promotions led to a loss of $100 million during the Christmas selling season of 1977.

Compensation for Checklist Employees

The system of compensation for the some 20,000 checklist employees of Sears was a prominent arena in the contest between the forces of decentralization and centralization within the corporation. Before the 1970s, checklist compensation policies represented vintage Sears managerial philosophy, for they combined a set of widely recognized, often invoked corporate principles with an almost total absence of centralized control. When Sears began to encounter profitability problems in the early 1970s top management responded by attempting to fundamentally reshape the structure of checklist compensation.

Prior to 1974 Sears had no centralized compensation system. Pay decisions were, according to the description offered by the EEOC in its administrative finding on Sears, "based largely upon the recommendation of the individual Unit Manager"; they were "totally discretionary" (Plaintiff's Tr. Ex. 22, pp. 162–63). Salaries for headquarters positions – consisting primarily of buyers – were decided by group merchandise managers; those for positions in retail stores were set by store managers; positions in catalog sales were governed by the General Managers of Catalog Merchandise Distribution Centers; by the early 1970s positions in Regional Credit Centrals were set by their respective regional managers (Sears Brief to 7th Cir., pp. 26–27). As a result, Sears's managers did not know what employees working outside their units did or what they were paid (Katz 1987, 28).

So profound was the lack of information about companywide pay practices that in 1970 a personnel official based in the Chicago Parent wrote to the personnel directors of the territories and national groups to ask what their policies were on the size and pace of pay raises for checklist employees.

> In conjunction with our current review of the checklist
> salary/earnings picture, we have a rather significant problem.
> No one seems able to describe what our existing
> compensation policy is for this group as a whole. . . . Toward
> this end, we thought it might be helpful to find out from the
> key people administering The Policy what they *think* The
> Policy is. (Sears Internal Corresp., dated Feb. 16, 1970;
> Attached to Tr. Ex.)

Even within territories there was little centralized control. One regional personnel director reported that salary guidelines for minimum and maximum pay existed but were not mandatory. He developed new guidelines in the late 1960s, but these were used only 50 percent of the time and fell into disuse (written testimony, Jt. App., Vol. 13, p. 21).

The unstructured, decentralized character of compensation practices mirrored the corporate philosophy that General Wood had developed for the company. The general rejected conventional management tools in favor of policies that depended on the individual initiative of employees. Reposing authority over compensation in unit managers was consistent with the view that low-level management should have the autonomy to run operations as they saw fit. They were ultimately responsible for the profitability of their units and would be under pressure to follow compensation practices that maximized profits. Nonetheless, pay practices were significantly shaped by a set of companywide principles. Four of the most important were:

1. Pay the person, not the job. During its dispute with the EEOC, Sears insisted that prior to 1976 and the adoption of a new compensation scheme, and even to certain degree after that time, the company philosophy was that individuals created their own jobs. The witnesses testifying on Sears's behalf asserted that "Store managers set the compensation of employees according to their talents and responsibilities" (Tr. Trans. 13, 796–97; written testimony, Jt. App., Vol. 13, p. 11). "The employees themselves created their own jobs and had maximum freedom to expand their roles within the company" (Tr. Trans. 15, 496–99; written testimony, Jt. App., Vol. 14, pp. 87 et seq.).

2. To get ahead at Sears, you have to move. Given the rapid expansion of the company after World War II and the resulting need to constantly move executive personnel to new assignments, relocation became a necessary and highly rewarded aspect of upward mobility within Sears. Relocations involving promotions led to significant increases in base salary. Because relocation raises became a part of an employee's permanent salary base, employees had incentives to move often and to move to high-cost-of-living areas. (The latter carried higher-than-average raises, which continued even after an employee was being transferred to a lower-cost area.) As a regional official testified, it was common for employees to relocate three or four times within a ten-year period and to receive an increase of at least $75 per month for each relocation (written testimony, Jt. App., Vol. 13, p. 12).

3. Never cut salaries, even if an employee is no longer working in a higher-paying position. Sears had developed the tradition of never cutting the pay of employees. If an employee in a high-paying job moved into another job, the pay would not be

reduced. But employees moving into the same position from a lower-paying job would not necessarily receive the same pay level as the higher-paid entrant (Sears Brief to 7th cir. at 33). "An employee moving from division management, rather than from a clerical job, could enter checklist with a particularly high salary" (written testimony, cited on p. 30 of Sears Brief to 7th Cir.).

4. Use bonuses as a major component of total compensation in checklist jobs. With the exception of jobs in credit units, most checklist employees received a substantial portion of their total income as a year-end bonus. (The bonuses were paid in the spring for the preceding calendar year.) The size of bonuses awarded depended on the profitability of the unit in which the employee worked as well as on the philosophy of the unit manager. Managers received bonus allotments each year. It was up to them to decide what portion they kept for themselves and what portion they divided among their subordinates. "Some Group Managers were known to be generous, while others had a reputation for being less willing to distribute bonus money" (written testimony, Jt. App., Vol. 13, pp. 12–13). Between 1974 and 1976 some guidelines were established to govern bonuses, but exceptions were often made. This resulted in considerable variability in bonus policies across units (Sears Brief to the 7th Cir., pp. 27–28).

In 1974, in response to dramatically slumping profit levels, substantial layoffs, and a growing sense of internal division and conflict among the various segments of the corporation, Chairman of the Board Arthur Wood turned to outside consultants to evaluate the company's executive compensation system (Katz 1987, 24–25). Sears retained Hay Associates, the preeminent firm of compensation consultants. From the outset it was clear that top management already had concluded that existing compensation practices were seriously flawed and required a major overhaul. In a letter embodying the proposal for the consulting project, the leader of the Hay team, C. Ian Sym-Smith, described the project goals articulated by Sears's management.

> You have reached the conclusion that this [the existing bonus] program no longer serves the purposes of the corporation, and wish to develop a base salary and incentive compensation program to replace it. You are pretty sure that the bulk of the compensation for the bulk of these [checklist employees] people should be in the form of base salary, and you wish to develop a base salary administration program based on job

> evaluation that will insure you of internal equity. (Letter from Sym-Smith to Charles Bacon, Vice President for Personnel, Sears, Mar. 11, 1974; Jt. App., Vol. 14, pp. 128–38.)

According to this initial letter, Sears was "asking for an Executive Compensation Program which will accomplish the following":

> Accurately measure the relative worth of the various executive positions within the Company.
>
> Accurately measure your competitive position with executives in other companies.
>
> Provide for uniform application throughout all of the units in your highly decentralized Company. . . .

Thus the three items of highest priority among a list of ten goals were internal equity, competitiveness in the market for managerial manpower, and uniformity across company units. In the context of the political conflict between territories and the parent, it is evident that the Hay consultants were being deployed in an area of keen sensitivity. In calling for a shift to a uniform compensation policy based on job evaluation, the parent corporation was seeking to constrain the vast amount of salary-setting discretion subunit managers possessed. According to one account, the Hay consultants suggested that to have a significant impact, the managers selected for the Sears Hay Committee should be a group of "young Turks" from both the field and the parent, who would be willing to fundamentally restructure the job system (Katz 1987, 28–29). The members of the Corporate Committee were handpicked by the personnel department and the Hay consultants. They became a "council of disaffected young colonels . . . . [who began to feel] disdain for many of the traditions they'd been taught to respect since their corporate infancy [that] grew more powerful with each new boondoggle they identified and so named" (Katz 1987, 40).

But the efforts of the outside consultants (both Hay's compensation study and a study of the managerial structure by McKinsey and Company) had to bow to the political reality of the field's power. The next letter in the court record from the Hay consultants and to Sears's vice president for personnel reflects this tension.

> We have had a number of discussions with you where you have been very concerned, and we feel properly so, about assuring that a substantial proportion of territorial jobs be evaluated within the territories themselves. At the same time, we have been very concerned with developing a way of achieving the volume of evaluations required by working with a number of committees while at the same time assuring

companywide internal consistency. (Letter from Ian Sym-Smith
of Hay Consultants to Charles Bacon, Vice President for
Personnel, Sears, Sept. 3, 1974; Jt. App., Vol. 14, pp. 119–22)

As a result, Hay Committees were established for each territory. These
were presided over by territorial personnel directors. Territorial reports
were reconciled at a national meeting attended by representatives from
Hay, the Corporate Staff, and representatives of each territory.

The Hay consultants produced two major reports, both sharply critical of the existing compensation system and the managerial environment
in Sears. After several jobs were evaluated according to the Hay System
for know-how, problem solving, and accountability, and assigned corresponding point totals, the Hay analysts plotted the relationship between
average compensation and company evaluation points. The results
revealed very significant variations in the pay levels of jobs with similar
point totals.

> Jobs at about 800 points are paid from $15,000 per year to
> $57,000 per year. Jobs at about 1000 points go from $26,000
> to $58,000. Jobs at 1300 points go all the way from $35,000
> to $67,000 per year. Jobs in the 1700 to 1800 point range get
> paid from $50,000 to $87,000 and so on. As can be seen, the
> cases picked out are not the extreme, jobs are spread fairly
> evenly throughout these ranges. Such dispersion raises big
> questions as to internal equity, effective use of compensation
> dollars, and management disciplines [*sic*] in the utilization and
> development of people. (Hay Associates, May 1975, p. 8; Jt.
> App., Vol. 14)

The return to points also varied systematically across functions and
territories. At 1,000 points, parent merchandising jobs averaged 30
percent higher total compensation than jobs in the credit function.

The Hay analysis also demonstrated that Sears's managers perceived
the system as inequitable. In the course of a "climate study" based on
interviews with a random sample of Sears's managers, the respondents
were asked how the equity of their total compensation relative to other
managers in the company compared with the equity of compensation in
other companies. All categories of respondents, including those from the
parent, the field, top management, and officers, rated the Sears's compensation system as less equitable than the industry average. "Both the
objective and the subjective data are in agreement that Sears' pay practices have not yielded a system in which people are paid in close relationship to their relative impact on the Company's functioning" (Hay
Associates, May 1975, p. 17; Jt. App., Vol. 14).

The Hay reports also compared Sears's compensation practices to those of 303 of their other industrial clients. (More specialized size and industry comparisons did not produce different results and were, therefore, not reported; Hay Associates, May 1975, p. 18; Jt. App., Vol. 14.) To compare the rate of compensation across companies, the point totals assigned jobs within each company were transformed into standardized Hay units, which in turn were plotted against annual compensation. Excluding officers and jobs with lower point totals, total cash compensation at Sears fell among the top 10 percent of companies analyzed (Hay Associates, May 1975, p. 22; Jt. App., Vol. 14).[4] Despite these high relative levels, the sample of Sears's managers in most parent and field positions perceived their compensation as below average for industry and as less satisfactory than the industry average (p. 35). Responses to questions about the bonus component of compensation indicated significant problems with the bonus system. Rather than acting as an incentive, it was seen primarily as a part of salary; it was thought to be unfair, not effective in motivating effort, and based on factors managers did not understand or could not control (pp. 36–38).

Given these results, Hay recommended adoption of its system for setting salaries according to a formula based on total compensation points. Most checklist jobs were to be moved from the 90th-plus percentile in industry to the 80th percentile. It suggested a number of implementation strategies that would gradually lower overpaid positions and gradually increase underpaid ones. The final pages of both Hay reports targeted raises based on geographical relocation as a major source of the chaos in salary system and a significant cause for Sears's overly generous compensation levels.

> Hitherto, Sears has had a practice when transferring people geographically to give them a substantial increase which was incorporated into their ongoing compensation program. The result of this has been that the compensation of many individuals has been more related to the number of geographical moves he has had than to any other factor. This is also part of the reason of [sic] the fantastic spread or scatter in your compensation practice for a given size job. It is our recommendation that when people are moved geographically

---

4   Officers at Sears were not so handsomely paid relative to industry. Officer compensation fell just above the overall mean, with some positions receiving pay levels below the industry average for top officers (Hay Associates, 27–33). This less well paid group constituted only a small fraction of checklist employees and therefore did not change the overall position of Sears compensation levels vis-à-vis other industrial companies.

for the convenience of the Company (i.e. not at their own request) that they be given a one-shot payment of 20% of their base salary. (Hay Associates, Jan. 1976, p. 64; Jt. App., Vol. 14)

It appears from Sears's compensation manuals published after 1976 that these recommendations became company policy.[5] It is interesting to note that among the elaborate procedures contained in the compensation manual are rules forbidding salary administrators from disclosing to employees the number of compensation points their positions carry and the salary ranges for positions. The concern that employees perceive the new salary system as fair did not translate into policies disclosing the results of job evaluations or how they were translated into salary midpoints.

Thus in 1976 Sears embarked on implementing a fundamentally new program for executive compensation. The new system played a pivotal role in the plaintiffs' allegations of pay discrimination. They argued that male-female pay disparities within jobs that were evaluated as one position in the Hay scheme were, when other individual characteristics were taken into account, compelling evidence of disparate treatment of men and women. Indeed, the plaintiffs retained as an expert witness a former Hay employee who had worked on the early phases of the Sears project.

The highly critical Hay reports also might have proved damaging to Sears's contentions that its early compensation policies reflected sound business judgments. Yet a series of Hay consultants came to the defense of their client at trial. The head of the Hay team, Sym-Smith, spoke in glowing terms of the unique organizational philosophy that had guided the earlier years of Sears's compensation system. According to Sym-Smith, the extremely decentralized pay practices of the earlier period were appropriate for the time in which they were conceived. They had served the organization well during the immense postwar expansion. Only recently had it become clear that these policies were no longer in Sears's best interests. Sears's management had acted responsibly, according to business judgment, both in establishing the decentralized system and in revamping it in 1976 (written testimony of Sym-Smith, Jt. App., Vol. 14, pp. 87–91). We now reexamine a portion of the data presented at trial to learn more about the nature of the work force to which this system was applied and what the system's consequences were for the relative pay of men and women.

---

5 See Executive Compensation Manual, Basic Company Policy, October, 1977, Jt. App., 14: 143–214.

An Empirical Reanalysis of Pay Inequality among Checklist Jobs: A New Treatment of Models Presented to the Trial Court

The ultimate focus of the EEOC's pay discrimination claim was a set of fifty-one checklist jobs in the period 1973–80. Prior to the entry of the final pretrial order in which the EEOC was required to specify the facts it would attempt to prove at trial, the number of jobs in which the EEOC alleged discrimination varied considerably from a low of some six job codes to a high of seventy-three job codes (Defendant's Post Tr. Brief, July 1985, pp. 61–63). The commission asserted that the jobs were selected because they each contained at least ten male and ten female employees for two consecutive years.[6]

One of the major complexities of the plaintiffs' statistical evidence was their treatment of the fifty-one job codes in the years 1973 to 1975, prior to the adoption of the Hay system of which the fifty-one jobs were a part. As noted, the Hay job classification scheme was not implemented until 1976. Prior to that time, Sears relied on a system which was identified as the "C-job" classification system, since each job number was preceded by the letter "C"; that is, job C196 was a general job designation for "Manager." In attempting to deal with within-job pay differences before 1976, the plaintiffs did not make direct use of the C-job system, probably because they viewed these titles as being so broad that it would have been exceedingly difficult to argue that the work performed within them met the legal criterion of being "substantially equal." Instead, the plaintiffs constructed what became known as the "artificial work force," placing individuals in the Hay codes based on the analysis of a sample of workers who had not changed jobs during the period in question. This attempt at matching earlier and later jobs was less than perfect. As Table 7.1 demonstrates, a substantially smaller number of employees were contained in the artificial work force the plaintiffs constructed than were contained in the jobs at issue analyzed for the post-1975 period.[7]

---

6 Although most of the tables in the plaintiffs' exhibits show fifty-one lines of results, that number is actually misleading insofar as six of the titles listed are simply renumbered versions in 1979 and 1980 of six identical job titles that appear from 1973 through 1978. Thus, in any particular year, the maximum number of jobs at issue is forty-five. That number is reduced further by the unavailability of data for some jobs in some years.

7 The data we reexamine here are based almost entirely on the reported characteristics of these fifty-one jobs. In contrast to the information available for UNI (Chapter 5) and for Coastal Bank (Chapter 8), the individual records underlying these occupational aggregates are not available for Sears. Where appropriate, these job-level data are supplemented by other aggregate statistics taken from the various reports prepared by the plaintiffs and the defendants.

Table 7.1. *Composition of Checklist Jobs at Issue in* EEOC v. Sears

Sex Composition & Size of Jobs at Issue	1973	1974	1975	1976	1977	1978	1979	1980
Actual work force								
1. Percent female	—	—	—	18.3%	20.2%	21.4%	22.1%	22.4%
2. Total no. of employees	—	—	—	5,169	5,397	5,208	5,393	4,994
Artificial work force								
3. Percent female	14.6%	15.8%	17.4%	—	—	—	—	—
4. Total no. of employees	1,937	2,606	3,943	—	—	—	—	—
C-job work force								
5. Percent female	10.5%	12.4%	14.3%	—	—	—	—	—
Checklist work force in "at issue jobs"								
6. Total no. of employees	6,978	7,076	7,829	—	—	—	—	—
7. Percent	40.5%	40.8%	40.8%	27.5%	28.7%	28.4%	30.8%	30.6%
Total checklist work force								
8. No.	17,286	17,309	19,067	18,632	18,721	18,203	17,397	16,229
9. Percent female	9.8%	11.6%	12.5%	13.6%	14.8%	15.7%	16.1%	17.0%
Job segregation (index of dissimilarity)								
10. Actual work force	—	—	—	42.8	39.9	40.2	35.9	37
11. Artificial work force	49.6	45.5	44.5	—	—	—	—	—
12. C-job work force	39.0	39.3	40.1	—	—	—	—	—

Sources: *Actual work force:* Defendant's Exhibit 6-QQQ; *Artificial work force:* Plaintiff's Exhibit Table 8; *C-job work force:* Plaintiff's Exhibit Siskin (pay) 38 (2); *Percent of checklist work force in "at issues jobs":* Defendant's Exhibit 6-QQQ (for 1973–75 percentages are values listed in Plaintiff's Exhibit Siskin (pay) 38 (2) divided by totals listed in Defendant's Exhibit 6-ZZZ); *Total checklist work force:* revised Siskin Pay Report, 5; *Job segregation actual work force:* calculated from data in Defendant's Exhibit 6-QQQ; *Job segregation artificial work force:* calculated from data in Defendant's Exhibit Table 8; *Job segregation C-job work force:* calculated from data listed in Plaintiff's Exhibit Siskin (pay) 38 (2) divided by totals listed in Defendant's Exhibit 6-ZZZ.

In Table 7.1, we first examine changes in the sex composition of the "jobs at issue" and compare them with what was happening in the overall checklist work force. Row 8 of Table 7.1 shows that Sears employed a large number of individuals in its checklist work force, with the total fluctuating between sixteen thousand and nineteen thousand. In row 7, however, one can observe the effect of the imposition of the criterion of a minimum of ten female and ten male employees. Workers included in the set of jobs that were statistically analyzed were less than half of the overall checklist work force. The introduction of the Hay plan had the effect of substantially increasing the overall number of job titles in use for checklist employees. From 1973 through 1975, the average number of C-job (pre-Hay) codes was 260; in the 1976–80 period, the average number of Hay codes was 1,971 (Siskin Report, 1984, p. 7; Jt. App., Vol. 13).

Regardless of which set of figures is examined, there is an unmistakable trend evident in rows 1, 3, and 5 of Table 7.1 – the labor force in the fifty-one jobs was steadily increasing its proportion of female workers. Depending upon the choice of earlier figures used, one would conclude that women increased their representation somewhere between 8 and 12 percentage points. Furthermore, the pace of this increase seemed to hover around 2 percentage points per year before leveling off substantially in 1978.

By inspecting row 9 of this table, one can make a comparison with the same trend in the overall checklist work force. First, in any given year, females were a higher percentage of the fifty-one jobs at issue than they were of the overall checklist group. This is to be expected given the selection rule that jobs had to have a minimum of ten female employees to enter the "at issue" category. However, the overall work force (row 9) shows almost the same trend of increasing female participation as occurred for the fifty-one jobs at issue, with the 1980 percentage being approximately twice as large as the 1973 percentage. On this dimension at least, the "at issue" and overall work force appear to be similar.

An increase in numbers does not necessarily indicate a trend toward equivalence of position within this group of jobs. Therefore, in the bottom three rows of this table, we have provided some additional data related to job segregation among male and female employees in any given year. The measure used is the widely adopted index of dissimilarity. After 1975, the pattern seems simple enough – job segregation declined in somewhat irregular fashion. Unfortunately, this clarity evaporates once the data from the earlier period are considered. If the artificial work force data are used to characterize the 1973–75 period, the trend toward decline seems more clearly established. When the data from the job classification system actually in use (the C-job codes) are examined, the whole series loses its earlier shape. Instead of a steady decline, the amount of job segregation now seems to fluctuate unsteadily around the high thirties for the entire period. The truth probably lies between these two possibilities, in part because there are about 60 percent as many C-job codes as Hay codes in this analysis. The dissimilarity index is sensitive to the number and "fineness" of the categories used.[8]

---

8 The decline in segregation for the artificial work force in the 1973–75 period also might be influenced by the process used to construct this population (i.e., counting only those who did not change c-jobs). If more men than women leave the lower-level jobs in question, the procedure may have the effect of decreasing the amount of measured job segregation.

Table 7.2. *Characteristics of Jobs at Issue in* EEOC v. Sears *Compensation Claim*

| Year | Total No. of Jobs | Jobs at Issue | | |
		N of Jobs	Range of Hay Salary Midpoints	Correlation of Hay Points with Percent Female
1976	2,102	38	$17,020–$31,728	−0.403
1977	2,110	39	$17,770–$34,026	−0.456
1978	2,014	39	$18,688–$37,002	−0.487
1979	1,935	41	$19,915–$39,735	−0.479
1980	1,786	39	$21,496–$43,290	−0.446
Hay Points				
Minimum		268		
Maximum		839		

Therefore, the most likely state of affairs is that job segregation was somewhat higher in the pre-1976 period than after, but that it was probably not much higher and probably did not change drastically in the years between 1973 and 1975. These figures almost certainly underestimate the amount of job segregation in the checklist job codes as a whole. According to the plaintiffs' statistical expert, "Using 1978 as representative of the period in which the Hay codes were in effect, nationwide at year-end there were 1,994 Hay job codes with active employees. Of these 1,994 job codes, 1,454 had no women and 275 had no men" (Siskin Report, 1984, p. 7; Jt. App., Vol. 13).

We begin our analyses of compensation practices per se by looking at the assignment of Hay job evaluation points to the jobs "at issue." The requirement of a minimum of ten female incumbents created a tendency for the "jobs at issue" to cluster toward the middle and bottom levels of the Hay point distribution. Although in general Hay point totals for individual jobs at Sears can range as high as 2,600 points, in the subset of jobs considered in the EEOC's compensation claim, the range was 268 to 839 points. Even within this sample of jobs, there is a tendency for jobs with a higher proportion of females to have lower point totals. As the last column of Table 7.2 shows, there is in each year a substantial negative correlation between the percentage female in each job and the Hay point rating of the job.

Interpretation of this correlation is facilitated by two additional pieces of information. First, once the point totals were established for the individual jobs in this sample, they remained completely invariant over this five-year period except for two jobs. Second, in any given year there is a completely deterministic relationship between the number of points for a job and that job's minimum salary level, its maximum salary level, and the midpoint of its salary range. (The latter is important since it is that value that is multiplied by each individual's "compa-ratio" to determine his or her salary.) It is also of interest that two different linear relationships apply to minimum salaries in any given year – one for jobs with point totals less than 830 points and one for jobs with higher point totals. Thus in 1976, the minimum salary in each job (in the lower point range) could be calculated from the following formula:

Minimum Salary = $7,820.60 + $19.71 * Haypoints.

As a concrete example, the minimum salary for an Assistant Buyer IV (M028) was:

$7,820.60 + $19.71 \times 571 = $19,075.$

As we have noted, the plaintiffs pursued the case against Sears on the basis of "within-job" discrimination. The upshot of the pay system just described is that a "between-job" claim of the comparable worth variety would have had to have been made on one of two grounds: (1) that the process of assigning points to the jobs was itself gender biased; or (2) that only a fraction of the Sears labor force is represented in the subset of jobs analyzed. (That is, one would have found more between-job inequality throughout the remainder of the company.) The compensation system for these jobs was not structured in such a way that male- and female-dominated jobs with the same points received different levels of pay. In fact, once the number of Hay points for a given job is taken into account, there would be a zero partial correlation between the job's gender composition and its position in the salary structure. Contrast this system – in which evaluation points define earnings differences – with the more typical role of job evaluation in defining between-job gender inequality. "In spite of the high probability that a priori job evaluation methods contain a built-in cultural devaluation of women's work, these systems have consistently demonstrated . . . that female-dominated jobs are underpaid when compared with male-dominated jobs with similar point scores" (Acker 1989, 69).

Bias in assigning points to jobs would not have been a novel occurrence, however. Acker (1989) discusses at length the conflict that emerged on Oregon's pay equity task force over the issue of how much importance should be given to the human relations subdimension of the know-how factor of the Hay system, which was being used to revamp pay practices in that state. Feminists on the task force lobbied to have the human relations component expanded from three to five levels, so that it would have greater weight in the overall composite scores.

Interestingly, the jobs at issue in the Sears case were almost all evaluated at level 3 of the human relations subscale (there were six exceptions rated at level 2). Thus, this subfactor contributed little to the overall variability of job point totals. While there is not much data here that bear on this issue, it is true that in 1980 if the Hay points had been assigned solely on the basis of either the "know how" component or the "problem solving" component, the correlation with the percent female in each job would have been only slightly lower than it actually was: −0.42 and −0.40, respectively, as compared with −0.446. Although these reductions are rather modest, it is still possible that a different system of evaluation might have produced a substantially lower correlation.

With regard to the second point, the place of the checklist work force in the larger division of labor at Sears, there are a multitude of lower-level "timecard" sales and nonsales positions that could be brought in, as well as the mass of excluded "checklist" jobs whose existence is documented in Table 7.1. The possibility of some sort of "pay equity" case being made would have been enhanced to the extent that different Hay point formulas were used to translate points into pay for different Hay point ranges (see previous discussion) or for different types of job classifications, where the overall proportions of females were much higher.

Nevertheless, within the range of jobs pursued in the lawsuit, it is difficult to prove that the generally lower level of female salaries resulted from the systematic devaluation of women's work. The correlations between gender composition and the salary levels of particular jobs primarily reflect differences in the salary of men and women *within* the same job title. Salary differences across jobs play a smaller part in total wage differences. Moreover, these jobs are not rigidly segregated by gender.

We now turn to the question of how the adoption of the Hay system affected the total earnings differences between men and women in this subset of checklist jobs. That is, if one grants that the ranking of the jobs in terms of points is largely gender neutral, there is also the issue of how males' and females' average salaries stack up with regard to the Hay-determined "salary midpoints" within their particular job classifications. We can anticipate several possible outcomes here that are informed by both within-job and between-job inequality processes. For example, given the pay consultants' concern with excessively high salary values for some individuals relative to external rates, it would not be surprising if the attempt to rein in salary growth among the highest earners – presumably males – had the effect of initially decreasing the level of gender inequality within certain jobs. A second possibility, and one put forward vigorously by Sears and its attorneys, is that the upgrading of females into higher level jobs might have initially tended to decrease their relative standing within jobs as these newly promoted women started at the bottom of a new wage hierarchy. Yet a third possibility is that gender integration between jobs and the gender equalization within jobs proceeded simultaneously as the company's commitment to "fairness" began to diffuse across more and more units of the firm. Or it is also possible that the forces of reaction won out with any gains from gender integration across jobs being counterbalanced by renewed efforts at holding the gender line within jobs.

What was the trend in male-female earnings? Here again we must contend with problems of data availability. Because the pay disparity issue was framed in the litigation by the notion of equal pay for equal work, almost all earnings figures reported for these jobs are differences between male and female earnings. The actual male and female means used to calculate those differences have been omitted. While these within-job gender differences are presented after several different types of statistical adjustment have been applied (including no adjustment at all), data on unadjusted male and female mean earnings within jobs were never explicitly presented in the trial or pretrial exhibits. However, for about two-thirds of the job-year combinations after 1975, the plaintiffs did provide estimates of dollar differences, which they calculated by multiplying the defendant's estimates of the percentage differences by the male within-job salary means. Working backward we were able, therefore, to construct the male means for these jobs in these years. (And because the unadjusted male-female differences were listed, we could also reconstruct the female mean earnings for those jobs as well.) For the missing one-third of cases, we were able to estimate successfully male and female mean earnings on the basis of salary data provided separately for entering male and female workers and for "stable" male and female workers across the various years (see Appendix 7.1).

In Table 7.3, we have provided data showing a comparison of weighted average male and female salaries across all the job classifications that were at issue in the litigation. The three data series reflect different treatments of missing values for mean salary levels (see Appendix 7.1). Series 1 (Sears Best data) contains no substitutions for missing values but includes a smaller proportion of the total work force. Series 2 (Sears Better data) incorporates substitutions where the substitutions met a criterion of accuracy in reproducing differences in mean salary levels (see Appendix 7.1). Series 3 (Sears Good data) contains substitutions for all missing data. With one exception, the three data series provide a consistent picture of the aggregate trend in the female to male salary ratio. The ratio increased noticeably between 1976 and 1977 and then leveled off at the higher value obtained. The

Table 7.3. *Trends in Male and Female Average Salaries, Sears "At Issue" Work Force, 1976–1980*

	Males		Females		F/M Salary Ratio (%)	Percent Female in Jobs
	Mean Salary	N	Mean Salary	N		
1976						
Series 1	$20,800	3,738	$16,800	774	81	17
Series 2	$20,600	4,063	$16,500	911	80	18
Series 3	$20,700	4,224	$16,500	941	80	18
1977						
Series 1	$22,400	3,139	$19,200	837	86	21
Series 2	$22,200	4,083	$18,900	1,047	85	20
Series 3	$22,400	4,284	$19,100	1,088	85	20
1978						
Series 1	$24,900	2,957	$21,300	913	86	24
Series 2	$24,600	3,858	$20,800	1,063	85	22
Series 3	$24,800	4,096	$20,900	1,112	84	21
1979						
Series 1	$27,300	3,393	$23,900	892	88	21
Series 2	$26,900	3,902	$22,300	1,138	83	23
Series 3	$26,700	4,201	$22,300	1,180	84	22
1980						
Series 1	$31,000	3,039	$26,800	783	86	20
Series 2	$29,300	3,851	$24,600	1,103	84	22
Series 3	$29,300	3,876	$24,600	1,118	84	22

Series 1 data show a continued increase in the earnings ratio between 1978 and 1979 and a subsequent return to the 1977 level in 1980. Without additional information, it is difficult to know whether to attribute this to a problem of selection bias or to a real change that is masked by adding in the inferior substitute data. The fact that the increase in the ratio was not sustained suggests that the selection bias interpretation may be correct.

To gain further insight into this wage gap, we can make use of the fact that the salaries of both male and female checklist employees are a function of the Hay points assigned to their jobs, the associated Hay midpoint of their salary range, and the deviation of their salaries from that midpoint. The male-female wage gap can be statistically decomposed into three components. The first of these components is a "between-job" aspect of the wage gap in which men are disproportionately represented in jobs with high salary midpoints in the Hay system. This component would be small in either of two instances: if men and women were equally distributed across all occupations; or if men and women were unequally distributed but if the female-dominated occupations had, on average, Hay point ratings equal to or better than those of males. Thus, compared with the index of dissimilarity used earlier, this component takes into account the salary levels of the jobs in which men and women are disproportionately represented. The second and third components are "within-job" salary inequalities. The second captures the extent to which men are in jobs where their salaries exceed the Hay midpoints and the third captures the extent to which women are in jobs where their salaries are below the Hay midpoints.[9]

While we have already seen that the extent of gender integration has been rather modest over the time period under study, examining these components and their change over time helps to evaluate whether the defendant's account of the wage gap is accurate or not. That is, Sears alleged that the wage gaps remained in place only because women were moving into higher-level jobs where they had less seniority and were starting at the bottom of a new within-job wage hierarchy. If this is so, then over time the first component of the wage gap (the "between-job" component) should diminish in size and the third component (the within-job female disadvantage component) should increase. The second component (the within-job male advantage component) should remain relatively stable as male movement does not play a role in this particular account of wage stability. Table 7.4 presents the relevant values from the decomposition of the total wage gap based on data series 2 in Table 7.3.

---

9   The wage gap between men and women in this sample of jobs can be expressed by the following formula:

$$\frac{\overline{\$}_m - \overline{\$}_f}{\overline{\$}_m} = \frac{\sum p_{mo}\overline{\$}_{om} - \sum p_{fo}\overline{\$}_{of}}{\overline{\$}_m}$$

A simple and somewhat informative decomposition of this gap can be accomplished by breaking the numerator of the right-hand side of this equation into three component parts.

$$\sum p_{mo}\overline{\$}_{om} - \sum p_{fo}\overline{\$}_{of} = \sum \$_{o \cdot mdp}(p_{mo} - p_{fo}) + \sum p_{mo}(\overline{\$}_{om} - \$_{o \cdot mdp})$$
$$+ \sum p_{fo}(\$_{o \cdot mdp} - \overline{\$}_{of})$$

where p_{mo} = proportion of all males in occupation o, p_{fo} = proportion of all females in occupation o, $\$_{om}$ = mean male salary in occupation o, $\$_{of}$ = mean female salary in occupation o, and $\$_{o.mdp}$ = Hay salary midpoint in occupation o.

Table 7.4. *Components of Male-Female Wage Gaps in Sears Checklist Jobs (%)*

| | Between Job Components | Within Job Component | | Total |
		High Male Salaries	Low Female Salaries	
1976	7.3	14.2	−1.5	20.0
1977	6.7	10.3	−2.3	14.6
1978	6.5	9.9	−1.0	15.3
1979	6.7	9.7	0.8	17.1
1980	6.2	9.0	1.0	16.2

As we have already seen, the largest yearly change in the wage gap occurred during the 1976–77 period. Interestingly, during this period all components of the wage gap decreased in size, with the largest decrease occurring for the male "within-job" wage component. In other words, the implementation of the Hay system seems to have had the effect of decreasing wage inequality by bringing male salaries closer in line with the newly established midpoint values. After this initial surge, however, there was not much change in either of the first two components. From 1977 through 1980 women closed the salary gap by moving into better-paying jobs (component 1), but the amount of change in the last four years on this component was no larger than the change that occurred in the first year. After decreasing by 4 percentage points, the second component only decreased by 1 additional point in the last four years. As for the third component, it did something of an about-face in the last four years. While women improved their within-job standing between 1976 and 1977 (negative values mean that this component tends to reduce overall gender inequality), women's relative position within jobs began to erode in the transition from 1977 to 1978 and thereafter. In fact, had this erosion not taken place, the amount of inequality in 1980 would have been nearly 2 percentage points lower than in 1977 (12.9 percent compared with 14.6 percent).

From Sears's point of view, this widening within-job inequality was a necessary concomitant of moving women into higher-wage-level jobs from which they had been previously excluded. What is interesting about the results shown here is that this pattern does not seem to explain much of what transpired. In the year when between-job inequality declined by the greatest amount, females' within-job salaries actually improved with regard to their midpoints. Moreover, the largest decrements in the wage gap associated with the implementation of the Hay system happened by the reduction of male salaries relative to their midpoints rather than by some process that involved women workers at all.

Further evidence on this point can be adduced by looking at these data from a slightly different vantage point. From 1976 onward, corresponding jobs can be identified across years. If gender integration of jobs is associated with an increase in the level of inequality between males and females within jobs, then we would expect the following to hold true: Controlling for the ratio of female to male salaries in year 1, and controlling for the sex ratio in year 1, the sex ratio in year 2 should be positively correlated with the salary ratio in year 2. That is, as jobs become more female (the sex ratio declines), the ratio of women's to men's salaries should decline because the women tend to enter at the bottom. The actual regression coefficients fail to support this prediction, however. Thus in the fifth column of Table 7.5, we see that although three of the four coefficients have signs consistent with the prediction, all are statistically insignificant (the highest t-value is 1.23). In short, these figures confirm the results shown from comparing the cross-sectional results: There is only weak evidence in favor of the idea that gender integration weakens women's salary position within jobs.

It is also possible from these data to examine the degree to which these trends varied by location within the organization. As we demonstrated in Chapters 5 and 6, organizational politics can play an important role in producing gender inequality. The effects of any organizational change, especially one that represents a sharp break with the past (as the Hay classification system did at Sears), will be molded by the constellation of interests and powers existing at the time of the implementation. To investigate this possibility, we have grouped the jobs at issue in the EEOC lawsuit into four broad functional groupings that correspond to various areas within Sears's organizational structure. These are credit jobs (which were in the process of being relocated from stores into "credit centrals"), merchandising (buying) jobs that were geographically centralized in either Chicago or New York, retail store jobs dispersed around the country, and other jobs, largely in retailing but more likely to be located in group or other branch offices. A list of jobs and their categories appears in Appendix Table 7.A2.

In Table 7.6 the change in the sex composition of the various jobs over the eight-year period is presented separately across these corporate functional categories. If we begin by examining the 1976–80 period, which has fewer problems of data consistency, there is a clear trend for the greatest change in gender composition to have occurred among the politically weakest sector of "credit." In this area, the proportion female increased by 10 percentage points (on a base of 13 percent), while the

Table 7.5. *Effect of Changing Gender Composition on Changing Within-Job Salary Ratios*

Year 1	Year 2	Effect of Year 1 Sex Ratio on Year 2 Salary Ratio	Effect of Year 1 Salary Ratio on Year 2 Salary Ratio	Effect of Year 2 Sex Ratio on Year 2 Salary Ratio	N
1976	1977	−0.003	0.637*	0.004	26
1977	1978	−0.002	0.556*	0.003	26
1978	1979	−0.001	0.549*	−0.002	24
1979	1980	−0.004	0.761*	0.003	29

* t significant, $p < 0.05$.

Table 7.6. *Sex Composition of Checklist Jobs by Corporate Functional Location, 1973–1980*

	Credit		Merchandising		Retail Store		Other Retail	
	% Female	Total No.	% Female	Total No.	% Female	Total No.	% Female	Total No.
1973								
Artificial work force[a]	6.9	58	24.2	289	8.1	670	16.7	920
C-job work force[b]	8.6	850	18.5	1,250	5.6	3,031	13.9	1,847
1974								
Artificial work force[a]	10.5	95	26.7	415	9.6	966	17.5	1,130
C-job work force[b]	11.4	915	22.4	1,214	7.2	3,225	15.5	1,722
1975								
Artificial work force[a]	10.7	178	30.3	574	12.5	1,707	18.8	1,484
C-job work force[b]	10.3	796	25.8	1,290	8.3	3,902	17.8	1,841
1976	13.0	292	32.8	793	14.1	2,368	18.9	1,784
1977	16.8	334	34.3	937	15.9	2,368	19.4	1,751
1978	20.7	430	42.4	948	15.7	2,142	21.3	1,689
1979	23.3	515	34.6	948	16.8	2,176	21.6	1,740
1980	22.7	563	35.8	938	16.6	1,931	21.6	1,557

[a] Sex composition values taken from Plaintiff's Exhibit Table 8.
[b] Sex composition values taken from Plaintiff's Exhibit Table 38 (2).

increases in the other more powerful sectors did not exceed 3 percentage points. This picture is muddied somewhat if the early years are also brought into consideration, with merchandising registering gains almost as large as those in credit. It is possible that this pattern represents an interaction among departmental power relationships, the affirmative action plan, and the implementation of the Hay system. Before 1976 it is likely that the retail area alone was able to resist corporate pressures for greater inclusion of women in the lower and middle management ranks. To some extent, the Hay plan was a "corporate" or "parent" creature from its inception. This being the case, it is at least possible that the buying organization, due to its concentration in Chicago and New York, was more immediately subject to control by the parent organization. Only later, after the adoption of a centralized compensation system, did the parent begin to achieve more success in controlling the remaining parts of the organization.

Some additional insight into this matter can be gleaned from Table 7.7, which breaks the compositional analysis of Table 7.4 down into the portions of each component associated with each corporate functional area. (Thus, if the values in Table 7.7 are added across columns, one obtains the contributions shown in Table 7.4.) Because the size of these units differs dramatically, it is not particularly meaningful to examine between-area differences within individual years. On the other hand, the areas can be compared with regard to trends over time. First, between-job contributions associated with merchandising and other retail are both larger at the end of the period than they are at the beginning. Also, as we noted in the aggregate analysis, there is little meaningful change in the female within-job inequality component. About all that can be said is that it increased a little in both the retail store and merchandising areas. Finally, these figures are interesting because they demonstrate that the decrease in male within-job wage advantage was almost entirely concentrated in the store and nonstore retail areas. In short, to the extent that the Hay system was bringing male salaries into check, it was doing this almost entirely in the most decentralized parts of the corporate structure.

Other Estimates of Trends in Male-Female Inequality

Finally we return to a consideration of the size of and the trends in the male-female wage gap. While there was a number of minor issues on which the parties disagreed, the major points of disagreement concerned two issues. The first was the number of additional variables that should be statistically controlled. Here the defendants included not only the variables used by the plaintiffs (job performance, time in present job assignment, time in other checklist job assignments, and time in other Sears nonchecklist jobs, the squares of the time variables, and the territory in

Table 7.7. *Contributions to Overall Gender Gap by Corporate Function and Source of Difference*

Year & Source of Gender Gap	Corporate Functional Area (%)				
	Credit	Merchandising	Retail	Other	Total
1976					
Between	1.72	−13.68	16.02	3.24	7.30
Male within	0.97	1.87	7.69	3.71	14.24
Female within	−0.32	1.55	−3.06	0.30	−1.53
Total	2.37	−10.27	20.65	7.25	20.01
1977					
Between	1.66	−15.81	14.16	6.65	6.66
Male within	1.08	1.27	5.28	2.66	10.28
Female within	−0.50	0.92	−2.20	−0.52	−2.30
Total	2.23	−13.62	17.24	8.79	14.65
1978					
Between	1.00	−14.13	15.60	3.99	6.46
Male within	1.25	1.74	4.39	2.48	9.87
Female within	−0.30	1.53	−1.89	−0.38	−1.04
Total	1.95	−10.86	18.10	6.09	15.29
1979					
Between	−0.16	−10.44	12.85	4.43	6.68
Male within	1.28	2.08	3.50	2.80	9.66
Female within	0.13	2.12	−1.41	−0.06	0.78
Total	1.25	−6.24	14.94	7.18	17.12
1980					
Between	0.08	−12.29	12.61	5.78	6.18
Male within	1.29	2.14	3.16	2.35	8.95
Female within	−0.04	2.77	−1.15	−0.54	1.04
Total	1.34	−7.38	14.62	7.59	16.17

which the employee worked),[10] but a host of other factors as well, including such things as veteran status, marital status, number of children, number of job relocations, and previous salary in a timecard position (if any). The second dispute concerned the proper functional form the model should take. In the defendant's reanalysis, several variables were multiplied by (interacted with) checklist seniority in an attempt to estimate the effect of each independent variable on two separate

10 These were the variables in plaintiffs' model 1. Their model 2 added a number of other variables, including education, but was not used since the results were the same as those from model 1.

Table 7.8. *Estimates of Adjusted Percent Salary Difference in* EEOC v. Sears *(%)*

Year	EEOC	Sears Replication of EEOC	Original Sears
1973	11.65	—	8.91
1974	10.76	—	9.90
1975	11.72	—	9.15
1976	8.63	9.12	5.83
1977	6.06	6.00	5.02
1978	5.54	5.00	3.89
1979	5.39	4.95	2.87
1980	5.07	4.46	3.21

salary components – the beginning salary of each employee and his or her rate of increase. However, as the plaintiffs' expert pointed out, this is a largely spurious exercise in the absence of true longitudinal data on each individual (the data were analyzed within year and job title as a series of cross sections). Table 7.8 shows how the various models produced different estimates of the gender gap across the various years. It is taken in its entirety from Defendants' Ex. 6-AAAA (Jt. App., Vol. 13, p. 119).

The statistical arguments in the trial focused on the pattern of statistical significance associated with these percentages, with the defendant succeeding in convincing the court that there was no pattern of meaningful differences. By looking at the size of the percentage differences themselves (which of course vary because of the different set of covariates included in each model), we can derive some alternative conclusions. First, even though these are adjusted salary differences between males and females, they follow largely the same pattern established in Table 7.3 for the unadjusted differences. The analyses of both plaintiffs and defendants show a substantial diminution of the wage gap across the eight-year period, with the largest reductions occurring in the years from 1975 to 1977 when the Hay system was first being implemented. Second, even though there are disparities between EEOC's and Sears's analyses, these are generally differences within a range of 2.5 to 3 percentage points. Based on this sample of jobs, there seems to be little doubt that our earlier assessment of diminished gender inequality during the period is accurate.

Before we consider the implications of these results for theories of wage determination and gender inequality, we take a closer look at how these and other data were treated by the trial and appellate courts.

The Litigation: A Sociological Review

The Origins of the Lawsuit

Like almost everything else in the case, the origins of the lawsuit were contested by the parties. According to Sears, the official who headed the EEOC's investigation had a conflict of interest, in that he served on the Board of Directors of the Women's Defense Fund and was personally involved with and later married a member of NOW's board (Opening Stmt., Charles Morgan, Sept. 23, 1984; Tr. Trans., p. 120). This official allegedly gave a presentation at the NOW convention in 1973 in a session on "Confrontations and Demonstrations," which spoke of a fictitious investigative target called "Snears & Doebuck." Five months later, in August 1973, the EEOC filed formal charges against Sears. The same official remained in charge of the Sears case at the EEOC while participating in various NOW campaigns against Sears (*Sears* II, p. 358). T-shirts sold at the 1975 NOW convention carried the slogan "N.O.W. Sears Action Task Force – 100 Million and Nothing Less." The "100 million" referred to was the goal for monetary damages – a figure that would have exceeded any previous antidiscrimination award (*Sears* II, p. 358). Although the EEOC official had resigned his membership on the NOW board on the suggestion of the commission chairman, he remained in charge of the investigation. He sought a $600 million predetermination settlement from Sears.

Sears rejected this proposal. In March 1977, Sears appeared before the commissioners of the EEOC and sought to convince them to negotiate a memorandum of understanding. The memorandum would constitute a consent decree in which the EEOC could monitor Sears's progress in achieving the goals of its internal affirmative action program. After questioning the basis for the earlier EEOC complaint, Sears argued that such an agreement would do more to advance equal opportunity than would litigation. " '[M]aking an example' of Sears is really doing little to frighten skeptics into voluntary compliance. Instead . . . voluntary compliance efforts in general are becoming tainted, as 'money down the drain.' We would like to suggest instead, that if Sears be used as an example, it should be used as an example to prove that voluntary compliance *can* work" (Tr. Ex., March 1, 1977, p. 30).[11] The Sears presentation did not prove persuasive. A month later, in April 1977, eighteen days after the EEOC official who had been accused of having a conflict

---

11 Jt. App. Vol. 12, Tr. Ex. Presentation to Commissioners and Gen'l Counsel of the EEOC, Mar. 1, 1977.

of interest left the agency, the commission adopted by a 2 to 1 vote a "reasonable cause" decision against Sears.

In the statutorily mandated conciliation procedure that followed the commission's decision, the EEOC reduced its demand for damages to $54.5 million. According to the court of appeals opinion, the reason the EEOC continued to seek a large monetary settlement was that "outside interest groups had to be satisfied" (*Sears* II, p. 358). Sears again rejected the commission's monetary claim. In the words of its defense counsel, Sears would pay "not one dime for political tribute" (Morgan Opening Statement, Sept. 23, 1984; Trial Tr., p. 142). The EEOC filed suit in 1979. The initial complaint included a broad range of charges that mirrored the earlier EEOC complaint. Many of the initial charges were dropped as the case moved to trial, including charges brought by named individuals.

The early history of the EEOC inquiry led to serious doubts about the objectivity and fairness of the government's case. Before the case was reassigned to Judge Nordberg for trial, Sears sought to have the suit dismissed because of the alleged conflict of interest. Its motion was denied, but the district court criticized the EEOC's handling of the matter (*EEOC v. Sears, Roebuck & Co.*, 504 F. Supp. 241 [N.D. Ill. 1980]). The court of appeals panel that later reviewed the case concluded that the EEOC had "badly abused the investigation, predetermination settlement, and conciliation statutory prerequisites to suit" (*Sears* II, p. 358). While the EEOC was allowed to pursue the case at trial, its credibility was in doubt at the outset. The strategy it chose to pursue at trial may have compounded these difficulties.

The Pay Discrimination Claim and the Statistical Evidence

As we have seen, the EEOC's pay discrimination claim was limited to jobs that each contained at least ten male and ten female employees for two consecutive years. The selection criteria thus reflected a fundamental principle of statistical analysis: To perform meaningful statistical tests of pay differences between male and female employees, it was necessary to have some minimum number of males and females to compare. The commission's experts never defended this rule of thumb by formal statistical proof, although it would have been a straightforward matter. Nor did they attempt to place the fifty-one jobs in the total context of the other jobs in the Sears system. The fifty-one jobs represented only 3 percent of the total number of job codes in the Hay scheme Sears adopted in 1976. Due to the minimum size requirements, the jobs contained a much larger percentage of checklist employees – some 30 percent in 1980 (see Table 7.2, row 7). The defendants accused the EEOC of arbitrarily selecting the jobs analyzed. But the trial court did not fault this aspect of the commission's case.

The EEOC constructed the case involving the fifty-one jobs according to the logic of an Equal Pay Act allegation, even though the pay claims were made pursuant to Title VII rather than the Equal Pay Act itself. (For a general discussion of the differences between Title VII theories and Equal Pay Act theories, see Chapter 2.) The plaintiffs only analyzed pay differences between men and women *within* job codes or families of related job codes. They asserted that the adoption of the Hay scheme of job evaluation and compensation indicated that the employees working within a job code were performing similar work. If women were paid substantially less than men assigned the same job code, this established a prima facie case of wage discrimination, which shifted the burden of proof to Sears. Sears would then be required to rebut the EEOC's findings through more refined statistical evidence or justify the pay differentials as resting on legitimate grounds. If it failed to meet this burden, Sears would be liable.

The commission analyzed the wage differentials between men and women within each of the fifty-one job codes for each of the eight years in contention. It ran separate regression models for each job by year combination. For the years 1973 to 1975, a period in which most jobs received bonuses, it compared earnings with and without bonus. (Thus the EEOC reported the results of 561 regression models.) The models included measures of sex, time in present assignment, time in present assignment squared, additional time in checklist (beyond present assignment), additional time in the company (beyond present assignment and other time in checklist jobs), additional time in company squared, territory of employment, job performance ratings, and Hay points.[12] The coefficient for sex in almost all instances was negative, indicating that women made less than men after controlling for other differences. The proportion of coefficients that were statistically significant (i.e., with t-values greater than 1.96 or two standard deviations below the estimated income of men) ranged in any given year from a low of 57 percent to a high of 80 percent. By chance alone, one would expect that 5 percent of the comparisons in any year would be statistically significant at this level. On their face the plaintiffs' statistical results were striking.

---

12 Report on Checklist Comp. Practices of Sears. (Revised Sept. 18, 1984, Table 7.9 at 21–22, Jt. App. Vol. 13.)

Sears attacked the plaintiffs' case in several ways. Judge Nordberg was persuaded by virtually all of Sears's arguments. Indeed, on the checklist compensation portion of the case, there is a close correspondence between the posttrial brief filed by Sears and the judge's opinion. Therefore, we can look to the trial court opinion to summarize the defense Sears mounted.

The court began by rejecting the legal theory advanced by the commission. In Judge Nordberg's opinion, the adoption of the Hay system by Sears did not alter the EEOC's burden of proof. He distinguished the Sears case from *Gunther* and other wage discrimination cases decided under Title VII in which the courts had shifted the burden of proof to the employer to defend its compensation practices. The preceding cases had involved manifestly unfair pay differences between predominantly male and predominantly female jobs. According to Judge Nordberg, the allegations against Sears did not involve job segregation or specific pay practices that disadvantaged women. Nor did the judge accept the EEOC theory that the incumbents of each Hay code were performing the same work. He held that even after the adoption of the Hay system in 1976 Sears paid the person, not the job.

> While the Hay evaluation system helped set the salary ranges, many other factors influenced the actual salary of individual checklist employees. . . . [T]hese included performance evaluations, previous job history, number of relocations, seniority, and geographic location. Under the new salary range system, Sears still compensated employees on these bases. (*Sears* I, p. 1337)

Having failed to establish the "equal work" component of a "classic" Equal Pay Act claim, the commission bore the burden of proving through direct evidence that the observed salary differences were the result of an intentional pattern of discrimination against women.

In the court's eyes, the EEOC did not carry this burden. The judge dismissed the 1973–75 portion of the case because the artificial work force created for those years excluded too many employees to be definitive. For the 1976–80 period he faulted the EEOC for using a data base that contained too many errors, for omitting important variables that might legitimately influence checklist compensation, for aggregating statistical results nationwide when actual pay decisions were made in territorial, functional, and local units, and for failing to produce testimony from individual victims of discrimination (*Sears* I, pp. 1343–46). In contrast, the court found that Sears proved it did not engage in pay discrimination. The defendant's more numerous, segmented analyses found statistically significant differences in only a handful of job-years. Its cohort analysis indicated that newly hired and promoted women in the recent period received higher rates of salary increases than men (*Sears* I, pp. 1346–52).

The court also was impressed with the testimony of Sears officials.

> More important than any statistical evidence in this case is the testimony of Sears' witnesses. . . . The witnesses' uncontradicted testimony helps "bring to life" Sears' statistical evidence, and lends strong support to the conclusion drawn from Sears' statistical evidence, that Sears compensated checklist men and women in a non-discriminatory way. The fact that Sears' affirmative action programs were in effect throughout this period, making it unlikely that Sears would be intentionally discriminating against women in pay at the same time, corroborates their testimony.
>
> In stark contrast to Sears' presentation, EEOC presented no credible witnesses with personal knowledge of Sears who could contradict the testimony of Sears' witnesses, or give any life to EEOC's inadequate statistical data and analyses. EEOC did not prove even one individual instance of pay discrimination by Sears. (*Sears* I, p. 1352)

A Summary Critique of the Evidence and Analysis

The statement just quoted suggests that in the end the qualitative evidence proved more dispositive than the statistical data in *Sears*. Even Judge Cudahy, who, in writing a dissenting opinion to the court of appeals decision, cast the only vote in favor of the commission, lamented that the "EEOC as much as gave the case away by failing to produce flesh and blood victims of discrimination" (*Sears* II, p. 360). Nonetheless, it is instructive to briefly consider the strengths and weaknesses of the statistical evidence presented at trial, as well as how Judge Nordberg treated it.

As we have demonstrated (Table 7.1), the data presented for 1973–75 were of questionable quality. Given the relatively large number of employees excluded from the data set in these years and the uncertain character of the bias produced by such exclusions, we do not feel comfortable relying on these data during this period. It is likely that the sample in the early years yielded conservative estimates of the male-female wage differentials, for it probably contained a disproportionate number of relatively immobile men and average women. The data quality for the earlier period was further compromised by missing data on the amounts of bonuses paid employees.

The EEOC is in a far better position in analyzing the data set assembled for the 1976–80 period. Judge Nordberg's opinion expressed some concern about inaccuracies in the data set that might artificially inflate estimates of the male-female wage gap (*Sears* I, p. 1343). Yet it is unclear whether Sears only performed audits on variables that, when controlled, would tend to reduce wage differences. Errors in complex data sets are inevitable. The ultimate consideration is how the distribution of errors is likely to affect estimates of the true characteristics of the population. It is possible that the correction of errors in other variables would have strengthened the findings of statistically significant wage differences.

Judge Nordberg was more concerned about the inadequacy of the measures the plaintiffs employed in their regression equations to control for otherwise legitimate bases for salary differences. It is important to note that there is considerable facial validity in the EEOC's regression results. There is some significance to the fact that the analysis involved individuals engaged in jobs assigned the same number of Hay points. While there might be considerable differences in actual work of individuals within job codes, the range of activities and responsibilities was certainly much more delimited than in other cases involving analyses of an entire set of work force categories. The EEOC employed an extensive set of measures that were objectively defensible as a means of operationalizing the human capital workers bring to their jobs. Additional measures might better explain wage differences at Sears, but the critical question is whether the attributes measured contributed to the productivity of a worker.

A number of the measures Sears included in its regression equations were clearly and predictably associated with gender but were of dubious business value. Perhaps the most striking of these was the number of geographical relocations. We noted earlier that an informal company slogan was that to get ahead at Sears, one had to move. Given the fact that women were more likely to be married to working spouses who preferred not to relocate, it is also likely that female employees of Sears were less willing to move than their male counterparts. Sears's tradition provided a substantial salary increment for every move made, which became part of the employee's base salary, even though the increase was unrelated to the responsibilities of the new job. Men received many more of these than women, which contributed to the salary differentials within checklist codes. While Judge Nordberg saw relocation raises as an unobjectionable business practice, the Hay consultants hired by Sears recommended that they be abolished because they were unnecessary and inefficient. The consultants suggested that relocating employees be given a one-time increment to cover the costs of moving but that their base salary remain the same (Hay Associates, Jan. 1976, p. 14; Jt. App., Vol. 14). Such arbitrary practices may have contributed to what the consultants depicted as an inefficient, illogical compensation system. For many checklist positions Sears paid at or near the top of the pay levels offered by other retailers (Hay Associates, May 1975, p. 22; Jt. App., Vol. 14).

Judge Nordberg found the alternative analyses performed by the defendants to be more probative than the regression models offered by the EEOC. Yet the alternative formulations were not demonstrably superior to the EEOC's approach. They suffered some obvious limitations for making inferences about overall levels of pay inequality in the company. The Sears analyses consistently subdivided the number of cases included in statistical tests, which necessarily reduced the probability of finding statistically significant differences by gender.

The Sears expert purported to separate salary differences resulting from differences in starting salary and rate of increase by including variables for sex and for the interaction of sex and seniority. She then reported separate t-values for each variable, rather than reporting the results of a test for the joint contribution of sex and its interaction terms. By effectively dividing the effect of sex on salary between the two terms, fewer of the t-values for the sex-related terms achieved high levels of statistical significance. Similarly, by performing analyses on the subset of employees entering checklist jobs in given years – the "cohort analysis" – Sears ignored the much larger portion of the checklist work force. Women who entered checklist jobs after the filing of the complaint by the EEOC in 1973 may have been compensated as well as the male members of their cohorts. But this did not demonstrate that men and women throughout the ranks of checklist jobs were paid in a nondiscriminatory fashion.

Other aspects of the trial court opinion reflect statistical naiveté that Sears turned to its advantage. The judge cited two instances of pairs of individuals who appeared identical according to the measures employed by the EEOC. But an in-depth review of their employment files revealed that they possessed very different career experiences and qualifications. The judge concluded from these instances that the EEOC's measures could not effectively control for relevant differences in individual qualifications (*Sears* I, p. 1348). Yet the judge did not discuss how these cases had been selected. Were they extreme aberrations that Sears had uncovered by pouring over the records in many cases? Or were they commonplace? Did these imperfections in statistical measures only underestimate the qualifications of females? Judge Nordberg did not interpret these examples statistically. Instead, the examples led him to doubt statistical analysis altogether.

The trial court opinion does not resolve some of the basic questions about the nature of gender inequality in Sears. In part, this is due to errors in statistical judgment by the court. But in part it results from the statistical approach of the EEOC. The EEOC strategy was in one sense extremely conservative statistically. It focused on a limited set of jobs that met certain minimal numerical criteria and evaluated the extent of discrimination by counting what proportion of the pay differentials within those jobs were statistically significant. By concentrating on a subset of jobs and devoting relatively little attention to the systemwide wage gap, it failed to develop a broad conception of the pay system and the position of women in it. This would have required an examination of the distribution of women across different job titles and the relative compensation of the full range of checklist jobs, and the commission did not follow this approach.

Conclusion

The conflict between several institutional forces at work in contemporary industrial societies became apparent in the *Sears* litigation. These forces include bureaucratic personnel and pay practices as represented by the Hay consultants and the system that they devised; a set of government policies, regulations, and enforcement agencies as represented by the Equal Pay Act, Title VII, and the EEOC; and a large, decentralized corporation with a markedly traditional climate and culture, as represented by Sears. Significantly, Sears itself had internalized the division of interests it confronted in its external environment. The company contained both enthusiastic advocates for affirmative action efforts and a large group of executives and managers who resisted the program as an unwanted diversion from a focus on profitability. A core group of Sears executives devoted considerable effort to redesigning and gaining central control of its job structure; other groups steadfastly resisted any intrusion into their cherished principle of "territorial" sovereignty.

Our reinvestigation of this case, although limited by the data available to us, reveals several insights into the effects of these clashing forces. First, the checklist work force as a whole was becoming increasingly open to female participation both before and after the redesign of the job structure and the rationalization of the pay system. The fact that the proportion of women in Sears lower and middle management doubled in an eight-year period suggests not only that progress was made but that progress needed to be made as well. Second, after the implementation of the pay plan, there was an immediate reduction in the level of salary inequality between male and female checklist employees. This reduction was evident not only in the aggregate ratio of female to male salaries but also in the heavily adjusted "within-job" percentage differences presented at trial by both Sears and the EEOC. Furthermore, if the data on which our reanalyses are based are representative, the reduction in salary difference was achieved less by promoting women into higher-status jobs than it was by bringing a set of "high-flying" male salaries closer to earth, particularly the salaries of those men in the more decentralized reaches of the corporation at large. Third, the EEOC had uncovered substantial evidence of unexplained salary differences between men and women in the same job classifications but failed to convince the court that these differences resulted from illegitimate means or were large enough to warrant the award of any compensatory benefits to female employees.

The empirical results do not provide unequivocal support for market, efficiency, or organizational inequality models. Market theorists have a difficult time explaining why Sears fostered a compensation system that veered out of control from market wage rates at other large corporate enterprises, and which, at least until the early 1970s, discriminated against women. Post hoc one can argue that the pay structure was intended to build in labor market pressures by giving discretion over pay to the same managers who were trying to maximize the profitability of their units. A market adherent also could take the long view. Sears departed from market wage rates and paid the price in its product market: It began to lose out to lower-cost competitors.

These are hardly persuasive explanations. To characterize the earlier era of the Sears system as a kind of internalized market approach borders on the absurd in view of the contentious relationship between the field and the parent throughout the history of the company. It is not necessary to cede wage-setting authority to unit managers to incorporate information on market rates into a wage system. Indeed, if Sears intended to mirror the market through a decentralized system, it was an act of faith. When the company began to formulate a centralized pay system, it became apparent that there was no agreement and, in fact, no information about what a given job was paid in different parts of the company.

The retail market did eventually begin to punish Sears for a series of managerial missteps. But what role did errant pay practices play in the diminished market position of the company compared with other strategic miscues? And how long did it take the market to begin to discipline Sears for an inefficient compensation structure? We can only speculate about the relative significance of pay practices in Sears's recent difficulties. Again, one would have to take the market view on faith.

The administered efficiency explanation for the patterns we found in Sears is somewhat more compelling. The introduction of the Hay compensation system from 1975 to 1977 appears to have been responsible for significantly reducing the gender gap in checklist compensation. Indeed, the rationalization of the pay system looks to have been a more potent force for equalizing compensation across gender groups during this period than was affirmative action. Consistent with the administered efficiency conception, the reform seems to have been informed by a managerial imperative to make the wage system function more efficiently in achieving company goals.

Yet there are large parts of the Sears story that are not easily reconciled with an efficiency account, which can only be squared with processes we assert are part of the organizational inequality model. First, that there were substantial inefficiencies and inequities built into the pay system prior to the mid-1970s indicates that the early system was not being run according to rational principles. Second, the Hay system reforms were very much a part of the political struggles within Sears. The Hay consultants did not operate simply as neutral, technical experts. The correspondence between the Hay project team and Sears management establishes that they were aware of the highly politicized context they were hired into. The Hay consultants advised Sears management to assemble "Young Turks" for the job evaluation committees. The sudden reduction in the gender gap that occurred after the new system was adopted strongly suggests that the new system had a major impact. We found evidence, however, that the pace of change varied inversely with the distance of a subunit from the parent company. More powerful and remote subunits reduced the wage gap between men and women more slowly than other subunits. Organizational politics offers the most straightforward explanation for this pattern.

Third, the reform of the wage system largely gave a one-time jolt to the gender inequality structure. After cutting the adjusted wage gap by one-half for the subset of checklist jobs that were the focal point of the pay claims, an unexplained wage gap between men and women of from 3 to 6 percent persisted and showed some signs of growing. The persistence of a residual differential implies the persistence of sexist employment practices.

Fourth, while the administered efficiency conception suggests that organizations have a self-correcting tendency, the shrinking of the wage gap in Sears was at least in part the product of an antidiscrimination mandate imposed from outside the organization. Indeed, management could employ the outside legal threat as an excuse to follow its own preferred managerial strategy, the centralization of compensation for checklist jobs. As Edelman (1992) found, the vulnerability of an organization to legal sanctions is a significant variable in explaining the rate at which it adopts internal compliance structures.

While we find much in the *Sears* case that supports the organizational inequality model, the trial court concluded otherwise. It rejected the plaintiffs' contentions not because it had examined the trend in gender inequality in Sears over time and believed that things were getting better. Rather it was persuaded that discrimination never existed at Sears in any widespread fashion. Several idiosyncrasies of the case contributed to this result: a government lawyer who had left himself open to charges of impropriety, a judge who seemed unwilling to deal with statistical evidence in a rigorous fashion, and a set of plaintiffs who were either unwilling or unable to present any living victims of the discrimination they alleged. But these are not the entire story.

The errors made in the presentation and analysis of employment data in the *Sears* case, which appear so obvious in retrospect, are not surprising given the pressures that contested litigation imposes on participants. There was no forum here for a frank exchange of information. Both sides were driven to offer extreme and in part distorted interpretations of the Sears compensation system. The EEOC could not acknowledge that Sears had made substantial progress. Sears could not admit to the failings of its earlier wage patterns.

In our view, the *Sears* case raises questions about the ability of the current regime of discrimination law to deal with problems of systemic discrimination. The statistical data provided by the EEOC indicated that something was wrong in Sears. The inequality in the pay and the position of men and women was pervasive and it was linked to general companywide policies and practices. Yet, because the actual agents of discrimination – the hundreds of store managers and group leaders who engaged in a patriarchal reward system – and the victims of the system – the many women who could not "move to get ahead" – remained faceless throughout the proceeding, they were assumed not to exist.

The government lawyers bear part of the blame for not finding "flesh-and-blood" persons who could "bring the statistics to life." This is not just a tactical problem, however. Our legal system remains focused on individualist conceptions of fault. Recent cases concerning affirmative action underscore this tendency in civil rights cases. Absent a finding of past discrimination, preferences based on race or gender will not pass constitutional muster. Thus the courts have condemned legislative attempts to deal with systemic patterns of discrimination. The dilemma that frequently arises in employment discrimination cases is how to assess responsibility for patterns of inequality produced in countless small acts, by a changing cast of characters, that incrementally and consistently limit the employment prospects of one group of workers compared with those of another. In the *Sears* case, in the absence of specifically identified, culpable behavior, the court rejected the view that the employer bore responsibility under the law for wide-ranging gender inequality in its work force.

Appendix 7.1

To estimate missing values for post-1975 male and female salaries, estimated salaries were derived by calculating weighted averages, separately for males and females, of the salaries of those individuals who were entering the job in question and the estimated salaries of those who had been in the job in question for two consecutive years. The estimated male and female mean salaries were then used to compute predicted salary differences between males and females in each job. Because the actual salary differences were available in the original data, a comparison of the predicted and actual values provides a rough check on the accuracy of the estimation procedure for missing values. Most of the analyses that we conducted were replicated using three different data series. These series were Sears "Best" data (i.e., those values with no substitution for missing data); Sears "Better" data (i.e., those values where substitutions were made when the actual and predicted male-female salary differences were

Appendix Table 7.A1. *Coefficients of Determination between Actual and Estimated Mean Salaries by Gender and Year*

Year	Females		Males	
	R^2	N	R^2	N
1976	0.974	28	0.949	28
1977	0.953	25	0.950	25
1978	0.995	24	0.980	24
1979	0.944	23	0.920	23
1980	0.993	22	0.991	22

Appendix Table 7.A2. *Jobs Classified by Functional Location*

Credit	*Other retail*
Coll Mgr-Cr Ctrl	Asst Merch Mgr-FDC
Cr Auth Mgr II	Grp Merch Mgr III
Cr Auth Mgr I	Grp Merch Mgr II
Div Mgr Coll	CSO Mgr III-W SVC
Div Mgr-Cr Auth	CSO Mgr II-W SVC
Coll Mgr-Cr Ctrl	CSO Mgr I-W SVC
	CSO Mgr II-W/O SVC
Merchandising	CSO Mgr I-W/O SVC
Copywriter D/744	CO Buyer (CMDC)
Buyer IV	CO Buyer (GRP CMDC)
Buyer III	CSO Mgr III-W SVC
Buyer II	CSO Mgr II-W SVC
Asst Buy IV(Buy 5+)	CSO Mgr I-W SVC
Asst Buy III(Buy 4−)	CSO Mgr II-W/O SVC
Asst Buy II (N-B 5+)	CSO Mgr I-W/O SVC
ASSt Buy I (N-B-4)	Cat Buyer-Logis
Mdse GRp Sls Coord	
Mdse Asst-Adm Asst	
Mdse Asst-Sls Promo	
Buyer 1	
Buyer 2	
Retail store	
Cust Conv Ctr Mgr I	
Cust Conv Ctr Mgr II	
Merch Mgr IV-Ret Str	
Merch Mgr III-Ret Str	
Sate/Appl Str Mgr III	
Sate/Appl Str Mgr II	
Sate/Appl Str Mgr I	
Area Sls Mgr I NotIHI	
Area Sls Mgr II-Not	
Display Mgr II-Ret Str	
Pers Mgr III-Str/Spt	
Pers Mgr IV-Ret Str	
Pers Mgr III-Ret Str	
Pers Mgr II-Ret Str	
Cr/Mgr II-WO/Coll	

within $1,000); and Sears "Good" data (i.e., those values where substitutions were made for all missing cases). Appendix Table 7.A1 shows the R^2 values between the actual and estimated mean salary values when both sets of figures were available.

8

The Financial Institution as a
Male, Profit-Making Club:
Glass v. Coastal Bank

Our last case involves Coastal Bank, a pseudonym for a major financial institution located in an international money center.[1] As institutions built on financial analysis, one might expect banks (and their pay systems) to embody principles of economic rationality. Yet banking traditionally occupied a distinctive place in American commerce. Before deregulation in the 1980s, bankers were at the center of commerce but also somehow above it. They kept "bankers' hours"; the architecture of their buildings made their places of business the temples of capitalism; and reserve requirements and government regulation underscored the fact that banks made up the institutional framework for the economy and were not ordinary actors in the marketplace. As such, the internal management of banks before the most recent era might have reflected customs that could not be reduced to means-ends calculations.

In the mid-1970s, Coastal Bank's pay system reflected both tendencies. On the one hand, it clearly bore the imprint of bureaucratic administration. The bank retained compensation consultants to evaluate and revamp its pay structure. It adopted a new set of job evaluation techniques. It collected and analyzed pay data from the banking industry generally and local competitors in particular. Compensation for senior managers in large measure was provided through a management fund that granted substantial bonuses based on the bank's overall profits. Such an incentive program would seem to guarantee the aggressive pursuit of profits and discourage discrimination in pay because, presumably, it eats into the potential profits of top officers and shareholders.

On the other hand, the bank's compensation structure bore characteristics of a male club. All thirty-three top officers were white males. The "members" of the club were selected based on status attributes: the college they graduated from, the nature of their ethnic and class origins, even whether they were outstanding athletes. Women, Jews, and African

---

1 Some dates and statistics have been altered to cloak better the identity of the case. For a discussion of the reasons for using a pseudonym, see Chapter 4.

Americans were excluded from the top group, even though some had generated significant profits for the bank. Discriminatory practices also operated at lower levels of the officer corps and in the large, nonofficer segment of the bank.

In Coastal Bank, as in the other organizations we have studied, patterns of gender inequality cannot be explained by market or administered efficiency considerations. Rather we find that jobs held predominantly by women suffered from organizational policies and practices that were shaped by the relative lack of power of women in the organization and the tendency of organizational pay practices to institutionalize male cultural advantages. Gender inequality persisted despite the fact that it might have cut into the profits of senior management. While we have doubts about assuming that the "costs" of discrimination are borne primarily by managers and shareholders, as some economists argue, it is not surprising that these inequities proved so resilient in Coastal. The tendency to disproportionately reward male workers and male work was built into the politics and managerial style of the organization. As such, until the lawsuit, some of these tendencies were unrecognized, and others were unchallenged.

After briefly describing the case study and data sources, we supply some organizational history about Coastal Bank and its pay system. We then analyze quantitative data on the Coastal work force that allow us to compare the explanatory power of market, administered efficiency, and organizational inequality models (for abbreviations used in the text, see the appendix on court documents and case materials). This same analytic objective guides our examination of documents concerning the evolution and operation of Coastal's pay system. We conclude with a discussion of the implications of our findings.

Coastal Bank: Case Study Characteristics and Data Sources

In the 1970s Coastal Bank was a major player in the banking industry, one of the largest banks within a leading commercial city and a presence among large banks nationally. During the early years of the decade, Coastal achieved high levels of profitability and growth. In 1977, after three years of organizing activity by women's groups and the processing of administrative complaints, women and minorities filed suit alleging that the bank had discriminated against them in promotion and pay decisions. After some nine years of litigation and the rendering of a trial court decision in favor of the plaintiffs, Coastal entered a settlement agreement in which it continued to deny wrongdoing, paid a multimillion-dollar award to the plaintiffs, and adopted an aggressive affirmative action program to advance women and minorities within the bank.

Several attributes of Coastal as an organization and the litigation surrounding the discrimination claims against it make it an appropriate case for our inquiry. First, Coastal is a bank of sufficient size and standing to represent a major institution in the banking industry. As an organization located within the mainstream of the banking field, it is less likely that its personnel practices would deviate very far from those of other major banks. Second, Coastal is nonetheless an employer of modest size. It retained some two thousand full-time employees during the 1970s. We possess at least some compensation data from the top to the bottom of the organization, which allow us to see very concretely who gets what in terms of economic rewards. We can combine these data with documents that detail the roles of various officials and groups within the compensation system. Thus we can directly examine the relationship between compensation practices and the interests of specific groups of actors in a profit-maximizing organization. While the *Sears* case also provided insights into compensation in the private sector, Sears is a much larger, more complex organization. Given the limited nature of the pay claims and the available data about Sears, we could not so directly analyze the link between compensation practices, the interests of various groups within the organization, and the overall configuration of inequality within the firm. The *Coastal* case gives us that opportunity.

The *Coastal* case also has some analytic limitations. First, *Coastal* was litigated as a traditional promotions and pay case rather than under a comparable worth (between-job) formulation and, therefore, the market defense was never an issue. As a result the parties never focused on market imperatives as such. Nonetheless, the labor "market" figures prominently in Coastal's pay documents. We gained enough relevant material to analyze Coastal's use of market data in pay decisions. Second, a portion of the documents in the case was subject to protective orders. This limited our access to data in ways we cannot fully assess. Third, the apparent sensitivity of Coastal officials curtailed the amount of personal interviewing we attempted to do. We spoke to lawyers and witnesses for the plaintiffs but not the defendants. While we have tried to take this potential bias into account by questioning the verisimilitude of informant observations, the interview data are not as useful here as they were in the *Christensen* and *AFSCME* cases (Chapters 5 and 6).

Despite these problems, we possess an unusually rich archive on the personnel and pay system at Coastal Bank. These include individual level career and pay data on officers and nonofficers for both 1974 and 1977. For some jobs in these same years we also have wage survey data, job evaluation ratings, and job grade within the organization. In addition to statistical data, case materials include an array of relevant organizational documents.

Coastal Bank: Background on the Organization

Coastal Bank was founded in the 1880s and by the 1970s was well established as one of the five largest banks in its home city and as one of the twenty-five largest banks in the country. In certain specialty areas, trust management and investment, for example, it was even more prominent and routinely was listed among the nation's ten largest banks. Its top officers were well connected to local elites, and, in the words of one informant, the bank was known for the "social connections" of its senior management (personal interview, May 1994).

Consistent with its carriage-trade client list, the bank also had developed a long-standing reputation for conservative business practices. A banking periodical noted, "[Coastal] has always been a conservatively run bank" (ca. 1983). A business magazine described it as "faceless and gray-suited" (ca. 1978). In the financially turbulent 1970s, the bank's role as an organizational tortoise amid a field of financial hares sometimes contributed to favorable results. As one story in the business press commented, "conservatism has paid off for [Coastal] in recent years as the bank avoided the big losses on real estate, tankers, and foreign loans that plagued many others" (ca. 1979). At the same time, the bank's traditionalist tendencies may have also contributed to its troubles as times changed from the 1970s onward.

In the early 1970s the bank posted strong advances in both total assets and net operating earnings. Between 1971 and 1975 assets increased at an average rate of 13.0 percent per year and net earnings by an even more impressive 16.1 percent per year. As the decade drew to a close, however, earnings growth had given way to earnings stagnation; the average yearly increase in earnings from 1975 to 1979 was a meager 1.1 percent. In the early 1980s, net earnings dropped below the 1975 level. One commentator disparaged it as "amongst the least profitable U.S. banks" (banking periodical, ca. 1984). Even in earlier and better days, questions had been raised about Coastal's slowness in diversifying and in developing a stronger retail base. For example, in 1974 its expansion into foreign markets was described as "brisk, if belated" (business periodical, ca. 1974). By the time of a major restructuring nearly a decade later, the bank was still characterized as having "a limited customer base" (banking periodical, ca. 1984).

Traditionalism also was a hallmark of the bank's stance toward its female employees and customers. Eight years after the passage of Title

VII and its prohibition against classifying employees on the basis of sex in ways that would limit their opportunities, Coastal continued to assign some new employees to the categories of "man-in-training" or "woman-in-training." For an additional two years, the bank maintained a separate "women's division" for its female retail customers.

Interestingly, the traditionalism of the bank's personnel policies on women was linked to the role of a de facto women's personnel department managed by a strategically placed female executive. Reigning over an operation that continued many explicitly gendered practices, this executive was thought to have powers equal to, if not greater than, those of the male vice president holding the title of personnel director. Her power was based in no small measure on her direct access to the president of the bank, with whom she had an acknowledged personal relationship (personal interviews, May–June 1994).

It is against this backdrop that one needs to see the development of the lawsuit against Coastal Bank. While its actual practices appear not to have diverged drastically from those typical in the banking industry at the time, in its reputation, in its approach to business, and in its dealings with a changing labor force, the bank was, at worst, hidebound and, at best, slow on its feet.

The Lawsuit

Origins

Starting in 1973 a grass-roots organization began a national campaign to improve enforcement of equal opportunity employment legislation. Among other corporate targets, the group singled out the banking industry in Coastal's metropolitan area and began distributing handbills to bank employees in January 1974 (banking periodical, ca. 1974). In May of that year, the group released a report in which it charged that extensive discrimination existed at Coastal and a small number of other large depository institutions. The group further alleged that mandated Treasury Department compliance reviews were not being carried out in a timely fashion, citing the fact that Coastal's last review had taken place two years earlier. Over the summer of 1974, the group continued its investigation and leafletting of bank employees. In several instances, meetings took place with bank officials, including a session that was held in late summer with the Coastal vice president and chief personnel officer. The Coastal official denied that any discrimination had occurred, but also refused to disclose the bank's affirmative action plan and rejected the advocacy group's request that it establish a job posting system –

which he labeled as "dismal and ineffective." One month later, Coastal was one of seven financial institutions against whom the group filed sex discrimination charges with the Equal Employment Opportunity Commission.

During the next three years, the group continued to exert pressure on the targeted banks. As a result of their actions, on-site compliance reviews were held in November 1974. Over the next two years, the group offered testimony to subcommittees of both houses of Congress, engaged in extensive lobbying of the relevant regulatory bodies, and renewed and updated its original formal charges. As time progressed, the advocacy group increasingly narrowed its enforcement agenda to a focus on one specific institution – Coastal Bank.[2]

The Trial Court Opinion

The lawsuit against Coastal asserted that women and minorities had been discriminated against in job assignment, promotion, and pay. Data on gender differences in pay were presented to measure the overall effects of various discriminatory practices. The case did not allege that predominantly female jobs were discriminated against compared with predominantly male jobs. Nonetheless, the Coastal data allow us to consider the nature of between-job gender inequality and whether it is explained by efficiency factors or market pressures.

The plaintiffs' class consisted of women and minority employees of the bank from 1974 to the time the case was concluded. They proceeded under the theory that Coastal had engaged in "a pattern or practice of disparate treatment of women and minorities," meaning that they sought to prove "that intentional discrimination was the defendant's standard operating procedure" (Opin. 1986, p. 7). Although the period for which Coastal was potentially liable began only in 1974, the trial court held that evidence of discriminatory actions in preceding years might be probative on the issue of whether Coastal was continuing to discriminate after 1973 (Opin. 1986, pp. 10–11).

The plaintiffs presented testimonial and statistical evidence to support their claim. A small group of past and present Coastal employees gave testimony concerning their treatment at the bank. The court entered almost one hundred findings of fact concerning these women, concluding in each case that "the Bank had discriminated against them and that

---

2 This targeting becomes especially clear when one examines the group's congressional testimony given during one year near the beginning of the dispute. In January allegations of discrimination were still being directed against the entire group of seven institutions. By August, Coastal had been singled out as the prime exemplar of gender discrimination in banking employment.

their experiences exemplified the types of barriers erected by Coastal to hinder the advancement of women" (Opin. 1986, p. 13). One of the female witnesses had been required to bring in some $25 million dollars in business to the bank before she was made an officer, a requirement that had never been imposed on male candidates for officer positions. Three other college-educated females were initially placed in clerical positions with no clear upward career tracks, while comparable males were given higher initial placements, more rapid promotions, and higher salaries.

The trial court cited other evidence of discriminatory practices against women and minorities. A Coastal official testified that between 1975 and 1977 one of Coastal's department heads had told him that "he did not want minorities assigned to the department because they might leave for better opportunities" (Opin. 1986, p. 15). The same official reported similar resistance to accepting minorities in three other subunits within the bank. Until at least 1971 the bank had maintained separate training programs for men and women, women were excluded from some bank departments, and female college graduates were historically placed in secretarial and clerical jobs. The strength of the testimonial evidence led the trial court to conclude that "absent any statistical evidence the record is replete with incident after incident of employment practices displaying discrimination. A *prima facie* case of discrimination has been shown without reliance on statistical evidence" (Opin. 1986, p. 15).

The court's view of the testimonial evidence meant that the bank had to present statistical evidence that was sufficiently powerful to rebut the conclusion that it discriminated against women and minorities in the normal course of things.

The trial court voiced skepticism about both sides' statistical tactics. "Expressed in simplest terms the Plaintiff's goal was to include every negative observation in the data base, while Coastal, on the other hand, wished to emasculate the data base as much as possible by removing any damaging data observations. Both sides also manipulated the selection of variables in the statistical equations in such a way as to benefit them" (Opin. 1986, pp. 47–48). In the end, the court viewed the plaintiffs' analyses as more persuasive. "It is in the nature of its exclusions, disaggregations and choice of variables, however, where Coastal fails. The Bank's explanations of its manipulations have so many subjective elements that they undercut the value of the results" (Opin. 1986, p. 48). After reviewing some judicial commentary on the appropriate role of statistical evidence in discrimination cases, the court asserted that it was viewing the sum of the statistical evidence as limited but useful evidence of the existence of discriminatory practices in Coastal.

After this general review of the evidence, the court examined the separate elements of the plaintiffs' claims. For each claim for each group, the court analyzed the strengths and weaknesses of the statistical evidence and then returned to the testimonial data to determine whether the plaintiffs had demonstrated discrimination by a preponderance of the evidence. In each instance, the court followed the gist of the plaintiffs' testimonial evidence. Thus, the only element of the case the court dismissed was the assertion that the bank had discriminated against minorities in promotion to officer. Because no minorities had come forward to testify that they had been denied promotion opportunities, the plaintiffs had not carried their burden of proof on the issue.

The court was not persuaded by some of the arguments employed to good effect in the *Sears* case. It recognized that the bank had an elaborate affirmative action program, but concluded that it "was not effective. . . . Coastal's actions speak louder than its AAP" (Opin. 1986, p. 81). Coastal also presented a job preference study that claimed to demonstrate that many members of the affected class had asked for the kinds of initial assignments they had received. The court decided that "this crude preference study falls far short of the more extensive and precise surveys conducted by the employer in the *Sears* case" (Opin. 1986, p. 82).

The Settlement

Some three years after the trial court judgment, the parties reached a settlement. Coastal did not admit to discriminating against the plaintiffs. Newspaper accounts reported that bank management was interested in putting the litigation behind it to halt speculation about the potential magnitude of its liability in the financial markets. Coastal agreed to pay more than $10 million in backpay to identified class members, to fund a special training program to enhance the career opportunities of women and minorities in the bank, and to implement an affirmative action plan that monitored the external availability of women and minority candidates and tracked the careers of these groups within the bank. Most plaintiffs received modest cash awards. One of our informants received $2,500; another was given about $2,000; the largest single award supposedly was $30,000.

It appears to us that the settlement did little to alter the basic structure of gender inequality at Coastal. Consistent with the legal theory pursued in the case, awards were determined on an individual pay and promotion basis. That is, for each affected group, formulas were developed to compensate for initial salary discrimination, discrimination in salary advancement, and discrimination in promotion. But virtually no attention was given to specific compensation practices that may have disadvantaged the plaintiffs, or to comparisons between jobs held predominantly by men and jobs held predominantly by women. The affirmative action plan went entirely to hiring and promotion considerations. No reforms of the pay system as such were included in the settlement.

The *Coastal* case presents a stark contrast with the *Sears* case. Persuasive testimony by individual victims was the cornerstone of the court's judgment in favor of the plaintiffs. Statistics played a supporting role and lent credence to the notion that the individual incidents were not isolated aberrations within Coastal. Even a judge who was very sympathetic to defendants in discrimination cases would have had a difficult time ignoring the testimony by individual plaintiffs. However, such a judge might have taken a highly critical attitude toward the plaintiffs' statistical evidence and found in favor only of selected individual plaintiffs rather than an entire class of plaintiffs.

Statistical Analyses of Gender Inequality in Coastal Bank

Coastal's Income Distribution

Before we focus on gender inequality in Coastal's work force, it is useful to present an overview of income inequality in the bank. Table 8.1 presents a categorical breakdown of the earnings in 1974 of all full-time employees and of males and females separately (cols. 2 and 3). Figure 8.1 plots the earnings distribution separately for each sex.[3]

The amount of income inequality in Coastal is striking, although perhaps not unusual among financial institutions. Most employees (61 percent) made less than $10,000. Another 30 percent made between $10,000 and $20,000 annually. Of the 10 percent who made more than $20,000 a year, most earned between $20,000 and $30,000. Less than 2 percent of the organization earned more than $40,000. If we had complete data on bonuses, we would probably find about forty cases moved up one or two income categories, mostly from the $20,000–$30,000 and $30,000–$40,000 income groups to the $30,000–$40,000 and $40,000–$50,000 groups. A small number of senior officers made many times more than other officers. The highest paid officer was paid

3   We do not have complete data on bonuses in 1974. In 1978, about sixty-six officers received bonus compensation. In 1974, we know the bonuses of twenty-six officers, including the highest paid officers. About thirty to forty officers, mostly in the municipal bond and government bond divisions, probably also received bonuses.

Table 8.1. *Distribution of Earnings by Gender: Coastal Bank, 1974 (Full-Time Employees Only) (%)*

Annual Earnings	All Full-Time Employees	Female	Male
$1–$9,999	60.9	82.6	36.8
$10,000–$19,999	28.7	17.0	41.8
$20,000–$29,999	7.1	0.3	14.7
$30,000–$39,999	2.0	0.1	4.2
$40,000–$49,999	0.3	0.0	0.6
$50,000–$59,999	0.2	0.0	0.5
$60,000–$69,999	0.2	0.0	0.5
$70,000–$79,999	0.0	0.0	0.1
$80,000–$89,999	0.1	0.0	0.2
$90,000–$99,999	0.0	0.0	0.1
$100,000 and over	0.3	0.0	0.6
Total	100.0	100.0	100.1
N of cases	(2,788)	(1,469)	(1,319)

$265,000, followed by officers earning between $176,000 and $106,000. Some seventeen officers garnered between $50,000 and $100,000. Among officers alone there is an earnings ratio of about 8 to 1 between the highest paid and the lowest paid. The earnings ratio between the highest paid and the lowest paid employee of the bank is roughly 56 to 1.

Equally striking were the earnings differences between male and female employees (see Figure 8.1). Women were overwhelmingly concentrated in the under $10,000 category – only 17 percent earned more than $10,000 – and no female employee earned more than $40,000. In contrast, the majority of male employees were not located in the lowest income category. More than twice as many men than women made between $10,000 and $20,000; almost one-quarter of the men but less than 1 percent of women made more than $20,000. The long upper tail of the income distribution described in the last paragraph was entirely a male preserve. Thus, it is fair to say that the earnings distribution at Coastal was highly skewed in a general sense, but also highly skewed in favor of male employees.

Figure 8.2 demonstrates the relationship between salary grade and earnings. There is a gap in the numbering of grades between nonofficer (1–21) and officer (31–50) positions, but the earnings function is relatively continuous across the officer-nonofficer divide. The earnings curve slopes up gradually until grade 42, when it accelerates rapidly. The height

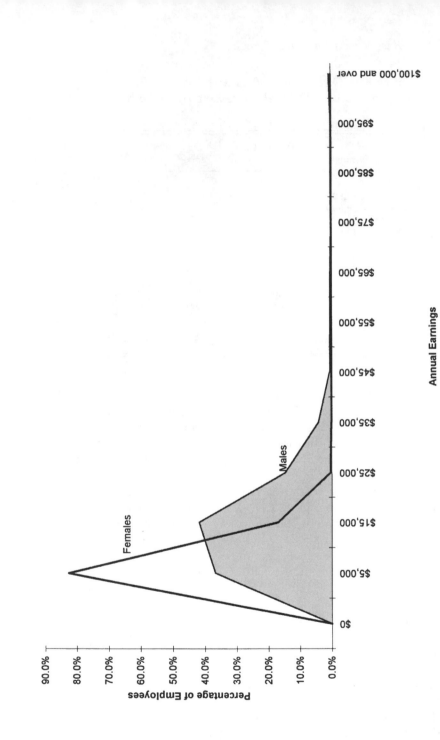

Figure 8.1. Earnings distribution by sex at Coastal Bank, 1974.

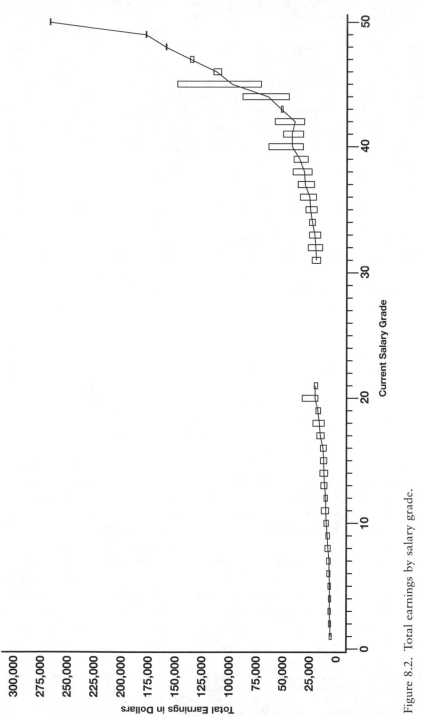

Figure 8.2. Total earnings by salary grade.

of the vertical bar in each column indicates the range of earnings within each grade. There is relatively little income variance within grade at the lower grade levels, but significant within-grade wage gaps exist at the upper end of the nonofficer grades and appear throughout the officer grades. While some of the spread within grades is attributable to missing data on bonuses, there appear to be quite dramatic income gaps (many as large as by a multiple of two) within grade at the upper end of the grade scale.

The kinds of income differences we find in Coastal clearly outstrip what we see in the public sector firms we studied, and probably are characteristic of private sector organizations. Sears no doubt contains a similar gulf in earnings between its top executives and low-level, full-time employees. The pay systems of the State of Washington and the University of Northern Iowa contain far more compressed salary ranges. Top officials in these systems, with the exception of men's football and basketball coaches, probably make ten to fifteen times what the lowest-paid state employees make.

Data

The analysis in this section makes use of data from a variety of sources. Court records contained employment data on individual employees at two points in time: December 1974 and March 1977. A slightly different set of variables was recorded for the two time points, but our analysis centers on a set of measures common to both.[4] For each year we were able to ascertain employees' sex, race, number of years of education, months of seniority, current job title with Coastal, and current salary. Neither data file contained information on the age or length of prior employment of individuals. Hence it was impossible to formulate even a crude total experience variable. This lacuna also showed up in the statistical analyses presented by expert witnesses in the litigation.

For those employees who had achieved officer status, a wide range of supplementary information was available, including external market salary data (Office Corresp., D48669–D48774; Ext. Mkt. Salary Data D48661–D48668), job evaluation points, and periodic recommendations for revisions in those points. Data listing each officer's rank and section assignment were available in directories issued semiannually by a commercial publisher.

---

4 Unfortunately, it was impossible to match the individual-level records across these two time points because there was not a common individual identifier in the two data sets. However, because the 1977 records contained the names of bank employees, it was possible to merge them with legal and other public records that contained other variables of interest, e.g., the rank of officers at various levels.

The salary observations available to us reflected the total population of individuals employed by the bank in the two time periods. Our reconstruction of the data sets produced samples of officers and nonofficers similar in number to those reported by the plaintiffs' expert witness.[5]

Overview

The 1970s was a decade of changing opportunity for women in the labor market in the banking industry as well as in the larger society. Figure 8.3 illustrates how these changes were realized at the officer levels of Coastal Bank and several of its competitors. The percentages graphed were calculated from listings provided in the aforementioned corporate directories. (Data for the two "larger competitors" were marred by the fact that beginning in 1974, the banks chose to list only higher-level officers in the published directories.) At Coastal Bank and at the two medium-sized competitors, a decrease in the proportion of officers who were male began as early as 1971. In fact, the decrease at Coastal was among the largest.

In Table 8.2 more details are shown where the changing proportions are identified by occupational level. These percentages show that all banks were similar insofar as the influx of women began at the lower ranks of the officer corps and spread slowly upward. (The rank category "other" is a residual category that contains predominantly men in staff

5   The smaller number of nonofficers analyzed by the plaintiffs is explained by their decision to exclude part-time workers, a group we included to maximize comparability between the 1974 and 1977 data sets. In analyzing the 1974 data, to make our sample as comparable as possible to that used by the plaintiffs' statistical expert, we excluded all employees who were from the bank's "outpost" operations in other U.S. and foreign cities. We also omitted the eight highest-ranking officers of the bank (all white males) because their compensation was determined by very different mechanisms (and was provided in very different ways) from the remainder of the bank's officer corps. After these restrictions were imposed, we were left with a 1974 sample size of 2,621 nonofficers and 410 officers. The plaintiffs' expert witness reported corresponding totals of 2,329 and 414.

   In 1977, because of a clerical error, data for a large number of employees were not entered into the working data base and were irretrievably lost. These employees made up about half of the surviving cohort of employees who were hired by the bank between 1965 and 1973. It is not known what impact this nonrandom pattern of missing data has on the results presented here, although one suspects that the statistical consequences of this loss of data may not have been enormous. If the number of observations in the available 1977 data set was inflated by a factor of two for these years, the resulting total number of observations would have been 3,432 instead of 2,761, or about 25 percent more cases. In addition, it was not possible to exclude part-time employees from the 1977 sample. The available number of observations for 1977 was 2,454 nonofficers and 363 officers. The corresponding values provided by the plaintiffs' expert witness were 2,466 and 483.

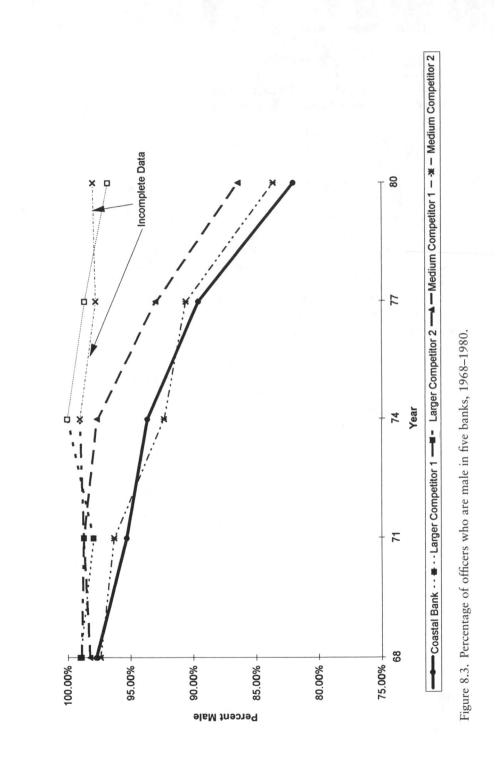

Figure 8.3. Percentage of officers who are male in five banks, 1968–1980.

Table 8.2. *Percent Male at Each Rank, by Bank by Year*

	All Ranks	Other	Officer	Lower VP	VP	Upper VP
			Rank			
Coastal Bank						
1968	97.7	100.0	96.1	96.8	100.0	100.0
1971	95.3	100.0	89.0	96.8	100.0	100.0
1974	93.6	100.0	88.1	95.7	96.5	100.0
1977	89.5	93.1	81.1	93.0	95.9	100.0
1980	81.9	96.9	66.7	83.9	93.7	100.0
Larger competitor 1						
1968	99.0	100.0	97.0	98.7	100.0	100.0
1971	97.9	98.1	94.4	99.3	100.0	100.0
1974	100.0[a]	—	—	—	100.0	100.0
1977	98.6[a]	—	—	—	99.3	100.0
1980	96.7[a]	—	—	—	99.0	100.0
Larger competitor 2						
1968	98.9	98.9	100.0	97.9	99.0	100.0
1971	98.7	98.5	97.2	100.0	98.3	100.0
1974	99.0[a]	—	—	—	98.6	100.0
1977	97.7[a]	—	—	—	99.0	96.2
1980	97.9[a]	—	—	—	97.8	100.0
Medium competitor 1						
1968	98.2	93.3	—	100.0	100.0	100.0
1971	98.7	95.8	98.0	100.0	100.0	100.0
1974	97.6	95.8	96.2	97.9	100.0	100.0
1977	92.9	100.0	86.3	95.8	97.1	100.0
1980	86.3	100.0	78.1	90.8	94.6	100.0
Medium competitor 2						
1968	97.4	94.1	—	98.3	100.0	100.0
1971	96.3	94.0	—	96.3	100.0	95.5
1974	92.3	91.9	85.2	96.7	97.4	95.8
1977	90.5	96.1	81.4	91.5	98.4	100.0
1980	83.5	95.2	67.3	89.0	96.6	100.0

[a] Data incomplete due to change in reporting practices.

positions who are outside the "officer," "assistant VP," "VP," and "senior VP" progression.) The limits of this upward percolation of women officers in all banks is revealed by the fact that, both at the beginning and end of the period in question, the upper tier of officers remained exclusively male at all institutions.

Again, it is worth emphasizing that compared with its closest competitors, Coastal showed no signs whatsoever of being a laggard in incorporating women into its officer ranks. Further evidence of this is contained in a summary of the 1973 EEO-1 reports for the same banks

Table 8.3. *Female Representation by Job Category in Five Banks,*
1973 EEO-1 Data

	Percent Female at Job Level				
	Officials and Managers	Professionals	Technicians	Sales	Office and Clerical
Coastal Bank	11.0	32.1	18.7	16.7	72.6
Larger competitor 1	12.6	25.3	4.8	52.4	68.6
Larger competitor 2	13.0	25.1	21.8	22.4	73.7
Medium competitor 1	11.9	10.5	NA	NA	73.6
Meduim competitor 2	7.3	71.4	35.4	NA	71.4

(see Table 8.3). (EEO-1 reports are mandatory reports of the gender
and minority composition of a firm's workforce.) As in Table 8.2,
there is nothing exceptional about Coastal's incorporation, or lack of
incorporation, of women into the hierarchy of bank jobs. And, as was
pointed out earlier, the other banks were being equally criticized at
this time for their treatment of female employees. Neither of these
data sources, of course, speaks to the issue of relative pay levels of
men and women officers in the various banks. But if there were unique
antifemale bias at Coastal, it does not appear in these hiring and
promotion data. The more likely case is that Coastal was typical of its
sister institutions.

Table 8.4 presents a summary of the characteristics, qualifications, and
pay of the Coastal work force. Results are presented by employee sex,
officer status, and year. For both 1974 and 1977 and for both officers
and nonofficers, males have about one more year of education than
females. The pattern for months of seniority at the institution are a bit
more complicated. In both years, female officers have put in more years
at the firm than their male counterpart, but the reverse is true below the
officer level, that is, male nonofficers tend to have more seniority than
female nonofficers. In 1974, about 16 percent of employees in nonofficer
jobs were black, but almost none in officer jobs were black. By 1977,
the proportion of black employees had increased for all groups. Women
increased their representation at the officer level from 9 to 14 percent
between 1974 and 1977. One fact of life in Coastal remained relatively
constant across the years, however. Women's pay lagged behind men's:
Their average earnings hovered between 70 and 77 percent of the male
average regardless of year or level in the bank.

As previous chapters have shown, gender inequality is often closely
intertwined with an employer's structure of jobs and job titles. Table 8.5

Table 8.4. *Individual Characteristics at Coastal Bank, by Gender and Officer Status, 1974 and 1977*

	Nonofficers		Officers	
	Female	Male	Female	Male
1974 data				
Mean education (years)	12.5	13.7	15.4	16.4
Mean tenure (months)	62.7	66.4	213.3	164.1
Mean salary grade	8.18	12.18	32.97	35.69
Mean salary ($/yr)	$8,150	$10,568	$20,150	$27,068
Salary ratio (F/M)	0.771	—	0.744	—
No. of employees	1,613	1,008	36	374
Pct. black at level	15%	17%	0%	1%
Pct. female at level	62%	—	9%	—
1977 data				
Mean education (years)	12.3	13.4	15.1	16.1
Mean tenure (months)	57.0	69.5	189.2	186.3
Mean salary grade	NA	NA	NA	NA
Mean salary ($/yr)	$8,876	$11,617	$20,990	$29,939
Salary ratio (F/M)	0.764	—	0.701	—
No. of employees	1,551	903	50	313
Pct. black at level	20%	19%	4%	2%
Pct. female at level	63%	—	14%	—
Supplementary officer data				
Assistant VP or higher	—	—	16%	53%
Mean salary	—	—	$22,115	$29,764
Salary ratio (F/M)	—	—	0.743	—
No. of employees	—	—	71	452
Pct. female at level	—	—	14%	—

recapitulates the information shown in Table 8.4, with the data aggregated to the level of jobs. For both officers and nonofficers, for both years, predominantly male jobs (i.e., 0–30 percent female) are occupied by employees with higher average levels of education – although these differences are less pronounced for officers than for nonofficers. Seniority patterns are mixed but indicate a change between the two years with predominantly female jobs having higher average seniority in 1974 and with the reverse being true in 1977. Among the officer job titles, this occurs because of a large drop in average tenure for predominantly female jobs – a pattern that is consistent with the firm having disproportionately hired women from outside the firm into these jobs between 1974 and 1977. It is interesting to note that the mean job size for these thirteen job titles in 1977 was exactly one, suggesting a practice of placing these women into idiosyncratic positions.

Table 8.5. *Job Characteristics at Coastal Bank, by Percent Female in Job and Officer Status, 1974 and 1977*

	Percent Female in Nonofficer Level Jobs			Percent Female in Officer Level Jobs		
	71%–100%	31%–70%	0%–30%	71%–100%	31%–70%	0%–30%
1974 data						
Mean education						
(years)	12.6	14.1	14.2	16.2	16.3	16.4
Mean tenure (months)	78.2	67.6	76.0	194.2	130.6	166.6
Proportion black	0.117	0.135	0.142	0.000	0.028	0.006
Mean salary grade	8.59	11.0	13.1	32.4	28.8	34.5
Mean salary($/yr)	$8,524	$9,898	$11,716	$18,437	$18,344	$26.245
Mean job size	3.99	6.54	3.44	1.40	4.78	6.29
No. of jobs	339	82	186	5	9	72
Pct. of jobs	(55.8%)	(13.5%)	(30.6%)	(5.8%)	(10.5%)	(83.7%)
1977 data						
Mean education						
(years)	12.6	13.8	14.1	15.5	15.1	16.3
Mean tenure (months)	82.2	62.7	89.4	140.4	147.0	182.2
Proportion black	0.151	0.200	0.150	0.000	0.045	0.018
Mean salary grade	NA	NA	NA	NA	NA	NA
Mean salary ($/yr)	$9,539	$10,709	$13,081	$19,468	$21,654	$30,972
Mean job size	3.84	6.32	2.64	1.00	4.36	4.96
No. of jobs	347	90	196	13	11	68
Pct. of jobs	(54.2%)	(14.8%)	(31.0%)	(14.1%)	(12.0%)	(73.9%)

As might be expected, average salaries also differ between predominantly male and predominantly female jobs. In 1974, the ratio of earnings in the 71–100 percent female category to the 0–30 percent female category was 0.73 for nonofficers and 0.70 for officers – values roughly comparable with those found for female and male individuals. By 1977, however, these ratios had moved further apart, with predominantly female jobs holding steady at a ratio of 0.73 at the nonofficer level but slipping to a ratio of 0.63 at the officer level. Such a shift implies either changes in the relative pay of these positions, or movement of better-paid women out of the nonofficer ranks and into the officer ranks. Finally, we note that the job structure – the percentage of jobs predominantly female, mixed, or predominantly male – hardly changed at all in the nonofficer tier of jobs. At the officer tier, however, the proportion of predominantly male jobs declined and was offset by increases in both the number of mixed jobs and the number of predominantly female jobs.

To this point the quantitative data depict a sex-segregated work force that was undergoing modest changes in gender inequality. Women constituted a higher proportion of officers in 1977 than three years earlier, although their salaries lagged further behind those of their male col-

Table 8.6. *Sex Segregation Indices for Job Titles, Officer Position Numbers, and "Officer Rank Titles" at Coastal Bank, 1974 and 1977*

	Minimum Job Size		
	1 Person	2 People	3 People
1974 data			
Nonofficers	73.4[a] (590)[b]	70.0 (303)	69.3 (202)
Officers	64.1 (86)	58.8 (39)	56.8 (29)
1977 data			
Nonofficers	68.8 (656)	63.2 (291)	61.3 (182)
Officers			
Job titles	53.4 (99)	41.7 (37)	39.0 (27)
"Rank" titles	58.8 (33)	57.4 (26)	57.0 (22)

[a] Index of dissimilarity.
[b] No. of job titles.

leagues than such salaries had in 1974. The degree of job segregation was declining as evidenced by the drop in the proportion of mostly male jobs. To confirm this latter point, we calculated the segregation index or index of dissimilarity across job titles for officers and nonofficers at the two time periods. Table 8.6 contains the relevant results. At both time periods (and regardless of the minimum size of job considered), nonofficer jobs are more sex-segregated than officer jobs. Likewise, for both levels, job segregation by sex declined between 1974 and 1977. (The larger decline shown when the minimum job size is two or three people is a necessary result of the pattern shown in Table 8.5 – predominantly female jobs in 1977 were exclusively single-person jobs.)

The level of gender segregation among officers in 1977 may be higher than indicated by the figures shown for job titles, however. An alternate basis of classification for officers is provided by the designations contained in the organization's listing in the aforementioned commercial directory. (There were about thirty-three such titles, e.g., Personnel Officer, Assistant Vice-President, Systems Officer, etc., which we refer to as "Rank Positions.") When the level of gender segregation is calculated across these positions, it is higher than what is found on the basis of functional job titles. In fact, segregation of officers by "rank position" is only slightly lower than segregation of nonofficers by functional job title. Because of the salience of hierarchical distinctions at the officer level of the bank, segregation by "rank" titles may be more meaningful here than segregation according to purely functional duties.

Market, Efficiency, and Organizational Inequality Models

Having set the context, we now assess the explanatory power of market, efficiency, and organizational inequality models of pay differences in Coastal based on a series of multivariate analyses. After presenting an ordinary least squares model of income that only includes individual-level data, we analyze models that also contain parameters for job-level differences in pay. Job-level variation in pay is, of course, of fundamental concern in the pay equity debate. Comparable worth advocates argue that gender inequality in pay operates in large measure through the devaluation of female jobs. They predict that, net of other variables, the gender composition of a job will decrease the earnings of its incumbents. In addition to job-level sex composition, we also possess market survey data on some jobs. This allows us to test the effect of market indicators on wage differences. The effect of market data can be juxtaposed with variables on the internal ranking of jobs by Coastal – job evaluation points and grade within the Coastal job grade system. If the latter prove more powerful in explaining gender-based wage differences, this would tend to reject market-based theories in favor of either efficiency or organizational inequality interpretations.

In Table 8.7, standard ordinary least squares regression predictions of the logarithm of income are shown for officers, nonofficers, and the combined work force for 1974 and 1977. (All regression coefficients are statistically significant *except* those indicated.) With the exception of one group, adjustments for "human capital" differences do not account for very much of the difference in earnings between men and women. (The implied percentage difference in earnings between females and males, or any dichotomous variable, can be obtained by applying the following formula: percent difference = $e^b - 1$; see Halvorsen and Palmquist 1980.) Thus, for officers, the models imply that women have adjusted earnings that are lower by 23.0 percent in 1974 and 22.6 percent in 1977 (compared with 23.2 percent and 27.2 percent lower before adjustments). For nonofficers in 1974, the percentage differences are 21.8 percent before controls and 16.4 percent after controls. In 1977 for nonofficers the controls for education and seniority lower the estimate of the income gap by slightly more: from a 20.3 percent gap to a 12.7 percent gap.

It is also important not to lose sight of the considerable salary difference attributable to officer status itself. In 1974, being an officer was associated with 87.2 percent higher adjusted earnings on average, and in 1977 it was associated with 70.2 percent higher adjusted earnings on average. The simple control for officer status decreases dramatically the implied salary gap between all men and women in the organization – a

Table 8.7. *Salary Determinants for Officers and Nonofficers, Coastal Bank, 1974 and 1977 (Standard Errors in Parentheses)*

	All Employees		Nonofficers		Officers	
	Model 1	Model 2	Model 1	Model 2	Model 1	Model 2
1974 data						
Intercept	9.470	8.400	9.215	8.387	10.158	9.103
	(0.011)	(0.026)	(0.009)	(0.027)	(0.015)	(0.110)
Female	−0.480	−0.185	−0.246	−0.179	−0.264	−0.262
	(0.015)	(0.009)	(0.012)	(0.009)	(0.051)	(0.046)
Education (years)		0.055		0.054		0.054
		(0.002)		(0.002)		(0.006)
Seniority (years)		0.017		0.019		0.012
		(0.001)		(0.001)		(0.001)
Black		−0.106		−0.099		−0.164[a]
		(0.013)		(0.012)		(0.117)
Hispanic		−0.102		−0.101		0.004[a]
		(0.023)		(0.022)		(0.184)
Officer		0.627		—		—
		(0.015)		—		—
N of cases	3,031		2,621		410	
R^2	(0.248)	(0.768)	(0.146)	(0.476)	(0.059)	(0.267)
1977 data						
Intercept	9.523	8.259	9.271	8.236	10.243	9.041
	(0.013)	(0.027)	(0.012)	(0.028)	(0.019)	(0.114)
Female	−0.450	−0.145	−0.227	−0.136	−0.317	−0.256
	(0.018)	(0.010)	(0.015)	(0.011)	(0.051)	(0.043)
Education (years)		0.068		0.069		0.059
		(0.002)		(0.002)		(0.007)
Seniority (years)		0.021		0.023		0.016
		(0.001)		(0.001)		(0.001)
Black		−0.084		−0.080		−0.007[a]
		(0.013)		(0.013)		(0.107)
Hispanic		−0.103		−0.099		—[b]
		(0.026)		(0.026)		—
Officer		0.532		—		—
		(0.018)		—		—
N of cases	2,752		2,393		359	
R^2	(0.190)	(0.760)	(0.090)	(0.550)	(0.095)	(0.380)

[a] Coefficient *not* significant, $p > 0.05$; all others significant.
[b] Coefficient not estimated; no Hispanic employees at officer level.

fact presumably not lost on the plaintiffs in the lawsuit, who chose not to do separate analyses for the two groups.

Perhaps the larger unexplained difference for officers is a reflection of a pattern we noted earlier: the increase in the number of women occupying officer positions in 1977. In other words, salaries in this organization might reflect time in *current* job more than they reflect

Table 8.8. *Salary Determinants by Officer Status, Coastal Bank, 1977*

	Nonofficers		Officers	
	Coefficient	Standard Error	Coefficient	Standard Error
Intercept	8.2459	0.0287	9.1858	0.1150
Female	−0.1404	0.0107	−0.2321	0.0420
Education (years)	0.0680	0.0020	0.0478	0.0066
Months in current job	0.0015	0.0002	0.0041	0.0006
Months in previous job(s)	0.0020	0.0001	0.0011	0.0001
Black	−0.0799	0.0129	0.0252	0.1028[a]
Hispanic	−0.1001	0.0259	—	—[b]
Hired from inside	0.0220	0.0103	−0.0027	0.0375[a]
N of cases	2,393		359	
R^2 (adj)	0.5510		0.4526	

[a] Coefficient *not* significant, $p > 0.05$; all others significant.
[b] Coefficient not estimated; no Hispanic employees at officer level.

general seniority within the organization. In particular, if current job experience is more highly rewarded than experience in general, women who are newly promoted into the officer ranks might suffer a wage penalty that is gradually made up over time as senior men retire and the women accumulate more job-specific seniority. Table 8.8 presents the required data.

For officers only, this refinement produces a slight reduction in the estimated level of gender inequality. At the officer level, for those who have had more than one job, months of seniority that are spent in the most recent job contribute more to earnings than months of seniority in earlier jobs. (There is no discernible influence of the simple fact of having had more than one job with the firm, as evidenced by the nonsignificant effect of the dummy variable for "hired from inside.") This differential is quite large, with seniority in the current job counting for nearly four times as much per month as previous job seniority. As suspected, male officers have longer mean seniority in their current jobs than do female officers – twenty-seven months for males compared to fourteen months for females. Taken in conjunction with the higher return for current job seniority, this difference does play a role in explaining why female officers are further behind their male counterparts than female nonofficers are behind their male counterparts.

Although differences in current job seniority explain a small amount of the gender wage gap among Coastal officers, they account for almost nothing at the nonofficer level. Thus, additional explanations need to be considered. There are three important factors worthy of more attention: (1) job segregation; (2) the gender composition of jobs; and (3) market wage rates. Furthermore, it is important to recognize that factors 2 and 3 are closely linked to factor 1. What matters in a "between job" wage inequality claim is the degree to which salaries are clustered by job, and the extent to which this job-level salary component is associated with the gender composition of jobs. Contrariwise, what matters from the viewpoint of administered efficiency is the extent to which the job-level component is associated with external market differentials.

A statistical technique well suited for this task is the so-called random effects regression model. An explanation of this procedure is presented in an appendix to this chapter, with a summary of key findings provided in Table 8.9. Essentially, the technique allows one to combine individual and group-level variables in a way that the importance of various aspects of the group (e.g., gender composition) can be assessed against the overall contributions that groups (i.e., jobs) make to earnings.

In the following summary tables (Tables 8.9, 8.10, and 8.11), we present data on the size of the individual-level gender effect (i.e., the "cost of being a female"), the size of various group-level effects (e.g., percent female in the job), and the degree of salary clustering by job (measured by the intraclass correlation coefficient). To the extent that these various group-level variables (in this case, percent female in the job) have important consequences, three results should occur: (1) their specific coefficients should be large and statistically significant; (2) they should reduce the effect of gender at the individual level; and (3) they should reduce (i.e., explain) the degree of salary clustering by job.

Results for both 1974 and 1977, reported separately for officers and nonofficers, are shown in Table 8.9. For statistical reasons, the analysis is restricted to individuals in jobs that have at least two incumbents. There are two central assertions of the between-job discrimination hypothesis: (1) most of the earnings disparity between male and female workers is located between jobs; and (2) the amount of clustering of earnings by job is considerable. For nonofficers in 1974 and 1977, both of these conditions seem to be met. That is, if we compare the value of the individual male-female earnings disparity from the first column of Table 8.9 (after controlling for education, etc., but prior to controlling the job vector) with its value in the second (after controlling job), it is reduced by 75 percent (from −0.176 to −0.044). Or stated somewhat differently, the unexplained earnings difference from the human capital model is mostly between jobs. As for the overall level of earnings clustering, that property is best indexed by the adjusted intraclass correlation ratio, which in this case equals 0.902. This is a very high degree of overall clustering, suggesting that the bank in this instance tended to "pay the job" rather than "pay the worker."

There is one additional implication from the between-job, gender dis-

Table 8.9. *Summary of Models with Job-Level Effects Including Percent Female by Officer Status, Coastal Bank, 1974 and 1977*

	Model 1: No Job-Level Effects	Model 2: Job-Level Effect Only	Model 3: Job-Level Effect with % Female
1974 results: Nonofficers (N = 2,324)			
Individual-level gender effect	−0.176	−0.044	−0.037
Degree of salary clustering by job	—	0.902	0.877
Effect of gender composition of Job	—	—	−0.328
1974 results: Officers (N = 367)			
Individual-level gender effect	−0.244	−0.136	−0.122
Degree of salary clustering by job[a]	—	0.521	0.513
Effect of gender composition of job	—	—	−0.204[b]
1977 results: Nonofficers (N = 2,045)			
Individual-level gender effect	−0.130	−0.028	−0.022
Degree of salary clustering by job	—	0.921	0.902
Effect of gender composition of job	—	—	−0.419
1977 results: Officers (N = 304)			
Individual-level gender effect	−0.234	−0.127	−0.120
Degree of salary clustering by job	—	0.666	0.632
Effect of gender composition of job	—	—	−0.468

[a] As measured by intraclass correlation coefficient.
[b] Coefficient not statistically signicant; all other significant, $p < 0.05$.

crimination hypothesis: The job feature of predominantly female jobs that is most responsible for the diminished earnings is the fact that the jobs are disproportionately female (see England 1992, 125ff). Or, in terms of our statistical model, the unexplained income variance associated with jobs should be substantially reduced when the gender composition of those jobs is taken into consideration. To investigate this possibility, the gender composition of each job has been added as an additional explanatory variable in the third column of Table 8.9. For nonofficers, there is some additional support for the gender segregation hypothesis in this model: The effect of percent female is large and statistically significant, and there is a small reduction in the degree of salary clustering.

Table 8.9 also shows parallel findings for officers. The results are in the same direction as those for nonofficers, but are not nearly as strong. For example, the cost of being female is diminished, compared with the estimate shown in Table 8.7, where job membership was not taken into account, but only by 44 percent, not by 75 percent as for nonofficers.

Second, the intracorrelation ratio is only 0.52 for officers, indicating less clustering of income by job. Finally, the effect of percent female at the job level is not statistically significant, and the addition of this variable to the model barely reduces the amount of unexplained job level variation.

For officers, the patterns are also similar in 1977 and 1974. Again, about half of the original gender gap in pay is explained by the job vector, and the degree of income clustering by jobs is also less than at the nonofficer level. However, the intraclass correlation has increased to 0.66, and the effect of job sex composition is large and statistically significant. Thus, there is some evidence that sex composition matters more for officers in 1977 than it did in 1974.

One possible explanation for the continuing, although reduced, differences between officers and nonofficers in the structuring of income by job is that the concept of "job title" does not play the same role at the two levels. In fact, at the officer level, other sets of classifications besides job titles are used to keep track of the work force. Particularly meaningful is a set of "position numbers" that are used to compare the level of pay of Coastal officers with those in other banks in the same city and in the same geographic region. Not all officers are identified in our data by these position numbers. They seem to function as an informal set of "benchmark" jobs, which facilitate comparisons between the Coastal pay system and the broader market for bank officers. Of the 304 officers on whom we have complete data in 1977, over half (177) are in positions with position numbers. When the statistical analysis of officers shown in the last panel of Table 8.9 is repeated for this group, the estimates of the intraclass correlations increase dramatically: to 0.813 when sex composition is not in the equation, and to 0.797 when it is in the equation.

We think two related interpretations of this increase are plausible. First, at the officer level, position numbers may be an inherently more meaningful basis of classification that structure income levels more consistently than job titles do. Second, the subset of jobs/individuals given position numbers may be those occupying more standardized positions – positions that can be compared externally. This standardization necessarily leads to less "within-position" income variance. To the extent that the latter is true, it means that at least some "officer-level jobs" have as much income clustering as nonofficer jobs.

Establishing that important between-job income differences exist is a different matter than identifying from where such differences come. Fortunately, the data available on the Coastal case include information on salaries paid in the external market for a large portion of the jobs in question. Therefore, we can assess, at least tentatively, the extent to which such differences are explained by Coastal's simply paying "going rates" for the jobs in question.

We begin by examining nonofficers. In the early 1970s the bank identified some sixty-one job titles as benchmark positions that were evaluated using an 11-factor point scheme. Many of these positions were also included on a list of positions for which external salary data were gathered from a number of different sources; the two most frequently used were American Management Association surveys and Federal Reserve Salary Surveys. When available, these salary data on the external market were merged into the nonofficer data base. All told, 515 nonofficers were in positions for which external salary comparisons could be made. In Table 8.10 this additional information is incorporated into the random intercept salary models for nonofficers examined in Table 8.9.[6]

A primary focus of attention in these models entails changes in the size of the "job-level" effects that occur when market variables and pay system variables (i.e., grade) are added and removed. That is, we know that for nonofficers job membership has an enormous impact on salary and gender differences in salary. Because market and grade are essentially job-level variables, one of the main consequences of bringing them into these models will be to reduce the variance in log earnings associated with jobs (as measured by the intraclass correlations). It is of considerable interest to learn which of these variables has the effect of producing larger reductions in job-level variance, for the results bear directly on the relative explanatory power of market or organizational models of pay determination. At the same time, it is also worth consid-

6 In each of these analyses, the clusters for the statistical models are defined by job titles. Variables included to represent the effect of market wages are (1) the yearly log dollar equivalent of the monthly salary for the job as reported in one of the external salary surveys mentioned earlier, and (2) a dummy variable for individuals for whom external salary data were missing. The salary grade number reported for each individual in the 1974 data base is reported for some models. Only individuals with valid salary grade scores are included in these tables. Thus the sample size is reduced to 1,835 nonofficer employees. (When the job is covered in more than one external salary survey, the minimum salary value is included in the model. Trials that used the mean or the maximum value in these cases had nearly identical results to those shown here. Individuals in nonbenchmark jobs were assigned the mean value of this variable calculated across the individuals who had such comparisons.)

The specific models are defined as follows: Model 1 includes the same variables as were included in Table 8.7 (gender, education, seniority, African American race, and Hispanic ethnicity); model 2, all model 1 variables plus terms representing membership in a given job group and a term representing the percent female in each job (i.e., models 1 and 2 parallel models 1 and 3 in Table 8.9); model 3, all model 2 variables plus a term representing the external salary for the job title; model 4, removes the external salary term from model 3 and adds the effect of Coastal salary grade; model 5, incorporates all variables including external salary and Coastal salary grade.

Table 8.10. *Summary of Models with Job-Level Effects Including Percent Female, External Market Salaries, and Salary Grade at Nonofficer Level, Coastal Bank, 1974*

	Model 1: No Job-Level Effects	Model 2: Job-Level Effect with % Female	Model 3: Job-Level Effect with External Salary, % Female	Model 4: Job-Level Effect with Salary Grade, % Female	Model 5: Job-Level Effect with All Job Variables
All nonofficers (N = 1,835)					
Individual-level gender effect	−0.182	−0.045	−0.046	−0.018	−0.018
Degree of salary clustering by job[a]	—	0.901	0.900	0.460	0.461
Effect of % female in job	—	−0.303	−0.302	0.014[b]	0.015[b]
Effect of external salary in job	—	—	0.425	—	0.020[b]
Effect of job salary grade	—	—	—	0.066	0.066
Nonofficers in jobs with external comparisons (N = 515)					
Individual-level gender effect	−0.238	−0.033	−0.033	−0.028[b]	−0.030
Degree of salary clustering by job	—	0.879	0.422	0.292	0.231
Effect of % female in job	—	−0.412	0.014[b]	0.027[b]	0.043[b]
Effect of external salary in job	—	—	0.910	—	0.305
Effect of job salary grade	—	—	—	0.061	0.044

[a] As measured by intraclass correlation coefficient.
[b] Coefficient *not* statistically signicant; all other significant, $p < 0.05$.

ering the size and significance of the direct effects of external market salaries and pay grades on individual earnings. To this end, the impact of external salary comparisons can be seen either by comparing models 3 and 2, or by comparing models 5 and 4, and the effect of internal salary grade is revealed in the comparison of models 4 and 2 and of models 5 and 3.

First consider model 3, which examines the impact of external salary level before "Coastal grade" has been taken into account. Here there is a strong positive relationship between the market salary that is associated with an individual's position and the individual's salary in the bank. When we compare models 2 and 3, however, we see that the intraclass correlation ratio is virtually unchanged, going from 0.901 to 0.900, indicating that for the entire population of nonofficers between-job salary differences are not influenced that much by market wage comparisons. This reduction may be so small for either of two reasons: Only about 25 percent of individuals are in jobs with external referents; and external market salaries are not inherently powerful determinants of job-level earnings. Furthermore, when Coastal grade is taken into account (see model 5), the residual effect of the market salary on the individual salary is nil. This means that the effect of market is wholly mediated by the salary grade system in place in Coastal. Seniority and education continue to have a direct impact on individuals' salaries, which is not surprising given that most "grade" systems allow for differentials within grade based on tenure and performance.

The comparison of models 4 and 2 shows the effects of introducing pay grade by itself. It yields some notable results. The intraclass correlation drops substantially, as do the effects of education and seniority. Moreover, the gender-salary relationship also changes significantly across these models. When salary grade is controlled, as in model 4, the disparity between male and female earnings diminishes considerably, from about 4.5 percent to less than 2 percent, and the difference between predominantly male and predominantly female jobs disappears completely. (The coefficient for percent female becomes insignificant.) This means that women are sorted into jobs with lower point ratings and correspondingly lower salary grades. This same diminution does not happen when only external market data are taken into account. Furthermore, after salary grade is taken into account, the male-female pay gap is not reduced by adding market salary data. (Compare models 3 and 2 and models 5 and 4.)

For the whole population of jobs, it is not the market wage structure that directly explains females' residual low earnings. Rather, the internal salary structure itself explains this pattern. Three more conclusions are relevant: (1) We know from the way the grade structure is derived that the internal rate structure is influenced by the market rates. (2) The internal rate structure is not completely determined by the market rates, that is, it is only partly influenced by them. (3) Even after all this is taken into account, female nonofficers continue to suffer a small but statistically significant wage penalty.

Further insight into these processes can be gleaned from the second panel of Table 8.10, which parallels the top panel but is restricted to the subset of workers in jobs with external salary comparisons. The results differ in several ways. For one, the addition of external salary data in model 3 drastically reduces the estimated income clustering effect within job titles – the intraclass correlation drops from 0.945 to 0.422. This suggests that market rates are more influential than we would have concluded by looking only at the first set of results. Interestingly, however, the addition of grade level, as in Model 5, provides an even further reduction of income clustering, down to 0.231. In other words, salaries, even in market-sensitive jobs, are affected by grade level in the pay system when market rates have been taken into account.

Another difference between the results for these jobs and for the broader population is the pattern of income differences associated with predominantly male and predominantly female jobs. In this subgroup, both external salary and numerical salary grade (taken either individually or together) explain away the effect of percent female in job.

Several conclusions can be drawn from these analyses. Perhaps most central is the importance of the pay grade system itself. Even in the subset of jobs where external comparisons are systematically made, the internal grade structure modifies individual earnings and is associated with a sizable component of job-level income differences. A second conclusion is that the pattern of earnings *in the benchmark jobs* is broadly consistent with the "tainted market" version of comparable worth theory. That is, almost all pay inequality experienced by individual men and women occurs between jobs, and market rates explain about half of the job-level income variance and all of the sex composition effect. Caution is required, however, in generalizing these properties to the entire nonofficer work force. The assignment of jobs to grades is a critical factor in determining job-level pay and in explaining the male-female pay gap. What is not clear is whether this assignment is done in a gender-neutral fashion. The analyses of many such pay systems by comparable worth scholar-advocates would suggest that it is not. Nor is it clear that the attempts to approximate market salaries by a loosely anchored linear grade system might not themselves end up re-creating existing gender differences that the market no longer sanctions or perhaps never did sanction.

Similar models were estimated for officers and the results are shown in the two panels of Table 8.11.[7] When the entire population of officers is considered, as in the first panel of Table 8.11, several conclusions are immediately suggested. First as noted earlier and in contrast to the nonofficer level, clustering by jobs, which in this case are "position numbers," continues to be a less salient feature of the pay process. Second, when education and seniority are taken into account, there are no negative effects of the sex composition of these officer-level jobs. Third, there is a larger residual, within-job, individual gender effect among officers that is not explained by market forces or by the job evaluation points.

7 The procedures we applied to this group differ in several minor ways from the previous analyses. First, the results shown are for 1977 only, because market data are available only for the later time period. Second, several variables are defined a little differently: (1) job clusters are defined by position numbers, not by job titles; (2) two measurements of external salaries were available for jobs with such measurements: a wage for comparable positions in the same city and a wage for comparable positions in the same region; (3) pay grades were not used by the bank in 1977 for setting officer salaries, so these models use job evaluation points instead; (4) finally, about half the individuals are in jobs in which external comparisons are made, which is about twice the proportion found for nonofficers.

Table 8.11. *Summary of Models with Job-Level Effects Including Percent Female, External Market Salaries, and Salary Grade at Officer Level, Coastal Bank, 1977*

	Model 1: No Job-Level Effects	Model 2: Job-Level Effect with % Female	Model 3: Job-Level Effect with External Salary, % Female	Model 4: Job-Level Effect with Salary Grade, % Female	Model 5: Job-Level Effect with All Job Variables
All officers (N = 333)					
Individual-level gender effect	−0.214	−0.186	−0.183	−0.078	−0.081
Degree of salary clustering by job[a]	—	0.244	0.122[c]	0.233	0.202[b]
Effect of % female in job	—	−0.070[b]	0.184[b]	0.103[b]	0.139[b]
Effect of external salary in job: City	—	—	0.412	—	0.024[b]
Effect of external salary in job: Region	—	—	0.375[b]	—	0.149[b]
Effect of job evaluation points (100 pts.)	—	—	—	0.079	0.077
Officers in jobs with external comparisons (N = 162)					
Individual-level gender effect	−0.202	−0.144	−0.129	−0.069[b]	−0.082
Degree of salary clustering by job	—	0.759	0.227	0.342	0.242
Effect of % female in job	—	0.111[b]	0.132[b]	0.082[b]	0.130[b]
Effect of external salary in job: City	—	—	0.460	—	0.138[b]
Effect of external salary in job: Region	—	—	0.378	—	0.207[b]
Effect of job evaluation points (100 pts.)	—	—	—	0.075	0.054

[a] As measured by intraclass correlation coefficient.
[b] Coefficient *not* statistically signicant; all other significant, $p < 0.05$.
[c] Intraclass correlation estimated via minimum variance quadratic unbiased estimator.

Again we conducted a separate analysis that is restricted to those individuals in "market-compared" positions (see second panel). For these positions the amount of income clustering by position is substantially larger initially and approaches what is found among nonofficers. In addition, controls for both market salaries and job evaluation points substantially reduce the intraclass correlations, indicating that both of these factors are important in explaining between-position inequality. Like the situation for nonofficers, there are residual effects of market wages on individual income, but no effects of job sex composition once job evaluation points have been controlled. Given the smaller amount of income clustering and the absence of a sex composition effect, it is not surprising that the plaintiffs in the lawsuit avoided framing their claims in the language of comparable worth.

These findings drive home the relative import of the internal job system to gender inequality at Coastal Bank. For all nonofficers, and for officers who are directly compared with the external market, salaries are strongly structured by job classification systems. The system of salary grades and evaluation points does incorporate information about the external market: Market rates are related to individual salaries. But that relationship disappears when an individual's position in the "internal" classification system is taken into account.

These results have three significant implications. First, they strongly support organizational models (of either an efficiency or inequality cast) of income determination over a market model. Market rates are not unrelated to the Coastal wage structure, but they do not by themselves eliminate gender differentials in pay and at the nonofficer level they explain less between-job variance in pay than the internal pay grade classifications. Second, within the same private sector organization we find two species of income inequality. For nonofficers, most of the unexplained variance in individual-level income is attributable to between-job pay differences. Percent female in job is a significant source of such between-job variance. For officers, within-job income variation is a primary source of gender inequality in pay. Third, after introducing extensive controls for individual human capital characteristics, between-job pay differences, external market data, and internal grade or job evaluation ratings, we still find statistically significant gender differentials in pay. The persistence of the gender gap throughout these analyses, coupled with the finding that percent female in job by itself accounts for a significant portion of between-job pay differences, is not readily explained by efficiency principles.

Coastal's Compensation System: Principles and Practices

At both the officer and nonofficer levels, the Coastal pay system appears to be a formally rational system. It was designed with the advice of outside consultants. It employs formal job evaluation techniques and market wage data. Compensation policy is set within the personnel department, based on technical analyses by the bank's own economists, and is implemented by department heads according to salary guidelines. The various documents that constitute the system articulate four paramount principles: efficiency, fairness, competitive market rates, and managerial discretion. If the system is true to these principles, it would not itself contribute to invidious gender differentials in pay. Indeed, it is somewhat difficult to understand how such a system could produce the kind of unexplained wage differences we found in the prior section or the kinds of testimonials to blatant discrimination that the plaintiffs presented at trial.

The critical question we will pursue in this section is whether Coastal's compensation system conforms to these principles. Based on a relatively comprehensive archive on the nonofficer and officer pay systems in Coastal, we will examine how these systems evolved, how they operate with respect to the market, and how they treat men and women. The results could support or contradict what we have found thus far. If we find only minor deviations from market or efficiency principles in how the system operates, it tends to support market and efficiency models and raise questions about our quantitative results. If we find systematic organizational tendencies that disadvantage female jobs or female workers, or advantage male jobs or male workers, the results would tend to reconfirm the quantitative analysis and lend further support to the organizational inequality explanation of gender inequality at Coastal.

The Nonofficer Pay System

A formalized salary administration plan for nonofficers was first established in 1920, when Coastal adopted a job evaluation scheme based on job factor analysis. This system was modified and refined in the 1930s and again in the 1950s. The bank abandoned the system early in the 1960s because "[c]onfidence was lost in the ability of the plan to establish equitable relationships" (Coastal Salary Admin. Study, D48290). Until 1970 the bank's personnel division administered salaries "based on its extensive knowledge of the Coastal organization and its employees" (Coastal Salary Admin. Study, D48290).

In 1970, an established compensation consulting firm, whom we will refer to as Ryan Associates, was retained to evaluate and complete a new formal salary administration program. Ryan Associates presented its report to Coastal's senior management in May 1971, setting out the objectives and procedures for the nonofficer salary plan. Market rates figured prominently in the language of the Ryan Associates' Report. The first numbered principle says: "Since the stated objective of the compensation program is to maintain salaries at an equitable level, this general level should be equal to that of the market average" (Coastal Salary Admin. Study, D48311). Note that equity is here defined in terms of market rates. That is, so long as jobs are paid the "going rate" offered in the marketplace, equity is achieved. The three remaining principles dealt with the size of the salary range for each salary grade, the differentials between the midpoints of grades, and the need to have salary ranges that are large enough to allow incentive or merit pay increases.

Like the other job evaluation systems we have examined in this book, Coastal defined the outlines of the nonofficer pay structure by assigning job evaluation points to a set of "benchmark" jobs. The benchmarks were described to be "representative of all positions and functions and/or as being representative of the extremes to be found in one or more factors in the job evaluation plan. Benchmark job evaluations were to serve as a guideline or ruler against which to measure other Bank jobs" (Coastal Salary Admin. Study, D48301). Sixty-one jobs were chosen as benchmarks for nonofficer positions, out of some 708 total nonofficer positions in the bank. These jobs were then used as comparisons in the point ratings of other jobs. Twenty-one job grades were established based on point ranges.

Despite the emphasis on market rates in the statement of principles, wage survey data played a relatively minor role in Coastal's benchmark and job evaluation system. In the State of Washington scheme analyzed in Chapter 6, benchmarks were explicitly chosen as jobs that could be compared with the market. Coastal chose its benchmarks because "they were well known within the bank." Although many of Coastal's benchmark positions appeared among the list of jobs for which market data were available from the Federal Reserve and other sources, the market data were not used as an independent measure of whether the assigned point values corresponded to the distribution of wages in the market. Nor were the market data used to establish a prediction line that could translate points into salaries for jobs not included in one of the surveys. Rather, the market survey data were employed informally to validate the assignment of points.

There is little in the Ryan Associates report that proves that the new nonofficer salary scale reflected a disinterested analysis of the internal value of positions or the market rates for jobs. The report describes three analyses that purport to show that the job evaluation process had achieved its goals. First, fifty-two jobs in the Federal Reserve Salary Survey were ranked according to average salary and according to Coastal evaluation points. The two rankings were reported to be "parallel" to each other (Coastal Salary Admin. Study, D48297–D48298). It is curious that the study reports findings about parallel rankings when it could easily have reported a correlation between points and average salary. It did not even provide a rank order correlation. We can infer that the two sets of ranks were inspected without any formal analysis.

Second, the sixty-one benchmark jobs were ranked by number of points and by the average salaries of incumbents in the jobs. "This analysis indicated there was a meaningful relationship. Also, evaluation indicated that in several cases, the plan established a more equitable ranking between jobs than average salaries" (Coastal Salary Admin. Study, D48297–D48298). The report is extremely vague about how the judgment of equity was made and by whom. Third, the report states that the compensation manager and his assistant subjectively ranked jobs and that these subjective rankings correlated positively with rankings by Coastal points. No specifics are provided about the strength of the correlation. Nor are any details given about the degree to which their subjective rankings may have been contaminated by what they knew of the evaluation results.

While the external validation of the job evaluation system is unclear, it is very clear that the job evaluation results ultimately were subject to control by managers and division administrators. The Coastal Job Evaluation Manual states that after jobs are evaluated by job analysts, "[r]ankings will be explained to the Managers and approved by the Division Administrators before they are entered as a permanent record. For jobs where serious discrepancies are uncovered, a re-write and re-evaluation will be scheduled. Division Administrators and Managers will be permitted access to job descriptions and salary ranges for all jobs within their own area(s) of responsibility" (Job Eval. Manual, D48260). Managers also have a primary role in initiating changes in job descriptions. The compensation unit reviews job descriptions every two years, but it is the responsibility of a supervisor to contact a job analyst "when a position changes significantly enough to warrant a rewrite or when a new job develops in an area" (Personnel Pol. and Proc'd. Manual, D48272).

The makeup of the Evaluation Committee that initially rated the benchmark jobs also reflected the existing managerial hierarchy in Coastal. It was composed of five male vice presidents from each of five departments: banking, operations, trust, investment, and staff departments. They were assisted by personnel staff, only one of whom was a woman, and by the Ryan Associates consultants. Despite the use of formal job evaluation techniques, such a decision-making group is unlikely to raise fundamental questions about the existing pay structure. Given the seniority and gender composition of the group, it is also unlikely that it would take a hard look at the possibility that job ratings and salary levels contain gender bias. Indeed, the empirical record contains an indication that the initial results of the 1970 job evaluation largely preserved existing gender hierarchies among nonofficer jobs.

Several better-paying, predominantly male jobs were treated as exceptions to the job evaluation scheme. After a review by key Coastal personnel officials, the Ryan Associates consultants agreed to delete two of the thirteen job evaluation factors from the factor point plan. The factors eliminated were "working conditions" and "physical effort." After these factors were jettisoned, those jobs in which the eliminated factors were perceived to be important were excluded from the pay plan. The positions so removed were "in the maintenance, security, records, and stock room areas" (Coastal Salary Admin. Study, D48295). The further recommendation was made that salaries in these areas be administered on an "informal basis."

A review of the available personnel records for 1974 reveals that there were five subunits of the bank that specialized in these functions. The job titles in these areas included "janitor," "matron," "receiving clerk," "police," "sergeant," "lieutenant," "stockroom clerk," and other related designations. All told, in 1974 some 124 persons were employed in these titles. Only 8 (6.5 percent) were female, whereas 61 percent of nonofficers were female at the time. Most important, occupying one of these "excluded" positions had relatively favorable earnings consequences for position incumbents. After we controlled for seniority, education level, and employee gender, we found employee earnings in these exempted areas to be 8 percent higher than earnings of other nonofficers.[8] Removing these better-paying jobs from the formally sanctioned pay plan also prevented comparisons with other, lower job grades made up largely of female, clerical employees. The separation may have eliminated pressures to increase the pay levels of other employees for purposes of internal equity.

The tendency to preserve traditional wage patterns can be seen more clearly in the grade-by-grade cost analysis contained in the consultants' report, reproduced here as Table 8.12.[9] We have added a column for percent female in the grade as of 1974. Otherwise, we have entered the numbers and table headings from the table in the consultant's report. The report recommends immediate salary changes for employees who are paid below the range of their jobs, that is, below the normal minimum for the grade to which their job is assigned. Some 394 of the 1,857 employees included in the table were paid below range. This group presumably received equity adjustments. The table also gives the number of employees who were paid above range. Presumably these employees were "redcircled," meaning that they did not get normal pay raises until the salary range caught up to them. Some 112 employees were above range.

8 The *t*-value associated with this difference is 3.88, a value greatly exceeds that required to achieve statistical significance.
9 We have added a column for percent female in the grade as of 1974. Calculated from our 1974 work force data base. Other entries were taken from the original table produced by the pay consultants.

Table 8.12. Consultant's Summary of Cost of Adopting New Nonofficer Pay Structure, 1970–1971, by Grade, Percent Female in Grade, and Other Variables, Coastal Bank

Cost Analysis Summary

% Female (1974)	Grade	No. of Employees	Present Grade Cost ($)	Present Average Salary ($ Monthly)	Proposed Midpoint Cost ($)	Proposed Less Present ($)	Index	No. below Range	No. above Range	No. below Midpoint	No. above Midpoint
100	1	63	24,800	394	26,460	1,660	93.7	13	1	57	6
100	2	33	14,820	449	14,355	−465	103.2	4	6	17	16
96	3	89	39,890	448	40,317	427	98.9	6	10	58	31
100	4	81	37,445	462	38,070	625	98.4	3	6	54	27
94	5	144	65,795	457	70,416	4,621	93.4	39	6	110	34
92	6	182	90,915	500	93,730	2,815	97.0	37	22	114	68
89	7	250	131,534	526	139,750	8,216	94.1	46	17	187	63
69	8	140	79,185	566	84,560	5,375	93.6	31	9	109	31
63	9	149	87,548	588	96,552	9,004	90.7	42	3	116	33
73	10	137	90,812	663	94,941	4,129	95.7	31	10	84	53
46	11	110	73,915	672	81,070	7,155	91.2	39	7	82	28
74	12	136	96,379	709	107,168	10,789	89.9	35	3	113	23
39	13	73	59,241	812	62,123	2,882	95.4	13	5	47	26
38	14	65	53,954	830	59,410	5,456	90.8	12	1	47	18
20	15	57	50,307	883	55,347	5,040	90.9	13	3	47	10
27	16	47	46,107	981	48,880	2,773	94.3	8	0	29	18
27	17	30	29,698	990	33,390	3,692	88.9	8	3	23	7
10	18	41	44,266	1,080	49,077	4,811	90.2	7	0	32	9
15	19	8	8,506	1,063	10,288	1,782	82.7	2	0	8	0
1	20	11	13,775	1,252	15,191	1,416	90.7	2	0	10	1
0	21	11	14,360	1,305	16,401	2,041	87.6	3	0	9	2

Note:: Additional statistics include the following: total no. of employees, 1,857; total present cost, $1,153,250; total proposed midpoint cost, $1,237,500; difference between proposed and present cost, $84,244; present cost as a percent of proposed cost, 93.19; total below range, $14,307; no. of employees, 394; total above range, $7,018; no. of employees, 112.

Table 8.12 vividly demonstrates the gendered nature of Coastal's nonofficer job grades at this time. The lower grades are made up almost exclusively of women. The upper grades, while containing smaller numbers of employees, are overwhelmingly male. The proportion of employees found to be below and above range is fairly similar across grades. Indeed, employees in grades occupied by a majority of men are slightly more likely to receive a compensatory increase than are employees in grades occupied by a majority of women (23.6 percent below grade vs. 20.5 percent below grade), while majority female grades contained slightly more workers paid "above range" (6.6 percent) than majority male grades (3.5 percent). While we do not know the impact of the new plan on male-female wage differences, the grade-level data imply relatively little change in a pay structure in which male workers held better-paying positions.

Despite the absence of a rigorous demonstration that the Coastal pay structure was determined by market wage rates, and quite compelling indications that the new job evaluation scheme left the relative pay levels of most jobs largely unchanged, Coastal personnel officials and their consultants employ the idiom of market rates when assessing the pay structure. The Ryan Associates Report declared:

> One of the most significant findings of the study relates to the fact that salary levels of nonofficer positions in the Coastal Bank are competitive in relationship to other leading employers. It will cost less than 3 percent in the long range to correct inequities and to increase base salaries. . . . Certainly this is a lower cost than in many similar installations where the policy has been to compete with a cross-section of leading employers in the community rather than the more limited (generally lower paying) financial community. (Letter from Ryan Assoc. to Coastal Personnel Dir., June 7, 1971, D482888)

The personnel director's memos on annual pay increases also are pegged to the market. The 1973 guidelines are typical. After stating that the bank's goal for the aggregate increase in salaries was 6 percent, it admonished supervisors to be tough in their salary reviews, only rewarding employees who have performed well, rather than automatically passing on percentage increases. The guidelines include a table that cross-classifies the evaluation of the employee's performance (unsatisfactory, satisfactory, above average, and superior) by whether the employee currently is below or above the control point (or midpoint) for the job. Larger percentage increases are allowed for better performance and when the employee is below the control point. A footnote defines the control

point in market terms; "Salary level appropriate to satisfactory performance where the incumbent meets the normal requirements of the position and the salary is representative of the value of the position in the
outside employment market" (Memo, Dec. 29, 1972, and 1973 Salary
Pol. Doc. D5764–D5770).

A memo for a later year states, "The Employee Services Division carefully evaluates several salary surveys and salary and economic forecasts
to establish salary ranges which accurately reflect the market for each
particular job" (Memo, Dec. 1, 1976, and 1977 Salary Pol. Guide,
D5727). The passage gives the impression that Coastal's compensation
group carefully monitors changes in market rates for detailed jobs. Yet,
with one exception – computer programming jobs, which we will discuss
in more detail – there are no indications in the pay system documents
that the pay levels of certain jobs were fine-tuned in response to changing market data. Nor, in contrast to what we find for officer positions,
are there records of discussions between administrators and compensation analysts over whether particular positions are properly evaluated or
properly paid.[10]

Documents generated in 1979 provide some intriguing insights into
how Coastal officials interacted with the market differently for male and
female workers. The documents also reveal that Coastal's own economists pointed out the inconsistency and recommended a policy change
without explicitly discussing the gender dimension of the problem. The
1979 memo by the bank's financial analysts predicted that the "market"
for officers and nonofficers would move 7.0 percent in 1979 (1979 Salary
Recomm., D48483). The economists suggested that to remain competitive the bank should raise the average salaries of its control points to the
1978 market levels plus 7 percent for the anticipated increase in 1979.
In support of the recommendation, they plotted the market midpoints
(control points) of the twenty-one nonofficer grades by Coastal job
points and monthly salary for 1978. The graph is reproduced here as
Figure 8.4.

Several aspects of the data as presented are interesting. Figure 8.4
depicts a substantial gap between market midpoints and Coastal control

10   We cannot be certain that all documents relating to Coastal's experience with the labor
market were produced through discovery. Yet given the kinds of detailed documents
that were produced, we think it unlikely that such documents exist. At the nonofficer
level, with the one exception of computer jobs, it appears that market data were used
to estimate changes in "average" market wages. These data informed Coastal's
decisions about annual across-the-board pay increments for nonofficers. If any more
detailed, job-by-job market comparisons were made, it was done by supervisors within
their zone of discretion. No records of such job-level market comparisons were produced. Again, we think it unlikely that supervisors were systematically incorporating
market data in their pay recommendations.

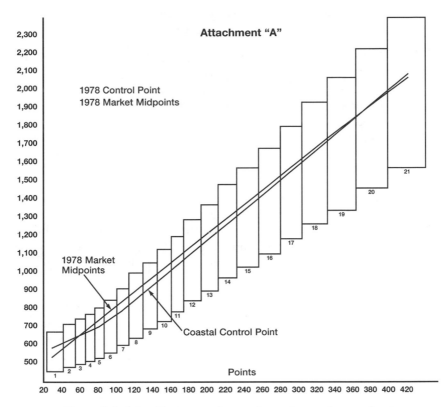

Figure 8.4. Monthly income by market points and control points, Coastal Bank, 1978.

points for the lower nonofficer grades. The differential is greatest for grades 6, 7, and 8 and then narrows to zero by grade 19. Inspection of the underlying data (not shown) reveals that the control points for grades 4 through 11 were paid an average of 2.7 percent to 5.8 percent below the market. Recall the data from Table 8.12 on the percentage of female employees by grade. All but one of the grades with disparities of this magnitude were predominantly female in 1974. We know that the gender composition of upper nonofficer grades and officer grades was changing between 1974 and 1979, as more women moved up within the bank. But it is unlikely that the gender composition of the lower nonofficer grades changed significantly. Therefore these data suggest that according to the bank's survey of market rates, they paid predominantly female grades lower with respect to the market than they paid gender-mixed and predominantly male grades.

The 1979 report alludes to earlier policy decisions to lower the minimum salaries paid to the lowest grades.

> Prior to 1976, our salary structure was based on a 80 percent to 120 percent spread of control points. But market studies at that time showed us that we could hire new employees at lower salary levels, even though the market value for experienced personnel continued to rise. Consequently, we went to a 76 percent to 116 percent spread to accommodate that particular market situation. (1979 Salary Recomm., p. 6, D48486)

The passage refers to "market studies" to indicate that a lower minimum was possible, but no explanation is given. Does it mean that the bank itself found it was able to hire at a lower minimum? Or was the decision based on reports of the minimums other employers were paying? The ambiguity continues as the report advises changing the spreads around market control points.

> However, current market analysis has shown us that our 76 percent to 116 percent range spread is too broad at the entry end of the range. The average low salaries (by grade) paid in the marketplace are substantially higher than our existing minimum salary levels. (1979 Salary Recomm., p. 6, D48486)

As a result of these findings, the bank's economists recommended raising the minimum pay of grades 1 to 5.

The only job grades for which Coastal attempted to fine-tune wage rates as a way of reducing labor costs in 1976 were populated primarily by women. Given that Coastal increased minimum wage rates for those grades only three years later suggests that it had gone too low in the market. In any event, it appears that Coastal had played tough with the market for predominantly female jobs, while paying at or above the market for predominantly male grades. Coastal was paying minimum wages that fell well below the market for virtually all grades. But given the large numbers of female employees in entry-level positions in lower grades, compared with small numbers of males in entry-level positions in the upper nonofficer grades, this practice put female workers at a disadvantage. Moreover, the Coastal maximums rose above the market maximums above grade 13. Grades 13 and above were predominantly male in 1974. This deviation from the market is likely to put male workers at an economic advantage.

Note that this pattern is consistent with the quantitative results we

reported in the previous section. Our random regression models indicated that a large portion of the male-female wage gap among nonofficers resided between jobs and that the earnings penalty for female
workers declined substantially when salary grade was controlled for.
Minimum market salary bore relatively little relationship to between-job
earnings. (See models 2, 3, 4, and 5 in Table 8.10.) Female nonofficers
suffer lower wages for two reasons: They are clustered in lower-pay
grades; and Coastal pays its lower-grade employees below the market
average, a practice they do not apply to employees in higher-grades. The
inconsistent use of market averages diminishes the explanatory power of
this variable in our statistical results.

Although the plaintiffs did not press any between-job wage claims
in the *Coastal* case, could Coastal's practice of playing tough with the
market for predominantly female grades have been another basis for liability under Title VII? The pivotal factual presumption in *Gunther* was
that the employer used job evaluation results to determine pay levels for
the male prison guards and the female prison matrons, but paid only 75
percent of the recommended pay level to the matrons. With that presumption in mind, the *Gunther* court ordered the trial court to give the
plaintiffs a chance to prove their case. In the *American Nurses* case,
Judge Posner stated that plaintiffs would have a valid Title VII claim if
they could prove that "the State has departed from the market measure
on grounds of sex" (*American Nurses' Association v. State of Illinois*,
783 F.2d 716, 725 [1986]). Thus, it appears that Coastal's pay policies
with respect to different jobs might also have been challenged by the
plaintiffs.

The 1979 memo may show that Coastal departed from the market in
paying women, but it also shows that at least one group in the organization – the economists – took the market data seriously. They were recommending pay adjustments tailored to bring particular grades into line
with "the market." We might wonder about the validity of their data.
We cannot tell, for example, whether any of their recommendations were
based on experience with turnover or difficulties in hiring replacements.
There is no mention of these sorts of internal data in their report. It
also may not be reasonable to talk about "the market" for some 700
nonofficer positions moving a given percentage. Depending on how comparisons are made to the outside market, it may be artificial to plot
minimum and maximum salaries by job grade. But if we take their analysis of the market as a given, their recommendations are consistent and,
from the standpoint of gender, progressive. They recommend larger pay
increases and raising the minimum pay levels for lower-level jobs held
predominantly by women. Whether the economists' recommendations
were followed in practice, we do not know.

The documents on nonofficers contain only one clear instance in which market pressures directly affect Coastal's wage rates. Coastal apparently encountered problems with its pay scales in the computer programming and systems analysis area. The personnel department reviewed all computer systems jobs, comparing Coastal pay rates with computer industry salary surveys and reported pay levels from other financial institutions in the region and the city. The memo from personnel concluded that Coastal's data processing salaries were competitive but that systems and programming salaries were not. The memo recommended raising the pay of twelve jobs, but gave the final decision to managers. One manager was singled out in the memo as having given special raises to programmers in his department, even though "market data didn't warrant it at this time" (1976 Memo on Systems and Prog. Mkt. Salary Survey, D48203). The personnel office treated the special pay raises as a temporary aberration in the market. The affected jobs were placed in separate salary grades, denoted with a "T," that paralleled the job grades they had been assigned to. By 1977 the personnel office began to suggest that the technical jobs soon could be merged back into the regular pay structure, because "the market for systems and programming positions is beginning to level off." Pay levels had "returned to normal" (Recomm. 1979 Coastal Bank Tech. Salary Structure, D48542–D48567).

The treatment of the programmers is an exception that proves the rule. The personnel department reacted to the proposal to change pay levels for these workers as an extraordinary event, indeed, almost as an unwarranted disturbance in the organization's pay system. It seems clear that the personnel office sought to maintain stable relative wage levels for different jobs in the nonofficer sector of the bank. Efforts to realign wage rates were likely to be met with hostility.

The data we have examined thus far on nonofficer pay indicate that women were paid less than men, at least in part as a result of conscious policies by Coastal officials. It may be, however, that the male wage advantage reflects the superior position of men in the labor market and that we have not adequately measured these resources. One way to investigate the prospect is to look at rates of turnover for men and women employees and assess whether the reasons they left indicate a different standing in the labor market.

Although it is not apparent that the bank routinely made use of turnover data in its salary deliberations, the case records contain some turnover statistics. Data for nonofficer terminations in 1978 are shown in Table 8.13. Rates of departures for economic and "family" reasons have been separately identified. When the numbers of voluntary terminations are compared with the estimated sizes of the male and female work forces, several patterns emerge. First, the overall rates of departure

Table 8.13. *Voluntary Terminations by Reason and Gender for Nonofficers, Coastal Bank, 1978*

	Males		Females		
	No.	Rate	No.	Rate	z
No. in work force[a]	932		1,523		
Voluntary departures[b]	37	0.0397	42	0.0276	$z = 1.55$
Economic departures[c]	32	0.0343	23	0.0151	$z = 3.12^*$
Family departures[d]	3	0.0032	17	0.0112	$z = 2.12^*$

[a] Numbers in work force are for 1977 and are taken from tables prepared by plaintiffs' expert. These numbers are reduced by the number of involuntary terminations in 1978: regular retirements, deaths, and firings for cause.
[b] Includes early retirements.
[c] Includes departures for dissatisfaction with promotion opportunities, with supervisor, and with pay, as well as for better offers, to return to school, and to take another job.
[d] Includes pregnancy/child care, relocation, "marriage," and other family reasons.
$^*p < 0.05$.

for males and females were not significantly different in that year. When the reasons for departures are considered, however, a more complicated picture emerges. Male nonofficers were significantly more likely than their female co-workers to leave the bank for economic reasons. Contrariwise, female nonofficers were more likely to leave for family and related nonjob reasons. Because the economic departures might have been much more responsive than the family departures to changes in Coastal's pay rates, one might ask whether the turnover differences shown here might justify not only higher pay rates for males than females but also higher rates than the males were receiving in 1978.

We cannot answer this question with the data we possess. The 3–4 percent departure rate for males is relatively low in absolute terms, but we do not know whether it was high enough to be considered problematic to the bank's operations or whether training and replacement costs were such that even small numbers of departures could be very expensive. Two points are perhaps significant. First, the turnover data do not suggest that the bank would have had much incentive to increase women's relative pay because of an excessive quit rate. Second, there is no evidence that the bank considered any of these data on overall quit rates in deciding how to administer its pay system.

The pay system documents on nonofficers suggest that despite the salience of market and efficiency considerations in the rhetoric of the nonofficer pay plan, many of the bank's pay practices are not well explained in market or efficiency terms. The job evaluation scheme was not validated by independent market data and appears to have preserved the existing wage hierarchy among nonofficer jobs. Several well-paying jobs held by men were exempted from the new scheme. Market data were used to determine overall salary increases rather than changes in relative wage levels. Before 1979 the bank paid predominantly female lower grades less with regard to the market average than it paid pre-dominantly male higher grades. Men were somewhat more likely to leave the bank for economic reasons than were women, but turnover rates among men and women were not statistically different.

Do similar mechanisms operate at the officer level of the bank? Recall that our statistical analysis suggested that a much smaller portion of gender inequality among officers was attributable to between-job pay dif-ferences. This pattern may reflect the relatively small number of women officers (14 percent by 1977) compared with women nonofficers (63 percent). We might well expect that a small group of recent entrants to the officer corps would be treated differently than workers in large, pre-dominantly female job grades. We now turn to the documents on the officer pay system to consider if this is the case.

Officers

The officer compensation system at Coastal was designed and periodi-cally reviewed from 1962 to 1975 by a major consulting firm (whom we refer to by the pseudonym Warren and Associates). (The Ryan firm was never involved in the officer compensation program.) The system was based on factor ratings of forty-five benchmark jobs, which were then "priced" against similar positions in other banks. After the benchmarks were evaluated and priced in the market, "the salary ranges of nonrep-resentative positions [were] fixed by referring to the salary ranges of the benchmark positions" (Warren Officer Job Eval. Guide, D5427).

The guide does not contain any specific listing of benchmarks or market data used to set benchmark salaries. The guide obviously was written at a time when officer status was equated with male gender. All pronouns used in the guide are male. For example:

> Position evaluation is a method of dissecting a position in terms of what a man does. . . . Of course, it is difficult to separate the "man" from the "job" at the officer level, but we will evaluate only the job as the man has made it (with higher management approval). (Warren Officer Job Eval. Guide, D5427)

A committee of senior management assigned points to each position based on its evaluation of the position on a set of factors. The total number of evaluation points determined the pay grade to which the job was assigned. Grade in turn set the salary range (Warren Officer Job Eval. Guide, D5438–D5439).

Thus the early officer pay system was moored to the market in ways that were not spelled out in pay system documents. And although jobs were evaluated according to a formal system, the application of the system was completely controlled by senior management.

Another consulting firm, Smith and Associates (a pseudonym), took a fresh look at the system in 1975. The Smith Report was only mildly critical; it found that the bank's current compensation practices were well designed and effective in maintaining the competitive position of the bank in the market for officer personnel. "[I]t appears evident that Coastal has developed a salary structure for its officers that closely follows normal business practice" (Smith Officer Comp. Strategy Report, Aug. 1975, D53710). Nonetheless, the Smith consultants had some suggestions for change.

The Smith firm began their report with a statement about the importance of officer compensation to overall bank performance.

> To assure the long-range continuance of the Bank's quality
> growth, Coastal has emphasized the acquisition and
> development of a high calibre officer staff, primarily through
> internal growth programs. . . . In order to acquire such people,
> satisfy their aspirations for growth, and obtain high
> performance through effective motivation, a well-conceived
> reward structure is essential. (Smith Officer Comp. Strategy
> Report, Aug. 1975, D5368)

The statement identifies a particular labor market strategy by Coastal: Individuals are recruited at the entry level and promoted into positions of increasing skill and responsibility. The report goes on to assess how well the compensation system is meeting that goal.

The core of the Smith firm's analysis was based on the application of its job evaluation system to some ninety-three benchmark positions in an officer work force of 445 in 1975. The Smith system assigns points for know-how, problem solving, and accountability. The ninety-three benchmarks "were chosen to represent all Officer levels in the Bank and all major functional areas. Included in this group were the positions of all Management Committee members" (Smith Officer Comp. Strategy Report, Aug. 1975, D5369). (The Management Committee includes the chairman and top seven officers/department heads.) The report does not disclose who decided which jobs would be used as benchmarks. The Smith consultants determined the number of points the chairman of Coastal received. (He received 6,240 points, some 2,500 more points than the next highest-rated officer, the vice chairman.) The Management Committee's points were set by the chairman and the consultants. The remaining benchmark jobs were evaluated by a group of Coastal's personnel professionals from the personnel department, assisted by Smith consultants. An Officers' Position Evaluation Committee consisting of the president, the general administrative executive, and the head of the banking department (all three of whom were among the top five officers in the bank in points and income) and the head of the personnel department reviewed the benchmark evaluations "to assure that they were consistent with the Bank's organizational policies and strategy" (Smith Officer Comp. Strategy Report, Aug. 1975, D5370). Just as with the prior officer system and the job evaluation system for nonofficer jobs, in the Smith evaluation scheme senior management retained firm control over the job rating process.

The results of the job evaluation process were then plotted against current salary. A "line of central tendency" was drawn by "inspection" (Smith Officer Comp. Strategy Report, Aug. 1975, D5370-A), bracketed by two lines showing a range between 80 and 120 percent of salary. Eleven cases fell outside this range, but the report concludes that "most deviations can be easily explained." Those below the minimum were rapidly promoted stars whose salary had not yet caught up with newly acquired positions. Those above the maximum were plateaued performers who were doing lower-level jobs while keeping higher salaries or whose positions were due to "special market conditions that have obliged the payment of unusually high salaries" (Smith Officer Comp. Strategy Report, Aug. 1975, D5371). The report thus concludes that Coastal's salary practices had been based on sound business judgment.

The Smith consultants provide legitimation to the existing pay structure through an exercise in which incumbent management is allowed to devise how many points it will allocate to various jobs. The deviations from this process are then rationalized as logical exceptions. Some exceptions are excused as responses to "special market conditions." But the report does not explain what "special market conditions" means. It might mean that these individuals had received outside offers and were given raises to retain them. Or it might reflect someone's judgment that these individuals' skills would earn a premium on the market, a premium that somehow escapes quantification in Smith's job evaluation scheme. The two largest deviations were for the manager of the special funds section (paid $9,916 more than expected) and for the manager of the savings section (paid $8,143 more than expected). These seem like relatively mundane bank control positions and not the kinds of jobs that get "hot" in the labor market.

More explicit attention to market comparisons was offered in the next section of the report. The Smith firm relied on its extensive list of clients to provide a profile of how compensation in a particular firm compared with others in the same industry or locale. Because all clients employed the Smith point system, Smith could plot the relationship between points and salary for an entire distribution of firms and then report where the point-salary line for the particular client lay within the distribution. The point system eliminated the need to rely on benchmark jobs and salary surveys. But the accuracy of the "market" measurement relied on the representativeness of the Smith client list, the choice of appropriate comparisons among the firms on the client list, and the reliability of point evaluations across different firms. The Smith consultants engaged in virtually no methodological introspection about these issues. Rather, they provided Coastal with a variety of comparisons and then concluded with an assessment of how Coastal's officer compensation structure compares with that of similar employers.

Compared with a "broad cross-section" of some 107 banks throughout the country, reported Smith, Coastal's base salaries were "strongly competitive" (Smith Officer Comp. Strategy Report, Aug. 1975, D5373). They slightly exceeded the third quartile (upper 75th percentile) of salaries at virtually all point levels along the salary curve. Coastal held a similar relative position compared with a group of fifty-four banks with assets over $700 million in 1974. Compared with nine very large banks, Coastal looked average at 500 points and 1,500 points, but was significantly below average at 5,000 points, the top pay level. Compared with other large area employers, it appeared average at lower point levels and somewhat above average at higher point levels (Smith Officer Comp. Strategy Report, Aug. 1975, D5373-A). Given the proximity of Coastal's base salaries to those of other banks and employers, the Smith consultants warned that "Coastal will have to remain alert if it is to maintain a competitive salary posture" (Smith Office Comp. Strategy Report, Aug. 1975, D5374). Because Coastal was so generous in benefits and bonuses, however, it was in a far stronger position in the market.

Figure 8.5 (Chart T) (Smith Officer Comp. Strategy Report, Aug. 1975, D5415) plots total cash compensation at Coastal and a group of other large financial corporations and banks that grant bonuses. (Total cash compensation includes benefits and incentive pay bonuses.) Coastal provided incentive pay to forty top officers in a program known as the Management Participation Fund and other functional incentive programs for specified positions in areas such as bond trading (Smith Officer Comp. Strategy Report, Aug. 1975, D5375). Below that level officers at 1,500 points and lower receive total compensation that puts them just above the third quartile. But there is a decisive break in compensation

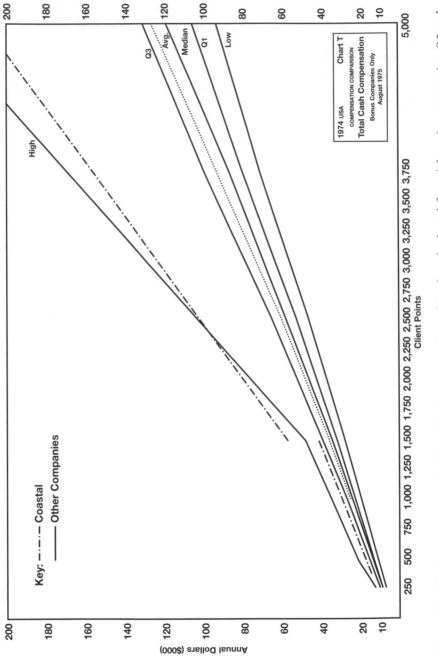

Figure 8.5. Total compensation by job evaluation points, Coastal Bank and selected financial services companies. Q3 and Q1 enclose middle 50 percent of company median lines.

policy at 1,500 points, which puts officers with over 1,500 points at average compensation of about $58,000 in 1974, some $20,000 higher than for officers with fewer points. The second, higher salary curve exceeds the highest pay line for the comparison group until 2,400 points and then remains just under the high pay line but still well above the third quartile for the comparison group.

When total compensation is the metric, we can more fully appreciate the nature of the relationship between gender, incentive pay, and the market in Coastal's inequality system. Officers as a group are well paid (at least at the 75th percentile for a cross section of large banks and employers); but the top officers are extremely well paid. They literally "cream" the market for top financial companies. And there is no readily available rationale within the Smith system to explain the sharp positive jump in compensation at the 1,500-point level. One mitigating factor is that there is no guarantee that all years will produce the same level of incentive payoffs, because bonuses largely are set based on the profit performance of the bank as a whole. The year 1974 was a good one, as were most in the late 1970s for the bank (Financial Pub., 1976, 1978; Coastal Annual Report 1979). Other years may not be as generous.

The gender consequences of incentive pay are transparent. In 1974 none of the Management Participation Fund participants and only a handful of other incentive pay positions were held by women. Records in 1978–79 also show a complete absence of women from the management fund and only five women in a group of forty-one other incentive pay positions. Moreover, two of these women received the smallest participation share in their respective incentive pool (1978–79 Pay Doc., D66078–D66361). Coastal's incentive pay system produces compensation for top management – all of whom are male – that exceeds the market value for their responsibilities.

Coastal's own consultants criticized the incentive pay system because it is not sufficiently linked to performance criteria. They acknowledged that the total compensation curve "exhibits a general sweep toward the upper right that seems to indicate knowledgeable, planned reward commensurate with job weight and performance" (Smith Officer Comp. Strategy Report, Aug. 1975, D5376). After laying out some eight goals that management incentive plans should seek to achieve, including management commitment to stockholder return, building a results-oriented management team, and instilling commitment to the organization and its long-term growth (Smith Officer Comp. Strategy Report, Aug. 1975, D5378–D5379), the report analyzed whether the Management Participation Fund operates to do this. It praised the fund for contributing to these goals. But it was critical of the link between payout and performance.

> The program currently suffers from the fact that participation units, once awarded, are seldom if ever withdrawn and the actual monetary reward associated with the granting of units is delayed for one year after the grant is made. Under these conditions, the link between an Officer's performance and his incentive reward is somewhat remote and, in fact, his overall effectiveness may actually decline over a period of years while he continues to receive substantial incentive payments. (Smith Officer Comp. Strategy Report, Aug. 1975, D5380)

The report offered suggestions to link reward to performance in the incentive year, to withdraw units of fund participation when individual performance lags, and to create a reward formula that considers performance in relation to overall industry profits, rather than setting rewards on net profits, even if they lag behind industry norms for a given year. The most radical suggestion was that the bank explore creating a trade-off between fixed and variable compensation for incentive eligible positions. Perhaps anticipating resistance to this last proposal, the consultants observed that doing so would be a major departure for Coastal and that their recommendations about salary levels did not contemplate such a shift in policy (Smith Officer Comp. Strategy Report, Aug. 1975, D5391–D5392).

Documents from later years strongly imply that the incentive pay policies did not change in response to these recommendations. Printouts of individual salaries and scheduled salary increases for December 1978 contain separate column entries for the number of units each officer had in either the management participation fund, the municipal bond fund, or the government bond fund (1978–79 Pay Doc., D66078–D66361). There was no indication of a link between fund units and salary levels, as the Smith consultants had suggested. The same is true of a document containing 1979 salary recommendations. Although it separated managerial fund participants from other officers, the report examined salaries for all officers without reference to bonuses (1979 Salary Recomm., D48508–D48518).

The latter document also is significant in that it shows a very different interpretation of how the pay of Coastal's officers compared with other banks from the interpretation offered by Smith and Associates. The document plotted salaries by points for Coastal and for local banks, regional banks, and New York banks (1979 Salary Recomm., D48508–D48516). The nonmanagerial fund participants (the term used in the report) show up just below the mean for local banks, well above the mean for regional banks, and well below the mean for New York banks. Managerial fund participants were paid at the mean for local banks for jobs with 1,500 to 2,000 points but then fall significantly below the local mean at higher point levels. Their salaries were higher than those paid at other regional banks but were substantially lower than New York salaries. The gap with New York increased as points increased. At the top point level, 5,000 points, New York bankers made almost double what Coastal bankers made. Thus by shifting from a comparison with Smith's client list to a comparison with other banks, Coastal's compensation levels for officers look far less generous.

Similar to what we found at the nonofficer level, Coastal's personnel professionals and its outside consultants employed a discourse of "the market" and engaged in elaborate efforts to locate the bank pay structure relative to other institutions. Yet more grounded manifestations of how the bank interacted with the labor market at the officer level were absent from these documents. There is no discussion of turnover, bargaining with potential hires or departees, hiring difficulties, and so forth. This leads skeptics like us to question whether Coastal's behavior was directly market driven, or whether Coastal was following a set of legitimated practices that are only loosely constrained by market forces. Some adherents of market models might argue that it is enough to validate the operation of effective markets: If the firm is making a profit, while managing a complex employment relations system, with no major personnel problems, it is meeting the requirements imposed by the market. The critical question is, given that there will always be a range of indeterminacy within which firms can manage their labor costs more or less efficiently, When is it no longer valid or useful to treat pay levels as responsive to market forces?

Even if Coastal's officer pay levels were not tightly linked to market pressures, did its pay practices systematically and unjustifiably disadvantage female officers? The managerial fund and the other incentive pay funds in the bank were overwhelmingly populated by men. The few women in them receive smaller numbers of bonus units than do men. Males received an average of 2.7 bonus units in municipal bonds compared with an average of 1.6 units received by women. Men in the government bond pool averaged 2.8 bonus units compared to the 1.1 bonus units that women earned on average.

Male officers also were disproportionately represented among the beneficiaries of special pleadings for exceptions to the new job evaluations implemented by the Smith consultants. The bank's Research and Compensation Division coordinated the point ratings of all jobs that had not been included in the initial ninety-three benchmark jobs. Before the compensation office's ratings were adopted, department heads had

Table 8.14. *Changes in Salary Resulting from Appeals to Compensation Committee, by Gender, Coastal Bank Officers, 1977*

	Change to Higher Salary		Salary Lowered or Same		Total	
	No.	%	No.	%	No.	%
Males	96	92.8	14	7.2	110	100
Females	4	57.2	3	42.8	7	100
All changes	100	85.5	17	14.5	117	100

Note: Chi-square probability = .028; Fisher's Exact Test = .062.
Source: Based on Job Evaluation Review, Oct. 7, 1977, D48625–D48635.

Table 8.15. *Reasons for Salary Changes by Type of Change and Gender of Employees, Coastal Bank Officers, 1977*

Reason for Change	Lowered Salary		Salary Stayed Same		Salary Increased		Total
	Males	Females	Males	Females	Males	Females	
Change in factor scores	7	1	5	1	42	1	57
Comparison with other employees	1	0	1	0	13	1	16
Personal request by department head	0	1	0	0	41	2	44
Total	8	2	6	1	96	4	117

Source: Based on Job Evaluation Review, Oct. 7, 1977, D48625–D48635.

an opportunity to review and question the results. A compensation office document listed all cases that were brought to the job evaluation committee for final resolution. It details the job title in question, the name of the incumbent, the job evaluation review committee's comments, the results of reviews by Compensation and Research, and the Final Approved Rating. Case files also contain memos from department heads in which they register their differences of opinion with the Compensation Division's decisions. Tables 8.14 and 8.15 report tabulations concerning these cases.

Table 8.14 reveals that a large proportion of officer jobs are reconsidered in the appeals process (117 out of 445, or 26 percent). Reconsideration overwhelmingly results in approval of a higher point total (and a commensurate increase in expected earnings). Some 100 out of 117 cases, 85 percent, are granted more points. Only a small number of cases (7) involve female employees. With 7 cases, each case constitutes 14 percent of the group, and shifts of one or two cases from one category to another would dramatically change the results. It is interesting, nonetheless, that the female success rate is drastically lower than that for men. Women gained higher points in 57 percent of their cases. Men got higher points in 87 percent of their cases. Despite relatively small numbers, this difference approaches statistical significance. (The chi square probability is 0.028. The more conservative Fisher's exact test shows that the probability of such a disparity in outcomes by chance alone is 0.062.)

Perhaps more important than the lower success rate is that a smaller proportion of women had their evaluations appealed. In 1977 about 14 percent of Coastal's officers were women. If the appealed cases reflected a randomly selected group, we expect to find some 16 women among the 117 contested decisions. Again the numbers are small, but less than half as many women as we would expect are involved in further considerations about their point totals.

Personal intervention by department heads plays a major role in modifications to the job evaluation results. As Table 8.15 demonstrates, the largest proportion of reviewed cases (57, or 49 percent) are disposed of by reviewing factor totals and, typically, increasing one of the factor scores. One in ten cases makes reference to what other officers are receiving, for example, that officer A should make close to the same as officer B. Of the 117 cases, 44 (38 percent) were reviewed at the request of department heads. All but 1 of these cases resulted in an increase in job evaluation points. The one exception involved the case of a woman, whose points were lowered in consultation with her department head. Of the 43 favorable outcomes initiated by department heads, 41 involved a man; 2 affected women.

These results are strikingly similar to what we found in the State of Washington pay system. In both instances appeals from an initial set of pay decisions were overwhelmingly successful in raising pay. In both cases, male employees or male jobs were disproportionately involved in appeals. In both cases, the result is a large number of pay increases for men, while relatively few pay increments are offered to women in proportion to their presence in the work force. Neither set of decisions involves gender in an explicit way. Yet within very different organizational contexts – a public employment system in which an employee union was an active participant and a private organization with no employee representation – we find incumbent management and other actors effectively altering a pay structure devised by compensation

Table 8.16. *Voluntary Terminations by Reason and Gender, Officers, Coastal Bank, 1978*

	Males		Females		
	No.	Rate	No.	Rate	Tests of Significance
No. in work force[a]	413		63		
Voluntary departures[b]	47	0.1041	9	0.1429	$z = 0.918$ (NS)
Economic departures[c]	33	0.0788	5	0.0794	$z = 0.015$ (NS)
Family departures[d]	4	0.0097	3	0.0476	NS (Fisher's Exact Test)

[a] Numbers in work force are for 1977 and are taken from tables prepared by plaintiffs' expert.These numbers are reduced by the number of involuntary terminations in 1978: regular retirements, deaths, and firings for cause.
[b] Includes early retirements.
[c] Includes departures for dissatisfaction with promotion opportunities, with supervisor, and with pay, as well as for better offers, to return to school, and to take another job.
[d] Includes pregnancy/child care, relocation, "marriage," and other family reasons.

analysts in ways that introduce (and perhaps reintroduce) more gender inequality. Both instances involve an unspoken alliance between male managers and male workers, in which managers support the workers' claims for higher pay. Such seemingly benevolent behavior is not neutral in its consequences for gender inequality. A series of decisions that are explicitly based on other grounds – merit, market demand, relative fairness in pay – reaffirm the greater value of the work done by men and the economic inequality between male and female workers.

Are there legitimate grounds for giving more favorable treatment to male officers? Again one way to assess this prospect is by comparing rates of turnover among Coastal's officers. As with nonofficers, it is possible to examine how male and female officers differed in their rates of voluntary exit from Coastal Bank and to examine differences in their reasons for leaving. While these data are from a point in time well after the Smith officer pay system had been put into place, they do provide some insight into one measure of how that system interacted with the external market. The relevant figures are shown in Table 8.16.

There are several differences between the officers' turnover patterns and those of nonofficers. First, the officer turnover rates are higher. Second, male officers do not have higher rates of departure for economic reasons than female officers do (as was true among nonofficers). In fact, statistically speaking, there are no differences whatsoever between males and females in the officer population – in economically motivated turnover, in family motivated turnover, or in total turnover. To the extent that male and female officers were being paid differently by the Smith system in 1978, there is nothing in the turnover patterns that would suggest that the bank was under extreme market pressure to maintain the existing pay differential.

As with the nonofficer pay system, the qualitative data on Coastal's officer compensation system identify significant departures from market and efficiency principles, many of which contribute to the gender gap in pay among officers. The data are broadly consistent with the model of organizational inequality we have seen operating in the other case studies, although in different form from one context to the next. In the concluding section of this chapter we define the particular form of organizational inequality embodied in Coastal bank.

Conclusion: The Male Profit-Making Club

Gender inequality in organizations often is a product of the interaction between a specific type of organizational inequality system and broader cultural forces. It is useful to think of Coastal Bank in these terms and then to pose the theoretical competition between market, efficiency, and organizational inequality models in these terms as well. One can think of the bank as a profit-making cooperative. The members of the cooperative are those senior officers of the bank who receive a substantial portion of their compensation through participation in the management fund. Other officers earn substantial salaries, occupy a distinctive and privileged status in the organization, and are eligible to move into the profit-sharing group. As a result they identify with and behave in ways similar to those of senior management. Yet, the reins of power and wealth are concentrated in the management fund group. This group controls the structure and management style of the organization, including the principles and practices that directly affect the position of women and minorities in the organization.

Economic theories of the firm explain the emergence and functioning of the profit-making cooperative in efficiency terms. According to this view, in an organization that combines a complex set of activities, the value of the organization as a whole is greater than the value of each worker's contribution taken by itself. Thus there is a surplus of value that must be allocated between management, workers, and shareholders. The profit-making cooperative creates a unity of interest between management and shareholders, in that top management will have a strong incentive to generate and retain as large an amount of profit as possible (generally see Mailath and Postlewaite 1990). Some workers, as individuals or as groups, may attempt to extract a larger share of this surplus by threatening to leave or by otherwise making claims that they deserve more. Top management ultimately is responsible for bargaining with workers. It is in management's interest to give up as little as possible while still maintaining the quality of staff necessary for effective performance. The labor market plays a role in such a model. If workers identify superior rewards for similar jobs in other organizations, it adds credibility to their wage demands. In this model it is not surprising that job evaluation schemes and wage surveys become political contests within the organization.

This conception can be readily applied to Coastal's incentive structure. Coastal's management group appeared motivated to maintain a skilled and committed work force, including an officer corps from which it could recruit new members of top management, without paying more than was necessary. Because discrimination typically is conceived of as inefficient (see Becker 1971; Donohue 1986), in that it involves paying some preferred group more than is necessary, Coastal's management group would appear to have had a direct interest in eliminating discriminatory pay practices. Indeed, Coastal had developed an elaborate administrative structure for determining pay levels at both nonofficer and officer levels. This system included state-of-the-art techniques for evaluating jobs and surveying market wage rates. Coastal's managers responded with indignation to charges that they discriminated. In their view, they had not intentionally discriminated against women and minorities. If discrimination imposes unnecessary costs on the employing organization, it was not reflected in overall profit levels. At least until the late 1970s, Coastal's top managers and shareholders alike enjoyed high profits.

Yet the efficiency explanation carries us only so far in this instance. The data indicate that Coastal's top management functioned not just as a profit-making cooperative, but as a male, profit-making club. That is, while senior management was ideologically committed to paying market rates and merit-based compensation, it allowed, even actively encouraged, gender and racial bias in pay determination. The result was an inequality system that penalized women and minorities in ways that were inconsistent with principles of market-based pay and efficient wage administration. The members of the top management group were exclusively white males. While they may not have thought of themselves self-consciously as a race- and gender-based group, it was their definition of merit, market, and efficiency that controlled the pay determination process and the pathways of upward mobility in the organization. Without explicitly discriminating against any group, they had imposed policies and practices that worked to the disadvantage of those employees who did not share their race and gender. That these patterns could persist in Coastal reveals that even in private sector firms, market and administered efficiency models cannot adequately explain the inequities that emerge in organizational pay systems.

The inability of market and administered efficiency models to explain patterns of gender inequality in Coastal again point to the need for a model that emphasizes the organizational bases for gender inequality. Statistical results lay the foundation for this interpretation. In both the officer and nonofficer segments of the work force, after taking account of education, seniority, market wage rates, and grades or evaluation points, gender has a statistically significant negative effect on earnings. In the nonofficer sector of the bank, much of the gender gap in pay is attributable to between-job wage differences. In the officer sector, where job in general has less force in setting earnings, a larger proportion of the gender differential resides within jobs.

While gender inequality takes a different form in the nonofficer sector than in the officer sector of the organization, it appears to derive from similar sources: the relatively less powerful position of women in the politics of the organization and the organizational reproduction of male cultural advantage. The decision to carve out exceptions to the nonofficer job evaluation scheme for jobs that were predominantly male was reached by a committee that had but one female member. She had a reputation for being a traditionalist on the role of women in Coastal. The managers who lobbied for higher point ratings for their employees were all men. On at least one occasion when a male manager advocated a promotion for a woman in his department, his male superior told him not to rock the boat if he knew what was good for his career. Other testimonial evidence indicated that certain department heads had the power to announce that they would not be bound by affirmative action goals, that they refused to hire women or minorities because they saw members of such groups as risky investments for training purposes. Management engaged in practices that discounted the value of female work, such as paying below market starting wages for lower, nonofficer grades. These practices were eventually challenged, somewhat ironically, not by the managers directly responsible for these employees, but by the economists who prepared the data on market rates by grade.

Coastal's personnel structure at the beginning of the 1970s clearly bore the imprint of traditional gender roles in the workplace. There were separate directors for male and female employees. The elite college recruitment program was denoted the college men's program. While these formal gender divisions were dissolved in the early 1970s, considerable testimonial evidence suggested that they persisted in practice. Women college graduates often were given initial placement in clerical jobs, whereas male college graduates moved directly into officer training positions. Women continued to receive lower pay than men holding essentially identical jobs. Before women were accepted into upper-level officer positions or invited to join "the million dollar club" (indicating they had brought in that much business), they had to meet requirements never before imposed on men (such as exceeding a specific amount of new business generation or bringing in a million dollars in two consecutive years).

In these and other more subtle ways, Coastal's management operated as a male club. Explicitly or implicitly certain social characteristics, including gender, class, and ethnicity, were required for admission to the top management group. According to one informant, older women often were given the job of training young rising stars, "fair-haired boys," prior to their ascent up the corporate ladder. When asked what attributes defined a "fair-haired boy," she replied,

> Well, they were usually some kind of star athlete. JW had been a star quarterback at the University of ••, and KW had been a championship golfer, JS had been an athlete or had been from a family in the carriage trade. His wife was from the •• family. CW, his parents had been famous architects. (Personal interview, May 1994)

Later in the interview, she added that there had been discrimination against other kinds of people as well, mentioning in particular the case of a male Jew who left Coastal to form a highly successful independent bank.

How was this possible in an organization in which the top management had a direct interest in profit maximization? I put the question directly to the same informant.

> Q: It seems so irrational for the bank not to have recognized the kind of work that people like you were doing. Why do you think they treated people that way?
> A: I think there was a mindset that things were just done in a certain way. The people at the bank just believed that only a certain style should be permitted. And I have heard similar things; I attend meetings of the National Association of Bank Women and I have heard rumblings about discrimination from lots of people who attend those meetings. . . . Nineteen sixty-eight I asked if I could be included in the college program. They said no because I was a woman and because I was Jewish and that I didn't have the right kind of educational background. I can remember when I finally was put in the officer training program. They brought in a professor from •• University,

who was not very kind to me. And he would put calculus proofs on the board. . . . He eliminated me from the program.

(Personal interview, May 1994)

It is informative to speculate about the cost to the top group of discriminating against women in favor of men. If we assume that the unexplained gender gap between male and female nonofficers in 1977 is a deadweight cost to Coastal, we estimate that Coastal paid $1.5 million more than was necessary in that year. This represents 3.3 percent of the total payroll and about 5 percent of Coastal's net income. In 1977 the top thirty-three managers received total compensation of $3.9 million of which about $2.1 million was paid in base salaries and $1.8 million was incentive pay linked to firm profitability. If officers' profit bonus increased by 5 percent, it would yield $91,800 for the top group, or some 2.4 percent more than their 1977 compensation.

Even in this idealized formulation, top officers do not have a large financial incentive to eliminate gender bias. It also is not clear, however, that they are the ones to bear the cost of the gender differential in pay. There is no inherent reason to treat the unexplained gender gap in pay as a premium to male workers. It is equally plausible to think of the difference as a wage penalty on female workers, a penalty they do not escape because they lack information about competitive wage rates or because they fear other costs in seeking better-paying employment in the labor market. As our informant told us, when she learned that a male vice president in Coastal was making $27,000 for doing a job like the one she did at $12,000, she figured she could make more money elsewhere. But it was not until her retirement policy became vested that she was willing to take the chance actually to leave Coastal and seek employment at another bank (personal interview, May 1994). From this perspective, men may enjoy the privileges of belonging to the club while others pay the dues.

Among the four cases we have studied, at Coastal we find the most evidence for the impact of the market on an organization's wage system. Certainly the market played a greater role here than in UNI. In UNI administrators not only chose to ignore the recommendations of outside consultants about how to deal with market data when they confronted a shortage of clerical workers in data analysis positions; they asked the competing employer not to hire their people away and announced a policy of refusing to rehire anyone who took a better offer elsewhere. (See Chapter 5.) In Coastal, they raised the pay of a similar category of workers – in the computer programming area – to respond to perceived market forces. And Coastal economists were true to their faith in recommending higher entry-level wages for some grades (indeed predominantly female grades) based on their reading of market data.

But even in this case, we find that the market influence on male-female earnings is heavily mediated by organizational forces. Both statistical and quantitative data support the view that much of the gender inequality in Coastal is attributable to organizational factors rather than market forces or efficiency considerations.

The question arises, Is Coastal unique? In one crucial respect, Coastal is a rarity. It lost a major discrimination lawsuit. When we reviewed the testimonial evidence presented at trial, the legacy of explicitly differential treatment of male and female employees, and its solitary resistance to external pressures on banks to change their personnel policies, we felt that Coastal appeared unusually backward, even clumsy, in its efforts to comply with the mandates of discrimination law. Yet, in other important ways, it seemed much like other major banks in the period. As our data on the percentage of women at Coastal and other major banks in the same city indicate, Coastal was if anything slightly more progressive than other banks in hiring and promoting women. Moreover, our informants told us that other banks anxiously awaited the outcome of the Coastal case, for they felt Coastal's practices were similar to theirs.

We cannot dispel doubts about the representativeness of Coastal as an organization. We are prepared, however, to argue that the features of sex-based wage inequality we found in Coastal are likely to be found in many large, private sector organizations. Indeed, we suspect that these patterns continue in Coastal itself. Despite the fact Coastal paid monetary damages and agreed to an externally monitored affirmative action plan for women and minorities, these remedies do not address between-job wage differences at the nonofficer level. Nor do they alter the formal structure or wage-setting politics of Coastal. Greater numbers of women and minorities may be hired into and promoted at Coastal, but invidious gender- and racial-based inequality in pay is likely to persist.

Appendix 8.1

As discussed in the text, a crucial issue in the statistical investigation of the organization's compensation patterns is the role of jobs as an influence on pay levels. Thus, it is important that our analysis properly take account of the lack of independence among individuals working in the same job category. Tables 8.9–8.11 in the text summarize results obtained under the assumption that there is a stochastic component of income associated with membership in a particular job category. These models are variously described as random intercept models, hierarchical linear models, or multilevel models.

Despite the fact that we attempted to obtain a complete census of individual workers in each company, there are several reasons why random effect models may be desirable in this instance. First, the population of *filled* jobs in any company at any time is more fluid than a classical model of bureaucracy might suggest. Not only do some job titles lie dormant until a suitable occupant appears on the scene, but new jobs are continuously created and old ones wither and die (Miner 1991). There are also instances of the kind reported by Granovetter (1974) in which positions are created to provide a niche for a valued, external candidate who happens to become available at a particular time. For these reasons, it is plausible to regard the set of jobs that contain incumbents at any particular time to be a stochastic realization of a larger population of positions that might have come into existence or that might have been filled.

The random effect or random regression model (RRM) approach that we use here is similar to that used by a variety of researchers under the rubric of the "multilevel model" (see Mason and Entwisle 1985; Mason, Wong, and Entwisle 1983). For this investigation, we restrict attention to a set of models that contain only one level 2 (job-level) random variable. Typically, these models can be represented by a set of equations grouped into two levels. Thus, in considering the Coastal bank data set we begin with the following set of equations. First, the "within-job" equation:

$$LOGSAL_{ij} = \beta_{0j}ONE + \beta_{1j}EDUC_{ij} + \beta_{2j}FEMALE_{ij}$$
$$+ \beta_{3j}BLACK_{ij} + \beta_{4j}HISPANIC_{ij} + \beta_{5j}TENURE_{ij}$$
$$+ \varepsilon_{ij}$$

This equation represents the effect of all individual-level variables on the dependent variable (log salary) within any job indicated by the subscript *j*. At the second level we write an equation in which the dependent variables are the coefficients in the first-level equation. Since we are restricting attention to a single random effect at the second level, the only coefficient with random variation at the second level is the intercept from the first level. Thus, the "between-job" equation is

$$\beta_{0j} = \gamma_{00}ONE + \upsilon_{0j}$$

In this equation, Y_{00} represents the overall intercept, while the additional random term, V_{0j} represents the random effect of membership in a given job on log salary. To investigate the effect of each job's sex composition, an alternative between-job equation is also estimated:

$$\beta_{0j} = \gamma_{00}ONE + \gamma_{01}PCTF + \upsilon_{0j}$$

Note that while this specification allows the aggregate sex composition variable to have an effect on individuals' salaries, the individual-level determinants of salary do not vary across job categories. There is no interaction of the job-level sex composition variable with any of these individual-level variables, nor are there any random differences among these coefficients across job categories. Neither of these models is considered since they do not seem to be an integral part of the pay equity framework. The estimates of the random regression models in the subsequent tables were obtained via SAS PROC MIXED and are identical to estimates obtained via another multilevel program ML3 (see Goldstein 1987; Prosser, Rosbash, and Goldstein 1991).

A particularly attractive feature of the random effects or, in this case, variance components model, is that it allows a partitioning of the "total" residual variance for each case into two components. The first of these components, which we will represent as σ_μ, is the variance component associated with jobs. The second, σ_Σ, is the residual variance associated with the within-job equation. The ratio of the first to the sum of the first and second is the intraclass correlation and provides a handy index of the amount of clustering within job categories.

Finally, it should be noted that the RRM methodology is likely to have particular advantages in the present case where many of the clusters are extremely small. The essence of the empirical Bayes estimation of cluster effects on the dependent variable is to take into account the degree of certainty associated with the empirical disparity of a given cluster mean from the overall mean. When clusters are small, the degree of certainty is similarly small and the estimation of the cluster effect is restricted to be closer to its prior value (assumed to be zero).

An alternate technique for taking into account within job similarities is the fixed effect model in which it is assumed that the clusters (jobs) included in the analysis represent the population of clusters in question. For reasons stated earlier, we do not believe this assumption is appropriate in the analysis of jobs within a changing corporate hierarchy. Nevertheless, analyses of these data using the fixed effect model produce conclusions that are consistent with those presented in the text. For example, in 1977 there was still more salary clustering by job among nonofficers and there is a higher residual individual male-female income difference among nonofficers than officers when this alternate technique is used. Summary sets of coefficients are provided in Tables 8.9 through 8.11; complete details are available from the authors on request.

Part III

Conclusion: Legalizing Gender Inequality

9

Rethinking the Relationship between Law, Markets, and Gender Inequality in Organizations

In an earlier era, the gendered division of labor was often seen as part of a natural order (Kessler-Harris 1982). Law was centrally implicated in this ideological structure. Not only did legal rules operate to constrain female labor force participation, but the opinions of judges articulated the gender ideology that made the rules reasonable and just. When the Supreme Court upheld the State of Illinois's proscription of women from law practice, it cited higher authority: "The paramount destiny and mission of woman are to fulfill the noble and benign offices of wife and mother. This is the law of the Creator."[1]

In the modern era, one would think, certainly both societal values about female employment and the role of the law in regulating labor markets have changed dramatically. A substantial proportion of American women work outside the home, even in years when they have young children. Now the law against employment discrimination stands to strike down the very sex stereotypes that it once invoked.

Yet what has changed? Women work, but, remarkably, they continue to "choose" jobs that pay less. According to orthodox labor economics, employing organizations are not responsible for this fact. The market sets the price of work independent of the gender of its incumbents. The highly gendered character of pay inequality in organizations is explained as the product of gender-neutral responses by employers to a gender-neutral labor market.

The market-based interpretation of gender inequality in organizations is not just one side of an academic debate. In terms of law and policy, it is the dominant interpretation. When it became clear by the mid-1970s that the Equal Pay Act's mandate of "equal pay for equal work" would not close the wage gap, women began to focus on "between-job" pay claims brought under Title VII. In *Gunther* a bitterly divided Supreme Court ruled in favor of the more expansive interpretation of Title VII by holding that the law against pay discrimination could reach cases involv-

---

1 *Bradwell v. State*, 83 U.S. 130 (1873).

ing male and female workers occupying different jobs. The abstract opening provided by *Gunther* was quickly shut, however. When federal courts confronted broader claims of pay discrimination against jobs held predominantly by women, they invoked the market explanation.

Judge Kennedy's words in the pivotal decision in the *AFSCME* case may have been more modern than the words of the Supreme Court in *Bradwell*, but they were equally sweeping. "Neither law nor logic deems the free market a suspect enterprise."[2] The courts had found a new deity to cite as the source of gender inequality: the market. While the struggle for pay equity continued in scattered legislative and collective bargaining arenas, the issue largely receded from public debate (see McCann 1994). The market view of between-job wage differences clearly had triumphed.

In this book we have tested the empirical claims of the dominant interpretation in the very arena in which it has had its most direct consequences – litigation involving claims of sex-based pay discrimination. We have analyzed four cases and four employing organizations. In three cases the plaintiffs lost based on the court's conclusions concerning market and efficiency explanations of observed wage differentials. In the one case in which the plaintiffs prevailed, there was no explicit attention to between-job pay differences and the settlement reached in the wake of the judgment did nothing to realign the organization's pay system. In that case individual plaintiffs received some compensation, and the employer agreed to new efforts to hire and promote women and minorities, but the pay system as such was left untouched.

Yet in each of these organizations, we find that gender inequality cannot be adequately explained by market forces or efficiency reasons. These patterns require a rethinking of the relationship between law, markets, and gender inequality in organizations. Contrary to the dominant interpretation in economics, the law, and in these organizations themselves, employing organizations bear considerable responsibility for the fact that men and women are paid less for work requiring similar effort, training, and skill. The results thus suggest the need for a new theoretical focus on the organizational dimensions of gender inequality, particularly on the processes through which organizations mediate market wages. Our findings also call for reopening policy debates on pay equity. If male-female wage differences are not the product of market forces or efficiency principles, how should these be dealt with through regulation or antidiscrimination law? Finally, our research has implications for theories about the relationship between law and gender inequal-

2 *American Fed'n of State, County, and Municipal Employees v. Washington*, 770 F.2d 1401 (9th Cir. 1985).

ity in American society. We will argue that the courts have "legalized" gender inequality. By giving authoritative approval to the market justification for between-job earnings differences, they have played a distinct role in the social construction of markets and female earnings. The law not only has granted legal protection to a given set of institutional pay practices, it has itself also been a powerful source of a gendered view of markets and unequal pay.

In this concluding chapter we rethink these questions. On each set of issues we include a synthesis of results from the empirical case studies, discuss whether the results generalize to other organizations, and suggest avenues for future research. We then address theoretical and policy questions.

Rethinking Gender Inequality in Organizations

Our central argument is that gender-based pay inequality in organizations is, in significant respects, the product of organizational forces. The extent to which this holds will vary by market and organizational context. It is a phenomenon to be examined empirically and theorized more fully based on additional data. We suggest that our thesis will apply quite broadly, especially within large organizations. We are so persuaded by what we learned in our case studies, which encompass a diverse set of organizations, as well as by research in other organizational contexts that also reveal mechanisms of gender inequality at work. In positing the importance of the organizational roots of gender-based inequality, we are not suggesting that market factors and efficiency principles do not affect wage differences. Market and efficiency imperatives play prominent roles in organizational pay systems. What we object to is the reification of market and efficiency influences and the tautological insistence that all wage differences are explainable in these terms. Nonetheless, it is possible to go too far in rejecting market- and efficiency-based explanations. Sociological research on gender inequality too often fails to take account of the effect of market conditions on wage differences. We advocate the development of a theoretical approach that attempts to explain the relative weight that market, efficiency, and organizational inequality processes have in determining the wages of male and female workers.

Throughout our case studies we explicitly compared the explanatory power of market, administered efficiency, and organizational inequality models. We developed the organizational inequality model in response to competing positions in labor economics. Our model identifies two significant sources of organizationally produced gender inequality: the subordinate position of women workers in organizational politics, and organizational practices that reproduce male cultural advantages.

Synopsis of Findings

We now turn to a brief synopsis of our empirical results. Our findings suggest the potential contribution of in-depth analyses of organizations as inequality systems. Not only do our results address the theoretical competition among models of inequality, they also challenge some existing notions in the labor markets literature based on aggregate-level studies.

Patterns of Gender Inequality. All four organizations exhibited significant gender-based pay differences. A variety of human capital characteristics, such as education and seniority, could not account for the gender gap. In the two cases in which we had the employer's market data, controlling for market pay levels did not eliminate the gender differential.

The male-female wage gap was largely the product of between-job wage differences among nonprofessional workers at the University of Northern Iowa (UNI), among state workers in Washington, and among nonofficers in Coastal Bank. Within-job pay differences figured more prominently in the Sears case and among the officer corps at Coastal. In *Sears* this result in part reflects the logic of the plaintiffs' case: They selected a subset of jobs with large enough numbers of men and women incumbents to compare earnings within jobs, a comparison similar to traditional Equal Pay Act claims. But the pattern suggests that gender inequality operates differently in the professional/managerial sectors of organizations (at least in private organizations) than in the lower levels. For lower-level positions organizations will structure compensation by the job, and gender differences in pay will depend on between-job pay differences. For upper-level positions, organizations will bend to pay the person rather than the job. As a consequence, a larger proportion of gender differences will occur within the same job categories.

Although we found a substantial amount of sex segregation by job in the four organizations, it appears that some estimates of "near total" sex segregation by position within organizations (see Baron and Bielby 1980) are exaggerated. UNI, the State of Washington, and the nonofficer level of Coastal were quite segregated by job. At UNI, for example, only about 25 percent of the work force held jobs in which one gender or the other occupied less than 90 percent of positions in the job. The Sears checklist jobs and the Coastal officer positions were more integrated, however. An index of dissimilarity of 1.00 indicates total sex segregation by job.

For the Sears jobs the index hovered around 0.40 for years for which we have data; in Coastal bank the measure varied between 0.50 and 0.70 for various years for officer positions.

These results underscore the need for organizational analyses of gender inequality. Closer scrutiny of male-female wage differences in terms of market conditions and efficiency concerns does not explain away wage differentials at the organizational level. Moreover, the contours of unequal pay vary across organizations and locations within organizations. Such variations imply the difficulty of mounting an adequate theory of organizational inequality without attending to organizational variation itself.

The Mediation of the Market. The case studies strikingly demonstrate how large organizations mediate between the price of labor in the labor market and wage schedules within organizations. Each of the organizations we studied had developed a bureaucratic personnel system that contained personnel officials who actively managed employment relations and devoted considerable resources to the promulgation and application of rules about pay practices. The least-developed personnel system was at UNI, the organization with by far the smallest number of employees, which we characterized as undergoing a transition in the 1970s from paternalistic employment relations to bureaucratic employment relations. Even at UNI, the pay system, which had been examined several times by outside consultants, made extensive use of job evaluation and salary surveys. The other organizations, public and private, contained even more elaborate and well-established systems. The archives of the Sears personnel office, for example, are truly massive, and included numerous kinds of psychological and aptitude tests.

These personnel bureaucracies did not simply attempt to incorporate market pricing into their organizations but instead pursued a course of technocratic pragmatism with respect to wages. On some occasions, pay bureaucrats and outside consultants openly rejected the market as a basis for setting wages, because it would have made wage administration too chaotic and uncertain. A pay official in the State of Washington talked about the job evaluation system he had constructed as a "fluid tool" through which he could maintain the proper relationships among jobs. He and his colleagues showed disdain for market rates by "averaging" the salary survey results for several jobs to create an internal wage benchmark. Coastal Bank followed an approach common to large organizations: It surveyed the market primarily to determine how large an across-the-board increase to grant each year. Of all four cases, Coastal was probably the most responsive to market forces. Except for pay raises for computer programmers and some tinkering with the entry-level salaries of lower-grade clericals, we found no evidence of attempts to track market movements for the pay of different kinds of work. The bank settled for referring to "the market" to set an administered wage increase.

In numerous ways we found that these organizations were only loosely following the market.

a. A small proportion of jobs was compared with the market. In all four organizations, the primary method employed to measure the market was a salary survey, done by another organization or by its own personnel office. The surveys generated salary data on a small fraction of the jobs in the organization. This left considerable discretion to personnel officials about how to use the survey results. In the State of Washington case, we found that unexplained gender inequality increased among jobs that were not used as market benchmarks or were not in job families with market benchmarks.

b. The salary survey methods were arbitrary. We found that how a salary survey was conducted could be crucial to its results, and that interested parties could influence such important decisions as what jobs to survey, what data to reject as inaccurate, and when additional data would be collected to correct or clarify results from an earlier round of data collection.

c. Appropriate market data for comparisons were chosen arbitrarily. We found in UNI and in Coastal Bank that the "market rate" for a given job varies substantially depending on the segment of the market chosen, such as unionized workers versus others or New York City banks versus banks in other cities or very large banks versus medium-sized banks versus other large financial institutions.

d. Traditional wage differences among organizational positions were preserved. Like Rosenbaum's (1984) findings on the continuity of between-job wage patterns after the formal revision of a pay system, we found that personnel officials often openly resisted changing the relative pay of positions. UNI refused to follow its own consultants' recommendation to put certain "male" and "female" jobs in the same job category. Testimonial data from the State of Washington revealed a similar imperative in operation: Wage survey results largely maintained historical pay patterns. Despite a wide-ranging set of job evaluations, relatively few Coastal Bank jobs were targeted for special treatment because they were overpaid or underpaid. It appears that the job evaluations, done largely by incumbent Coastal management, reproduced the existing job and pay hierarchy.

e. Managerial discretion was often used to set pay levels. In the private sector firms, we find that managers have substantial discretion about how to pay the employees they supervise. Pre-1970s Sears presents an extreme case of decentralized pay authority. Store managers and other division heads apparently could strike their own deals with employees already in the organization to assemble their own managerial team. As a result, the outside pay consultants found that pay levels varied widely and, overall, were well above what other comparable employers were paying. Coastal Bank also bestowed considerable discretion on managers in determining annual wage increases for employees. Supervisors could recognize "potential" as well as performance. The market set the parameters on managerial discretion only in the most limited way. The compensation committee's decision about the overall pay increase in the organization set the bounds on how an increase could be awarded without special justification. Within those bounds, however, managers could make their own judgments about what was an appropriate increase.

These practices would have less significance if we found that the organizations continuously responded to market forces in other ways. What is the evidence on this score?

a. Absence of systematic turnover/retention studies. One mechanism for assessing whether wage rates are adequate would be to analyze the effects of wage levels on the ability to hire and retain workers. We did not find such studies in any of the four organizations. When we attempted to determine whether turnover rates correlated with male-female wage patterns, we had to calculate the statistics from the data we possessed.

b. Rarity of market exceptions to the administered wage schedule. Given the great variety of jobs contained in these four organizations, we were struck by the almost total absence of documented instances in which organizations had to adjust pay levels to get and keep workers. UNI reported having difficulty keeping clerical and computer programming personnel during the boom years of employment at John Deere and Company. Curiously, the university did not respond by raising the salaries of clericals but instead approached its competitor and asked it to stop hiring their workers. UNI adopted an informal policy of not hiring back anyone who left for better-paying jobs. Coastal Bank was forced to raise the pay levels for computer programmers. It did

so on a temporary basis by creating a separate technical classification. After a few years the technical jobs were merged back
into the regular pay schedule.

c. The particularism of market exceptions. For certain jobs, UNI,
the State of Washington, and Coastal Bank all created exceptions for certain jobs from the regular salary schedule. The jobs
excepted were stereotypically male – craft workers at UNI and
in Washington, blue-collar workers in Coastal. In UNI and
Washington the decision to grant the exceptions was transpar-
ently political. That is, they were concessions to organized
labor's insistence that government pay "prevailing" (i.e., unionized) wage rates. Did this concession have a basis in the market?
Yes, but only in the sense that unionized wage rates typically
define the upper end of wages paid in a local market. There was
no pretense in either case of a shortage of workers at lower rates.
This "market" exception stands in sharp contrast to the decisions on granting nurses an exception to the regular wage levels.
It was not until turnover in state nursing positions had reached
almost 50 percent that personnel officials approved ad hoc pay
increases for nurses. At Coastal, the exception for blue-collar
workers was based on personnel managers' decisions that the
jobs did not fit within the overall job evaluation system. The
excepted jobs clearly gained a premium within the internal
system. There was no discussion of whether the market
demanded that such positions receive higher pay.

In sum, in these four very different organizations, there are very few
manifestations of active interactions between market forces and pay decisions. If this kind of articulation takes place, it occurs invisibly from the
standpoint of the centralized pay records. The managers in Sears and
Coastal did have considerable discretion in wage setting. They may have
been reacting to the market offers their workers received. It is somewhat
surprising that there would be no records of such actions, however, especially when such information might have been useful in defending against
allegations of discrimination. One also has to wonder how significant
such interactions are in the broad scheme of things if the personnel office
does not bother to collect any data about responses to competing offers.
Our impression from the four case studies and from our reading of the
other pay discrimination cases in which the market defense figured
prominently is not that the employers attempted to defend their pay practices based on responses to actual competing offers. Rather, they
defended their practices as an administered wage system that took some
account of market wage rates. In that sense the organizations followed

an idiom of a market-based system. Actual pay practices may have been quite loosely coupled with market exchange.

Internal labor markets also are important to our theory of how organizations mediate the effect of labor markets on pay. If a work force is made up of internal labor markets, in which workers are hired for entry-level positions but then progress up a series of organization-specific job ladders, many jobs in the organizations cannot be readily compared with jobs in the external market – no genuine comparisons exist. As a consequence, pay levels for such jobs must be set within the organization without market referents. Our case studies indicate that in some large organizations, internal labor markets function to decouple pay setting from the market. Job ladders figured prominently in some job families in the State of Washington bureaucracy. Both Sears and Coastal relied heavily on entry-level recruitment and promotion in some areas of their operations. It was unclear how one would compare many of these positions with jobs in the external market.

Yet internal labor markets are not completely coincident with systems of organizational inequality. UNI filled relatively few of its work force positions through internal promotion. The director of personnel during the time we conducted interviews on campus, well after the conclusion of the *Christensen* case, spoke of his desire to institute more job ladders. But the job chains he described, as well as those we observed in the job titles at the time of the lawsuit, were laughably simple. UNI represents a case where internal labor markets do not figure prominently in the organizational mediation of pay determination, even though we find convincing evidence that organizational politics rather than market forces were responsible for maintaining pay differentials between male and female jobs.

The Difference between Public Sector and Private Sector Organizations. Our research, both the in-depth case studies and our survey of pay discrimination cases, confirms the perception that public and private firms operate pay systems in very different ways. It is striking that, with the exception of the *I.U.E. v. Westinghouse* case, no comparable worth lawsuits were prosecuted against private firms. Can this be explained by differences in the nature of gender inequality between these organizational types? As Sorensen (1994) and others have pointed out, there appear to be somewhat larger pay differentials by gender in the public sector than in the private sector. The issue is empirically complex, for there are many other differences between public and private sector firms. It is less clear whether, after taking into account organization size and the occupational composition of public organizations, you would still find more gender inequality in those contexts. Yet it would be surprising if the size of the gender gap is an adequate explanation. Private firms still display significant amounts of gender inequality. McCann (1994) found that the relative amount of pay differentials was not a factor that distinguished among more or less intense pay equity campaigns.

Another possibility is that it is the shape of gender inequality rather than the magnitude of differentials that is the crucial difference between sectors. Public sector systems are more rigidly structured by grade and step classifications than are private sector systems. It would not be surprising if a greater proportion of wage inequality in a grade and step system resided between jobs rather than within job classifications. The latter are determined by grading and, typically, seniority. People in the same grade and step will be paid the same. Private systems at least formally allow more individualized treatment. Managers have discretion over how large an increase to grant employees working in similar classifications. There were no indications of the managerial discretion to grant high or low raises at UNI or the State of Washington personnel system such as we saw in Sears and Coastal. If public systems have more between-job inequality, whereas private systems have more within-job inequality, one might expect to see comparable worth lawsuits primarily in the public sector because they uniquely target between-job differentials.

The results of our case studies also belie this explanation. At both Sears and Coastal we found between-job pay differences as well as within-job pay differences. Indeed, our statistical partialing of within- and between-job inequality for the UNI work force and for the Coastal nonofficers yielded strikingly similar results: Lower-level positions in both organizations contained a predominance of between-job wage inequality. It is very plausible that pay bureaucracies in large organizations, public and private, will construct relatively rigid job- and grade-based pay arrangements for lower-level positions precisely to avoid constant dickering and uncertainty over wages.

A more likely explanation is the difference in political milieu between public sector and private sector firms. Fundamentally different norms govern employment relations in the two sectors. One very telling difference is the nature of information available about earnings. State law typically requires public organizations to publish the earnings of employees. It is quite possible in public contexts to determine what fellow employees make. Such information is jealously guarded in private sector firms. At both Sears and Coastal, pay manuals instruct managers that they are not to disclose the earnings of other employees to their subordinates. The control of such information is seen as essential to the preservation of managerial authority in private contexts.

Employment relations in the public sector also are intrinsically more political. Public workers are not just employees under contract, but are agents of the state. The very character of the state is intimately connected with how it manages public employment. Civil service reform was a fundamental element of Progressive Era reform, after all (Wiebe 1967; Skowronek 1982). The elaborate rules that govern public employment are manifestations of its unique normative climate.

In such an environment, public workers enjoy much more power than most of their private sector counterparts. Even when not formally unionized, they have considerable political leverage with elected officials. Not only do they have access to decision makers through sheer proximity, but they also hold the power to affect the performance of governmental functions. They can make people and programs look good or bad. They also have standing to make public claims about the fairness of the terms of their employment. The litigation in the State of Washington began with complaints by public employees, which prompted the liberal Republican governor to launch a pay equity study. As McCann (1994, 107) reports, the political climate in a jurisdiction was crucial to the initiation and eventual outcome of pay equity campaigns. States and municipalities with traditions of progressive politics were far more likely to foster pay reform movements than were more conservative governments.

It is extremely rare that such organizing takes place in a private setting. When it does, the politics of the activity are very different. Workers who feel they are victims of discrimination in a private firm do not have a public forum for expressing such grievances. It is virtually unthinkable that the CEO of Sears would launch a pay equity investigation if he received complaints from a woman's group within the organization. In fact, when the National Organization for Women attempted to mobilize women and minority employees at Sears, it was later characterized by defense counsel as a malicious conspiracy to make an example of Sears. An EEOC official with authority over the Sears case, who also held an advisory position with NOW, was branded as having a conflict of interest. The defense allegation effectively raised doubts about the good faith of the EEOC in pursuing the Sears litigation. The Coastal case is another instance in which female workers turned to government authorities in charging Coastal and other banks with discrimination. Coastal management dug in its heels in public and eventually became involved in litigation. Other banks avoided such a direct confrontation, apparently accommodating government regulators by offering to make additional efforts to hire and promote minorities and women. It was only by appeal to a public authority in a government-regulated industry that women had leverage with their employers (short of litigation itself).

Political differences best account for why comparable worth as a legal reform effort was attempted in the public sector and not in the private sector. It is also accurate to say that bureaucratic politics were demonstrably more significant as sources of gender inequality at UNI and in the State of Washington than at Sears or Coastal Bank. The "meatpackers" in UNI and the Washington Federation of Labor embodied male interests. At Sears and Coastal Bank it is more difficult to point to the specific actions of a male constituency. At Sears, managerial discretion, indeed male managerial discretion, must have been implicated in producing wage advantages for men. At Coastal, the profit-making club was male and acted to be exclusively male. At both Sears and Coastal, organizational politics figured in the production of gender inequality but in less obvious ways than in the explicitly politicized pay systems at UNI and the State of Washington. Whether this is a general pattern for public and private sector organizations requires further research.

Changes in Gender Inequality in Response to Equal Employment Laws. In three of the four cases we can observe changes in gender inequality over a span of time in the 1970s, after the organizations became subject to Title VII. At UNI we see a small reduction in unexplained wage inequality between 1973 and 1974, mostly as a result of the elimination of certain job classifications in the new pay scheme adopted in 1974. At Sears we find significant improvement in the integration of women into various positions as well as a modest decline in the unexplained wage differential between 1973 and 1979. Part of Sears's defense was that it was aggressively pursuing affirmative action for women and minorities. While it had not eliminated gender inequality in the subset of checklist jobs under scrutiny in the case, it had significantly narrowed the gap. Coastal Bank exhibited almost no change in gender inequality at the nonofficer level between 1974 and 1977, but it did show a modest decline in the amount of gender inequality at the officer level. By 1977 a number of women had moved into officer positions once held almost exclusively by men. As women moved up in the officer ranks, overall wage differences declined. But because women moved into the lowest-paying rung of various job clusters, the amount of within-job pay differences actually grew during the period.

These patterns of change are instructive. Taken together they suggest that organizational attempts to rationalize compensation systems had some salutory effects on gender inequality. The exercise of systematically reviewing pay levels under the supervision of outside consultants, even though such an exercise was hardly free of organizational politics, reined in some anomalies in the pay system that contributed to a male earnings advantage. The shadow of Title VII also may have been a spur to organizational efforts to improve the relative position of women and minorities. Both Sears and Coastal Bank already were targets of some governmental attention by the start of the period analyzed. Their efforts to hire and promote more women clearly had some effect. It also should be noted, however, that a significant gender gap in pay remained in these organizations. Much of this differential resided between jobs.

It is unlikely that the market alone can account for the relatively rapid changes we observe in these organizations. It seems clear that the changes we observe resulted from changes in personnel and pay administration rather than in underlying market conditions. We take this as further evidence of how wage determination is an organizational as well as a market domain. The results in these organizations in this very limited time frame suggest that legal mandates and efforts at rationalization can quickly reduce otherwise unexplained gender inequality. Our findings are consistent with Donohue's assertions (1986, 1989) that antidiscrimination law can have dynamic effects that hasten the movement from inefficient, discriminatory behavior to more efficient, less biased personnel practices.

Critics of antidiscrimination law might scoff at the interpretation that a decline in the male-female wage gap in these organizations is an indication of progress. They could insist that declining differentials might simply reflect a kind of tax that the law imposes on employers, rather than a reduction in invidious discrimination (Epstein 1992). To use lawyers' words, such an argument is overbroad. It can be made with respect to virtually any equalization of employment or earnings status by women and minorities. Neither it nor its obverse are readily subject to empirical test.

The Case for the Organizational Inequality Model

While some may concede that we have made a pretty good case for the existence of invidious, gender-based pay inequality in organizations and for the proposition that organizations mediate between the market and organizational pay practices, some might challenge us to prove the connection between the two. That is, have we established that organizational pay systems tend to advantage jobs held predominantly by men over those held predominantly by women, more so than what we would expect based on the labor market generally? It is true that some parts of our analysis have proceeded to establish gender inequality and market mediation separately. Those aspects of the case studies require a speculative leap to make the connection.

But there is much evidence that directly links the two phenomena. In our analysis for UNI, the State of Washington, and Coastal Bank, we introduced statistical controls for various kinds of market data to

322   *Conclusion*

assess whether market patterns would explain patterns of inequality in the organization. They did not. At Sears, we were comparing individuals occupying the same job title. Market-based occupational differences could not explain these patterns. The failure of market variables suggests that the employing organization is a major source of inequality.

A variety of organizational process data reveals that several aspects of organizational pay practices directly contribute to gender inequality. The most active participants in debates about wage surveys and job evaluations are male – male workers, male union representatives, and male managers. We observed this directly at UNI, the State of Washington, and Coastal Bank. It is implicit in what we know about Sears as well. At Washington and Coastal we were able to code appeals of the compensation committee's decisions about pay levels. These overwhelmingly were made on behalf of incumbents of male jobs and were overwhelmingly successful in raising wages.

At UNI male administrators were fearful of the response of male physical plant workers to proposals to change the starting wages for some positions but enjoyed paternalistic control over female clerical workers. As a result they refused to adopt revisions in the pay scheme that would have somewhat closed the gender gap in pay.

Many of the principles that Sears fostered in its pay and promotion system tended to disadvantage women or left male managerial discretion relatively unchecked. The axiom that "to get ahead you had to move" clearly put women employees at a disadvantage for promotions and relocation pay raises. Judge Nordberg found the practice defensible on grounds of business judgment but did not deny the effect of the practice on women. Sears's outside consultants advised a change in the policy of permanent pay raises based on relocations, not on grounds of gender inequity but on grounds of economic inefficiency.

Documents produced by Coastal Bank's personnel office suggested that the bank had played tougher with the market for lower-level clerical positions in which women predominated, while paying starting rates that were higher relative to the market for other nonofficer positions that contained larger numbers of men. Several predominantly male blue-collar positions were exempted from the regular job evaluation system and paid at levels that exceeded those of most nonofficer positions. The bank had until the late 1960s maintained separate personnel systems for men and women; had referred to its officer recruitment and training program as the "College Men's" program; and had systematically steered female college graduates into clerical or lower-level managerial positions. More recently, women were not admitted to the bank's "million dollar club" made up of officers who brought in $1 million in business, even though some women had exceeded that level of performance. The top group of profit-sharing officers was all male. Our informants suggested that the basis for the selection and promotion of individuals into some of the top positions was the nature of their social connections, even past athletic prowess. Other aspirants to senior management were disqualified due to their gender, minority status, or religious background.

These data establish the link between organizational pay practices and gender inequality. To a certain extent, the mechanisms that generate inequality are unique for each organization. The character and magnitude of wage differences are not the same across each organization. But in each case, we find significant unexplained wage differences between male and female jobs. And the roots of these differentials lie in organizational practices.

Are These Minor Deviations from Rational Pay Practices?

Are the wage differences we observe minor deviations from the ideal of rational wage setting? One of the fundamental insights of organizational theory and research is that organizations seldom work perfectly. Formally rational organizations often depart from principles of rationality, resorting instead to garbage can decision making (Cohen, March, and Olsen 1972) or to satisficing behavior (Simon 1957a, 1957b). Sociologists long have observed the significance of informal group processes to how organizational structures actually work (Roethlisberger and Dickson 1939; Roy 1954; Burawoy 1979). Organization theorists might object to our organizational theory of inequality because it relies too heavily on a contrast between idealized principles of pay determination and the messy ineptitude that characterizes so many aspects of organizational life, not just wage determination. In other words, have we attached exaggerated importance to relatively minor deviations from the principles of rational pay administration?

First, the "deviations" we have identified do not appear insignificant, whether measured in dollars and cents or in terms of the validity of the pay standards in question. Substantial sums of money are implicated in the pay decisions we have analyzed. The initial judgment in the State of Washington case, for example, was $400 million. At UNI the unexplained wage gap was 11 percent of an average annual wage of $7,247 for some 576 workers in female jobs or some $459,000. The amount of the Coastal settlement for back pay was never made public, but we estimated the unexplained gender gap at $1.5 million for the nonofficers alone. Thus what may seem like relatively small effects on individual incomes, when multiplied for an entire work force, assume much greater magnitude. Moreover, as the judge in the Coastal case observed, wage penalties have a cumulative effect. Victims of pay discrimination suffer a loss in every succeeding paycheck.

Our investigation of how organizations set wages suggests that the process often involves arbitrary judgments about the value of a job within the organization, what an appropriate comparison would be in the labor market, and even what the market rate is for a given job. The apparent certainty of organizational wage structures is bottomed not on defensible, objective criteria (as managers and personnel officials tend to believe) but on convention. The organizations that we have studied and reports from other scholars about case studies (Baron 1991, 125–27; Rosenbaum 1984) indicate that organizations follow incremental changes in pay levels. Because almost every employee enjoys annual wage increases, with more significant jumps based on promotions, more radical reconsiderations of the wage structure are seldom considered. The closest thing to it in private firms is a review of the system by outside consultants. Even these are not very radical. The consultants are hired by incumbent management and rely heavily on organizational incumbents in evaluating the wage structure. Indeed, the consultants also construct a reified conception of the firm's compensation structure and its location in the market. Consultants transmute jobs into evaluation points, which in turn are plotted by income, and compared with the points-earnings slopes of other clients of the consulting firm. After reviewing the reports of several consulting firms, we began to think that the clients of pay consultants were like the children in Garrison Keillor's Lake Wobegon: all above average. We have yet to come across a consulting report that finds its clients paying below the midpoint of other clients that retain the consulting firm.

We would be going too far if we suggested that the emperor had no clothes. At some level, organization pay levels are constrained by market conditions. But just as clothing is only partially determined by weather and locally available materials, and is heavily influenced by fashion and tradition, organizational pay structures are not just products of economic necessity. They also are creatures of convention and tradition. When we took the unusual step of looking at what organizations actually did in setting wages, we found considerable indeterminacy.

Many of the mechanisms we identified as producing gender inequality in these organizations are consciously designed practices that cannot be dismissed as mere quirks in an otherwise rational system. The concessions to male workers at UNI, the relocation bonuses in Sears, and the incentive pay program in Coastal Bank all involved direct managerial decisions. Interestingly, all three practices were in some way challenged by outside pay consultants as inefficient or unfair.

Finally, if the practices we have identified as departures from rational pay principles are minor deviations, they do not appear to have random effects across gender groups. That is, one would expect that if organizational pay systems depart from ideal practices, at least sometimes they would benefit women more than men. This is not the case either in our four organizations taken as a whole or in many of the specific organizational processes we have looked at. Indeed, it appears to us that these organizations have a systematic tendency to pay workers in female jobs less than workers in male jobs.

The Significance of the Organizational Component of Pay Inequality

Is the portion of gender inequality attributable to organizational dynamics a small part compared with gender inequality rooted in the labor market? Comparable worth advocates might argue that the organizations we studied are aberrations that can make up only a relatively small part of the market. According to the argument, not all employers could pay their female jobs below the market, or their male jobs above market, or else the concept of market-based differentials would become meaningless. A few organizations might deviate from market rates for male and female jobs (which would add to the wage gap), but most of the wage gap tracks with market rates. (These may be historically tainted market rates, but they are market rates.)

We should note that many economists would take a similar view of the relative importance of organizational and market determinants of between-job gender inequality. Indeed, in the *Nassau County* case, 799 F. Supp. 1370 (E.D.NY. 1992) (discussed in Chapter 2), the court gave great weight to the finding by the defendant's expert that controlling for market rates eliminated most of the gender difference in pay.

Our first response is to point out the difficulty of obtaining "true market rates." Our case materials make abundantly clear that this is not straightforward. Wage levels for standardized jobs vary significantly. Employers often must choose what segment of the market they want to compare themselves with. They may choose different segments for different kinds of positions. We also have learned that many large organizations only in fact survey the market for a small proportion of the jobs in the organization. It is not clear how organizations should treat firm-specific jobs when attempting to arrive at their market pay levels. We also have seen that organizations do not use dispassionate, objective criteria in selecting benchmark jobs and collecting data. What data are collected and used often is a highly politicized process that tends to define the market in the organization's own image. Thus the notion of finding a "true market wage" is, from the standpoint of any given organization, somewhat illusory. The "market wage" is a statistical construction that large organizations seldom test against actual experience by engaging in spot hiring or individualized price negotiation.

Our second response is to concede that a vector of average occupational wage levels should bear a pretty high correlation with organizational wage levels. If female secretaries average $17,000 and male craftworkers average $30,000 and largely male middle managers make $50,000 as a market average, we would be surprised if that did not correlate quite strongly with the organization's pay levels for those jobs. But if the organization is cheap with secretaries, paying them only $16,000, and is a bit too generous with craftworkers, paying them the market average that includes seasonal workers and unionized craftspersons, when it could hire such workers for $27,000, we now find that $4,000 of the $14,000 difference between secretaries and craftspersons involves deviations from the market. And if middle management is paid 10 percent too much, $6,000 of the $34,000 difference between secretaries and managers is attributable to the organization's departures from the hypothetical true market. Deviations of such a magnitude are easily possible in the sorts of wage systems we have studied. And they can account in our hypothetical cases for between 15 percent and 25 percent of the between-job pay differences. England (1992) reports that most job evaluation studies show that predominantly female jobs are underpaid by about 20 percent when evaluation points are controlled for.

Our results suggest the need to reconsider what has been taken for granted in theories of gender-based pay inequality. Research should begin to analyze more systematically the relationship between markets and organizations as it relates to male-female wage differences. The theoretical framework we propose is conceptually straightforward. It requires empirical investigations of organizational pay systems as systems of inequality. The relative absence of such studies to date derives in part from ideological and disciplinary differences – the idealization of markets and organizations by economists, the vilification of markets and organizations by sociologists. But a significant reason is lack of access to data on the internal workings of organizational pay systems. The main reason we have relied on concluded lawsuits as the source of our information is the difficulty of getting inside organizations. The same kind of organizational power that blocks access to organizational pay data works to make the gendered character of inequality invisible within the organization.

The case studies embody our best efforts to work with organizational and market data to specify the nature of organizational inequality. They do not offer templates, for each organization was different, each case generated different kinds of data. Yet they are suggestive of several analytic strategies. More, better case studies would add to our knowledge in this field. Researchers might also consider other designs that systematically pursue an organizational framing of inequality. Surveys of employers, such as Edelman's work on the development of equal employment opportunity structures (1990, 1992), Bridges and Villemez's study of the hiring and employment practices of employers (1994), and the National Organization Study (Kalleberg et al. 1994) are useful efforts that begin to relate organizational practices to theories of inequality. These studies have not turned to sex segregation by job or income determination processes, issues that are salient for the organizational inequality approach we advocate. But similar research designs could be employed for these purposes. It also may be possible to build synthetic data sets from existing sources. Just as we employed data from the census in our analyses of UNI and of the State of Washington, it is possible to identify employees of large employers in certain locales and perform multivariate analyses of their earnings functions and how their earnings functions compare with those of other workers in the locale.

Further research is needed, but the results of this study have implications for current policy debates and for theories of law and inequality. Just as our findings indicate a need to rethink theories of gender inequality in organizations, they urge a rethinking of policies on pay equity and theories of discrimination law.

Rethinking Policy on Gender Inequality in Pay

If we accept the conclusion of the foregoing analysis – that there is a significant amount of between-job gender inequality in pay in organizations – what policies should our society adopt to redress this problem? In Chapter 2 (Fig. 2.1) we set forth three paradigms of antidiscrimination law based on different conceptions of the relationship between law, labor markets, and employing organizations. The paradigms imply legal and regulatory strategies that vary on a continuum of state intervention into employer's pay practices from noninterventionist market approaches to interventionist comparable worth rules. We now return to these models to discuss the advantages and disadvantages of each in terms of antidiscrimination policy. We only briefly consider existing free market approaches, for these have been significantly undercut by our empirical findings concerning wage determination in organizations. We offer a far more extended discussion of comparable worth models, drawing on research into efforts to implement such pay equity reforms. Our analysis of comparable worth projects has theoretical as well as policy implications. We interpret the problems of implementation as evidence for the organizational inequality approach we have developed. We then offer our own recommendations for policy and legal reforms to address invidious gender-based wage differences.

Free Market Approaches

Strong Free Market Approach. The purest market approach is suggested by Richard Epstein in his book *Forbidden Grounds* (1992). Epstein's jurisprudential approach toward virtually all fields of law, not just employment discrimination, is based on a fervent belief in the primacy of freedom of contract. His general view on employment discrimination is that the state should impose antidiscrimination laws only to remove the effects of past state-sanctioned discrimination or in instances in which the market cannot effectively operate, such as in some public sector contexts or where union contracts frustrate market processes. Beyond the normative element of his argument, that undue state interference is an unacceptable violation of freedom, he argues that the costs of discrimination laws outweigh the benefits. In his view, laws against sex discrimination are particularly problematic. While few employment policies based on racial classifications are rational, many sex-based employment practices are.

There is little doubt that Epstein would disagree with the results of our empirical analysis. He interprets male-female wage differentials as reflecting unmeasurable differences between workers and is highly critical of statistical analyses that interpret unexplained wage differentials as the result of discrimination (1992, 375–85). But even if he accepted our empirical conclusions, he rejects the notion that legal rules can sensibly deal with the problem. Instead he would rely entirely on the market. Enterprising employers will move to employ and pay female workers better than their discriminating competitors, thus providing ambitious women with new opportunities. He would not distinguish between different kinds of discrimination: In his view, employers would be free to discriminate against women in hiring, promotion, and pay. The same market pressures will work equally effectively with respect to all kinds of discrimination. Indeed, we might expect that Epstein would be especially critical of efforts to redress between-job pay differences, for they might entail even more intrusive and complicated interventions into decisions made by employers than hiring and promotion rules.

Epstein's position is not well supported empirically. Our case studies demonstrate the indeterminacy of market wage values in organizations, the significant limitations on administrative rationality in the pay-setting process, and organizational mechanisms that introduce irrational gender bias in pay decisions. He discounts a large body of empirical evidence that finds that male-female wage differentials are not attributable to differences in the nature of work performed by women or by the human capital endowments of women compared with men (generally see England 1992 and Chapter 3). Our society does not accept Epstein's view of markets and discrimination, with good reason. To accept a laissez faire view of gender discrimination in all its manifestations would mean allowing irrational and unfair gender discrimination to remain, indeed possibly to again increase.

The Lesser Market Position. Other legal scholars and economists who are critical of comparable worth take a less extreme, free market position. Fischel and Lazear's (1986) article on comparable worth can be taken as a representative. Fischel and Lazear argue that the correct approach to accusations of between-job pay differences is to rigorously enforce rules against discrimination in hiring, promotion, and sex segregation, and unequal pay in the same job but to reject comparable worth. In this view, as discrimination in hiring and promotion are broken down through the law, it will shrink the portion of the between-job wage gap attributable to sex differences. This is a lesser market position because it relies on the long-run effect of gender integration by job; wages paid particular occupations are still determined by the market.

Fischel and Lazear are highly critical of comparable worth because it risks distorting market wages. They suggest that if our society wants to pursue a course of pay equity, it can do so by giving victims of gender-based pay discrimination a direct subsidy rather than by adopting job evaluation as the basis for pay decisions.

The Fischel and Lazear approach is an improvement over Epstein, in that they acknowledge that irrational discrimination may exist in the world and not be fully remediable by market processes alone. The main difficulty with their analysis is that they do not recognize between-job wage discrimination as a violation that can be remedied by law. Their solution to the problem of an employer that unfairly pays secretaries less than truck drivers (as measured by some objective principle) is for the secretaries to become truck drivers. Studies by Jacobs (1989) and others indicate that such occupational shifts will not be a solution. Women remain reluctant to move into the hostile territory of many male jobs; in recent years many women who have moved into male jobs soon move out. The data indicate that women still face massive amounts of sexual harassment when they attempt to enter previously male domains (Martin 1988; Walshok 1981; Gutek 1985; Gutek and Morasch 1982; Rhode 1997). Theoretically, hostile treatment is itself actionable. We know from

Bumiller's (1988) work that female workers often are afraid to pursue their rights. Donohue and Siegelman suggest this is particularly true until a worker becomes unemployed. While workers are still employed by the same organization, they are reluctant to sue for fear of damaging the relationship with their existing employer (also see Rhode 1989, 182–83; 1997).

We agree with some of Fischel and Lazear's criticisms of comparable worth. It may not help the actual victims of discrimination, it may lead to allocative inefficiencies in labor markets (see also Killingsworth 1985), and it may harm the employment prospects of women. Forcing an employer to pay jobs held predominantly by women more than they were paid previously will give that employer an incentive to reduce the amount of female labor performed by the firm. It does not follow, however, that just because comparable worth is not the proper solution, nothing should be done in law and policy with respect to between-job pay differences.

*The Current Post-*Gunther *Regime.* The current law might be characterized as a lesser market position with nominal provisions against egregious between-job pay discrimination. As we found in our review of cases in Chapter 2 and in the in-depth case studies, the courts have not given *Gunther* any practical effect. They consistently have rejected between-job claims, largely on the basis of their belief that the market or efficiency reasons explained the difference in male and female wages.

Our case studies reveal the inadequacies of the present regime. The courts' authoritative pronouncements in these cases presented a distorted image of the sources of gender inequality in the pay systems in question. Women workers who read those opinions would come away thinking that they were the victims of marketwide practices rather than of decisions by their own employer's managers and other workers. If the courts had simply pointed out that the women had not made out their case, or that male workers were better organized than female workers and thus got larger pay from management, the women might have understood their situation. Instead, female plaintiffs have been asked to accept the dominant ideology as reality. They have not been wronged. There is no solution from law.

The current regime has a disingenuous character. It holds out the formal possibility of legal remedies for between-job pay discrimination. In practice, most cases do not take the women's claims seriously. Our results, if recognized by the courts and parties, could begin to change the treatment of pay discrimination claims within the framework of existing law. The analytic strategies we developed post hoc for these case studies might be employed by plaintiffs and their lawyers in new litigation. If plaintiffs more clearly focus on how employers depart from the market and from rational compensation principles in ways that negatively affect women's pay, courts may be more receptive to their arguments. One clear lesson from these four cases is the importance of testimony by actual victims of discrimination. In the one case in which this kind of evidence was presented, the *Coastal* case, the plaintiffs prevailed. The absence of such testimonial evidence doomed the case against Sears.

Comparable Worth Approaches

Comparable Worth as a Wage Policy. The virtual disappearance of pay equity from the courts has slowed but not eliminated its promotion as a possible remedy for the gender earnings gap in society at large and in specific organizations. Pay equity advocates continue to propose that the best solution for the problem of gender-based wage inequality is comparable worth, that is, paying jobs according to the evaluated worth of the jobs to employers rather than the market value (see generally England 1992; Steinberg 1992). (Because there is some danger in confusing a broader concern with reducing between-job, gender disparities in pay that some have labeled "pay equity" and the specific remedy of comparable worth, we discuss the comparable worth proposals under the heading of "CW/pay equity.") But questions remain about the fairness and effectiveness of CW/pay equity. Having looked at the inner workings of four different compensation systems, we have learned a great deal about the sources of continuing gender inequality in pay within organizations. Our inspection of these systems sheds light not only on the potential usefulness and fairness of CW/pay equity remedies but also on their relevance. That is, as a treatment, does CW/pay equity reach all the basic conditions that produce diminished earnings for female workers? We shall first address this question leaving aside the issue of the proper role of markets in setting wages for predominantly male and female jobs. This will be a temporary delay, not a permanent oversight, however. The influence of external markets is a crucial, although not solely determinative, factor that must be brought into the picture.

Considering CW/Pay Equity

What Is CW/Pay Equity? At the outset, it is necessary to recognize that CW/pay equity is not a single, clearly defined policy. Jurisdictions that have adopted equity initiatives differ dramatically in the range of employers to which the policy applies. Some, like the states of Oregon and Washington, have limited equity initiatives to state government employees. Others, Minnesota, for example, have extended coverage to all nonfederal governmental employees. Most far-reaching have been jurisdictions like the Canadian provinces of Ontario and Quebec that have mandated that equity adjustments be implemented by *all* employers, public and private, with more than a specified number of employees (ten in the case of Ontario) (Smeenk 1993).

Equally, if not more, important are differences in the specific changes that each piece of legislation mandates. At one extreme are legislative directives of the type implemented in Minnesota for its state-level employees. (Subsequent legislation covering local government bodies in Minnesota differed substantially.) These policies assume the existence of job evaluation systems that are more or less fair and mandate that female-dominated job classifications and male-dominated job classifications with equal evaluated worth ("points") be paid equal amounts (see Evans and Nelson 1989, 79–82). Implementation of this policy then takes the form of legislative allocations of state funds to achieve the desired upgrading of pay in female-dominated jobs. Summarizing this process in Minnesota, Evans and Nelson report:

> When implementation was complete on June 30, 1987, the full cost of pay equity was 3.7 percent of the 1983 base payroll, a bit under the initial estimate. As reported by the Commission on the Economic Status of Women, approximately 8,500 employees in 200 female-dominated job classifications received pay equity increases. Most of the people receiving pay equity raises worked at clerical or health care jobs; about 10 percent of the recipients were men. The estimated average increase from over four years for pay equity raises was $2,200. (1989, 98)

Outside of Minnesota, this form of CW/pay equity implementation characterized efforts in states such as Washington.

At the other extreme of proactivity is legislation like that passed in the Province of Ontario which requires employers to evaluate the worth of female- and male-dominated job classes and to remove any nonpermissible differences in compensation between jobs of comparable worth[3] (Smeenk 1993; Gleason 1994; Agarwal 1990). This approach is more thoroughgoing in three related aspects. First, it prescribes the use of job

---

3 Wage differences stemming from seniority, temporary training assignments, merit pay, redcircling, and skill shortages are regarded as permissible. The latter would seem to leave room for the intrusion of market differences, but this is not a widely discussed feature of the system.

evaluation as a compensation mechanism in settings even when there may be no precedent for the use of this method in compensation decisions. As Agarwal (1990, 523) writes, "Then there are those organizations that do not use job evaluation at all in determining pay rates of their employees. . . . a mandated job evaluation approach simply does not fit all circumstances." Second, the legislation adopts a skeptical stance toward existing evaluation systems by requiring that the evaluation process itself be purged of invidious gender biases. "The important thing is that the system be 'gender neutral.' In other words, it cannot undervalue or overlook aspects of jobs that are done predominantly by one sex or the other" (Miller 1993, 31). Based on the belief that job evaluation systems embody some of the same sexist tendencies to devalue women's work that exist in the external labor market, CW/pay equity proposals call for technical controls to eliminate gender bias in job evaluations. Among these are controls, known as policy-capturing techniques, that reweight evaluation points to "remove" the gender component.

Third, as Agarwal (1990, 523) notes, "The Ontario Pay Equity Act imposes an additional requirement on the job evaluation process. The Act implies the usage of a job evaluation scheme that is universally applied to all jobs covered in a single pay equity plan and potentially, to jobs across all pay equity plans, i.e., across all jobs in the establishment."

Not surprisingly, the majority of legislated CW/pay equity initiatives falls between these two extremes. As Cook (1990, 527) states, "These laws run a gamut from fairly broad generalizations to the specifics of authorizing studies and implementation procedures." Typical of these initiatives is the comparable worth legislation and implementation process in the State of Oregon, which is described in considerable detail by Acker (1989). Although it covered only employees of the state government, it did mandate a comprehensive job evaluation for the purpose of eliminating gender bias in the ratings of predominantly female jobs.

Problems with Implementation. One prerequisite for CW/pay equity legislation to be useful as a policy tool is that it actually be implemented. In part, this depends on whether the remedies are ambitious and thoroughgoing, as in Ontario, or more restrained, as in Minnesota at the state government level. Not surprisingly, less radical plans have enjoyed smoother sailing in both their ease and completeness of implementation. Thus, Cook (1990, 528) states, "Unquestionably, the most successful case of the institution of pay equity in state and local government is that of Minnesota."[4] In large part, this success, even in the context of well-established collective bargaining, was due to the fact that, "the process of job classification and evaluation and the pay equity law were not connected" (Evans and Nelson 1989, 169). In both the United States and Canada, however, the more usual situation is for legislation and job evaluation to be connected.

Where this is the case, implementation has been delayed, protracted, or watered down. Joan Acker (1989) provides an insightful account of how comparable worth in Oregon fell far short of the expectations of its supporters and advocates. While a state task force wrestled with issues of points, weighting, and pay lines, the final solution represented the result of a continuing struggle among several labor unions, a number of different occupational groups, and the state pay bureaucracy. The end product was that, "Instead of a comprehensive comparable worth plan, they decided to (1) decouple compensation and classification, (2) use the job evaluation data to identify individual workers with the largest wage inequities, (3) propose that the remaining $5 million for comparable worth in the state budget be used to rectify these inequalities" (Acker 1989, 165). In Acker's words, the shift could be summarized as the abandonment of "true comparable worth" in favor of "poverty relief." Results in New York State were not altogether different according to Alice Cook (1990, 527): "In New York, the consultants and the unions both found themselves on the outside without a peephole, as the professional bureaucrats in compensation and budget took over the details and procedures of the implementation."

The implementation of CW/pay equity in Iowa followed a similar path. In fact, in a 1990 study of the implementation process, Orazem and Matilla undertook a statistical analysis of several pay plans that were subject to varying amounts of interest group and political influence. With the unique data available to them, they were able to compare CW/pay equity plans, many of which were never adopted, at various stages in the implementation process to determine how women and other constituencies fared under each. Their summary states,

> Our major conclusion is that the ultimate impact of
> comparable worth on the wage structure of state employees in
> Iowa was greatly modified by various interest groups through
> the political process of legislation and implementation.
> Potential gains of 8.8 percentage points in female pay relative

---

4   Her inclusion of *local* government in this glowing assessment is somewhat misleading. Evans and Nelson (1989, 125ff.) describe in painstaking detail the tortuous process that accompanied attempts to implement comparable worth in local government units.

to male pay under the original statistical plan ended up as a gain of only 1.4 percentage points once comparable worth was fully implemented and appeals were resolved. (1990, 149)

Problems of implementation in Ontario are, because of the wide scope of the statute's reach, more diverse and, therefore, harder to summarize. It is clear that implementation has been neither quick nor painless. In November 1993, the Ontario provincial treasurer moved the final date for implementation in the public sector from 1995 to 1998. Despite the fact that the enabling legislation was passed in 1987, wage adjustments for the smallest category of employers – those with 10 to 49 employees – were not even scheduled to begin until 1994 (Miller 1993). In sectors where the law has taken hold it has met with considerable resistance. Thus, by the end of 1993, over 3,500 complaints had been lodged with the provincial Pay Equity Office. Of these, 56 percent remained unresolved at the end of the year (Gleason 1994, 39).

A second set of issues involves the extent to which those working in female-dominated jobs have benefited under the Ontario plan. Among large, private sector Ontario employers (500 or more employees), only a bit over 20 percent of female-dominated jobs were found in a 1990 study to have been eligible for pay equity increases. (Of the total set of female-dominated jobs – defined as 60 percent or more female by this legislation – about 50 percent already had earnings as high as those in the "male comparator" jobs. Another 28 percent of such jobs were in establishments where no appropriate male comparison could be identified.)[5] However, adjustments were found to be necessary for relatively more female-dominated job classes in the public sector – 40 percent (Smeenk 1993, 60).

Questions have also been raised about the potential for the Ontario system to fall prey to the same confluence of political forces that "distorted" implementation in Oregon and other U.S. jurisdictions. Commenting on the implications of the Ontario Pay Equity Act for collective bargaining in various settings, Agarwal turns to a consideration of "differences in bargaining power." He writes (1990, 525), "But after pay equity has been achieved in an establishment, the Act does not prevent such pay differences [between equally valued male and female jobs] if the employer is able to show the difference is the result of differences in bargaining strength." As one might expect, Agarwal avoids considering

5 Because of this problem, the act was amended in 1993 to provide adjustments by means of a "pay-line" system to supplement the job-to-job comparison method that the original act had stipulated. This amounts to a gain in coverage at the expense of intrusiveness, i.e., requiring employers not only to implement job evaluation and point-based ratings, but also to adopt a particular mechanism for linking points to pay.

what exactly "difference in bargaining strength" means. For us, the critical issue is whether such differences occur solely because of factors that reside in the employee groups themselves (i.e., those in predominantly male vs. those in predominantly female jobs), or whether differential bargaining power emerges out of the relationship of these groups to employers and employers' differential reaction to them. As noted earlier, the latter situation prevailed at both UNI and in the Washington State employment bureaucracy.

While advocates recognize the politics of pay as an obstacle to the successful implementation of comparable worth, they fail to come to terms with the ultimate implications of their observations. Unless they believe that political maneuvering over job classes and their pay rates only come into being in response to CW/pay equity legislation, they ought to realize that these organization-level processes have been a potential source of pay inequity for a long time. This conclusion is precisely what our research has shown to be true. But the CW/pay equity paradigm, with its single-minded focus on cultural devaluation operating through tainted markets, misdiagnoses a large part of the problem. Is it any surprise that a remedy based on a tenuously proven diagnosis might leave the patient feeling better for awhile but still suffering from a long-term malady? Specifically, without changing the fundamental aspects of organizational politics or how an organization tends to reproduce male advantages through the pay system, changing the metric by which jobs are evaluated and paid will not work.

CW/Pay Equity and Markets. The second front on which CW/pay equity requires careful scrutiny is in its stance vis-à-vis labor market effects on earnings. There is a voluminous literature on this topic, almost all of which is highly critical of the comparable worth position (see, e.g., Gold 1983; Rhoads 1993; Killingsworth 1985; O'Neill 1984; Fischel and Lazear 1986). The four most frequent points of attack are (1) that it relies on subjective values rather than market-based valuation and is, therefore, open to a wide range of biases and manipulation; (2) that CW/pay equity solutions would introduce market distortions and a misallocation of resources by failing to recognize differences in wages that result from legitimate differences in labor supply; (3) that, partly because of this distortion, CW/pay equity adjustments would help to perpetuate the gender segregation of the labor force by paying workers what is in essence an above-market premium for working in female-dominated jobs; and (4) to the extent that it raises the price of women's jobs, it will lead employers to reduce demand for those jobs and will result in a reduced number of jobs for women. Our view of the relationship between external labor markets and nondiscriminatory wages for predominantly female jobs is that these concerns are sometimes, but not always, justified.

Before considering their differences, it is important to recognize that the neoclassical and the CW/pay equity positions do not disagree about everything. In fact, CW/pay equity and the neoclassical model of wage determination are in a much more ambiguous relationship. Comparable worth arguments and policies accept almost uniformly the proposition that the source of diminished wages in predominantly female jobs is the existence of marketwide discrimination in the valuing of such work. Individual employers participate in this discrimination when they set wages at the market level and pass along this disadvantage. It is for this reason that the one common element in all comparable worth policies is a deep suspicion of any provision in a wage determination system that would incorporate comparisons or references to market wages. (The Province of Ontario allows an exception for "skill shortages" but carefully avoids labeling such effects as paying market wages.)

Thus, CW/pay equity supporters embrace the market model of wage determination as an explanation for between-job wage differences in one breath but condemn it in the next as an illegitimate source of any earnings differences. (One wonders what their evaluation would be of markets in a hypothetical world in which *only* women worked for pay.) Surely, it is the case that market forces at some time, and in some place, must have operated to reduce an invidious, preexisting wage difference between a predominantly female and a predominantly male job. That the market can be a powerful engine for the improvement of historically subordinate groups is shown in Heckman and Payner's (1989) study of the South Carolina textile industry. Their investigation illustrated that once federal law struck down restrictions on employment in the industry, African Americans quickly rose to wage parity with white workers. Nurses historically have had to struggle to get employers to recognize the value of their labor. Severe shortages in the 1980s forced employers to raise dramatically the level of nursing salaries.

In our view, a sensible policy must recognize this possibility, alongside the equally plausible notion that some external markets may undervalue female-typed jobs. But we depart from both of these bodies of conventional wisdom (CW/pay equity and the neoclassical model) in arguing that the organizational aspects of pay determination are the central missing consideration in nearly all extant discussions of the problem. Our results suggest that organizations often tend to mediate markets in ways that disadvantage workers in predominantly female jobs. Markets that are mediated in this way may be quite ineffective in raising the salaries of historically disadvantaged groups.

In general, without concrete knowledge about the pay-setting practices of particular organizations, it is nearly impossible to weigh the conflicting claims of CW/pay equity and neoclassical theorists. Thus, whether or not a pay equity adjustment would distort a historically equilibrated pay rate for a particular job depends critically on whether or not the pay policies of the employer have already introduced a significant distortion. If current wage structures are not determined by market processes, how do we know that shifting to comparable worth will significantly increase misallocation over the current system? If the current wage structures are *not* so distorted, we can more readily accept the neoclassical critique of the CW/pay equity paradigm.[6]

Similar considerations also apply to whether wages that are initially determined by job factor point evaluations should be adjusted to reflect external market comparisons. In this case, the issue is not whether a particular adjustment of this type would increase or decrease the earnings of a female-dominated job but the specifics of the comparison process itself. Are such comparisons applied uniformly across the organization? (They were not, for example, at Coastal Bank.) Are the comparisons meaningful? Or are they artificially contrived and heavily "constructed"? (They were not especially meaningful, for example, in the State of Washington.)

In addition, although economic theory would predict a decline in demand if the price of female jobs rises, it is difficult to determine how large the effect would be on female employment. We do not know how price-sensitive demand is for female occupations. If organizational demand is relatively inelastic for some positions, a price gain would not lead to major cuts in female jobs. Furthermore, within large organizations that have many jobs that are only loosely linked to market values, a rescaling of the value of different positions, with some positions gaining value and others declining in relative value, is least likely to affect demand. The organization will continue to look for efficient means of reducing overall labor costs. But there is no reason to expect that predominantly female jobs would be the special target of these efforts just because their relative valuation in pay had increased.

To conclude, CW/pay equity does present some serious problems in relation to external market influences on wages. Significantly, these are not always the problems imagined by economic theory, nor are they the ones that trouble CW/pay equity advocates.[7]

---

6 Rhoads (1993) argues that such problems appeared in Minnesota's comparable worth reform. Yet the problems he identified seem quite modest.

7 Paul Weiler (1986) offers a more modest proposal that comparable worth be adopted through executive order by federal agencies. Weiler arrives at this position after reviewing the empirical data on male-female wage differentials and concluding that comparable worth will have a relatively modest effect on the wage gap. See our discussion of

Recommendations

Once one comes to terms with the full range of organizational practices that contribute to gender differences in pay, the limitations of putting comparable worth as an overlay on existing compensation systems becomes immediately apparent. Less clear is what exactly should be done to reach further to the core of the organizational sources of pay inequality between predominantly male and female jobs. In this section we outline a two-pronged approach to the issues. The first line of attack addresses the issue as an institutional problem that could be partially solved through the development of a "best practice model" of gender-neutral wage administration. This model, or a similar one, could be put in place in federal, state, and local jurisdictions in the belief that over time it would diffuse to the private sector. (According to some scholars, this has been a pattern in employment relations for much of the twentieth century [see Baron et al. 1988].) The second front involves

Weiler's analysis in Chapter 3. He nonetheless argues that comparable worth is a desirable policy, because it tends to cure some of the consequences of discrimination in labor markets. He rejects the idea that job evaluation should become the legal standard for determining discrimination under Title VII, largely on practical grounds. The cost of assessing liability through job evaluation on a case-by-case basis, through the process of contested litigation, would outweigh the potential gains. If the federal government adopts comparable worth as a standard practice, it will have an impact on the labor market and may lead other employers to adopt a similar approach.

If there are problems with comparable worth as a policy solution, however, either in terms of ineffectiveness or the harms it may cause, does it make sense to limit that policy to the federal government? One rationale is that pay discrimination is more of a problem there than elsewhere in the economy. Another is that federal employment is uniquely decoupled from the market, which makes the adoption of a nonmarket pricing system less problematic in that context than others.

The empirical data provide only weak support for these distinctions. The gender gap does tend to be larger in public sector employment (see Sorensen 1994), which is consistent with the notion that there may be more discrimination in that sector. Certainly various studies of public agencies, including our own studies of UNI and the State of Washington, demonstrate gender bias in wage and promotion systems (see Baron, Mittman, and Newman 1991; DiPrete 1989). The difficult question that is not answered in the literature, however, is whether this is worse in the public sector. There are many other differences between the public and private sectors, such as organization size and the composition of job titles, that also may affect the relative size of wage disparities. We certainly found significant between-job differences in our private sector case studies. The data are not so clear to call for a sharp distinction in pay policy between public and private sector organizations.

The same can be said of the issue of market decoupling. The private organizations in our case studies did not show markedly more sensitivity to market prices than did the two public sector firms. While we concede that private sector management may have a greater interest in lowering labor costs vis-à-vis the labor market than would public sector management, why should we expect the incentive to work differently for male and female jobs? Again, the public-private sector differences are not so clearly established to merit different policies.

renewed efforts at achieving results through selective litigation and other forms of antidiscrimination regulation.

Gender-Neutral Pay Administration

One of the more beneficial results of the comparable worth movement has been the emergence of numerous studies devoted to the question of how job evaluation can be purged of its inherent male biases (e.g., Steinberg and Walter 1992; Steinberg and Haignere 1987; Treiman 1979). The most important points from these efforts seem to be the following. First, inventories of job factors must not ignore or take for granted traits, abilities, and skills that are associated with female roles while they simultaneously reward traits, abilities, and skills associated with male roles. Second, in devising new lists of job factors and their related evaluations, analysts need to do more than simply add compensable factors relevant to "female" jobs on top of the sometimes rather long list of factors relevant to existing jobs. Instead, gender neutrality often requires reformulation of extant job factors to broaden the definition of particular job traits (Steinberg and Walter 1992). Along these lines, several efforts are underway to develop evaluation systems that would give equivalent credit to high level skills in activities such as care-giving, conflict resolution, and manual dexterity.

Nevertheless we believe that any "best practice" model of wage administration must go beyond technical reforms in job evaluation. One must confront a number of crucial issues that are conveniently avoided as long as the focus remains on the relatively sterile exercise of proposing factors and assigning them points. For example, proposed reforms must take into account whether the wage differentials that are already in place in a given wage plan are supported by norms of equity and justice. In organizations where internal labor markets exist in more than a nominal sense (where clusters of jobs are filled primarily from inside the organization by moving people between sets of "feeder" and "receiver" jobs), wage differentials also must be kept in line with sequences of promotions. In settings where some or many jobs can be filled from outside the organization, wage levels must be equilibrated to the quality of external applicants that are needed. Furthermore, there is also the strong possibility that pay practices that resolve one of these issues simultaneously create or exacerbate problems on one or more of the other dimensions. Because of these concerns, the recommendations that we offer must be seen as tentative guidelines rather than as a tried and true recipe for eliminating gender bias. It is crucial to raise pay equity concerns in the context of market influences on wages. This perspective on the pay equity debate has been missing for too long.

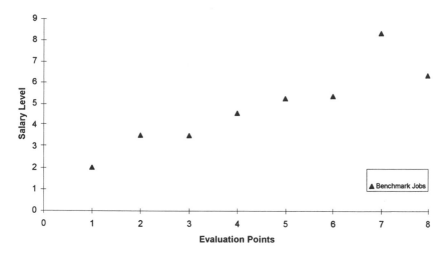

Figure 9.1. Benchmark jobs in hypothetical organization.

Our first proposal is that organizations should resist establishing separate job families on the basis of criteria that are gender-linked or even implicitly gender-related. A blatant violation of this principle occurs when organizations establish separate series for "clerical" and "physical plant" workers as in the UNI case. This point has already been raised in CW/pay equity literature, but mostly with regard to the inequities that arise when separate job families are established for the purpose of establishing job factors and conducting job evaluations. However, the point is even more compelling when separate gender-typed job families are established for the purpose of external market comparisons.

In Figures 9.1 through 9.3 we present hypothetical data that illustrate the nature of the problem. Let us imagine an organization with eight benchmark jobs that can be matched to external salary referents through market surveys. Figure 9.1 plots the salary level for each job against its number of evaluation points. Let us assume in addition that there are other jobs in the organization for which no external salary data exist. A typical practice in the field of organizational compensation is to establish, through least squares or otherwise, an approximate line of best fit to the benchmark data that can then be used to establish salaries for non-benchmark jobs. While such a salary line could be established on the basis of the complete set of benchmark jobs, organizations often choose to establish distinct subsets or families of jobs and to fit the salary practice lines separately within subgroups.

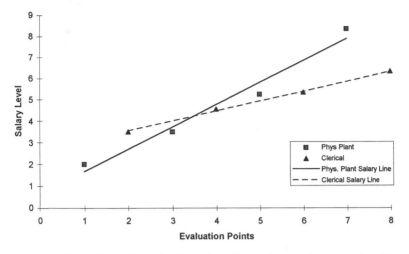

Figure 9.2. Hypothetical salary lines with gender-typed families.

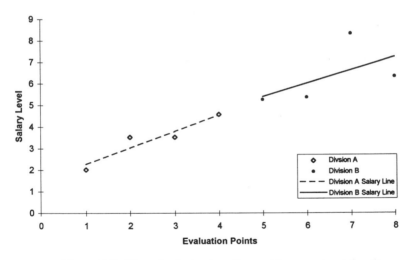

Figure 9.3. Hypothetical salary lines with status-level families.

Suppose in this hypothetical situation that jobs evaluated at 1, 3, 5, and 7 points are jobs associated with a "physical plant" classification, and are disproportionately male. Jobs 2, 4, 6, and 8 we will stipulate as members of a "clerical" classification and as disproportionately female. Figure 9.2 illustrates how salary lines fit by least squares would appear if salary comparisons were made *within* these stereotyped and gendered job categories. Nonbenchmark jobs in the upper range would receive considerably lower salaries if they were part of the clerical series than if they were part of the physical plant series (compare the salary lines corresponding to the physical plant job at 5 evaluation points to the clerical job at 6 evaluation points).

But keep in mind that the assignment of jobs to families is neither automatic nor free from arbitrary judgments. Although it would be understandable if compensation bureaucrats felt obliged to keep jobs in the same family that were linked by promotion and transfer ladders, this practice is often followed, as at UNI, when internal labor markets are noticeably absent. Suppose that instead of the thinly veiled gender-loaded categories of "physical plant" and "clerical," our hypothetical organization grouped together jobs at 4 points and below (division A) and jobs at 5 points and above. Figure 9.3 shows how salary lines fitting within those status-related categories would appear. In the lower half of the salary structure, salaries would remain virtually unchanged except for the male-dominated job at 3 evaluation points whose salary would be subject to a modest reduction. In the upper half of the distribution, however, there would be consistent improvements in salary for the two female-typed jobs (6 and 8), and a sizable reduction for one of the male-typed positions (7).

Although these data are purely hypothetical and inappropriate for any specific conclusions (e.g., "form job families by status level wherever possible"), they do illustrate that there are potentially drastic consequences of the manner in which job families are formed. Because of the widespread disparities that do occur when implicit gender categories are used for this purpose, we suggest that the burden of proof falls on those who propose to form job families along these lines. This burden could be carried, for example, if real promotion progressions existed among jobs within a job family, but in general the likelihood of abuse from these systems seems to far outweigh their potential benefits.

A second area in which most existing pay systems could be reformed is in the use of other indicators of market wage levels beyond the routinized, and to an extent ritualized, industry salary survey. In the four cases examined here, it was remarkable how sporadic organizations were in their collection of data related to hiring difficulty and turnover problems. Even in those organizations where these data existed, there did not appear to be any systematic triggering mechanisms that linked changes in recruitment and turnover trends to reviews of the wage levels for particular jobs. Instead, these indicators often seemed to function as yet one more implement wielded by one faction or another in the unceasing struggle for organizational advantage.

The absence of strong centralization in the collection and interpretation of this kind of market data may seem surprising given that organization compensation specialists appear eager to expand their roles and gain control over as many aspects of the salary setting process as possible (see Acker 1989, 55ff.). Part of the explanation may be the lack of organizational power associated with "human resource" functions in general and with pay specialists in particular. We believe that a more important factor is the internal conflict between different imperatives located within the role of the pay administrator itself. Certainly, personnel bureaucrats realize the necessity of taking external market wages into account in some fashion. Were it not for this perceived obligation, the machinery of salary surveys and benchmark jobs would have long since disappeared. At the same time, salary administrators act almost instinctively to enforce what might be labeled the "principle of order." The structure of this order derives not only from traditional differentials between jobs but also from the scientifically analyzed content of jobs, as reflected in job evaluation, and from the notion that the salaries of "related" jobs should move together.

The external market, however, knows of no such order. To the extent that wages in clearly defined labor markets are influenced by changing tastes and fashions, on both the supply and demand side, they will of necessity have a degree of unpredictability or even randomness. More than the weakness of the personnel department in the modern organization, it is this basic dilemma that restrains salary administrators from more closely monitoring and measuring the market for specific jobs and adjusting wage rates accordingly. Often a compromise is struck: Measure the external wage rates for individual jobs but then average the results for broad groups of related jobs. This strategy was widely followed by the department of personnel in the State of Washington in the 1970s.[8] In its most extreme form, all jobs in a firm are averaged together and a common "market movement" adjustment is applied uniformly to each.

Given that predominantly female jobs are currently disadvantaged in many pay systems, this method of introducing market corrections is nearly guaranteed to eliminate upward movements in salary in the external market for predominantly female jobs from being translated into increases for specific job categories of women workers inside organizations. The alternative solution would be to institutionalize the collection

---

8   Interestingly, the penchant for averaging has crept into the implementation of pay equity legislation in Canada. One practitioner advises, "it may be easiest to create an evaluation system based on only a very few pay levels, with broad classifications" (Conklin 1989). Another states, "Group jobs together for evaluation purposes. A lot of companies get bogged down when they try to use each job as a separate job class for determining male and female dominance and for evaluation purposes" (Miller 1993).

of detailed hiring, turnover, and market salary data for relatively fine-grained job categories.

Consider, for example, the salary structures shown in Figures 9.2 and 9.3 and the salary level that would be assigned to the (male) job at 7 evaluation points. One could make the argument that the structure shown in Figure 9.2 is to be preferred over the one in Figure 9.3 because it more closely reproduces the external salary for this particular job (although it misses the external rate for the job at 5 points by a wider margin). Rather than introducing an implicit gender bias into the structure and adopting the wage curve of Figure 9.2, a reasonable solution would be to regularize a process for granting market exceptions in those cases where the "systematic" wage clearly underestimates the wage for a particular job or jobs. Although the details of this process would have to be tailored to particular organizations and particular settings, one can easily imagine a set of criteria being established that would reflect not only external salary levels as measured in surveys but also internally generated data on hiring and turnover. While external data would, by definition, be lacking for jobs located entirely within internal labor markets, statistics related to problems in internal transfers in and out of particular jobs could serve as proxy hiring and turnover data. If such a process were implemented, one could even imagine that the so-called internal labor market might become a market in fact rather than being merely a market in name only.

An additional issue for salary systems with a mix of internal and external market job segments is the choice of a scheme to link salaries of specific jobs in the two segments. Perhaps the most widely used techniques are those that resemble the systems shown in Figures 9.2 and 9.3. In these "salary-line" methods, data on benchmark jobs in the external market are used to establish a translation of evaluation points into salary levels. For nonbenchmark (internal labor market) jobs, points become the coin of the realm that set the terms of placement in the actual system of grades. This method is not the only solution to the problem at hand, however. Specifically, the system used by the State of Washington DOP (Chapter 6), operated not on a logic of best-fitting lines but rather on a logic of job clusters. Each job that was not itself directly compared with an external job – that was not a benchmark – was indexed by means of a point system as being so many salary grades above or below its corresponding benchmark job. (Although in Washington State job evaluation points seemed to play a minor role in the establishment of the size of these indexing relationships, one can easily imagine a system in which they would play a much larger role.) What the cluster method avoids is the kind of reification that occurs when the market wage for two possibly unrelated jobs, such as grounds keeper and police sergeant, is used to construct a fictive linear translation between internally derived evaluation points and level of salary, on the supposition that what the market is really rewarding is job points. Instead, the cluster method, under ideal circumstances, tries to establish meaningful relationships among jobs based on patterns of internal movement and "sociotechnical" distance. (By the latter we mean that two jobs may be organizationally related in such a fashion that even though no movement takes place between the positions, they serve as routine points of comparison for each other. Jobs that provide technical support for related line positions might fall into this category.) In terms of the logic of administered efficiency, the cluster technique seems to have much in its favor.

But, of course, one must remember that each of these systems is implemented in a world that is shot through with organizational politics. As our investigation of the Washington State system revealed, the job cluster method is noteworthy for the multitude of decision points that it contains. The relationship between each job (the jobs number in the thousands) and its benchmark is subject to discretion, and, therefore, to interested manipulation, at several different decision points each time the salary structure is revised. Compared with a system of this type, the job evaluation/salary-lines systems have a much lower density of decision making despite the fact that individual job evaluations must be made for each job. Which of these are fairer to women and those working in predominantly female jobs? In employment settings where women have been historically underrepresented in unions and other employee interest groups, perhaps both systems disadvantage women equally. But as women begin to assert themselves through employee interest groups, it would seem that the job cluster methodology presents more formidable obstacles to getting equitable consideration until these groups achieve parity in influence with more traditional male-dominated associations. This would be especially true where women's political muscles are flexed on behalf of particular occupational groups such as nurses or librarians, as their coverage of the spectrum of jobs in the organization would be exceedingly narrow. The salary-line methodology provides the opportunity for increased wages in a few visible and relatively powerful benchmark occupations, such as nursing, to be leveraged into wage gains for other predominantly female lines of work. If these salary-line systems are favored for political reasons, we believe that organizational and economic efficiency requires that provisions be made for the kind of market-based, individual job adjustments we have described earlier. On the other hand, if the seemingly more rational cluster systems are chosen, it will be necessary to find some technique for guaranteeing that the relationship between nonbenchmark jobs and their market points of reference would not, in the words of one of the

Washington State participants, be "bargained to death." Continuing legal scrutiny of such systems, as authorized in *Gunther* but as abandoned in the wake of *AFSCME*, may be the most workable method of enforcement.

Legal Scrutiny of Between-Job Pay Differences

Reformulating Tests of Impact, Intent, and Treatment. Perhaps the pivotal issue in current law is whether plaintiffs can go beyond a demonstration of disparate impact from an employment practice to a showing of disparate treatment. Disparate impact theories do not require proof of discriminatory intent. If a practice has a disparate impact on a protected group and is not justified by business necessity, it is a violation of Title VII. Disparate treatment theories require proof of discriminatory intent. That is, the plaintiffs must present direct or indirect proof that a gender-based animus lies behind a practice that harms women.

The federal courts have been increasingly reluctant to employ disparate impact formulations in discrimination cases. As we discussed in Chapter 2, in 1989 in the *Wards' Cove* case (490 U.S. 642 [1989]) the Supreme Court largely vitiated disparate impact theories in a hiring and promotion case. The Civil Rights Act of 1991 overrode that opinion. That act is not likely to change the approach of the courts to pay discrimination claims, however. In *Spaulding* (740 F.2d 686 [9th cir. 1984]) and *AFSCME* (770 F.2d 1401 [9th cir. 1985]), the courts held that disparate impact theories were not appropriate for pay discrimination cases, because decisions about pay involved too many considerations to be treated as a single, discrete policy for purposes of a disparate impact analysis.

The courts' logic may hold for attempts at broadly invalidating pay systems through a disparate impact approach. For example, we agree that it is unwieldy to ask an employer to defend a market-based system only because women make statistically significantly less than men in such a system. The market principle is not a focused decision-making policy, but rather involves myriad judgments about particular jobs and individuals. Yet we do not understand why some more specific policies, such as relocation bonuses or overseas living allowances, cannot be subjected to a disparate impact analysis. In both cases if the policies disadvantage women, the employing organization should be able to mount a satisfactory explanation for why the practice is used. Those policies, although they deal with pay, do not involve individualized judgments. Therefore, courts should not automatically decline a disparate impact approach to all types of pay claims.

Indeed in *Donnelly v. Rhode Island Board of Governors for Higher*

Education (929 F. Supp. 583 [D. Rhode Island 1996]), the court held that it would subject the use of distinct market tiers in a university pay plan to a disparate impact analysis. Distinguishing the *Spaulding* case, the court refused to equate the use of tiers with actually paying market rates. ". . . [D]espite the fact that [the wage] Plan generally mirrors the differences in interdisciplinary compensation revealed by [a wage] survey, it is more than simply a mechanical application of market rates" (p. 590). Ultimately the university prevailed because the plaintiffs could not demonstrate that they were injured by the plan.

A broader point within the context of the current law is that our results point toward the need to expand the concept of intent and disparate treatment in pay discrimination cases. We find that pay differentials between male and female jobs are produced through an accumulation of organizational practices that tip the balance in favor of male jobs and away from female jobs. No single actor in an employing organization needs to be aware of the gender implications of behavior that disadvantages women. An objective review of pay practices will tend to reveal such biases. But one would be hard-pressed to attribute invidious intent to the many officials within the organization who had a hand in creating and maintaining unjustified gender-based wage inequality.

Under current law, if plaintiffs can demonstrate that disparate treatment is part of the employer's normal operating procedure, they make out an effective claim. One route to such an inference is testimonial evidence. What distinguished the Coastal case, where the plaintiffs prevailed, from the other three cases we analyzed was the powerful testimony of a group of women from various parts of the bank that they had been victims of discrimination. That testimony put a face on both the victims and perpetrators of discrimination. And it showed that the problem was not an isolated instance. When combined with statistical data showing widespread, unexplained pay differentials, it persuaded the judge that discrimination was systemic in the bank.

Another route to the inference of systemic discrimination gives greater emphasis to historical patterns and statistical data. In *Bazemore v. Friday*,[9] the Supreme Court ruled that evidence that an employer engaged in discrimination prior to the effective data of Title VII, and that such policies or practices continued, would support a finding of disparate treatment during the period covered by Title VII. *Bazemore* led some plaintiffs to dig deep into the histories of pay systems in an effort to trace out the origins of allegedly discriminatory practices. In *California State Employees' Association* (682 F. Supp. 1044 [N.D. Cal. 1987]), for example, the plaintiffs focused on pay practices that were designed in

9   478 U.S. 385 (1986).

the 1930s. The court rejected the argument based on its conclusion that the state employer seemed to be following the market in establishing the pay levels in question.

Our empirical results are consistent with the spirit of *Bazemore*. We found that critical examinations of the roots of pay systems, their historical positioning in the labor market for male and female jobs, their tendency to preserve existing wage differentials between male and female jobs, and the practical politics of systems in action contributed much to understanding the nature of gender inequality in organizations. Historical patterns should be particularly significant to legal judgments about pay discrimination. In cases on affirmative action in hiring, promotion, and government contracting, the federal courts have been increasingly hostile to historical justifications for preferential treatment for minorities and women, except in circumstances in which there is a demonstrated nexus between past discrimination and the current remedial program.[10] The use of historical patterns in pay cases presents a very different issue. Arguably, unlike the situation in affirmative action cases, paying female workers more fairly does not work an injury on their male counterparts (unless the men are hurt by loss in relative wage superiority within the organization). Moreover, evidence that the historical disadvantage of women has been preserved over time is relevant to proving ongoing harm. To paraphrase the opinion of the judge in *Coastal*, pay discrimination in the past, if not corrected, continues to show up in every succeeding paycheck.

In our view the courts in pay discrimination cases should begin to move away from a standard of culpability, in which the touchstone of liability is evidence of invidious intent, toward a standard of responsibility, in which the touchstone of liability is wage differentials that cannot be explained by genuine market and efficiency considerations. In large organizational contexts, the concept of intentional discrimination – which implies individual animus against women – is a kind of construction. Absent the smoking gun, the courts are forced to draw inferences about what motivated various employer policies. Rather than continue this fiction, we suggest that courts begin to give greater weight to the systemic aspects of pay determination to decide whether a pay system operates to produce and maintain unjustified male-female wage differences.

There may be little hope for change through a revitalization of existing antidiscrimination law based on more sophisticated empirical conceptions of the sources of gender inequality. Absent a major new initiative

10 See, e.g., *Adarand Constructors v. Pena*, 515 U.S. 200 (1995); *City of Richmond v. J.A. Croson Co.*, 488 U.S. 469 (1989).

by the EEOC, it is unlikely that plaintiffs would be willing to undertake the expense, risk, and uncertainty that a new set of legal challenges would entail. A new set of test cases might be valuable primarily as a means of lengthening the shadow of discrimination law over pay systems. If employers were prompted to reconsider the equity and defensibility of their practices, such efforts might have significant effect. For many employers who themselves do not recognize the gendered character of their wage determination systems, they are not likely to be moved by case-by-case adjudication. They are more likely to think their pay systems are legitimate and that they will never face a truly damaging judgment.

Moving from a Model of Rights Adjudication to Regulated Fairness. Given the likely limitations of adjudication as a mechanism for address-ing between-job gender inequality, are there other legal strategies that might prove effective? One possibility that might be explored would entail a shift from primary emphasis on the adjudication of claims to the regulation of pay practices. The law already extensively regulates how employers pay their workers. Yet an effort to police the relative wage levels of male and female jobs would be a regulatory undertaking of a much more massive scale. The reader should be clear, by now, that we take the decentralized character of American labor markets seriously. There is daunting variety in the organizational and market contexts in which pay systems operate. This variation counsels against any regula-tory scheme that relies on an inflexible template.

An approach that is sensitive to local variation is to mandate pay equity studies or audits. As we discussed in the previous section, the Canadian province of Ontario has required such studies of employers. The Ontario system grants a form of limited immunity from discrimi-nation lawsuits to companies that agree to a timetable for adopting the recommendations of equity studies. If the United States adopted a similar law, even if only limited to very large employers, the results might be quite dramatic. If the law required that the audit be conducted by an autonomous firm, so that the study was relatively independent of the bureaucratic politics of the subject organization, audits could provide a fresh look at gender inequality in pay. At the very least, mandated inquiries would raise the salience of pay equity as an issue in organiza-tional life. If studies identified irrationalities and bias that the employer was not previously aware of, they might stimulate voluntary efforts to reduce wage differentials. If some version of the results were made avail-able to workers, it would provide workers with a better sense of whether they were being treated fairly. Such information might spur collective action to reform the organization's compensation policies.

In endorsing pay equity studies, once again we are not endorsing comparable worth. If an audit showed that pay rates closely tracked genuine market rates for jobs, we would be inclined to accept those wage levels as legitimate. Another crucial question is how study results might be used in traditional Title VII litigation. If the results could be incorporated into discrimination claims, employers will have strong incentives to distort or compromise such a study. However, the audits might considerably strengthen the hand of deserving plaintiffs in litigation, which might give greater bite to a largely ineffective litigation regime.

More research and experimentation is necessary before it is reasonable to offer detailed proposals about the regulation of pay systems. Yet our results suggest that if this society is interested in pursuing the goal of social justice in the pay of male and female workers, such efforts are essential.

Reverse Discrimination as a Potential Roadblock to Pay Equity Initiatives. Just as affirmative action plans generally have come under legal attack for violating the constitutional rights of majority groups, voluntary pay equity initiatives also are potential targets. In *Smith v. Virginia Commonwealth University*, 84 F.3d 672 (4th cir. 1996), male faculty members challenged a university's pay equity program as sex discrimination. The program was adopted in response to a university study of gender-based pay disparities. After controlling for several independent variables, including national salary average by discipline and rank, possession of a doctorate, tenure status, years of experience at the university, general academic experience, and so forth, the university found that women faculty were paid an average of $1,354 less than male faculty (84 F.3d at 685 [dissenting opinion]. The male plaintiffs contended in their lawsuit that the regression analysis did not include some variables that would explain the gender difference. As a result, they argued that the pay equity increases given to female faculty (which varied between 1 to 40 percent raises based on reviews of individual cases, and had a median value of $1,414) constituted pay discrimination. The trial court dismissed the plaintiffs' case before trial on the grounds that the plaintiffs had not demonstrated that including more variables would in fact explain the gender differential, nor apparently were they planning to do so at trial. The Fourth Circuit Court of Appeals, sitting en banc (i.e., the entire court rather than a three-judge panel), overruled the trial court and ordered that the plaintiffs be given a chance to prove their case before a jury.

In the majority opinion (the court split 6 to 5), the court referred to the test for the legality of voluntary affirmative action plans under Title VII: whether the purpose of the plan was to break down old patterns of discrimination; whether the plan did not unnecessarily trammel the rights of those outside the protected group; and whether it was designed to eliminate a manifest racial or sexual imbalance. (The court cited *United Steelworkers v. Weber*, 443 U.S. 193 [1979] and *Johnson v. Transportation Agency*, 480 U.S. 616 [1987].) While the plaintiff bears the burden of proving that an affirmative action plan does not meet these criteria, the court agreed that the male faculty members had raised a material question about whether the university had demonstrated a manifest sexual imbalance in its pay system. The court relied heavily on the plaintiffs' expert witness, who said that adding more variables to the regression equation might eliminate the gender effect. One concurring opinion, by the chief judge of the circuit, was especially hostile to the university's equity initiative.

> It is not at all difficult to see how policies such as these threaten to poison the university environment. . . . Class-based raises and promotions will predictably spawn, as they have here, litigation by representatives of excluded faculty groups. They will stoke animosities among friends and colleagues and they will postpone the day when empathy among the races and understanding between the sexes is achieved. (84 F.3d at 677, 678)

In the wake of the court of appeals decision, the parties settled the lawsuit (personal communication with the university's attorney, Sept. 1998). At the very least, the case indicates that in the current judicial climate employers must be careful about establishing the grounds for pay equity raises, and that they must implement plans in a way that is fair to male and female workers. The case also raises the specter of a broader set of challenges to pay equity efforts that are not grounded on adjudicated findings of sex-based pay discrimination.

Rethinking Theories of Law and Gender Inequality: Legalizing Gender Inequality

After examining the rise and fall of pay equity as a theory of discrimination, and having studied in depth some of the cases that were pivotal in that history, we are left to consider the implications for the sociology of law. We turn first to the explanation of how the federal courts dealt with these cases. We then develop the implications of our findings for theories of the relationship of law to social inequality in American society.

Explaining the Case Outcomes: Doctrine, Politics, or Ideology?

The pay discrimination cases present a puzzle. Why did the federal courts open the door to between-job discrimination cases in *Gunther*, 452 U.S. 161 (1981), but then shut it by adopting the conventional market-based explanation for the wage differences at issue? We consider three broad categories of explanation: doctrinal, political, and ideological. These are not mutually exclusive interpretations. Each perspective elucidates some aspects of the phenomenon. In the end, we find the ideological explanation contributes the most to understanding the pattern of judicial decisions.

It is useful to begin by considering the conventional doctrinal explanation: The courts applied the law to the facts and concluded that the plaintiffs had not made out their case. There are some grounds for interpreting the outcomes of these cases in this fashion. The doctrinal basis for applying Title VII to wage differences involving different jobs was contested from the very beginning. *Gunther* was a bitterly divided opinion. Rehnquist's dissent is widely quoted in both law review articles and succeeding pay cases. As such, any case that relied on anything less than powerful, direct evidence of intentional discrimination stood little chance in the courts. The attempt to use job evaluation results to prove discrimination or to establish that employers knew they were discriminating was too ambitious within this fragile doctrinal structure. Plaintiffs sometimes added to the difficulties by propounding that the employer discriminated "by following the market." They thus set up an opposition between the market and Title VII that courts were unlikely to accept.

The state of social-scientific opinion might also be cited in support of a doctrinal view. It should be clear by now that we think the courts in these cases did not come to the correct conclusion about the extent to which the market determined the male-female wage differences at issue. But expert opinion in these cases did little to question the link between market and wages. Thus one could plausibly argue that the conflicting nature of the social science data presented to the courts led them to conclude that the plaintiffs had not established their case.

Yet it is clear from the in-depth case studies and the reading of other opinions that the courts typically went well beyond merely stating that the plaintiffs had failed to carry their burden of proof. With few exceptions, the opinions offered sweeping pronouncements that market forces or efficiency considerations explained the wage differences between male and female jobs. Recall Judge Posner's declaration in the *American Nurses* case, 783 F.2d 716 (1986) at 719, that the lower earnings of women are explained by the fact that "most women take time out of the labor force in order to take care of their children. As a result they tend to invest less in their 'human capital' . . . and therefore tend to be found in jobs that pay less."

Posner is no ordinary judge, of course. And the quotation is *dicta* from an opinion granting the women plaintiffs another chance to prove their theory of discrimination. Yet it is just a more erudite and explicit statement of a set of beliefs that run through most of the cases in this subfield. To be sure, the opinions do occasionally refer to the fact that a finding for the plaintiffs would raise difficult issues of how to design an appropriate remedy, but such statements usually go hand in hand with statements that the wage determination process is better left to market forces and the business judgments of employers. These deeper beliefs seem to motivate the courts to interpret the doctrine the way they do.

Political explanations of judicial decisions emphasize the institutional forces that affect how judges decide cases. One species of this approach is an interest group model. It predicts that the more powerful participant will prevail before the courts, just as it is presumed to do in the legislative or regulatory process. Given that women workers were less powerful than male management, the argument goes, they lose. The problem with this explanation is that sometimes women do win. They won in the *Coastal* case. And, as we showed more comprehensively in Chapter 2, they win quite frequently in equal pay act cases. If political power were a sufficient explanation, *Gunther* should have come out the other way, effectively sealing off claims about between-job wage differences.

A more subtle form of political explanation relies on the courts' own view of institutional capacity (for a general discussion, see Rosenberg 1991). From this perspective, courts that confront cases that seek to broaden the role of law and the courts must calculate the political costs of alternative courses of action. Applying this framework to pay discrimination cases, institutionalists would argue that the political costs of invalidating the pay systems of large employers were too high. It would embroil the courts in controversial and complicated efforts to develop an appropriate remedy, with no certainty that such difficulties would ever be effectively resolved.

This interpretation is quite plausible for the cases we have studied. Opinions occasionally refer to worries about the courts getting bogged down in decisions about pay levels they are ill equipped to deal with. One of the reasons the courts may be more inclined to rule for plaintiffs in Equal Pay Act cases is that a smaller number of individuals typically are involved and the damages and remedy are more straightforward to design than if a court invalidated an entire pay system.

Still this explanation only carries us so far. The courts sometimes have taken on significant supervisory responsibility to correct the illegal, unconstitutional, or discriminatory practices of large institutions (see, e.g., Chayes 1976; Johnson 1981). One of the points of contention in the pay cases is the complexity of the remedy called for. The plaintiffs' attorneys we spoke to tended to minimize the difficulties a judgment would involve (personal interviews, 1988). Indeed, the *Christensen* case and the checklist compensation segments of the *Sears* case did not seem to pose practical difficulties. UNI could have adopted the first set of recommendations from its own consultants. The calculation of damages and remedial pay raises in *Sears* appeared quite straight-forward. Coastal Bank was able to work out a settlement with the plaintiffs in the aftermath of losing at trial, without recourse to extensive judicial intervention.

Moreover, the courts in these cases did not concede that the plaintiffs may have had a valid point but just one not recognized at law. Instead, the opinions almost universally deny that any systemic wrong exists, or at least they reject the plaintiffs' argument that they have proved a systemic wrong attributable to gender bias.

A more radical political view is that courts created a mythical right to redress in order to bolster the appearance of legal responsiveness to inequality but then refused to give those symbolic rights any practical effect (see generally Scheingold 1974; Freeman 1990; Taub and Schneider 1990). This contention cannot be tested directly but also does not seem to fit. The *Gunther* case hardly has the look of judicial manipulation. The majority and dissenting opinions gave voice to sharply contrary interpretations of Title VII. The *Gunther* majority was unwilling to interpret Title VII in a fashion that would countenance blatant forms of intentional pay discrimination just because the workers involved held different jobs. We are more inclined to read *Gunther* as evidence of the normative appeal of the antidiscrimination principle than as a merely symbolic gesture toward gender equality.

Indeed, we see in the pay cases an ongoing dialogue about the reach of the antidiscrimination principle. Several opinions explicitly discuss the purpose of Title VII as providing "equal opportunity" and of removing artificial barriers to employment opportunities rather than guaranteeing equal outcomes in the labor market. The courts are quite explicit in announcing the limits of the employment rights at issue.

Where the courts are wrong and, in our view, somewhat disingenuous is in their treatment of the evidence on the sources of male-female wage differences. In *Christensen* and *AFSCME*, appellate court panels authoritatively announced that the wage differences were the product of the market, rather than gender bias within the employing organization. The opinions revealed no self-doubt about the court's knowledge of the true state of affairs in the organizational pay systems under scrutiny. The plaintiffs had not merely failed to prove their case. They had no case.

Thus we come down in favor of an ideological explanation of these cases. That is, the courts saw the evidence presented in these cases through the lens of the dominant discourse on between-job gender inequality. As a result they consistently invoked the market as the explanation for wage differences, despite only weak evidence in the record to support the conclusion. It is difficult to prove that a particular ideological frame is at work in any text, but this is especially true in the case of dominant ideologies. For an ideology to be hegemonic means that it is taken for granted, rendered invisible (Bourdieu 1977; Comaroff and Comaroff 1991). Yet we gain a glimpse of the dominant ideology in these cases. The texts of the opinions by Posner and Kennedy reveal an extraordinary certainty of vision. Posner's opinion in *American Nurses' Association* reads like a passage from a somewhat dated labor economics textbook. Even a promarket economist might agree that Kennedy's assertion that the State of Washington bore no responsibility for the male-female wage differences in state employment was overreaching.

In only a few cases do we find the courts making any serious attempt to assess whether the wage levels in question actually reflect market conditions. In most cases the courts simply assume that the compensation structure is designed to meet the market. If the opinions explicitly acknowledged that the law gave employers virtually total autonomy in designing wage systems, absent specific demonstrations of intentional gender discrimination, there would be no need to refer to the market at all. The fact that the courts cite the market, while seldom actually analyzing it, suggests that they take the market for granted.

In a provocative essay reviewing Susan Estrich's book, *Real Rape*, Kim Scheppele develops the notion of perceptual "fault lines" (1987). Scheppele argues, based on psychological studies, that men and women view the sexual dimensions of interactions differently, which leads to misunderstandings concerning the consensual nature of sex. Similar perceptual disjunctures infect the drafting of rape laws and their administration by law enforcement and the courts. Scheppele's insight is that the law not only is written from a male point of view, but men do not understand many sexual encounters in the same way as do the female victims of those crimes. A broad implication of Scheppele's argument is that the construction of facts is a crucial but poorly understood aspect of legal decision making.

We could characterize the judicial treatment of the market issue in the pay discrimination cases as another instance of perceptual fault lines. The courts in these cases would acknowledge the antidiscrimination principle articulated by *Gunther* but were largely unwilling to question the dominant explanation of "the facts" before them. The market ideology that shaped their decisions did not correlate with the gender of judges. Both male and female jurists adopted the dominant view. Yet in the context of these cases, the market ideology interacts with a gendered worldview in a way that produces clear gender-based consequences.

Schultz and Pettersen (1992) mount a similar argument to explain the higher success rates of African American plaintiffs than female plaintiffs in Title VII job segregation cases. After attempting to refute alternative explanations for the pattern, they assert that judges have fundamentally different worldviews about how race and gender affect job choice. The lack-of-interest defense by employers resonated with the judges' conceptions of gender roles, but they did not have such a cultural script for why African Americans would choose different jobs than whites. Consequently, they attributed racial segregation to discrimination and gender segregation to lack of interest by female employees.

The ideology we see operating in the pay discrimination cases is a specific combination of gender ideology and market ideology. In several other areas in which laws against gender discrimination conflicted with market imperatives, the courts ruled in favor of the antidiscrimination principle. It is no defense to the Equal Pay Act, for example, that other employers in the market pay men and women different wages for the same job (see Chapter 2, note 16). Similarly, the Supreme Court held that charging female employees more for retirement insurance than male employees was a violation of Title VII, even though the defendants could show that the differences were based on actuarial calculations and were used throughout the market.[11] The latter decision was harshly criticized by some legal scholars on the grounds that the Court did not understand the market forces at work (Kimball 1979). The position the Court took was that there was a clear difference in how female employees were treated in the retirement plans. The defendants did not unequivocally meet their burden of demonstrating that such discrimination was necessary and legitimate.

---

11 *Los Angeles Dept. of Water and Power v. Manhart*, 435 U.S. 702 (1978).

In cases where employers clearly are treating male and female employees differently, the courts will not entertain a market defense. In cases where the source of the gender differentials is not clear, the market defense comes into play. In the contested terrain of explaining why predominantly male jobs pay more than predominantly female jobs, the market explanation is a gendered explanation. In uncritically accepting the market as the source of the disparities, the courts legitimate a particular theory of the social world that holds that women choose an economically inferior position within organizations.

Considering the Impact: Material and Ideological Consequences

The courts' decisions had both a practical and ideological effect. The practical effect was to block the efforts of women to use the law as a mechanism for redressing wage inequality. At UNI and Sears, the legal defeats closed the chapter on women's demands for wage reform within those organizations. As our review of pay discrimination cases from 1982 to 1994 shows, the string of legal defeats cut short the campaign for wage reform through the law begun after *Gunther*. By 1990 plaintiffs had abandoned the field.

The decisions' ideological effects also are both local and more global. The message within the organizations where defendants won in court was that the law had validated the status quo. Pauline Christensen still felt that she was a victim of discrimination and that her case had not prevailed because of "politics." But hers was a lonely voice. We found no signs in our interviews that the lawsuit had galvanized a sense of injustice in other clerical workers. UNI was left a bastion of paternalistic gender relations.

The opinions also affect the broader discourse about gender inequality. In a sense, the courts gave authority to the very ideology on which the opinions rested. Many economists would applaud the promarket pronouncements of the courts. Other observers who are not intimately involved in problems of gender inequality may tend to equate the certainty of judicial opinion with the certainty of the market explanation. If Bourdieu is correct to observe that humans tend to accept, even idealize, the inevitable parts of our lives, it may be that scholars begin to accept, even positively evaluate, the explanation of gender inequality offered in these decisions. We suspect that this is what lies behind the question we almost always get from colleagues with whom we are discussing this project: "Isn't that a dead issue now?" The failure of these cases removed pay equity as a topic of active policy debate. Some advocates continue to argue for pay equity reforms, but the relative silence about the topic is testimony to the ideological effects of these case outcomes.

In *Rights at Work*, Michael McCann (1994) reaches a different conclusion about the effects of pay equity litigation. Surveying some twenty pay equity campaigns, he argues that the legal rights framework propounded in the lawsuits often was crucial as a catalyst to local efforts. Even in situations where a lawsuit ultimately failed, he cites the impact of the lawsuit as a vehicle for mobilization, as a source of rights discourse, and as a spur to some kind of official action. McCann acknowledges that pay equity has had only modest effects on the male-female wage gap and that it now is relatively moribund as a social movement. Yet he suggests that the more lasting legacy of pay equity litigation was that it raised the consciousness of women workers about wage injustice.

It seems to us that McCann celebrates limited victories in a small number of battles without recognizing that pay equity lost the war. We have a hard time reading the history of the pay equity movement as a political or legal success. McCann may be right in observing the catalyzing effect of litigation at a local level. He may also be right in concluding that movement activists were not misled by the rhetoric of rights. They saw the law as an instrument to be used but not as a substitute for political organization. Yet he does not count the vast number of workplace contexts where there have been no wage reform efforts. Even within the relatively small number of organizations where there were active movements, he draws most of his interviews from a handful of activists. We are left to wonder whether they represent rank-and-file women.

A more realistic reading of the pay equity movement in law was that it failed to overcome a powerful promarket ideology. The plaintiffs never found a legal strategy that could move the courts beyond the conventional view that gender inequality between jobs was a product of market forces. *Gunther* was both the beginning and end of legal theories of between-job pay discrimination. Absent the kind of direct evidence of intentional discrimination present in *Gunther*, the courts were unwilling to entertain the notion that such wage differences were the responsibility of the employing organization.

The effect of these decisions was to undercut the movement for wage reform, both in the specific employment contexts in which the suits were filed, and in the broader context of national debate. We think it ironic that McCann attributes so much power to the legal rights framework as a catalyst for social movement activity, without recognizing the force of legal arguments and outcomes in defining the limits of rights claims. Debates about the legal contours of Title VII's prohibition against pay discrimination are largely confined to elite circles of lawyers, government policy makers, academics, and movement activists. The opening provided by *Gunther* and briefly realized by the trial court judgment in *AFSCME v. State of Washington* was communicated from experts to organizers and employers quite rapidly. As that new possibility for achieving wage reform through the courts was closed, the effect also took hold quickly. Some public sector organizing continued, but little new activity proceeded. And the movement never achieved a threshold in the private sector.

McCann's effort to talk about a legal rights framework on the shop floor is laudable. We are not satisfied that he correctly makes the link between litigation and shop floor legal consciousness. Movement activists no doubt continued to use the rhetoric of rights as they tried to mobilize workers after the legal defeat of comparable worth. We think it implausible that the failure of pay equity litigation did not affect the dynamics of shop floor organizing. As the threat of legal sanction became more remote, the activists lost a source of leverage with employers. As the idea of comparable worth was attacked in policy circles and rejected by the courts, the centerpiece of organizing efforts must have lost some legitimacy.

We see the courts engaged in legitimation and denial. The *Gunther* decision declared that the law would respond to glaring instances of inequality, even if there were some question about the formal correctness of such an interpretation of the law. In light of that declaration of jurisdiction, the courts then consistently refused to find instances of pay inequality worthy of judicial intervention. In this two-step move, the courts simultaneously legitimated the law as an institution and denied that there were problems with the pay practices of employers. The courts effectively legalized a fundamental aspect of gender inequality in organizations.

Law, Ideology, and Inequality

The significance of law as an ideological force, both in erecting and maintaining social hierarchies and as a forum for resisting domination, has become a salient concern of contemporary sociolegal scholarship (generally see Hirsch and Lazarus-Black 1994). Comaroff captures the reason for the theoretical interest.

> If power lies in the relative capacity to construct reality, and law appears as "reality itself" [quoting Carlos Fuentes], it is obvious why the connection between the two, between law and power, should feature so prominently and problematically

in the historical consciousness of those who feel disempowered; of those who would alter the existing order of things, be it in the name of constitutional rights, private self-interest, or identity politics. To the degree that law *appears* to be imbricated in the empowered construction of reality, it also presents itself as the ground on which to unravel the workings of power, to disable and reconstruct received realities. Which is why, when they begin to find a voice, people who see themselves as disadvantaged often do so either by speaking back in the language of the law or by disrupting its means and ends. (1994, xii)

The failed effort to define some kinds of between-job pay differences as discrimination is an illustration of how the law's capacity to "construct social reality" can dampen, as well as encourage, resistance to inequality. Just as the *Bradwell* case reconfirmed the gender ideology of separate spheres for men and women, the post-*Gunther* cases reconfirmed the ideology of the market as the source of gender inequality in pay. The cases did not "unravel the workings of power" or lead to a "reconstruction of received realities." Rather they reinforced the social constructions of the existing gender order in organizations.

The fate of pay equity as a legal reform illustrates the paradoxical role that law plays in American society. The laws against gender-based pay discrimination and sex segregation clearly have affected explicitly sexist employment practices. Indeed, the regime of antidiscrimination law creates the appearance that the law stands available as a remedy against gender injustice in the workplace. It is one element in the set of legal mechanisms that supposedly deliver what Lawrence Friedman characterizes as "total justice" – the expectation that all wrongs are compensable under law (1985). Yet as E. P. Thompson demonstrated so vividly for eighteenth-century England, as law curbs certain injustices it creates others (1975). Antidiscrimination law, as interpreted by the courts, struck down unequal pay within the same job. It held open the possibility that intentional between-job discrimination would give rise to liability. But it embraced as legitimate the most pervasive and entrenched form of gender-based wage inequality in organizations – wage differences between traditionally male and female jobs. The underpinning for this judicial mandate was a social construction – that such wage differentials were, in the absence of direct evidence of gender bias by the employer, the product of market forces.

Perhaps one reason these cases proved so devastating to the pay equity movement was that the courts gave authority to a particular social theory of wage inequality. In some circumstances the less powerful will continue to challenge through the law a set of practices they see as unjust. Shamir (1990) found that Palestinians continued to legally challenge evictions by Israeli authorities, even though it was only a symbolic act, that virtually never succeeded unless the authorities had committed an egregious procedural error. The legal contests for the Palestinians were part of an expressive ritual for denouncing a substantive injustice; they never suffered the delusion that the evictions were just. Indeed, the Israeli courts only certified that the proper procedures had been followed by the authorities. In the pay discrimination cases the courts reaffirmed the dominant ideology within the workplace. In effect, they rebuked an alternative vision of wage inequality, and thus discouraged women workers from questioning the validity of their pay levels. McCann's assertions notwithstanding, the ideological power of the law was brought to bear in silencing women's voices within the workplace.

Our interpretation of the fate of pay discrimination litigation may seem pessimistic about the prospects for redressing gender inequality through the law. But there is nothing inherent or unchangeable in the stance of the courts. If the expert view of the link between markets and organizational pay systems changes, it is possible that the courts would reconsider an appropriate set of claims by female workers that they were discriminated against. Such a shift in expert conceptions is unlikely to occur. Orthodox economics retains its dominant position within the body of social science consulted by the courts, at least on questions of wage inequality. Most economists show little inclination to reexamine empirically the issues we have raised about the relationship between markets, organizations, and gender inequality.

The academic and policy debate about the male-female wage gap has been polarized in ways that have impoverished both our understanding of the phenomenon and the range of possible responses through law and regulatory policy. The assertion by comparable worth advocates that the market is the problem has left undeveloped alternative sociological conceptions of the sources of wage inequality. If sociologists construct programs of empirical research that better articulate the relationship between organizations, markets, and wages, they may produce more powerful explanations of pay determination than economists and comparable worth advocates have thus far. The rise of new theories of organizational pay practices may break through the current stalemate in academic circles.

This ferment may in turn change the legal and regulatory climate. But such intellectual change requires a measure of power. The law currently gives employers the right to control access to the kinds of data that are required to rigorously examine organizational pay practices. Until such data are made available, social scientists, policy makers, and the courts will not be able to make informed judgments.

Appendix: Court Documents and Case Materials Used in Case Studies

Chapter 5

Depositions

1. James A. Hughes, Principal with firm of Robert H. Hayes and Associates, Aug. 3, 1976 (Dep. of JAH, Aug. 3, 1976).

Trial Court Documents

2. *Christensen v. State of Iowa*, U.S. District Court, N.D. of Iowa Eastern Division, No. C 74-2030 (1976). Trial Transcripts, Aug. 18–19, 1976 (Tr. Trans.).

> *Witnesses cited*: M. Clark Turney, retired member of the management consulting firm of A. T. Kearney, Inc., pp. 363–414. Mr. Donald Walton, Assistant to the Vice-President for Administrative Services at the University of Northern Iowa, pp. 415–63. Mr. Don Volm, Director of Regents Merit System, pp. 463–507. Mr. James Hughes Jr., Principal with the firm of Robert H. Hayes and Associates, pp. 508–76. Dr. Robert D. Stansbury, Vice-President for Academic Services, pp. 578–96. Dr. David Whitsett, Associate Professor of Psychology and also employed by the New York consulting firm of Drake, Beam, & Associates, pp. 597–665.

3. Trial Court Opinion, Nov. 11, 1976, N.D. Iowa, p. 2, n. 3. *Christensen v. State of Iowa*, C 74-2030, N.D. Iowa Eastern Division. 111076SiD (Tr. Ct. Opin., Nov. 11, 1976, N.D. Iowa).
4. Defendants' Brief and Argument, Trial Brief, Oct. 1976 (Tr. Brief).
5. Judgment, Nov. 11, 1976. U.S. District Court, N.D. Iowa, Eastern Division, No. C 74-2030 (Judgment, Nov. 11, 1976, p. 2).

Appellate Court Documents

6. *Christensen v. State of Iowa*, 563 F.2d 353 (8th Cir. 1977).
7. Joint Appendix to the Court of Appeals for the Eighth Circuit, No. 77-1071 (Jt. App.).

    a. Order on Final Pretrial Conference, May 13, 1976, pp. 34–41 (Order on Final Pretr. Conf.).
    b. Affirmative Action Plan, p. 58, p. 74 (Aff. Action Plan).
    c. Master Report, filed Apr. 26, 1976, in response to Plaintiffs' Interrogatories (Master Report).

8. Brief for the Equal Employment Opportunity Commission as Amicus Curiae for the Plaintiffs/Appellants (EEOC Brief).

Other Documents Produced in Discovery

9. Robert H. Hayes and Associates, Inc., A Preliminary Presentation on Update of the Merit System Pay Plan for 1975–76 for Iowa State Board of Regents, Nov. 1974 (Hayes and Associates Report, Nov. 1974).
10. Robert H. Hayes and Associates, Inc., A Preliminary Presentation on Update of the Merit System Pay Plan for 1975–76 for Iowa State Board of Regents, July 23, 1974 (Hayes and Associates Report, July 23, 1974).
11. Robert H. Hayes and Associates, Inc., A Preliminary Presentation on Update of the Merit System Pay Plan for 1975–76 for Iowa State Board of Regents, Dec. 1974 (Hayes and Associates Report, Dec. 1974).
12. Robert H. Hayes and Associates, Inc., A Preliminary Presentation on Update of the Merit System Pay Plan for 1975–76 for Iowa State Board of Regents, June 29, 1974 (Hayes and Associates Report, June 29, 1974).

Chapter 6

Depositions

1. Manager of Standards and Surveys, Department of Personnel, May 25, 1983 (Dep. I); May 26, 1983 (Dep. II); June 23, 1983 (Dep. III); June 24, 1983 (Dep. IV).
2. Assistant Director, Higher Education Personnel Board, June 30, 1983 (Dep. V).

Trial Court Documents

3. *AFSCME v. State of Washington*, U.S. District Court, W. Wash., No. C82-465T (1983). Trial Transcripts, Aug. 30, 1983–Dec. 1, 1983 (Tr. Vol. I–XIII).

> *Witness cited*: Director of Personnel Board Activities, Washington Federation of State Employees.

Appellate Court Documents

4. *AFSCME v. State of Washington*, U.S. Court of Appeals, 9th Cir., No. 84-3569 (1984).
5. Brief of Defendants/Appellants.
6. Reply Brief of Defendants/Appellants.
7. Brief of Plaintiffs/Appellees.
8. Washington State Legislature 1975–76 Salary Survey. Vol. 1 Management Summary. Arthur Young and Company. Feb. 1976. Pp. 3333–397, Volume VIII, Supplemental Excerpt of Record.

Chapter 7

Trial Court Documents

1. *EEOC v. Sears, Roebuck & Co.*, 628 F. Supp. 1264 (N.D. Ill. 1986). No. 79-C-4373 (*Sears* I).

    a. Trial Transcripts, Sept. 23, 1984, Opening Statements of Charles Morgan and James Scanlon (Opening Stmt., Charles Morgan, Tr. Trans.; Opening Stmt., James Scanlon, Tr. Trans.).
    b. Trial Transcript 13, pp. 796–97, 13, 933 (Tr. Trans. 13).
    c. Trial Transcript 15, pp. 496–99 (Tr. Trans. 15).

2. Sears's Post Trial Brief, July 1985 (Defendant's Post Tr. Brief, July 1985).
3. Plaintiff's Exhibit 22 (Plaintiff's Tr. Ex. 22).
4. Sears Internal Correspondence, dated Feb. 16, 1970. Attached to Trial Exhibit (Sears Internal Corresp., dated Feb. 16, 1970. Attached to Tr. Ex.).

Appellate Court Documents

5. *EEOC v. Sears, Roebuck & Co.*, 839 F.2d 302 (7th Cir. 1988) (*Sears* II).

6. Joint Appendix to the 7th Circuit Court of Appeals, Vols. 12–14 (Jt. App.).

Vol. 12
a. Trial Exhibit, Presentation to Commissioners and General Counsel of the Equal Employment Opportunity Commission, Mar. 1, 1977 (Tr. Ex., Mar. 1, 1977).

Vol. 13
b. Written Testimony (Jt. App., Vol. 13).
c. Report on Checklist Compensation Practices of Sears, Roebuck. Revised Sept. 18, 1984. Bernard Siskin. Appendix 6. List of Jobs Grouped by Job Family. Pp. 365 et seq. (Siskin Report 1984, Jt. App. Vol. 13).
d. Defendants' Exhibit 6-AAAA, p. 119 (Defendants' Ex. 6-AAAA).

Vol. 14
e. Report of Bernard Siskin, Plaintiffs statistical expert, 1984. Report on Checklist Compensation Practices of Sears, Roebuck and Co. Revised Sept. 18, 1984. Bernard Siskin (Jt. App. Vol. 14, Siskin 1984).
f. Hay Report, May 1975, Rewarding Managers in Middle and Upper Management Jobs: Current and Recommended Management Processes, Report Prepared for Sears, pp. 216–317, PX 173A (Hay Associates, May 1975).
g. Letter from Sym-Smith to Charles Bacon, Vice President for Personnel, Sears, March 11, 1974, pp. 128–38, JX6.
h. Letter from Ian Sym-Smith of Hay Consultants to Charles Bacon, Vice President for Personnel, Sears, Sept. 3, 1974, pp. 119–22, JX 1.
i. Hay Associates Report, Jan. 1976, Compensation of Checklist Employees: Updated Recommendations, Report Prepared for Sears, pp. 339–405. PX 254 (Hay Associates, Jan. 1976).
j. Executive Compensation Manual, Basic Company Policy, October 1977, pp. 142–98, PX 167 (Executive Comp. Manual, Basic Company Pol., Oct. 1977).
k. Written testimony of Sym-Smith, pp. 87–98.

7. Sears's Brief to the Seventh Circuit, Oct. 28, 1986 (Sears's Brief to the 7th Cir.).

Chapter 8

Trial Court Documents

1. *Glass v. Coastal Bank*. Trial Court Opinion, 1986 (Opin. 1986).
2. Position Salary Comparison. Office Correspondence (Office Corresp., D48669–D48774).
3. External Market Salary Data (Ext. Mkt. Salary Data, D48661–D48668).
4. Coastal Bank Salary Administration Study: Non-Officer Personnel. Prepared by Ryan Associates, D48290 et seq. (Coastal Salary Admin. Study, D48290 et seq.).
5. Coastal Bank Job Evaluation Manual, Salaries Above or Below the Salary Range (Job Eval. Manual, D48260).
6. Personnel Policies and Procedures Manual (Personnel Pol. and Proc'd. Manual, D48272).
7. Letter from Ryan Associates to Coastal Personnel Director, June 7, 1971 (Letter from Ryan Assoc. to Coastal Personnel Dir., June 7, 1971, D482888).
8. Memo, Dec. 29, 1972, and 1973 Salary Policy Document (Memo, Dec. 29, 1972, and 1973 Pol. Doc., D5764–D5770).
9. Memo, Dec. 1, 1976, and 1977 Salary Policy Guidelines (Memo, Dec. 1, 1976, and 1977 Salary Pol. Guide, D5727).
10. Coastal Bank 1979 Officer and Non-Officer Recommended Salary Structure, D48483 et seq. (1979 Salary Recomm. D48483ff.).
11. 1976 Memo on Systems and Programming Market Salary Survey (1976 Memo on Systems and Prog. Mkt. Salary Survey, D48200 et seq.).
12. Recommended 1979 Coastal Bank Technical Salary Structure, ca. Nov. 1978 (Recomm. 1979 Coastal Bank Tech. Salary Structure, D48542–D48567).
13. Officer Job Evaluation Guide, Warren and Associates Method 1962 through 1975, D5427 et seq. (Warren Officer Job Eval. Guide, D5427 et seq.).
14. Coastal Bank: Officer Compensation Strategy, Smith and Associates, Aug. 1975, D5368 et seq. (Smith Officer Comp. Strategy Report, Aug. 1975, D5368 et seq.).
15. 1978–79 Employee Pay Documents (1978–79 Pay Doc., D66078–D66361).

References

Abbott, Andrew. 1992. "What Do Cases Do? Some Notes on Activity in Sociological Analysis." In C. Ragin and H. Becker, eds., *What Is a Case? Exploring the Foundations of Social Inquiry.* Cambridge: Cambridge University Press.

Abraham, Katherine G. 1990. "Restructuring the Employment Relationship: The Growth of Market Mediated Work Arrangements." In Katherine G. Abraham and Robert McKensie, eds., *New Developments in the Labor Market: Toward a New Institutional Paradigm.* Cambridge, Mass.: MIT Press.

Acker, Joan. 1989. *Doing Comparable Worth: Gender, Class, and Pay Equity.* Philadelphia: Temple University Press.

Addison, John T., and W. S. Siebert. 1979. *The Market for Labor: An Analytical Treatment.* Santa Monica, Calif.: Goodyear.

Agarwal, Naresh. 1990. "Pay Equity in Canada: Current Developments." *Labor Law Journal* 41:518–25.

Akerlof, George. 1984. "Gift Exchange and Efficiency-Wage Theory: Four Views." *American Economic Review* 74 (May):79–83.

Aldrich, Mark, and Robert Buchele. 1986. *The Economics of Comparable Worth.* Cambridge, Mass.: Ballinger.

Althauser, Robert P. 1989. "Internal Labor Markets." In W. Richard Scott and Judith Blake, eds., *Annual Review of Sociology,* vol. 15. Palo Alto, Calif.: Annual Reviews.

Althauser, Robert P., and A. Kalleberg. 1981. "Firms, Occupations, and the Structure of Labor Markets: A Conceptual Analysis." In Ivar Berg, ed., *Sociological Perspectives on Labor Markets.* New York: Academic Press.

Anderson, Cynthia, and Donald Tomaskovic-Devey. 1995. "Patriarchal Pressures: An Exploration of Organizational Processes That Exacerbate and Erode Gender Earnings Inequality." *Work and Occupations* 22:329–56.

Antilla, Susan. 1995. "Three Women vs. a Broker: Olde Is Accused of Blatant Job Discrimination." *New York Times,* Apr. 26, p. C1, C3.

Applebaum, Eileen. 1987. "Restructuring Work: Temporary, Part Time, and At-Home Employment." In Heidi Hartmann, ed., *Computer Chips and Paper Clips: Technology and Women's Employment.* Washington, D.C.: National Academy Press.

Baldus, David C., George Woodworth, and Charles A. Pulaski Jr. 1990. *Equal*

Justice and the Death Penalty: A Legal and Empirical Analysis. Boston: Northeastern University Press.

Baron, James N. 1991. "Organizational Evidence of Ascription in Labor Markets." In Richard Cornwall and Phanindra Wunnava, eds., *New Approaches to Economic and Social Analyses of Discrimination.* New York: Praeger.

Baron, James N., and William T. Bielby. 1980. "Bringing the Firms Back In." *American Sociological Review* 45:737–65.

Baron, James, N. Davis-Blake, and W. T. Bielby. 1986. "The Structure of Opportunity: How Promotion Ladders Vary within and among Organizations." *Administrative Science Quarterly* 31:248–73.

Baron, James N., P. Devereaux-Jennings, and Frank R. Dobbin. 1988. "Mission Control? The Development of Personnel Systems in U.S. Industry." *American Sociological Review* 53:497–514.

Baron, James N., F. R. Dobbin, and P. Devereaux-Jennings. 1986. "War and Peace: The Evolution of Modern Personnel Administration in U.S. Industry." *American Journal of Sociology* 92:350–83.

Baron, James N., Brian Mittman, and Andrew Newman. 1991. "Targets of Opportunity: Organizational and Environmental Determinants of Gender Integration within the California Civil Service, 1979–1985." *American Journal of Sociology* 96:1362–1401.

Baron, James N., and Andrew E. Newman. 1989. "Pay the Man: Effects of Demographic Composition on Prescribed Wage Rates in the California Civil Service." In Robert T. Michael, Heidi I. Hartmann, and Brigid O'Farrell, eds., *Pay Equity: Empirical Inquiries.* Washington, D.C.: National Academy Press.

    1990. "For What It's Worth: Organizations, Occupations, and the Value of Work Done by Women and Non-Whites." *American Sociological Review* 55:155–75.

Bartlett, Katharine T. 1990. "Feminist Legal Methods." *Harvard Law Review* 103:829–88.

Becker, Gary S. 1971. *The Economics of Discrimination.* 2d ed. Chicago: University of Chicago Press.

Bergmann, Barbara R. 1974. "Occupational Segregation, Wages, and Profits When Employers Discriminate by Race or Sex." *Eastern Economic Journal* 1:103–10.

Bernhardt, Annette. 1995. "Are American Firms Creating a More Segmented Labor Market: Issues and Preliminary Evidence." Presented to American Sociological Association Annual Meetings. Washington, D.C.

Bielby, William T., and James N. Baron. 1986. "Men and Women at Work: Sex Segregation and Statistical Discrimination." *American Journal of Sociology* 91:759–99.

Blau, Francine, and Lawrence Kahn. 1992. "The Gender Earnings Gap: Learning from International Comparisons." *American Economic Review: Papers and Proceedings* 82:533–38.

Bourdieu, Pierre. 1977. *Outline of a Theory of Practice.* Cambridge: Cambridge University Press.

Bridges, William P. 1995. "Where Do Markets Go To: An Analysis of Change in Internal and External Mobility Patterns." *Research in Social Stratification and Mobility* 14:71-98.

Bridges, William P., and Robert L. Nelson. 1989. "Markets in Hierarchies: Organizational and Market Influences on Gender Inequality in a State Pay System." *American Journal of Sociology* 95:616–58.

Bridges, William P., and Wayne J. Villemez. 1991. "Employment Relations and the Labor Market: Integrating Institutional and Market Perspectives." *American Sociological Review* 56:748–64.

——— 1994. *The Employment Relationship: Causes and Consequences of Modern Personnel Administration.* New York: Plenum Press.

Bumiller, Kristin. 1988. *The Civil Rights Society: The Social Construction of Victims.* Baltimore: Johns Hopkins University Press.

Burawoy, Michael. 1979. *Manufacturing Consent.* Chicago: University of Chicago Press.

——— 1991. *Ethnography Unbound: Power and Resistance in the Modern Metropolis.* Berkeley: University of California Press.

Bureau of National Affairs. 1981. *The Comparable Worth Issue: A BNA Special Report.* Washington, D.C.: Bureau of National Affairs.

——— 1985. "Current Developments." *Labor Relations Reporter,* May 10, Daily Labor Reports section, no. 91, p. A2.

——— 1986. "Pay Equity in Ohio's State Jobs." *Labor Relations Reporter* Apr. 7, p. 242.

Burstein, Paul. 1989. "Attacking Sex Discrimination in the Labor Market: A Study in Law and Politics." *Social Forces* 67:641.

Chandler, Alfred D., Jr. 1962. *Strategy and Structure: Chapters in the History of the American Industrial Enterprise.* Cambridge, Mass: MIT Press.

Chayes, Abram. 1976. "The Role of the Judge in Public Law Litigation." *Harvard Law Review*: 89:1281–1316.

Chicago Sun Times. 1998. "Women's Wages Rise." *Chicago Sun Times,* June 10, p. 1.

Cockburn, Cynthia. 1991. *In the Way of Women: Men's Resistance to Sex Inequality in Organizations.* Ithaca, N.Y.: Industrial Labor Relations Press.

Cohen, Michael, James March, and Johan Olsen. 1972. "A Garbage Can Model of Organizational Choice," *Administrative Science Quarterly* 17 (March):1–25.

Cohn, Samuel. 1985. *The Process of Occupational Sex-Typing: The Feminization of Clerical Labor in Great Britain.* Philadelphia: Temple University Press.

College Blue Book. 1965, 1975, 1981. New York: Macmillan Information.

Comaroff, Jean, and John Comaroff. 1991. *Of Revolution and Revelation: Christianity, Colonialism, and Consciousness in South Africa.* Chicago: University of Chicago Press.

Comaroff, John L. 1994. Foreword. In Mindie Lazarus-Black and Susan F. Hirsch, eds., *Contested States: Law, Hegemony, and Resistance.* New York: Routledge.

Congressional Research Service. 1985. *Summary of Pay Equity/Comparable Worth Activities by State Governments.* Washington, D.C.: Library of Congress.

Conklin, David. 1989. "How to Cope with Pay Equity Legislation." *Business Quarterly* 54:90–93.

Cook, Alice. 1990. "Current State of Comparable Worth in the United States." *Labor Law Journal* 41:525–31.

Corcoran, Mary, Greg J. Duncan, and Michael Ponza. 1984. "Work Experience, Job Segregation, and Wages." In Barbara F. Reskin, ed., *Sex Segregation in the Workplace: Trends, Explanations, Remedies.* Washington, D.C.: National Academy Press.

Crane, Jonathan. 1991. "The Epidemic Theory of Ghettos and Neighborhood Effects on Dropping Out and Teenage Childbearing." *American Journal of Sociology* 96:1226–59.

Culp, Jerome. 1985. "A New Employment Policy for the 1980's: Learning from the Victories and Defeats of Twenty Years of Title VII." *Rutgers Law Review* 37:895–919.

Cunningham, Clark D., and Charles J. Fillmore. 1995. "Using Common Sense: A Linguistic Perspective on Judicial Interpretations of "Use a Firearm.'" *Washington University Law Quarterly* 73:1159–1214.

Cunningham, Clark D., Judith N. Levi, Georgia M. Green, and Jeffrey P. Kaplan. 1994. "Plain Meaning and Hard Cases." *Yale Law Journal* 103:1561–1625.

Dalton, Melville. 1959. *Men Who Manage.* New York: John Wiley & Sons.

Delgado, Richard. 1984. "The Imperial Scholar: Reflections on a Review of Civil Rights Literature." *University of Pennsylvania Law Review* 132: 561–78.

Dickens, William T., and Kevin Lang. 1987. "Where Have All the Good Jobs Gone? Deindustrialization and Labor Market Segmentation." In Kevin Lang and Jonathan Leonard, eds., *Unemployment and the Structure of Labor Markets.* New York: Basil Blackwell.

Diebold, Francis X., David Neumark, and Daniel Polsky. 1996. Comment on Kenneth A. Swinnerton and Howard Wial, "Is Job Stability Declining in the U.S. Economy?" *Industrial and Labor Relations Review* 49:348–52.

DiMaggio, Paul J., Jr., and Walter W. Powell. 1983. "The Iron Cage Revisited: Institutional Isomorphism and Collective Rationality in Organizational Fields." *American Sociological Review* 48:147–60.

DiPrete, Thomas. 1989. *The Bureaucratic Labor Market: The Case of the Federal Civil Service.* New York: Plenum Press.

——— 1993. "Industrial Restructuring and the Mobility Response of American Workers in the 1980's." *American Sociological Review* 58:74–96.

Doeringer, Peter. 1967. "Determinants of the Structure of Industrial Type Internal Labor Markets." *Industrial and Labor Relations Review* 20 (Jan.):206–20.

Doeringer, Peter, and Michael Piore. 1971. *Internal Labor Markets and Manpower Analysis.* Lexington, Mass.: D. C. Heath.

Donohue, John J. 1986. "Is Title VII Efficient?" *University of Pennsylvania Law Review* 134:1411–31.

1989. "Prohibiting Sex Discrimination in the Workplace: An Economic Perspective." *University of Chicago Law Review* 56:1337–68.

Dunlop, John T. 1957. "The Task of Contemporary Wage Theory." In G. Taylor and F. Pierson, eds., *New Concepts in Wage Determination.* New York: McGraw-Hill.

Dunworth, Terence, and Joel Rogers. 1996. "Corporations in Court, Large Firm Litigation in the U.S. 1971–1991." *Law and Social Inquiry* 21:497–592.

duRivage, Virginia, ed. 1992. *New Policies for the Part-time and Contingent Work Force.* Armonk, N.Y.: Sharpe.

Dworkin, Ronald. 1977. *Taking Rights Seriously.* Cambridge, Mass.: Harvard University Press.

Edelman, Lauren B. 1990. "Legal Environments and Organizational Governance: The Expansion of Due Process in the American Workplace." *American Journal of Sociology* 95:1401–40.

1992. "Legal Ambiguity and Symbolic Structures: Organizational Mediation of Law." *American Journal of Sociology* 97:1531–1576.

Edelman, Lauren B., Steven E. Abraham, and Howard S. Erlanger. 1992. "Professional Construction of Law: The Inflated Threat of Wrongful Discharge." *Law & Society Review* 26:47–83.

Edelman, Lauren B., Howard S. Erlanger, and John Lande. 1993. "Internal Dispute Resolution: The Transformation of Civil Rights in the Workplace." *Law & Society Review* 27:497–534.

Edwards, Richard. 1979. *Contested Terrain.* New York: Basic Books.

England, Paula. 1982. "The Failure of Human Capital Theory to Explain Occupational Sex Segregation." *Journal of Human Resources* 17:358–69.

1984. "Wage Appreciation and Depreciation: A Test of Neoclassical Economic Explanations of Occupational Sex Segregation." *Social Forces* 62:726–49.

1992. *Comparable Worth: Theories and Evidence.* New York: Aldine de Gruyter.

Entwisle, Barbara, and William M. Mason. 1985. "Multilevel Effects of Socioeconomic Development and Family Planning Programs on Children Ever Born." *American Journal of Sociology* 91:616–49.

Epstein, Richard A. 1992. *Forbidden Grounds: The Case against Employment Discrimination Laws.* Cambridge, Mass.: Harvard University Press.

Evans, Sara M., and Barbara J. Nelson. 1989. *Wage Justice: Comparable Worth and the Paradox of Technocratic Reform.* Chicago: University of Chicago Press.

Ferber, Marianne A., and Helen M. Lowry. 1976. "The Sex Difference in Earnings: A Reappraisal." *Industrial and Labor Relations Review* 29:377–87.

Ferguson, Kathy E. 1984. *The Feminist Case against Bureaucracy.* Philadelphia: Temple University Press.

Filer, Randall K. 1989. "Occupational Segregation, Compensating Differentials, and Comparable Worth." In Robert T. Michael, Heidi I. Hartmann, and Brigid O'Farrell, eds. *Pay Equity: Empirical Inquiries.* Washington, D.C.: National Academy Press.

Fineman, Martha. 1991. *The Illusion of Equality: The Rhetoric and Reality of Divorce Reform*. Chicago: University of Chicago Press.

Finkelstein, Michael O., and Bruce Levin. 1990. *Statistics for Lawyers*. New York: Springer-Verlag.

Finlay, William. 1983. "One Occupation, Two Labor Markets: The Case of Longshore Crane Operators." *American Sociological Review* 48:306–15.

Fischel, Daniel R., and Edward P. Lazear. 1986. "Comparable Worth and Discrimination in Labor Markets." *University of Chicago Law Review* 53:891–918.

Fligstein, Neil. 1987. "The Intraorganizational Power Struggle: Rise of Financial Personnel to Top Leadership in Large Corporations, 1919–1979." *American Sociological Review* 52:44–58.

Freeman, Alan. 1990. "Antidiscrimination Law: The View from 1989." In David Kairys, ed., *The Politics of Law: A Progressive Critique*. New York: Pantheon.

Freyer, Tony A. 1984. *The Little Rock Crisis: A Constitutional Interpretation*. Wesport, Conn.: Greenwood Press.

Friedman, Lawrence M. 1985. *Total Justice*. New York: Russell Sage Foundation.

Frug, Gerald E. 1984. "Ideology of Bureaucracy in American Law." *Harvard Law Review* 97:1276–1388.

Galanter, Marc. 1983. "Reading the Landscape of Disputes: What We Know and Don't Know (and Think We Know) about Our Allegedly Contentious and Litigious Society." *U.C.L.A. Law Review* 31:4–71.

Gardner, Jennifer M. 1995. "Worker Displacement: A Decade of Change." *Monthly Labor Review* 118:45–57.

Gartrell, C. David. 1982. "On the Visibility of Wage Referents." *Canadian Journal of Sociology* 7:117–43.

Gitelman, H. M. 1966. "Occupational Mobility within the Firm." *Industrial and Labor Relations Review* 20 (Oct.):50–65.

Gleason, Nancy. 1994. "Canada's Experience with Pay Equity: National and Provincial." *Government Finance Review* 10:38–39.

Gold, Michael Evans. 1983. *A Debate on Comparable Worth*. Ithaca, N.Y.: Industrial and Labor Relations Press.

Goldstein, Debra H. 1995. "Sex-Based Wage Discrimination: Recovery under the Equal Pay Act, Title III, or Both." *Alabama Law Review* 56:294–301.

Goldstein, Harvey. 1987. *Multilevel Models in Educational and Social Research*. London: Charles Griffen.

Gooding, Susan Staiger. 1994. "Place, Race, and Names: Layered Identities in *United States v. Oregon*, Confederated Tribes of the Colville Reservation, Plaintiff-Intervenor," *Law & Society Review* 28:1181–1229.

Grandjean, Burke D. 1981. "History and Career in a Bureaucratic Labor Market." *American Journal of Sociology* 86:1057–92.

Granovetter, Mark S. 1974. *Getting a Job: A Study of Contacts and Careers*. Cambridge, Mass.: Harvard University Press.

Grossberg, Michael. 1994. "Battling over Motherhood in Philadelphia: A Study of Antebellum American Trial Courts as Arenas of Conflict." In Mindie

Lazarus-Black and Susan F. Hirsch, eds., *Contested States: Law, Hegemony, and Resistance*. New York: Routledge.

Gutek, Barbara. 1985. *Sex and the Workplace*. San Francisco: Jossey-Bass.

Gutek, Barbara, and Bruce Morasch. 1982. "Sex-Ratios, Sex-Role Spillover, and Sexual Harassment of Women at Work." *Journal of Social Issues* 38:55–74.

Halaby, Charles. 1986. "Worker Attachment and Workplace Authority." *American Sociological Review* 51:634–49.

Halvorsen, Robert, and Raymond Palmquist. 1980. "The Interpretation of Dummy Variables in Semilogarithmic Equations." *American Economic Review* 70:474–75.

Harding, Sandra. 1986. *The Science Question in Feminism*. Ithaca, N.Y.: Cornell University Press.

Harrison, Bennett. 1994. *Lean and Mean: The Changing Landscape of Corporate Power*. New York: Basic Books.

Heckman, James, and Brook Payner. 1989. "Determining the Impact of Federal Anti-Discrimination Policy on the Economic Status of Blacks: A Study of South Carolina." *American Economic Review* 79:138–77.

Hildebrand, George. 1963. "External Influences and the Determination of the Internal Wage Structure." In J. L. Meij, ed., *Internal Wage Structures*. Amsterdam: North-Holland.

Hirsch, Susan F., and Mindie Lazarus-Black. 1994. "Introduction/Performance and Paradox: Exploring Law's Role in Hegemony and Resistance." In Mindie Lazarus-Black and Susan F. Hirsch, eds., *Contested States: Law, Hegemony, and Resistance*. New York: Routledge.

Hodson, Randy. 1983. *Workers' Earnings and Corporate Economic Structure*. New York: Academic Press.

Horrigan, Michael W., and James P. Markey. 1990. "Recent Gains in Women's Earnings: Better Pay or Longer Hours?" *Monthly Labor Review* 113:11–17.

Horwitz, Morton. 1977. *The Transformation of American Law, 1780–1860*. Cambridge, Mass.: Harvard University Press.

International Labour Office. 1994. *1993 Year Book of Labour Statistics*, Vol. 52. Geneva: International Labour Office.

Iowa Board of Regents. 1976. *State Board of Regents Merit System Rules*. Iowa Administrative Code, Chapter 3 of Chapter 681.

Jackall, Robert. 1988. *Moral Mazes: The World of Corporate Managers*. New York: Oxford University Press.

Jacobs, Jerry. 1989. *Revolving Doors: Sex Segregation and Women's Careers*. Stanford, Calif.: Stanford University Press.

Jacoby, Sanford. 1984. "The Development of Internal Labor Markets in American Manufacturing Firms." In Paul Osterman, ed., *Internal Labor Markets*. Cambridge, Mass.: MIT Press.

——— 1985. *Employing Bureaucracy: Managers, Unions, and the Transformation of Work in American Industry, 1900–1945*. New York: Columbia University Press.

Johnson, Frank M., Jr. 1981. "The Role of the Federal Courts in Institutional Litigation." In Symposium on Judicially Managed Institutional Reform. *Alabama Law Review* 32:271–280.

Kalleberg, Arne L., David Knoke, Peter V. Marsden, and Joel L. Spaeth. 1994. "The National Organizations Study: An Introduction and Overview." *American Behavioral Scientists* 37:860–71.

Kalleberg, Arne L., and Mark Van Buren. 1996. "Is Bigger Better? Explaining the Relationship between Organization Size and Job Rewards." *American Sociological Review* 61:47–66.

Kalleberg, Arne, Michael Wallace, and Robert Althauser. 1981. "Economic Segmentation, Worker Power, and Income Inequality." *American Journal of Sociology* 87:651–83.

Kanter, Rosabeth Moss. 1977. *Men and Women of the Corporation.* New York: Basic Books.

Katz, Donald R. 1987. *The Big Store: Inside the Crisis and Revolution at Sears.* New York: Viking.

Kerr, Clark. 1954. "The Balkanization of Labor Markets." In *Labor Mobility and Economic Opportunity.* New York: Wiley.

Kessler-Harris, Alice. 1982. *Out to Work: A History of Wage-Earning Women in the United States.* New York: Oxford University Press.

Kilbourne, Barbara, Paula England, and Kurt Beron. 1994. "Effects of Individual, Occupational, and Industrial Characteristics on Earnings: Intersections of Race and Gender." *Social Forces* 72:1149–76.

Killingsworth, Mark. 1985. "The Economics of Comparable Worth: Analytical, Empirical, and Policy Questions," in Heidi Hartmann, ed., *Comparable Worth: New Directions for Research.* Washington, D.C.: National Academy Press.

Kimball, Spencer L. 1979. "Reverse Sex Discrimination: *Manhart.*" *American Bar Foundation Research Journal* 1979:83–139.

King, Gary, Robert O. Keohane, and Sidney Verba. 1994. *Designing Social Inquiry: Scientific Inference and Qualitative Research.* Princeton, N.J.: Princeton University Press.

Kluger, Richard. 1976. *Simple Justice: The History of Brown v. Board of Education.* New York: Knopf.

Knoke, David, and Arne L. Kalleberg. 1994. "Job Training in U.S. Organizations." *American Sociological Review* 59:537–46.

Larson, Arthur, and Lex K. Larson. 1994. *Employment Discrimination.* New York: Mathew Bender.

Lee, Yong S. 1989. "Shaping Judicial Response to Gender Discrimination in Employment Compensation." *Public Administration Review* 49:420–30.

Lehrer, Evelyn L., and Houston H. Stokes. 1985. "Determinants of the Female Occupational Distribution: A Log-Linear Analysis." *Review of Economics and Statistics* 67:395–404.

Levi, Edward H. 1949. *An Introduction to Legal Reasoning.* Chicago: University of Chicago Press.

Livernash, E. Robert. 1957. "The Internal Wage Structure." In G. Taylor and F. Pierson, eds., *New Concepts in Wage Determination.* New York: McGraw-Hill.

    ed. 1980. *Comparable Worth: Issues and Alternatives.* Washington, D.C.: Equal Employment Advisory Council.

Lozano, Beverly. 1989. *The Invisible Work Force: Transforming American Business with Outside and Home-Based Workers.* New York: Free Press.

Mack, Raymond. 1954. "Ecological Patterns in an Industrial Shop." *Social Forces* 32:351–56.

Madden, Janice F. 1973. *The Economics of Sex Discrimination.* Lexington, Mass.: Lexington Books.

Mailath, George, and Andrew Postlewaite. 1990. "Workers versus Firms: Bargaining over a Firm's Value." *Review of Economic Studies* 57:369–80.

Marini, Margaret Mooney. 1989. "Sex Differences in Earnings in the United States." *Annual Review of Sociology* 18:348–80.

Martin, M., ed. 1988. *Hard Hatted Women; Stories of Struggle and Success in the Trades.* Seattle: Seal Press.

Mason, William, George Wong, and Barbara Entwisle. 1984. "The Multilevel Linear Model: A Better Way to Do Contextual Analysis." In *Sociological Methodology, 1984.* San Francisco: Jossey Bass.

Matsuda, Mari. 1988. "Affirmative Action and Legal Knowledge: Planting Seeds in Plowed-up Ground." *Harvard Women's Law Journal* 11:1–17.

McCann, Michael. 1994. *Rights at Work: Pay Equity Reform and the Politics of Legal Mobilization.* Chicago: University of Chicago Press.

McEvoy, Arthur F. 1995. "The Triangle Shirtwaist Factory Fire of 1911: Social Change, Industrial Accidents, and the Evolution of Common-Sense Causality." *Law & Social Inquiry* 20:621–51.

Merry, Sally Engle. 1990. *Getting Justice and Getting Even: Legal Consciousness among Working Class Americans.* Chicago: University of Chicago Press.

Mertz, Elizabeth. 1990. "Consensus and Dissent in U.S. Legal Opinions: Narrative Control and Social Voices." In C. Briggs, ed., "Narrative Resources for the Creation and Mediation of Conflict." Special Issue of *Anthropological Linguistics*, vol. 30.

Meyer, John, and Brian Rowan. 1977. "Institutionalized Organizations: Formal Structure as Myth and Ceremony." *American Journal of Sociology* 83: 340–63.

Milkman, Ruth. 1987. *Gender at Work: The Dynamics of Job Segregation by Sex during World War II.* Urbana: University of Illinois Press.

Miller, Nancy. 1993. "The Scales of Injustice." *CA Magazine* 126:28–32.

Mincer, Jacob, and H. Ofek. 1982. "Interrupted Work Careers." *Journal of Human Resources* 17 (Winter):3–24.

Miner, Anne. 1987. "Idiosyncratic Jobs in Formalized Organizations." *Administrative Science Quarterly* 32:327–51.

——— 1991. "Organizational Evolution and the Social Ecology of Jobs." *American Sociological Review* 36:772–85.

Minow, Martha. 1990. *Making All the Difference.* Ithaca, N.Y.: Cornell University Press.

Mnookin, Robert H. 1985. *In the Interest of Children: Advocacy, Law Reform, and Public Policy.* New York: W. H. Freeman.

New York Times. 1997. "As U.S. Bias Cases Drop, Employees Take Up Fight." *New York Times*, Jan. 12, p. 1, cols. 1–2; p. 10, cols. 4–9.

Noonan, John T. 1976. *Persons and Masks of the Law: Cardozo, Holmes, Jefferson, and Wythe as Makers of the Masks.* New York: Farrar, Straus & Giroux.

O'Neill, June. 1984. "An Argument against Comparable Worth." In U.S. Commission on Civil Rights, *Comparable Worth: Issue for the 80's.* Washington, D.C.: Government Printing Office.

1985. "The Trend in the Male-Female Wage Gap in the United States." *Journal of Labor Economics* 3 (Jan.):S91–S116.

Orazem, Peter F., and J. Peter Mattila. 1990. "The Implementation Process of Comparable Worth: Winners and Losers." *Journal of Political Economy* 98:134–52.

Osterman, Paul. 1984. "Introduction: The Nature and Importance of Internal Labor Markets." In P. Osterman, ed., *Internal Labor Markets.* Cambridge, Mass.: MIT Press.

1988. *Employment Futures: Reorganization, Dislocation, and Public Policy.* New York: Oxford University Press.

Parcel, Toby. 1989. "Comparable Worth, Occupational Labor Markets, and Occupational Earnings: Results from the 1980 Census." In Robert T. Michael, Heidi I. Hartmann, and Brigid O'Farrell, eds., *Pay Equity: Empirical Inquiries.* Washington, D.C.: National Academy Press.

Perrow, Charles. 1970. "Departmental Power and Perspective in Industrial Firms." In Meyer Zald, ed., *Power in Organizations.* Nashville, Tenn.: Vanderbilt University Press.

Petersen, Trond, and Laurie A. Morgan. 1995. "Separate and Unequal: Occupational-Establishment Sex Segregation and the Gender Wage Gap." *American Journal of Sociology* 101:329–65.

Pfeffer, Jeffrey. 1981. *Power in Organizations.* Marshfield, Mass.: Pittman.

Pfeffer, Jeffrey, and James Baron. 1988. "Taking the Workers Back Out: Recent Trends in the Structuring of Employment." In Barry M. Staw and L.L. Cummings, eds., *Research in Organizational Behavior.* Greenwich, Conn.: JAI Press.

Pfeffer, Jeffrey, and Yinon Cohen. 1984. "Determinants of Internal Labor Markets in Organization." *Administrative Science Quarterly* 29:550–72.

Pfeffer, Jeffrey, and William Moore. 1980. "Power in University Budgeting: A Replication and Extension." *Administrative Science Quarterly* 25:637–53.

Polachek, Solomon. 1975. "Discontinuous Labor Force Participation and Its Effect on Women's Market Earnings." In Cynthia Lloyd, ed., *Sex, Discrimination, and the Division of Labor.* New York: Columbia University Press.

1981. "Occupational Self-Selection: A Human Capital Approach to Sex Differences in Occupational Structure." *Review of Economics and Statistics* 63:60–69.

Pondy, Louis R. 1970. "Toward a Theory of Internal Resource-Allocation." In Meyer Zald, ed., *Power in Organizations.* Nashville, Tenn.: Vanderbilt University Press.

Prosser, R., J. Rosbash, and H. Goldstein. 1991. *ML3 Software for Three Level Analysis: User's Guide for V. 2.* London: Institute of Education, University of London.

Ragin, Charles C. 1992. "Introduction: Cases of 'What Is a Case?'" In Charles C. Ragin and Howard S. Becker, eds., *What Is a Case? Exploring the Foundations of Social Inquiry.* Cambridge: Cambridge University Press.

Reinharz, Shulamit. 1992. *Feminist Methods in Social Research.* New York: Oxford University Press.

Reskin, Barbara, and Irene Padavic. 1994. *Women and Men at Work.* Thousand Oaks, Calif.: Pine Forge Press.

Rhoads, Steven E. 1993. *Incomparable Worth: Pay Equity Meets the Market.* Cambridge: Cambridge University Press.

Rhode, Deborah L. 1989. *Justice and Gender: Sex Discrimination and Law.* Cambridge, Mass.: Harvard University Press.

——— 1997. *Speaking of Sex.* Cambridge, Mass.: Harvard University Press.

Roethlisberger, Fritz J., and W. J. Dickson. 1939. *Management and the Worker.* Cambridge, Mass.: Harvard University Press.

Rosenbaum, James. 1984. *Career Mobility in a Corporate Hierarchy.* New York: Academic Press.

Rosenberg, Gerald N. 1991. *The Hollow Hope: Can Courts Bring about Social Change?* Chicago: University of Chicago Press.

Roy, Donald. 1954. "Efficiency and 'the Fix': Informal Intergroup Relations in a Piecework Machine Shop." *American Journal of Sociology* 60:255–66.

Saks, Michael J. 1990. "Judicial Attention to the Way the World Works." *Iowa Law Review* 75:1011–31.

Saks, Michael J., and Charles H. Baron, eds. 1980. *The Use/Nonuse/Misuse of Applied Social Research in the Courts.* Cambridge, Mass.: Abt Books.

Sarat, Austin, and Thomas R. Kearns. 1993. *Law in Everyday Life.* Ann Arbor: University of Michigan Press.

Scheingold, Stuart A. 1974. *The Politics of Rights: Lawyers, Public Policy, and Political Change.* New Haven, Conn.: Yale University Press.

Scheppele, Kim Lane. 1987. "The Re-Vision of Rape Law." *University of Chicago Law Review* 54:1095–1116.

Schultz, Vicki. 1990. "Telling Stories about Women and Work: Judicial Interpretations of Sex Segregation in the Workplace in Title VII Cases Raising the Lack of Interest Argument." *Harvard Law Review* 103:1749–1843.

Schultz, Vicki, and Stephen Pettersen. 1992. "Race, Gender, Work, and Choice: An Empirical Study of the Lack of Interest Defense in Title VII Cases Challenging Job Segregation." *University of Chicago Law Review* 59: 1073–1181.

Scott, James. 1985. *Weapons of the Weak: Everyday Forms of Peasant Resistance.* New Haven, Conn.: Yale University Press.

——— 1990. *Domination and the Arts of Resistance: Hidden Transcripts.* New Haven, Conn.: Yale University Press.

Scott, Joan Wallach. 1988. *Gender and the Politics of History.* New York: Columbia University Press.

Selznick, Philip. 1969. *Law, Society, and Industrial Justice.* New York: Russell Sage Foundation.

——— 1992. *The Moral Commonwealth: Social Theory and the Promise of Community.* Berkley: University of California Press.

Sewell, William H., Jr. 1992. "A Theory of Structure: Duality, Agency, and Trans-formation," *American Journal of Sociology* 98:1–29.

Shamir, Ronen. 1990. "'Landmark Cases' and the Reproduction of Legitimacy: The Case of Israel's High Court of Justice." *Law & Society Review* 24:781–805.

Shapiro, Martin. 1981. *Courts: A Comparative and Political Analysis.* Chicago: University of Chicago Press.

Siegelman, Peter, and John J. Donohue III. 1990. "Studying the Iceberg from Its Tip: A Comparison of Published and Unpublished Employment Discrimi-nation Cases." *Law & Society Review* 24:1133–70.

Silbey, Susan S., and Patricia Ewick. 1995. "Subversive Stories and Hegemonic Tales: Toward a Sociology of Narrative." *Law & Society Review* 29: 197–226.

Silbey, Susan S., and Austin Sarat. 1987. "Critical Traditions in Law and Society Research." *Law & Society Review* 21:165–174.

Simon, Herbert A. 1957a. *Administrative Behavior.* 2d ed. New York: Macmil-lan.

——— 1957b. *Models of Man, Social and Rational.* New York: John Wiley.

Skowronek, Stephen. 1982. *Building a New American State: The Expansion of National Administrative Capacities.* Cambridge: Cambridge University Press.

Smeenk, Brian P. 1993. "Canada's Pay Equity Experiments." *Human Resources Magazine* 38:58–61.

Smith, Dorothy. 1990. *The Conceptual Practices of Power: A Feminist Sociol-ogy of Knowledge.* Boston: Northeastern University Press.

Smith, Michael. 1990. "What Is New in 'New Structuralist' Analyses of Earnings?" *American Sociological Review* 55:827–41.

Sorensen, Elaine. 1994. *Comparable Worth: Is It a Worthy Policy?* Princeton, N.J.: Princeton University Press.

Steinberg, Ronnie J. 1992. "Gender on the Agenda: Male Advantage in Organi-zations." *Contemporary Sociology* 21:576–581.

Steinberg, Ronnie J., and Lois Haignere. 1987. "Equitable Compensation: Methodological Criteria for Comparable Worth." In C. Bose and G. Spitze, eds., *Ingredients for Women's Employment Policy.* Albany, N.Y.: SUNY Press.

Steinberg, Ronnie J., and Jerry A. Jacobs, 1994. "Pay Equity in Nonprofit Organizations: Making Women's Work Visible." In T. Odendahl and M. O'Neill, eds., *Women and Power in the Nonprofit Sector.* San Francisco: Jossey-Bass.

Steinberg, Ronnie, and W. Lawrence Walter. 1992. "Making Women's Work Visible, The Case of Nursing: First Steps in the Design of a Gender-Neutral Job Comparison System." Paper presented at the Third Women's Policy Research Conference, Institute for Women's Policy Research, Washington, D.C. May 15–16.

Stewart, James B. 1983. *The Partners.* New York: Simon & Schuster.

Strang, David, and James N. Baron. 1990. "Categorical Imperatives: The Structure of Job Titles in California State Agencies." *American Sociological Review* 55:479–95.

Sullivan, Charles A., Michael J. Zimmer, and Richard F. Richards. 1988. *Employment Discrimination*. 2d ed. Boston: Little, Brown.

Sunstein, Cass R. 1991. "Why Markets Don't Stop Discrimination." *Social Philosophy & Politics* 8:22–37.

Swinnerton, Kenneth A., and Howard Wial. 1995. "Is Job Stability Declining in the U.S. Economy?" *Industrial and Labor Relations Review* 48:293–304.

Taub, Nadine, and Elizabeth M. Schneider. 1990. "Women's Subordination and the Role of Law." In David Kairys, ed., *The Politics of Law: A Progressive Critique*. New York: Pantheon.

Taylor, Patricia A. 1979. "Income Inequality in the Federal Civilian Government." *American Sociological Review* 44:468–79.

Thomas, Robert J. 1985. *Citizenship, Gender, and Work: The Social Organization of Industrial Agriculture*. Berkeley: University of California Press.

Thompson, Edward P. 1975. *Whigs and Hunters: The Origins of the Black Act*. London: Allen Lane.

Tilly, Chris. 1992. "Dualism in Part-Time Employment." *Industrial Relations* 31:331–40.

Tomlins, Christopher. 1994. *Law, Labor, and Ideology in the Early American Republic*. Cambridge: Cambridge University Press.

Treiman, Donald J. 1979. *Job Evaluation: An Analytic Review*. Interim Report to Equal Employment Opportunity Commission. Washington, D.C.: National Academy of Sciences.

Treiman, Donald J., and Heidi Hartmann, eds. 1981. *Women, Work, and Wages: Equal Pay for Jobs of Equal Worth*. Washington, D.C.: National Academy Press.

Trubek, David. 1984. "Where the Action Is: Critical Legal Studies and Empiricism." *Stanford Law Review* 36:575–622.

Trubek, David, and John Esser. 1989. "'Critical Empiricism' in American Legal Studies: Paradox, Program, or Pandora's Box?" *Law and Social Inquiry* 14:3–52.

U.S. Bureau of the Census. 1974. *Statistical Abstract of the United States*. Washington, D.C.: Government Printing Office.

——— 1980. *Alphabetical Index of Industries and Occupations*. Washington, D.C.: Government Printing Office.

Villemez, Wayne, and William P. Bridges. 1988. "When Bigger Is Better: Differences in the Individual-Level Effect of Firm and Establishment Size." *American Sociological Review* 53:237–55.

Walshok, M. 1981. *Blue Collar Women: Pioneers on the Male Frontier*. Garden City, N.Y.: Anchor Press.

Weeks, David A. 1976. "Compensating Employees: Lessons of the 1970's." Report 707. New York: Conference Board.

Weiler, Paul. 1986. "The Wages of Sex: The Uses and Limits of Comparable Worth." *Harvard Law Review* 99:1728–1807.

Wiebe, Robert. 1967. *The Search for Order, 1877–1920.* New York: Hill & Wang.

Williams, Patricia J. 1991. *The Alchemy of Race and Rights: Diary of a Law Professor.* Cambridge, Mass.: Harvard University Press.

Williamson, Oliver. 1975. *Markets and Hierarchies.* New York: Free Press.

Index

385